Ethnicity in Canada
Theoretical Perspectives

Alan B. Anderson
Associate Professor of Sociology,
University of Saskatchewan

James S. Frideres
Professor of Sociology and Anthropology,
University of Calgary

BUTTERWORTHS   Toronto

Ethnicity in Canada: Theoretical Perspectives

© 1981 Butterworth & Co. (Canada) Ltd.

Printed and bound in Canada

The Butterworth Group of Companies

Canada:
Butterworth & Co. (Canada) Ltd., Toronto
Butterworth & Co. (Western Canada) Ltd., Vancouver

United Kingdom:
Butterworth & Co. (Publishers) Ltd., London, Borough Green

Australia:
Butterworths Pty. Ltd., Sydney, Melbourne, Brisbane, Perth, Norwood

New Zealand:
Butterworths of New Zealand Ltd., Wellington

South Africa:
Butterworth & Co. (South Africa) Ltd., Durban

United States:
Butterworth (Publishers) Inc., Boston
Butterworth (Legal Publishers) Inc., Seattle
Butterworth & Co. Ltd., Ann Arbor
Mason Publishing Company, St. Paul

Canadian Cataloguing in Publication Data

Anderson, Alan B., 1939-
    Ethnicity in Canada

ISBN 0-409-81110-6

1. Ethnicity.   2. Canada – Population – Ethnic groups.*   3. Canada – Ethnic relations.   I. Frideres, James S., 1943-   II. Title.

FC104.A54   305.8 00971   C80-094844-0
F1035.A1A54

Printed by Hunter Rose
Cover design by Brant Cowie

Contents

Part I
Defining Ethnicity

Chapter 1

Introduction: Theoretical Approaches

The central purpose of this book is to provide an integration of theoretical perspectives on ethnic identification, persistence and change, relations and policies in Canadian society.

During the past decade or so a large number of edited readers on various Canadian ethnic minorities have been published: J. L. Elliott (ed.), *Minority Canadians* (1971); P. M. Migus (ed.), *Sounds Canadian: Languages and Cultures in Multi-Ethnic Society* (1975); H. Palmer (ed.), *Immigration and the Rise of Multiculturalism* (1975); W. Isajiw (ed.), *Identities: The Impact of Ethnicity on Canadian Society* (1977); L. Driedger (ed.), *The Canadian Ethnic Mosaic* (1978); J. L. Elliott (ed.), *Two Nations, Many Cultures: Ethnic Groups in Canada* (1979); D. J. Lee (ed.), *Frontières Ethniques en Devenir* (1979); K. Ishwaran (ed.), *Canadian Families: Ethnic Variations* (1980); J. E. Goldstein and R. M. Bienvenue (eds.), *Ethnicity and Ethnic Relations in Canada* (1980); K. V. Ujimoto and G. Hirabayashi (eds.), *Visible Minorities and Multiculturalism* (1980); B. S. Bolaria (ed.), *Oppressed Minorities in Canada* (forthcoming). This rather lengthy list excludes books which were single-, co-, or joint-authored (in contrast to the above edited books), as well as the numerous authored and edited books on specific ethnic groups.

Yet for all this attention devoted to Canadian ethnic minorities, there have been too few attempts to develop theoretical generalizations out of a multitude of empirical case studies, and virtually no attempt to bring together into a single volume an integrated framework for analysing ethnicity in Canada.

That this is a difficult task the present authors realize only too well, but the attempt should be made. It is difficult for several reasons. First, there are different levels of theorizing ranging from empirical generalizations to grand theory. Second, the field of ethnic studies is interdisciplinary, and any one of the contributing social sciences include a bewildering array of theoretical approaches. Third, correspondingly, one finds divergent approaches in professional ethnic studies. Fourth, Canada is admittedly an extremely complicated country in which to study ethnicity. Let us now examine each of these difficulties in some detail.

Levels of Theorizing

Our first point was that there are different levels of theorizing in the social sciences in general and particularly in sociology. As Mitchell (1968) has concisely explained, sociology was born out of two traditions—one speculative, the other fact-finding. Martindale (1960) contrasted social scientists who are "architects of fantasy," producing theory which is abstract, grand, and large-scale, with social scientists who could be viewed as "esoterics operating in the shadowy realm of semi-darkness"; elusive, obscure, ephemeral. Surely, he agreed, the real function of theory should be to illuminate. This implies the constant improvement of theory, involving the search for alternative explanations of social phenomena and reviewing and updating existing theories. Martindale argued that the re-evaluation of sociological theories is long overdue, and also that more synthesization of theories could have been undertaken.

Any number of sociologists have insisted that sociological theory can be developed by following scientific procedure. Combining the suggestions of Timasheff (1967) and Blalock (1967: 194-196), this would involve five basic steps:

(1) observation
(2) generalization
(3) statement of theory, given the following conditions:
  (a) The propositions must be couched in terms of exactly defined concepts. Blalock calls this "formulation of a schematic diagram."
  (b) They must be consistent with one another, or—as Blalock puts it—the focus must be narrowed.
  (c) They must be such that, from them, the existing generalizations could be deductively derived.
  (d) They must be fruitful, i.e., show the way to further observations and generalizations.
(4) verification and systematic statement of findings
(5) testing of alternative models and revision of the schematic diagram.

Such a systematic approach to theory construction was provided by H. M. Blalock in his book, *Toward a Theory of Minority Group Relations* (1967). This author has explained that the main thrust of his theory-building effort is a "propositional approach"—i.e., the formulation of numerous (almost two hundred) propositions "rather loosely connected by semi-deductive arguments" (p. 190). In fact, Blalock has suggested that an even more systematic effort (in building his model of ethnic minority relations) could produce upward of a thousand such propositions, all of which would be "reasonably consistent with common sense and/or available empirical evidence." He has explained that his original strategy was to take a set of empirical generalizations and attempt to fill in the gaps and introduce conceptual clarifications until the ideal of a deductive theoretical system could be reasonably approximated; the researcher was to simultaneously appraise the adequacy of the empirical evidence bearing on each proposition. Whether one accepts his own model or not, Blalock argues some sort of theoretical framework is needed; any reasonably tight deduction system requires a relatively small number of basic concepts that are either self-evident or explicitly defined in terms of each other (pp. 190-191). Blalock outlined three general strategies (pp. 191-193): *First*, we must continue to collect and construct empirical generalizations or propositions that are rather loosely interrelated, but that tend to include large numbers of variables and perspectives. This author admitted that in the study of ethnic relations, such propositions might not be stated on a very high level of abstraction; thus they may not be generalizable to other aspects of social behavior. But the more concrete they are, the better chance they stand of being tested and properly qualified. *Second,* the researcher should attempt to explain particular phenomena by subsuming them under more general ones. *Third,* the researcher should attempt to develop causal models of complex processes. (For a pertinent discussion of various causal relationships, the reader should refer to H. L. Zetterberg, *On Theory and Verification in Sociology,* 1965.)

Impressive as this outline may seem, it implies only a single level of theorization. What exactly is a sociological theory? We do not have the space, much less the inclination, to repeat here the arguments in which sociologists have engaged over the past several decades as to whether their findings might be regarded as durable theories, working hypotheses, concepts, or simply observations. However, it may be useful to note R. K. Merton's (1945) typology of levels of theorizing. According to Merton the phrase "sociological theory" has been used to refer to at least six types of analysis which differ significantly in their bearings on empirical research: (1) methodology (or the logic of scientific procedure), (2) general sociological orientations (constituting only the point of departure for the theorist), (3) analysis of sociological concepts (i.e., conceptual clarification, or the instituting of observable indices of the social data with which empirical research is concerned), (4) *post factum* sociological interpretations (the subjection of collected data to interpretative comment, which remains at a low level of plausibility), (5) empirical generalizations (isolated propositions summarizing observed uniformities of relationships between two or more variables), and (6) sociological theory *per se* (a sociological generalization which is a statement of invariance derivable from a theory).

General Theoretical Approaches in Sociology and the Social Sciences

Ethnic studies are interdisciplinary, and virtually all of the social sciences— sociology, anthropology, history, geography, economics, political science, psychology, education, and religious studies—have contributed substantially to the study of ethnic minorities, ethnic relations, and ethnic identity. Our own perspective, and largely the perspective of this book, is sociological, although reference will be made to research in all of these academic disciplines. It would be rather pointless to attempt to distinguish between these fields by virtue of their each having a unique approach to ethnic studies, although some rather obvious methodological differences could be noted (historians are most likely to make use of oral histories, psychologists to focus on attitudinal surveys, political scientists on policies, and so forth).

The problem is that even within a single discipline many theoretical approaches could be discovered, which have a great deal to do with how one goes about studying ethnicity, what one perceives, and which conclusions are likely to be drawn. Just within sociology, for example, one could discern at least five general theoretical traditions, which in turn may be subdivided into any number of more specific theoretical approaches. *First,* the Marxist tradition has included classical or orthodox Marxism, pre-Marxist communism and utopian socialism, various types of reform socialism (e.g., evolutionary socialism, syndicalism, Fabian socialism, etc.), left anarchism, Marxism-Leninism (Leninism, Stalinism, Trotskyism, revisionism, Maoism, etc.), neo-Marxism, the left conflict perspective, and left structuralism, to mention just some of the schools of thought which have had the most influence on sociological theory. *Second,* there are several theoretical traditions which could be summed up as social evolutionism, or the historical-comparative tradition. This has included Enlightenment rationalism and Comtean positivism, social Darwinism, environmental determinism and geographical possibilism, technological determinism, neoevolutionism and comparative macrosociology. *Third,* structural-functionalism has incorporated such approaches as sociologism (Durkheim, Mauss, Halbwachs), socio-structuralism (Radcliffe-Brown), biopsychic functionalism (Malinowski), structural anthropology (Levi-Strauss), microfunctional equilibrium theory (Parsons), middle range theory (Merton), the order perspective and normative theory. *Fourth,* for lack of a better term we can label a variety of related approaches as socio-demographic or descriptive sociology. This would include, for example, much of demography, social or factorial ecology, social solidarity continuums, community theory, and most empirical and quantitative sociology. *Fifth,* a wide variety of approaches are socio-psychological, behavioral, and/or phenomenological, including symbolic interaction, field theory, social exchange theory, modern systems theory, role theory, the Weberian social action approach or systematic sociology, behavioral social psychology, phenomenological sociology, sociology of knowledge, cognitive sociology, ethnomethodology, metasociology, and so forth.

It should be clear that all of these five general traditions, as well as most of the more specific sub-categories, have applied to the sociological study of ethnicity and ethnic relations, although relatively few sociologists have consciously labelled the particular approach being used or their theoretical orientations. In view of this vast range of theoretical predilections, indeed it seems presumptuous to attempt an integrated perspective.

Divergent Theoretical Approaches in Ethnic Studies

Apart from the aforementioned disciplinary approaches to the study of ethnicity, a number of divergent theoretical approaches may be discerned between a generally psychological/social-psychological and what we call a more explicitly sociological orientation. Or between a neo-Marxist orientation which stresses a social conflict perspective in ethnic relations, and views ethnic minorities as subordinate collectivities within a social structure controlled by the dominant society, on the one hand, versus a "bourgeois" orientation which focuses on the assimilation, containment, or integration of ethnic minorities.

In suggesting that we are attempting an integration of theoretical perspectives, it is our intention to stress that various theoretical orientations might have their validity, depending on what exactly is being studied. Thus it is obvious that the conflict tradition in sociological theory is most relevant to our discussion of ethnic conflict in Canada (Chapter 8), whereas assimilation theories are most relevant in discussing ethnic identity persistence or change (Chapter 6) or in reviewing traditional sociological models of Anglo-conformity (Chapter 11). Again, a "left" structural approach will be utilized to put ethnic minority subordination in the context of dominant social control (Chapters 10-13), whereas—in striking contrast—psychological research will prove most useful in describing subjective attitudes toward ethnicity (Chapter 4).

Intergroup behavior, then, has been studied from a wide range of perspectives. Any one of these major approaches may not totally exclude variables that might be taken into account by other approaches but it determines which variables will be considered secondary in import in terms of explanation. In essence, then, the theoretical approach determines what the unit of analysis will be.

Individuals are often inclined to categorize theorists or researchers as belonging to one school of thought or another. It is often heard that "he's a system theorist" or "she uses nothing but conflict models." Somehow this is supposed to negate or make suspect all of the theory or empirical findings, and thus render their research useless. This type of assessment does not allow us to advance science nor does it answer any practical problems. Each piece of research must be evaluated in terms of its theoretical goals, its methodology and its data analysis. To suggest that because a model is social-psychological, conflict, or whatever and thus not important, is to engage in superficial, petty and self-serving analysis.

We will begin to identify the major themes or theoretical perspectives used in past research in the area of intergroup behavior. This will allow the reader to discern the major factors that have been taken into consideration by individual researchers and will also allow the reader to better understand what is meant by a psychological, social-psychological, or sociological theoretical approach.

The real issue in contrasting these disciplinary theoretical approaches is the question of whether one confines oneself to the study of society *per se* or the individual. For example, a sociological approach argues that society controls and directs the behavior of the individual. On the other hand, one could argue—as a psychological approach has tended to—that there are only individuals who find that they must interact with one another, and thus the operative force is the individual.

The psychological analysis focuses on the unit of analysis which is the individual and generally, the focus is upon *attitudes*. Research by proponents of this perspective suggests that certain personality types hold specific (usually prejudicial) attitudes toward out-group members. Hence, intergroup relations are thought to be a product of a variety of psychological syndromes that emerge in the individual because of specific family training processes as well as some built-in psychological tendencies. The work by Allport (1958), Adorno, et al. (1950) and Bloom (1971) reflects this basic psychological approach.

Other researchers (Kovel, 1970; McLean, 1940; Baughman, 1971; Bettelheim and Janowitz, 1950) have utilized a more traditional Freudian (psychological) analysis in interpreting what they call ethnic relations. Factors such as "instinctual fantasies," "anally rooted symbolism," and "frustration-aggression" are common in research conducted by these theorists.

While each psychological theorist may place greater emphasis on one factor or another to explain intergroup behavior, the point remains that the central object of study is the individual and certain personality attributes of the individual are used to explain why an individual is acting in a specific manner.

The social-psychological approach attempts to identify the social relationship between the individual and the social group. In addition, this approach specifies networks between groups (both dominant and subordinate) and the societal context in which these networks are established and maintained. The theoretical question raised by this approach is, "To what extent is man affected by the social order and how does that social order determine man's behavior?" The works of Richmond (1961), Blumer (1958), Bagley (1970), Pettigrew (1971), Hughes and Kallen (1974), Williams (1947), Shibutani and Kwan (1965), and most recently Dashevsky (1976) have used this type of an approach in the study of intergroup relations. The major factors taken into consideration by proponents of this approach would reflect the interest in the group (racial/ethnic group contact, institutionalization, situational patterning); the individual (internalization, projection, racial/ethnic identity); and the processes that link the individual to the group (reference group, sense of group position).

The strictly psychological, social-psychological, and sociological dimensions, then, are interrelated. As Kinloch (1974) points out:

> psychological factors, such as projection, are reinforced by the group context through institutionalization of values and are linked through racial identity. While at the next level, group relations are closely defined by the characteristics of the minorities involved, the nature of the elite and factors governing intergroup relationships. (86)

In his explanation of theoretical frameworks in the social psychology of ethnicity, Dashevsky (1976) has suggested that:

> These theoretical orientations may be classified along two axes as shown in Table 1: their *ontology* (theory of reality) and their *methodology*. On the ontological axis, a theoretical orientation may be classified according to its emphasis on the extent to which the individual's behavior is best understood as part of a larger whole, pattern, or system *(holistic)* or best understood as an element, part, or atom *(elementalistic)*. On the methodological axis, a theoretical framework may be classified on the basis of its reliance on *experimental* methods of research, such as those of laboratory or field experiments, or *nonexperimental* methods, such as clinical, survey, or field studies.

Table 1. Theoretical Frameworks in the Social Psychology of Ethnicity

		Methodology	
		Nonexperimental	Experimental
Ontology	*Holistic*	Psychoanalytic	Configurationist
	Elementalistic	Interactionist	Behaviorist

In the upper left cell is the *psychoanalytic* perspective, which represents a holistic nonexperimental approach in that ethnic identity is studied in terms of unconscious processes that transcend the physiological functioning of the human body and affect the personality structure. The upper right cell contains the *configurationist* (microfunctionalist, group dynamicist or gestalt) position. It is a holistic experimental approach, in which identity is studied in relation to the larger context of the group, perceptual field, or life-space. The lower left cell represents the elementalistic nonexperimental social psychology of the *interactionist* (role theory) tradition. Here, identity is studied in relationship to the mediating symbols in social relationships as they affect the individual. Finally, the lower right cell contains a fourth theoretical framework, the elementalistic experimental approach embodied in the *behaviorist* (reinforcement or learning theory) tradition, in which identity may be studied as reinforced responses to stimuli operating on the individual. There is little research on ethnicity in this framework because of the difficulty of studying ethnicity (a) in the laboratory and (b) in terms of the mechanistic stimulus-response model, both of which are fundamental assumptions in this tradition. (51-52)

The integrating aspect of research using a sociological approach centres on the social attributes of the social system. These factors, the proponents of a sociological approach argue, determine the relationships that exist between groups. Several different *macro* approaches have been delineated (Kinloch, 1974)—the societal characteristics approach, the ecological approach, the demographic approach and the institutional approach. We shall briefly discuss each.

In the *societal characteristics* approach (Van den Berghe, 1967; Mason, 1970; Lieberson, 1961; Rex, 1970; Cox, 1959), the concern is upon delineating types of society which determine intergroup relations. For example, Van den Berghe characterizes race relations as "paternalistic" or "competitive" according to the nature of the system's economy, division of labour mobility pattern, population ratios and value conflict. A variation of this approach places a greater emphasis on the contact situation for understanding ethnic relations.

The *ecological-frontier* approach analyses race relations, utilizing the economic and political factors controlling the intergroup relations. This approach has resulted in a number of authors (Park, 1950; Glick, 1955; Lind, 1969) postulating "phases" of race relations. Hence, once contact is established, race relations follow a particular sequence.

The *demographic* approach investigates the attributes of the population (both dominant and subordinate) as it affects intergroup relations. Changes in these attributes will produce changes in the relationships between ethnic groups. One last perspective utilizing a macro-sociological approach is the *institutional* approach. This approach focuses on the relevance of racial definitions provided by an individual's reference group. The central notion in this perspective analyses how ethnic-relations are changed as a society moves toward what some have called mass society.

Each of the appproaches discussed here has shortcomings as well as theoretically important contributions. The psychological approach assesses ethnic relations in terms of attitudes held by particular personality types. A number of shortcomings in the psychological approach to ethnic relations have been identified by Kinloch (1974):

(1) It concentrates on very high levels of prejudice, neglecting average or normal prejudice.

(2) It neglects the factors producing a particular personality type.

(3) Inter-racial contacts are viewed mainly as individual phenomena with little regard to group characteristics and identity.

(4) This approach fails to delineate different kinds of minorities and minority situations.

(5) Power and power structures are neglected. (66-67).

In summary, the psychological approach focuses on personality factors behind extreme racial prejudice. It neglects the social context in which these attitudes have developed, are reinforced and operate. Skidmore (1975) argues that if one focuses solely on the individual as the major operative force in explaining human behavior, it tends to destroy the concept of society.

On the other hand, the *macro* model ignores the individual and focuses on the social system. For example, one problem in the sociological approach is in its treatment of social change. While there is nothing inherent in the sociological approach that precludes its treatment of social change, past work completed using this model tended to ignore change or treated it in a most simplistic fashion. The *contact* theorists have developed elaborate models of ethnic group relations at the time of contact which supposedly have far reaching effects on the relationships today. While the model may be most applicable to the relationships at the time of contact, this approach lacks analytical focus. It tends to be simplistic in its description partly because it also tends to approach the problem in typological terms.

The conceptual approach to be used in the present text will utilize elements of all three approaches discussed above. The central focus of our work is to explain social behavior. If one focuses on structural factors, one explanation emerges. On the other hand, if the centre of one's investigation is the individual, a very different explanation emerges. The goal, as we see it, is to bring about a synthesis of these two basic orientations (social-psychological). Hence, some readers' inabilities to pigeon-hole the approach will make it unpalatable and thus they will reject it, not on the merits of the model but rather on the basis that it does not neatly fit into a pre-existing conceptual framework.

Perhaps one might more realistically refer to the ideas presented in this book as an explanation sketch. This explanation sketch will have a structural basis but it will not ignore the individual nor the processes relating the system to the individual. This explanation sketch is also an intermixture of structural functionalism, value analysis, system analysis and Marxian analysis. We prefer to define and use a theoretical orientation that contains an element or several elements of general variables that can be applied to more than one kind of analytical unit.

The end result, we feel, should produce an explanation sketch that is high in scope (generality), precise in prediction and accurate in explanation. Our task, therefore, is to utilize elements of various theoretical orientations that can provide us with a maximization of the above criteria.

Complexity of Canadian Society

A single model of ethnic survival for Canada is possible, if improbable, to formulate. The difficulty lies in the fact that while every ethnic group within Canadian society is a minority, at least at the national level (however this is not necessarily the case at a local, regional, or even provincial level), there are at least fifty clearly defined ethnic categories in Canada (not to mention further subgroup distinctions), ranging in size from several thousands to millions, many exclusively urban and others completely or primarily rural, and most embracing a wide range of opinions among their members as to what exactly constitutes ethnic identity and to what extent this identity should be stressed (Anderson, 1975).

Ethnic relations in Canada are unique even though some parallels from other countries are evident. Canada exists within its own social-economic-political framework and for that reason must be examined in that context. Our argument is similar to that set forth by Pike and Zureik (1975).

Thus along with a number of other academic observers of the Canadian social scene, it would seem to us that the following characteristics are peculiarly relevant to an understanding of our history and of our present social condition:

1. A weak sense of national identity accompanied by a strong sense of regional identification. In the case of certain provinces and regions (for example, Quebec), the regional identification is interlinked with particular ethnic group loyalties.
2. A hierarchical social class structure which is associated with the existence of class-based inequalities in educational and occupational opportunities.
3. An ethnic stratification system based on familial, religious and linguistic allegiances which is intertwined with existing class structure.
4. An official ideology which espouses the doctrine of cultural pluralism rather than assimilation. (viii and ix)

In this book, then, we are attempting to integrate theoretical perspectives and, in applying them, to make sense out of the enormous complexity of a country which is at once unicultural (represented in Anglo-Canadian dominance or—within Quebec—the *francization* policies of the Parti Quebecois), bicultural (e.g., French minorities outside Quebec or English-speaking minorities within Quebec), yet multicultural (especially in the larger cities and in the Prairie provinces).

In the first part of the book the concepts *race, culture, nationality,* and *minority* will be distinguished from *ethnic groups* (Chapter 2). *Ethnicity* will be defined not simply in terms of objective criteria (Chapter 3) but also in terms of subjective criteria and stereotyping (Chapter 4).

The second part of the book focuses more specifically on ethnicity in a changing Canadian society, describing the failure of biculturalism in many respects as a traditional mode or theme (Chapter 5), and the recent emergence of the concept of multiculturalism (Chapter 6). This portion of the book also presents a historical as well as a contemporary socio-demographic profile of immigration (Chapter 7).

In the third part of the book we will introduce the reader more systematically to theoretical perspectives on Canadian ethnic relations, through an application of conflict theory (Chapter 8), an analysis of racism (Chapter 9), and a description of dominant social control mechanisms (Chapter 10).

The fourth part of the book describes differential minority responses to and outcomes of domination and subordination. Ethnic minority subordination will be related to ethnic identity change (Chapter 11). The next chapter describes ethnic stratification and accommodation (Chapter 12). A third alternative, survival and revival, is discussed (Chapter 13). In our concluding chapter (Chapter 14) we will evaluate the implications of these minority responses and outcomes for government policies at the federal, provincial, and local levels.

REFERENCES

Adorno, T. W., et al. *The Authoritarian Personality.* New York: Harper, 1950.

Allport, G. W. *The Nature of Prejudice.* Cambridge Mass: Addison-Wesley, 1958.

Anderson, A. B. "Ethnic Groups: Implications of Criteria for the Examination of 'Survival'," a paradigm presented in a workshop on "Ethnicity and Ethnic Groups in Canada," at the annual meeting of the Canadian Sociology and Anthropology Association, University of Alberta, Edmonton, May 1975.

Bagley, C. "Race Relationships and Theories of Status Consistencies," *Race,* Vol. XI, No. 3 (1970): 267-289.

Banton, M. *Race Relations.* New York: Basic Books, 1967.

Baughman, E. E. *Black Americans: A Psychological Analysis.* New York: Academic Press, 1971.

Bettelheim, B. and Barbara Janowitz. *Dynamics of Prejudice: A Psychological and Sociological Study of Veterans.* New York: Harper, 1950.

Blalock, H. *Toward a Theory of Minority-Group Relations.* New York: Wiley, 1967.

Bloom, L. *The Social Psychology of Race Relations.* London: G. Allen, 1971.

Blumer, H. "Race Prejudice as a Sense of Group Position," *Pacific Sociological Review,* Vol. I, No. 1, Spring (1958): 3-7.

Bolaria, B. S. (ed.) *Oppressed Minorities in Canada.* Toronto: Butterworths, forthcoming.

Cox, O. C. *Caste, Class and Race.* New York: Monthly Review Press, 1959.

Dashevsky, A. (ed.) *Ethnic Identity in Society.* Chicago: Rand McNally, 1976.

Driedger, L. (ed.) *The Canadian Ethnic Mosaic: A Quest for Identity.* Toronto: McClelland and Stewart, 1978.

Eliott, J. L. (ed.) *Minority Canadians, Vol. 1: Native Peoples and Vol. 2: Immigrant Groups.* Scarborough, Ontario: Prentice Hall of Canada, 1971.

Elliott, J. L. *Two Nations, Many Cultures: Ethnic Groups in Canada.* Scarborough, Ont.: Prentice Hall of Canada, 1979.

Frazier, E. "Race Relations in World Perspective," *Sociological and Social Research,* Vol. 41 (1957): 331-335.

Glick, C. "Social Roles and Types in Race Relations," in A. Lind (ed.) *Race Relations in World Perspective.* Honolulu: Univ. of Hawaii Press, 1955.

Goldstein, J. E. and R. M. Bienvenue (eds.) *Ethnicity and Ethnic Relations in Canada.* Toronto: Butterworths, 1980.

Hughes, D. R. and E. Kallen. *The Anatomy of Racism.* Montreal: Harvest House, 1974.

Isajiw, W. W. (ed.) *Identities: The Impact of Ethnicity on Canadian Society.* Toronto: Peter Martin, 1977.

Ishwaran, K. (ed.) *Canadian Families: Ethnic Variations.* Toronto: McGraw-Hill Ryerson, 1980.

Kinloch, G. C. *Sociological Theory: Its Development and Major Paradigms.* New York: McGraw-Hill, 1974.

Kovel, J. *White Racism: A Psychohistory.* New York: Pantheon Books, 1970.

Lee, D. J. (ed.) *Frontieres Ethniques en Devenir.* University of Ottawa Press, 1979.

Lieberson, S. "A Societal Theory of Race and Ethnic Relations," *American Sociological Review*, Vol. 26 (1961): 902-910.

Lind, A. *Hawaii: The Last of the Magic Isles.* London: Univ. of Oxford Press, 1969.

Lohman, I. and D. Reitzes. "Note on Race Relations in Mass Society," *American Journal of Sociology*, Vol. 58 (1952): 241-256.

Martindale, D. *The Nature and Types of Sociological Theory.* Boston: Houghton Mifflin, 1960.

Mason, P. *Race Relations.* London: Oxford University Press, 1970.

McLean, H. "Psychodynamics Factors in Racial Relations," *Annals of American Academy of Political and Social Science*, (1940): 244.

Merton, R. K. "Sociological Theory." *American Journal of Sociology*, Vol. L, May 1945.

Migus, P. M. (ed.) *Sounds Canadian: Languages and Cultures in Multi-Ethnic Society.* Toronto: Peter Martin, 1975.

Mitchell, G. D. *A Hundred Years of Sociology.* Chicago: Aldine, 1968.

Palmer, H. (ed.) *Immigration and the Rise of Multiculturalism.* Toronto: Copp Clark, 1975.

Park, R. *Race and Culture.* Glencoe, Illinois: Free Press, 1950.

Pettigrew, T. *Racially Separate or Together.* New York: McGraw-Hill, 1971.

Pike, R. and E. Zureik (eds.) *Socialization and Values in Canadian Society*, Vol. 2. Toronto: McClelland and Stewart, 1975.

Rex, J. *Race Relations in Sociological Theory.* London: Weidenfield and Nicolson, 1970.

Richmond, A. "Sociological and Psychological Explanations for Social Prejudices: Some Light on the Controversy from recent Researches, in Britain," *Pacific Sociological Review*, Vol. IV, No. 2 Fall (1961): 63-68.

Schermerhorn, R. *Comparative Ethnic Relations: A Framework for Theory and Research.* New York: Random House, 1970.

Shibutani, T. and K. Kwan. *Ethnic Stratification.* New York: Macmillan, 1965.

Skidmore, W. *Theoretical Thinking in Sociology.* London: Cambridge University Press, 1975.

Timasheff, N. S. *Sociological Theory: Its Nature and Growth.* New York: Random House, 1967.

Ujimoto, K. V. and G. Hirabayashi. *Visible Minorities and Multiculturalism.* Toronto: Butterworths, 1980.

Van den Berghe, P. *Race and Racism.* New York: Wiley, 1967.

Williams, R. *The Reduction of Intergroup Tensions: A Survey of Research on Problems of Ethnic Racial and Religious Group Relations.* New York: Social Science Research Council, 1947.

Zetterberg, H. *On Theory and Verification in Sociology.* Totowa, N.J.: Bedminster Press, 1965.

Chapter 2

Race, Culture, Nationality, Minority

Few individuals writing in the area of ethnic relations or ethnic groups provide clear, unambiguous definitions of the key concepts used. A rather bewildering variety of terms have tended to be used more or less interchangeably with *ethnic group*—race, species, culture, subculture, folk, people, nation, nationality, minority group, ethnic minority, ethno-linguistic group, ethno-religious group. We feel that it is imperative that the student of ethnic relations should understand the different theoretical and practical bases for these terms, as well as for the concept of ethnicity, before we attempt to explain how ethnic groups act and react toward each other, particularly in Canadian society.

We will first identify and then explain how we establish the boundaries of the group we wish to analyse. Our task, then, is to show how one goes about "labelling" groups. We will provide for the reader characterizing attributes which allow us to make distinctions between groups. We do this because we wish to achieve conceptual clarity and to identify what kinds of groups we are attempting to analyse. Hence, we begin by discussing one of the most common (and improperly used) terms in the area of intergroup relations.

Race: Physical Versus Social Definition

The concept *race*, as initially used by physical anthropologists and biologists, referred to a specific group of people who could be phenotypically isolated into distinct categories. These traits bore no relationship with culture, personality or other social behaviors. The concept was only used to make distinctions between categories of people, i.e., statistical identification. It was a natural typological grouping of men displaying a particular set of common hereditary characteristics. However, since its conception, the term has been confusing and frustrating because of the diverse explicit (and implicit) meanings attached to it.

Van den Berghe (1967) outlines four of the most common definitions attached to the concept of the race.

(1) A sub-species of homo sapiens characterized by selected phenotypical (the physical make up resulting from genetic and environmental factors) and genotypical traits (the genetic make up of a person or group). This definition was (and still is) used by many physical anthropologists.

(2) A human group that shares a particular cultural characteristic, e.g., language or religion. The layman attributes this meaning to the concept.

(3) A species, i.e., the human race. A definition utilized by some sociologists and biologists.

(4) A human group that defines itself, and/or is defined by other groups, as different from other groups because of innate physical characteristics.

With the wide diversity of the meaning of the concept, it becomes clear to the serious student of human behavior that this multiplicity of meanings must be reduced.

When the concept of race was first introduced, it was not used in any clear scientific sense. Generally it referred to a group of human beings set apart from other groups of human beings by one or more marks of physical differences (McAllister, 1975). As Nash (1962) points out:

> the study of race is the pursuit of certain kinds of information about biological phenomena. People who are involved in the description and analysis of the population dynamics of groups with differing genetic frequences and physical features are studying race. They seek to find the scale, origins, causes, distributions, and correlates of genetic and morphological diversity of the breeding populations called races. (285)

This definition is multi-faceted, but it illustrates for the reader the overall focus of concern for those people who studied (or still use) the concept in its initial conceptualization.

The reader should be aware that while this general focus was (and still is) pursued by those studying race in the biological sense, changes in how this theoretical definition was linked to empirical data are evident over time. Bernier (1625-1688) was perhaps the first scholar who tried to divide the world's population into four races: Lapps, Asiatics, Africans and inhabitants of Europe and certain parts of Asia. This, of course, was not a strictly biological definition but rather a geographical-biological definition and was subsequently proved useless as a scientific tool, but it began a trend for pseudo-scientists to attempt to develop taxonomies and categorize man into one of several races.

Linnaeus (1707-1778) was the next major scientist to set forth typologies of races of the world. The categories he set forth were Europeans, Albus, Americanus Rubesceus, Asiaticus Luridus and Afer Niger. His discussions of the attributes that allowed "scientists" to place individuals into these categories were social-biological. For example the Afer Niger were characterized as slow and cunning. Leclerc (1707-1788) concluded in 1749 that he had indeed solved the problem by distinguishing six varieties, or races of mankind: Laplander, or Polar race; Tatar, or Mongolian race; Southern Asiatic race; European race; Ethiopian race, and American race. After these initial attempts to classify races, a host of others followed suit (Snyder, 1962). Perhaps the one person who had the greatest impact on the social sciences and its involvement with the concept of race was Blumenbach. In 1795, Blumenbach attempted to classify mankind into five races—Caucasian, Mongolian, Ethiopian, American and Malay. Because his work was subsequently translated into a number of languages and published in both scholarly journals and non-scholarly outlets, his typology has had a lasting impact on North American thinking and subsequent usage of the term.

These were not necessarily the first attempts to categorize people into different groups. Nor were these the first attempts to attribute different social characteristics to various groups. They were, however, the first to use biological criteria as characterizing attributes of a race in the name of science. Slobodin has commented, "the race concept, as we know it (in the biological sense) was absent from pre-modern thought. Clearly, the Chinese . . . and Incas . . . conceived of their ways as superior to other people, but this was a feeling of what in modern times would be called cultural rather than racial superiority" (Slobodin, 1966: 2).

Authors prior to the 17th century also built classification schemes. The Roman Vitruvius had reflected on the superiority of Romans to other peoples. It was due (he claimed) "to rarity of atmospheres and to the heat. The less fortunate northern peoples being involved in a dense atmosphere, and chilled by moisture from the obstructing air have but a sluggish intelligence" (Gosset, 1968: 6). He was, of course, simply echoing some of the same claims made by the Greeks. Thus, the differentiating attributes of people reflected different climates, particularly heat and cold. Other people, such as Bodin, writing during the 17th century, elaborated on these explanations and attempted to set up classification schemes on these bases. In addition, cultural and religious differences were invoked as criteria for classifying people. The argument being made is not that discrimination did not occur before the biological definition of race was introduced, but that biological differences were outside the field of orientation for man at that time.

As Snyder (1962), Gosset (1968), and Nash (1962) have indicated, a continual upgrading and revision of the biological criteria to define race was evidenced throughout the 18th and 19th centuries. Because of a lack of technology, attributes initially selected to represent racial differentiation were at best superficial, i.e., phenotypical traits. General emphasis rested upon color of skin, texture of hair, bone structure and body stature.

The initial attempts to differentiate groups of people (on the basis of biological attributes) began with a sincere scientific belief that these attributes could be used in a most meaningful manner, i.e., to predict and understand human behavior. However, two results have been produced by this continual insistence that there are meaningful biological differences: first, racism (as an ideology) has been able to develop; and second, there has been a shifting from outside appearance criteria for differentiating races on a biological level to genetic criteria. This latter development was nurtured by the increasingly sophisticated technological tools that became available to the scientists. As has been repeatedly pointed out by social scientists, two crucial problems seem to have been overlooked (and still are) by those proponents of studying biological races. First, exactly who they were to measure and, secondly, which precise measurement procedures were to be used.

In their investigations, social scientists have tried to identify various groups and then show how the criteria they have set forth apply. It is important to note that most of the researchers made several a priori assumptions before asking this question. The most important one was that there were distinct biological differences between groups and concurrently that cultural differences were minimal. The scientist took arbitrary, relatively superficial biological differences between groups of people and, on the basis of these, tried to find other cultural attributes which correlated quite closely (e.g., social/personality attributes). Many others have followed the theoretical models set forth by these early scientists. To mention but one recent example, Coon, in The Origin of Races (1962), established elaborate typologies dealing with physiological features inherent in various groups of people throughout the world.

When using this biological definition, the investigator is concerned with trying to isolate some phenotypical or genotypical characteristics that are common to a particular group of people (or animals) which set them apart from other groups of people (or animals). Thus, physical anthropologists tried to isolate, or more accurately set up a typology of biological attributes common to groups. Among the principal classification criteria employed by physical anthropologists, apart from skin color, have been the cranial index (ranging from dolichocephalic, i.e., long-headed, through mesocephalic, i.e., medium-headed, to brachycephalic, i.e., round-headed); the nasal index (leptorrhine or sharp-nosed, mesorrhine or medium-nosed, platyrrhine or broad-nosed); the hair index (straight, wavy, curly, wooly); the degree of prognathism (the extent to which the jaw juts out); and epicanthic folding (the extent to which the eyelid covers the eyeball). Supposedly less reliable criteria have included stature, body hair, body odor, lip form, eye color, blood type and even blood pressure, not to mention a wide variety of psychological attributes, utilized less by scientists than by laymen in recent years, e.g., differential IQ and learning ability, natural propensity for aggressiveness, and moral character. However, with increased technological innovations, genotypical attributes are now being utilized; chromosomal and gene structures are now being introduced into the taxonomy in an attempt to differentiate groups of people. What effect this will have on the construction and predictive value of typologies is not yet known.

These typologies may have some merit in terms of classifying humans but what theoretical (or practical) usage do they have for social scientists (or man in general) in explaining human behavior? The scientific benefit of typologies may be heuristic for the biologist or zoologist solely interested in setting up classifying schemes. However, it may be that in the future we will discover that certain biological attributes have universal social implications (Van den Berghe, 1978). This approach also hinges upon the assumption that these genotypical and phenotypical differences are important determinants in the social behavior individuals emit. These researchers use the following model as a guide to explaining man's behavior:

Antecedent condition	Intervening condition	Dependent variable
Genetic structure ⟶	Physical characteristics ⟶	Social behavior

The argument is that the genetic structure of man determines social behavior. An intervening variable of phenotypical traits sometimes affects the otherwise direct relationship.

Implicit in our discussions thus far, we have tried to convey to the reader that the concept of race (at least up until the present) has not yet yielded any new information about man's *behavior*. Thus, we wish to elucidate some of the inadequacies and limitations of the concept.

First, the traditional strictly *physical* (as opposed to a social) definition of race refers to a set of categories based on clusters of physical, hereditary characteristics. These classifying criteria are biological trivia, having little survival value (although, as we shall see, socially these characteristics may be very significant). These criteria, moreover, are phenotypically continuous rather than discrete invariable entities. They overlap, and are dynamic from generation to generation. Thus racial typologies are never more than mere approximations, indeed as many competent physical anthropologists (such as Ashley Montagu, 1962) have cautioned. Contemporary physical anthropology (and thereby cultural and social anthropology, cultural and human geography, and sociology) has stressed that there are these basic races (Caucasoid, Mongoloid, Negroid) and innumerable sub-races (Nordic, Alpine, Mediterranean, Negrito, Malay, Amerindian, and so forth). Yet the more complicated the classification becomes (in other words, the more sub-races are enumerated), the less will be the actual physical distinctiveness of each classified group.

Second, the question of first origins has repeatedly been raised. Where did man originate, and in what form? Are all races and sub-races derived from a common origin? To what extent are they all interrelated, and how? Physical anthropologists, archaeologists, and historical geologists and palaeontologists continue to literally dig up new evidence challenging previous notions. However, in tracing man's evolution and racial migrations many gaps still remain to be solved. For example, what is the relationship (if any) between the Negroid sub-races in Africa, India (Vadda), Malay (Semang, Sakai), Indonesia, Melanesia, and Australia (Aborigines)?

Third, there is the problem of the incorrect application of the term race, if it is defined strictly in physical rather than cultural terms, to human groups more appropriately differentiated by cultural attributes: Jews, Britons, Scandinavians, Germans, French, Hindus, Japanese, and the like. However, it is a fruitless task to attempt to draw a sharp dividing line between sub-races (defined by physical criteria) and primarily cultural groups. The point being made here is that we must be wary of imputing too much into physical differentiation. For example, while a relatively high proportion of Scandinavians are blond-haired, the majority of them are not; conversely, while most Mediterranean people are dark-haired, some may be fair-haired.

Fourth, in the contemporary age physical mixing of races has become commonplace. In fact, racial amalgamation has been operating as long as human migrations have occurred, as has been exemplified for centuries in the Finno-Ugrian peoples of Eastern and Northern Europe and Siberia, the Hamitic peoples of East Africa, and the diverse peoples of the Indian sub-continent and Southeast Asia. Mulattoes, Mestizos, Eurasians, Anglo-Indians, Metis, and many other groups owe their origins to racial mixing. Of course, given the fact that races and sub-races represent a phenotypical continuum, it is problematic just how we are to define racial mixing; there can be no precise definition. At any rate, it hardly needs to be pointed out that skin color tends to acquire social significance far beyond any biological relevance. Considerable differences in skin color may even occur within a single, supposedly non-mixed family.

Fifth, there are numerous misconceptions about the physical, not to mention the psychological, attributes of races. Races do not represent different stages in evolution (all races exhibit certain apelike features). Race is not necessarily related to stature or physical capabilities, much less to differences in intelligence. All races produce body odor.

Sixth, in utilizing the biological definition of race, the assumption often was that there were unique genetic or physiological attributes among groups of people and these physical differences somehow influenced an individual's behavior. Thus, people having red skin pigmentation somehow would act in a different manner than people having white skin pigmentation. In essence, the argument went: the red skin actually *caused* the behavior, e.g., getting drunk. Of course, through selective perception, these assumptions were always upheld. The theoretical model in this set of explanations is one borrowed from the natural sciences. Internal structures were assumed to be the initiating forces; the behavior by the object was due to the internal structure of the object. This was, of course, an easy model to generalize to humans. However, in doing so, the entire notion of external conditions was ignored, if not eliminated from their thinking. Even today, while natural scientists would agree that one cannot ignore the external conditions, they would argue that they are less important than the internal conditions. Today the social scientist claims that this is an untenable position to hold in understanding human behavior. One cannot begin to explain human behavior with only knowledge of the physiological make up of man. One must understand the culture in which the individual acts. However, as we have stated, science should be a cumulative and self-correcting procedure, therefore new evidence being collected must be evaluated.

Our general conclusion is that the concept of race should be omitted from social science terminology and that it should be used carefully only by individual scientists who recognize some utility in building physiological or genetic taxonomies. The concept of race has little empirical utility explaining human behavior.

As Blumer (1955) suggests:

> In my judgement the appropriate line of probing is with regard to the concept. Theory is of value in empirical science only to the extent to which it connects fruitfully with the empirical world. Concepts are the means, and the only means of establishing such connection, for it is the concept that points to the empirical [that] . . . Contraverse, vague concepts deter the identification of appropriate empirical instances and obscure the detection of what is relevant in the empirical instances that are chosen. (4)

Before we discuss the social implications of race, the reader should be aware of a number of other essentially physical concepts which have been used to delimit group boundaries when the focus of the study has been on the issue of intergroup behavior. It is important to point out again at this time that while many of these concepts have been used interchangeably by other authors, it is our contention that the attempt to equate the terms was and still is illegitimate and misleading. We are not suggesting that these terms are not useful concepts. They have theoretical and practical import depending upon the goal of the researcher. For these reasons we will characterize several concepts that are used in the explanation of intergroup relations.

Viewing human differentiation and distribution from another perspective, anthropologists have suggested that an alternative concept to race be invoked. Livingstone (1962) as well as a number of others has suggested the concept of *clines*. The general meaning of this concept is that groups of people can be identified in terms of statistical combinations of adaptive features which have geographical relationships. In other words, clines locate a trait or a gene on a "map" similar to mapping the barometric pressure over a geographical area. The result is that it expresses traits that vary continuously in space or gradual progression of some feature (Molnar, 1975). For example, skin pigmentation gets gradually darker as you go from north to south; hair texture becomes more wooly as you go from northeast Asia to India to Africa.

The proponents of this concept argue that populations cannot be categorized in such a manner so that inclusiveness and mutually exclusive categories can be achieved. They, on the other hand, tend to view populations as merging in and out of adjacent populations with regard to any criteria (phenotypical or genotypical) that are utilized to distinguish populations. Thus the populations of the world are a series of categories with extremely porous boundaries. Just where one category begins and another ends can only arbitrarily be established by the use of some statistical dimension, e.g., when 75 or 80% of a population exhibit a similar characteristic(s), then they could be called a cline. The fact that the distribution pattern for each trait (skin pigmentation, hair texture, etc.) varies makes the establishment of meaningful categories even more tenuous. The conceptualization involved in this concept is productive in that it attempts to link geography and physical adaptive features of man. However, it, like the concept race, fails to show how these interrelationships affect man's behavior in general and intergroup behavior in particular.

A *species* is a genetically related population, all members of which are fertile within their own group but unable to produce offspring with members of another species. Species, then, are genetically closed systems, or, put another way, species are reproductively isolated. Gene interchange between species cannot take place. Subspecies are groupings of individuals or populations within a species, who have in common a number of characteristics. However, it should be added that no single characteristic is sufficient to differentiate between subspecies.

While no clear-cut criterion is available to assess whether or not two groups are subspecies, the most generally accepted criterion is that if 75% of a group can be distinguished from another group (on the basis of some feature, i.e., blood type, hair texture) we would call them a subspecies (Osborne, 1971). As we have noted, obviously man, no matter what his skin pigmentation, hair texture, or body stature, can interbreed. Hence human populations are sympatric (geographically intermingled in a common territory). This process encourages the amount of gene flow for man. The conclusion to be reached then, is that *the species* refers to all humans. Hence, its delineation simply makes a distinction between human and non-human.

What we are suggesting is that even if a biological typology were constructed (which allowed meaningful distinctions between groups of people), this would not necessarily allow us to make truthful, important statements about human behavior. This typology would not allow us to predict the different kinds of behavior emitted by (and towards) different groups of people. What are important, however, are the assumptions that underlie the entire typology or conceptualization. Thus, it would be our task to discover what these assumptions are, why they are considered important and how they affect man's behavior. This, of course, is why a social definition of race is so important.

Drawing upon Park's (1928) discussion, we will try to build upon this social definition of race. As Park conceived it, we should not be talking about biological races, but rather "social supposed races." This, of course, relies upon the W. I. Thomas dictum of the "definition of the situation." Since we define something, e.g., some person or group, to have certain characteristics (and these characteristics are assumed to be important for an individual), then we see the person or the group as actually having the characteristics which produce certain positive or negative reactions in interacting with other persons or groups. However, this concept (social supposed race) still invokes the usage of the concept of race. Of course, differences exist, but we want a term to describe the existence of these differences without invoking the problematic concept of race, implying physical distinctiveness. We do not want a term which injects differences into meanings which are not there (Montagu, 1962).

Phenotypic attributes are used to classify individuals with respect to a single character—black, red skin—or to refer to an entire complex of attributes held by an individual: fair hair, white skin, and thin lips. The focusing on phenotypical traits allows almost any individual to quickly define certain people as belonging to a particular group. It also allows people inside a particular group to define themselves as a member or non-member of that particular group.

> As is probably evident by now, the term 'Indian' is used . . . to mean all those persons living in Canada who perceived themselves, and who are defined by others, as people of Indian ancestry. This is not to argue that the difference between the legal concept of 'Treaty Indian', the kinship category 'Metis', and the term 'Non-Treaty Indian'—not to mention other minor classifications—are not important in certain relations. . . . Similarly, Treaty Indians and Metis living in towns face basically the same range of problems, life prospects, and living conditions. (Davis, 1968: 219)

Man communicates by the use of symbols. He gives certain meanings to these symbols which then take on evaluative content—emotions. Depending upon the social system that one is discussing, the stimuli (symbols) generated to regulate behavior, will vary from strictly physical features to cultural traits such as body gestures (Banton, 1967: 65). An excellent example of this is the fact that in the U.S. skin pigmentation is the major stimulus which evokes certain kinds of behavior (with emotive overtones). Wagley (1952), on the other hand, found that people residing within the interior of the Amazon Basin perceived hair styles and shapes as the stimuli with emotive overtones. Dingwall (1946) found that nonphysiological traits were used. For example, English-speaking Canadians are generally able to distinguish themselves from Americans, not through the use of physiological attributes, but by linguistic differences; they say "eh," not "uh," they use some different words ("bloody," "pub"), and generally have a slightly different accent on certain words ("schedule," "route," "roof," "about").

The popular notions of group labeling held in Canada are not always evident or, in fact, utilized in other countries. In the U.S. descent plays an important role in race classification. However, in Brazil it plays a negligible role in determining the race of an individual. Even more different is the classification of groups in Japan, where skin color (a widely used attribute in the West) does not usually enter in the popular classification of people. Social economic status is the critical classifying variable, e.g., the Eta of Japan (Marshall, 1968).

45326

The discussion above once again suggests that any expedient set of physical and cultural behavioral attributes may be used as the basis for group classification. Marshall (1968: 155) goes on to say that "the assignment of individuals to the various racial categories recognized in different societies is often based on *perceived* behavioral differences rather than on demonstrable physical differences."

These symbols are passed on (along with meanings and emotions, and become stereotypes) to the next generation through formal and informal socialization procedures. They then become standards by which individuals act, and that generation establishes its own social reality. People then behave toward other people on the basis of the assumptions they make about the subjective and objective attributes of these individuals.

The following figure illustrates how the process of communication proceeds as well as how symbols take on meanings. We begin our discussion at time one (T_1) when group members exhibit certain symbols. Whether it be skin color, hair structure, body stature or linguistic ability makes no difference. They are recognizable symbols, perceived by others. Once perception takes place, definitions are made with regard to that symbol. At this time, the definitions are made with regard to the symbols that have been perceived in terms of what the perceivers have learned during their socialization. The next step in the process is the placement of valuation on the symbols. That is, each symbol is assessed on a number of evaluation dimensions, e.g., good-bad, worthwhile-worthless, intelligent-ignorant. After the evaluation is made, members of society then act with an appropriate behavior congruent to the symbol (Osgood, et al., 1957).

FIGURE 1   PROCESSES OF INTERACTION SEQUENCE

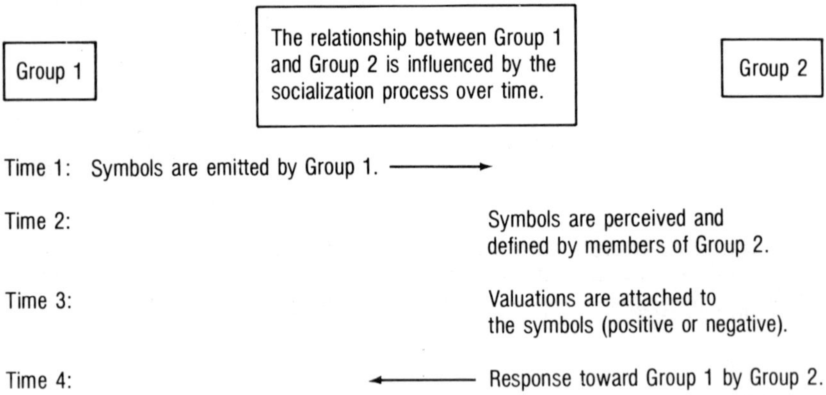

Group 1	The relationship between Group 1 and Group 2 is influenced by the socialization process over time.	Group 2

Time 1:   Symbols are emitted by Group 1. ⟶

Time 2:   Symbols are perceived and defined by members of Group 2.

Time 3:   Valuations are attached to the symbols (positive or negative).

Time 4:   ⟵ Response toward Group 1 by Group 2.

But how do these symbols attain their meaning? One of the most widely used symbols by people in North America in intergroup behavior is skin pigmentation (color) (Bastide, 1967). But why does it have such evaluative meanings? Why is it that Sargent (1923) and Birren (1962) found that in a variety of cultures, black meant gloom, evil, death, bad, despair, darkness, while white had very positive meanings: pure, good, and virtuous. How did colors come to take on these valuations? Bastide (1967) attempts to trace the history of "color, racism and Christianity." He provides a detailed documentation as to how certain colors attained their meanings through an evaluation of the tenets of Christianity. In his tracing of the history of Catholicism and Protestantism (via Calvinism), he clearly shows that Christian ideology systematically transformed neutral colors into symbols with high positive (white) and negative (black, red, yellow) evaluations.

Once the symbols have been recognized, defined and appropriately evaluated, these social psychological processes will be transmitted to each succeeding generation through the appropriate socialization apparatus set up in the society. For example, once the symbol of black is defined as dirty, unclean, or bad, members of society will then learn, through both intentional and unintentional socialization processes, how to act toward this symbol.

We are attempting to invoke the notion of individual perceptions. Because individuals perceive certain attributes, they act upon these notions. How this affects man's behavior is indeed a legitimate area of study. Whether or not various individuals (or groups of individuals) can *objectively* be placed into various specific categories is of little consequence. If, in fact, people perceive various individuals to belong to various races, ethnic groups or nationalities, this will determine their behavior toward that group and subsequent reactions.

The point is that people in various objectively *different* groups can be placed in *one* perceived appearance group if another group (generally with some kind of power) defines them as such. Many people may belong to or identify with groups but may be considered by others as if they are part of a larger group, e.g., Inuit and Amerindian peoples being treated as "Natives," or Canadian Negroes of diverse Caribbean and American origins being lumped together as "Blacks." In short, it doesn't make any difference in an objective sense to what group a person belongs, as long as another group defines it differently and then acts toward the individual or group on that basis. Legal definitions and stigmas of various sorts are utilized in establishing consensual symbols so that man can interact with his fellow man. Let us present a very real example from Pretoria, South Africa:

The Supreme Court here today upheld the classification of 11 year old Sandra Laing as coloured (mixed race) although her parents and their children are all classified as whites.

Sandra was classified coloured by the race Classification Board in February last year. She was said by South African officials to be a genetic throwback, showing strong non-white characteristics.

Dismissing an application by her father, Abraham Laing, for Sandra to be classified as white, Justice Oscar Calgut said the girl might still become white under legislation now before Parliament that would make descent, rather than appearance and general acceptance, the standard for race classification. (*New York Times*, May 3, 1967)

Canadians have knowledge and images of their own society (and the groups within) which determine the basis of action initiated between groups and subsequent reaction by the group toward which the action is directed. Society, then, may be viewed as a maze through which man must find his way.

We can get some idea of how complex this task is by imagining isolated individuals placed in an environment so new that their previous mental tools were of no use. How shall they respond to what they encounter? The task is very demanding for:

> The world of experience of any normal man is composed of a tremendous array of discriminably different objects, events, people, impressions. No two people we see have an identical appearance and even the objects that we judge to be the same object over a period of time change appearance from moment to moment with alterations in the light or in the position of the viewer. (Bruner, et al., 1956: 1)

The picture becomes still more complex when we add that much of man's maze consists not of a stable physical structure but also of other people whose reactions are important but not completely predictable.

If we assumed our isolated man to be in the natural human state, we would expect not a Hobbesian war of each against all but rather a willy-nilly randomness in which individuals responded uniquely to whatever concrete stimuli caught their attention for an instant. It is in this context that we understand the importance of Mannheim's (1936) statement that a society is possible in the last analysis because the individuals in that society carry around in their heads some sort of picture of that society. These *pictures in the head*, which are those aspects of the culture that provide information about the nature of the world, especially the social world, provide men with general orientations that are essential before men can act. (Parsons, 1964).

It will be our task to examine the nature of these pictures in the head, and show how we use them in finding our way through the maze that is society. They not only help man choose, but chain us to particular paths. In considering ethnic relations in particular, we will note that the pictures which some people hold in their heads lead them along paths that end at places other than brotherhood.

Tolman (1951) suggests that the individual deals with the diversity of stimuli by means of cognitive maps which permit him to respond selectively to the stimuli which he experiences. Tolman further elaborates his idea under the heading of a *belief-value matrix*, which he sees as one of the most important mechanisms by which the individual sorts stimuli. A belief-value matrix includes:

> Typed (not concrete) images of objects which the individual possesses by virtue of the differentiations and categorizations of the object world . . . which he has previously acquired, means-ends beliefs which indicate the types of ends for which different means are appropriate and range of objects which will serve for various means, and values (in the individual psychological sense) attached to the different cognitive elements. (Tolman, 1951: 290-291)

As students of society we are not primarily concerned with how an isolated individual reacts to all stimuli he encounters. Our main concern is how similar patterns of action emerge in response to the stimuli which are social in nature. Tolman moves us toward this goal by suggesting that a belief-value matrix may become "a culturally and sociologically determined belief and value system as shared by a community of individuals" (p. 294).

Our interest is now brought to bear on a cognitive pattern that is more or less common to the members of some society or segment of a society. As Albig (1956) points out:

A consideration of the life of an individual, a people or an age must begin with an inventory of its systems of thought. There are always complexes of popular convictions and beliefs that are fundamental and decisive for the life of the time. Underlying such popular thought are the systems provided by the professional philosopher, theologian, political theorist and economist. (13)

Madge (1964) also addresses this issue when he states:

Each of us has in his mind some sort of a picture (seldom clearly in focus) of society, just as he has a picture of the universe and a picture of himself. If and when we scrutinize the picture, there become detached from it certain elements which I shall call ideas: an inexact word which will be readily understood. While it is possible to consider such ideas either cognitively or evaluatively, these aspects are seldom separated by anyone but a philosopher or a sociologist. I would describe their function as the validation, or invalidation, of social institutions. Validation can be considered cognitively as a form of explanation or evaluatively as a form of justification. The emphasis is now on one, now on the other, and in most everyday thinking and expression, the distinction simply does not arise. (13)

Thus far we have raised several general points about thought patterns and their role in society. We will now summarize these points and show how we intend to use them in the study of ethnic relations.
(1) Man relates to his world by means of ideas. These ideas simplify the world in several ways.
(2) They provide categories or classes for events and objects. Rather than responding to each unique event man assigns individual events to categories and responds in a similar way to all members of a category.
(3) The categories are related to each other in "maps" in the mind. These relationships provide further organization to man's thoughts and actions.
(4) These ideas provide not only information (cognition) but also evaluations which provide man with a basis for judgment and feeling.
(5) Many of these ideas are shared by members of a society so that the pictures and the reactions are common to members of a society or group.
(6) These ideas are sufficiently related to each other that they can be viewed as systems of thought.

In a given society there will be ideas which deal with those things that are of concern to the members of the society. It is possible to talk about the socially accepted ideas that deal with courtship, child rearing, food habits, the supernatural, or any other topic that might be mentioned as important in a society. Our broad concern is with relationships between groups, and our specific concern is with the understanding of the relationships between ethnic groups.

Culture and Subculture

We have agreed that many groups popularly defined as races or sub-races are in fact primarily cultural rather than physical entities. While race may be *socially* significant, strictly speaking it should be viewed as a basically biological rather than sociological concept. Thus a race as a major grouping of people is generally biologically inbred to the extent that these people possess certain similar physical features which are biologically inherited from generation to generation unless amalgamation, or race mixing, occurs. Culture is manmade and is transmitted not through biological heredity but through learning. Culture has traditionally been divided by anthropologists into material culture (consisting of material objects, such as artifacts, and the ways in which these are used) and non-material culture (beliefs, customs, languages, social institutions, mentifacts).

While a physical definition of race may be a basis for differentiating mankind, and may be one element in defining ethnicity, most differentiating criteria are clearly cultural. Thus cultural anthropologists have equated cultures with ethnic groups and possibly subraces. Moreover, the slightly more specific term subculture has been used both by anthropologists (Steward, 1955) and sociologists. Assuming that groups with certain common interests tend to evolve behavior patterns differing from those of other groups and from the larger society's conventions, anthropologists and sociologists have employed the term subculture to refer to the more or less different folkways and mores developed by each group within a society. Hence the term has been applied to a wide variety of sub-groupings within a larger society, including disadvantaged, deviant, and ethnic groups. The problem is that culture and subculture are not very specific concepts, having limited empirical or theoretical utility.

Nation, Nationality, and Nationalism

Hans Kohn (1955: 9) has described nationalism as "a state of mind, in which the supreme loyalty of the individual is felt to be due the nation-state." Such a definition presupposes an understanding of what is meant by the term *nation-state*. And any reference to the nation-state as a particular type of political state depends in turn upon the concepts of *nation* and *nationality*.

What, then, is a nation? It is, in the simplest sense of the term, an ethnic group or people; the term does not *necessarily* refer to a political entity, although as Azkin (1964: 11) has pointed out at considerable length, this term has been used (especially in the English language) to denote concepts intimately linked to the state at least as much as with phenomena connected with ethnic groups, if not more so. Stalin wrote in 1914, "a nation is a historically evolved, stable community of people, formed on the basis of a common language, territory, economic life, and psychological make up manifested in a common culture."

It should be noted that the first characteristic which Stalin listed was "historical evolution." Indeed, among the criteria of nationhood, common heritage has repeatedly been singled out as a prime factor. Thus as early as 1782 Burke was writing that "a nation is an idea of continuity in time . . . ." And in an essay written in 1861 John Stuart Mill argued that "the strongest cause for the feeling of nationality . . . is identity of political antecedents; the possession of a national history, and consequent community of recollections; collective pride and humiliation, pleasure and regret, connected with the same incidents in the past." In 1862 the French writer Renan referred to "the soul and spiritual principle" of a nation as the "resultant of a long historic past, of sacrifices and efforts made in common, and of a united will and aspiration in the present; to have done the present." Bauer wrote in Austria (1924: 135) about a "community of character." And more recently we may note the British historian E. H. Carr (1945: 39) summing up concisely that "the modern nation is a historical group."

It should also be noted that Stalin appropriately referred to the "psychological make up" of a nation; this subjective aspect of national identity has aroused the attention of many writers. We may cite Disraeli's (1836) mention of a "national mind," Barker's (1927: 17) of a "common stock of thoughts and feelings acquired during the course of a common history," and Bauer's (1924: 135) of a "national character." Or we could cite Spengler's (1941: 6, 58-59) definition of nations as "spiritual unities," Lamprecht's (1905) as "social souls," Meinecke's (1908: 2) as "mental communities," and Don Sturzo's (1946: 13-17) as "collective personalities."

But all of these criteria and definitions have been subject to a good deal of criticism. For example, Renan (1887) pointed out at considerable length that a nation is not *necessarily* based on race, or on language, or religion, or a "community of interests," or the geographical factor (i.e., natural frontiers). Again, Deutsch (1953: 18) has remarked that "some of the most frequently cited objective characteristics of a people do not seem to be essential to its unity"; he criticized theories which base nationhood on common language, territory, conditions or experience, or on a community of history and memories, and common heritage. As for common heritage as a factor in national identity, Huxley and Haddon (1940: 16) remarked that "the nation is a society united by a common error as to its origins and a common aversion to its neighbors." Hertz (1944: 12-13) has, in turn, pointed out some of the difficulties in using such terms as *consciousness* and *will* in discussions of national identity; he has written, "a nation . . . is a community of fate, to a large extent brought together and molded by historical events and natural factors, and the individual has practically little opportunity of choosing his nationality or changing its fundamental traits." Thus, E. H. Carr (1945: 34) could safely conclude that "the nation is not a definable and clearly recognizable entity," in view of all these criticisms. Despite Disraeli's (1836) warning that "the phrase 'the people' is sheer nonsense," it still seems reasonable to retain our original definition of the nation, in the very simplest sense, as an ethnic group or people, if we remember that each people have their own unique historical development, culture, etc., and hence their own identity and *raison d'etre*.

Does a nationality differ from a nation, and if it does, how does it differ? English-language dictionaries (e.g., Webster's) define *nation* either as (a) "a people connected by ties of blood, language, religion, and culture, and by a sense of mutual interest" (i.e., in an essentially non-political, ethnic sense), or as (b) "the people in a country united under a single independent government," (i.e., in a political sense). Similarly, the ethnic and political factors enter into these standard dictionary definitions of "nationality"; by "nationality" is meant "national character or existence," or "the fact of belonging to one particular nation or state by birth, allegiance, etc."

The Canadian writer William Moore (1918: 3-5) seems to have equated the term nationality with definitions of the nation through conditional enumeration of objective criteria; he has written, "while we cannot define nationality satisfactorily, we can set forth the factors that usually, but by no means always, enter into it: ethnic identity, identity of language, the unity of religion, common economic interests, habitation subject to common geographical conditions, common history and traditions, and a uniform theory of government." He has added that "the word 'nationality' should not be confused with the word 'nation' in the sense of a state; the state is the encasing, the nationalities . . . the encased."

The late Louis Wirth (1936), a prominent American sociologist, has described a "nationality" as "people who, because of the belief in their common descent and their mission to the world, by virtue of their common cultural heritage and historical career, aspire to sovereignty over a territory, or seek to maintain or enlarge their political or cultural influence in the face of opposition." In thus describing a nationality as a conflict group in the sociological sense, Wirth has closely linked the ethnic and political factors.

In relating the two concepts of nation and nationality, Deutsch (1953) has written:

> a "nation" is often said by . . . writers to be a people living in a state "of its own". By this is meant, it seems, that the ruling personnel of this state consist largely of individuals who share the main characteristics of this people, and that the administration of this state is carried on in this people's language and in line with what are considered to be its characteristic institutions and patterns of custom. . . . A "nationality" in this widespread usage is, then, a term which may be applied to a people among whom there exists a *significant* movement toward political, economic, or cultural autonomy, that is to say, toward a political organization, or market area, or an area of literary or cultural interchange, within which the personnel and characteristics of this people will predominate. (17-18)

Here we may note the suggestion that, although both nation and nationality apparently may refer to the ethnic group *per se* (at least according to usage of these terms in continental European languages), these terms should be restricted at least to *politically significant* ethnic groups. Akzin (1964: 35, 41) has repeatedly made this point explicit. He has stated that there can be a point where the ethnic group begins to loom either as an active factor in an existing political structure or as a challenge to such a structure; and it is at this point that one can begin to refer to the ethnic group as a nation or nationality. He has added that such a distinction between an ethnically based nationality which becomes an active factor in politics and an ethnic group that does not yet amount to a real nationality (in this sense) is not necessarily marked but uncertain and subject to change.

Akzin (1964: 39-40) has further pointed out that this political significance of an ethnic group may result either from the demographic and cultural strength of the group (without any deliberate organized effort to gain political significance) or from a concious movement to influence a political structure in which the values of the ethnic group can best be realized. In the first case a nation may have become organized as a nation-state prior to the era of nationalism, according to Akzin, whereas in the latter case nationalism as a social movement has either already resulted in the creation of a nation-state or is in the process of establishing such a state.

A nation-state is, therefore, more or less coterminous in its extent with the area occupied by a particular nation or nationality. The government of such a state should identify with the nationality and adopt policies conducive to the welfare of the group. Conversely, the nationality owes a primary loyalty to its state and must accept, by and large, the authority of the state. Moreover, according to the classic definition by Max Weber (1968), the early twentieth century German scholar, the modern political state must have differentiated national level governmental and economic institutions, as well as a highly developed legal-rational bureaucracy (as defined by Weber) and a certain psychological basis for national coherence. (Though Weber did not specifically emphasize real or imagined ethnicity as this basis, in the case of the *nation-state* national unity ultimately rests upon ethnic solidarity, according to many writers.)

The concept of the nation-state is intimately related to that of nationalism, as Kohn has suggested. Shafer (1955) has summarized:

> at present by the word (nationalism) may be denoted that sentiment unifying a group of people who have a real or imagined common historical experience and a common aspiration to live together as a separate ethnic group in the future. This unifying sentiment expresses itself in loyalty to the nation-state whatever the government, in love of native land however little known, in pride in common culture and economic social institutions though these may not be understood, in preference for fellow nationals in contrast to disregard for members of other groups, and in zeal not only for group security but for glory and expansion. (10)

Nationalism is essentially a social movement. Wirth (1945) has succinctly defined nationalism as the social movements, along with the attitudes and ideologies, of nationalities striving to acquire, maintain, or enhance their position in the world vis-a-vis other nationalities. But just what is meant by nationalism depends upon the particular case studied. As Shafer has explained:

> Nationalism is what the nationalists have made it; it is not a neat, fixed concept but a varying combination of beliefs and conditions. It may be in part founded on myth, but myths like other errors have a way of perpetuating themselves and of becoming not true but real. The fact is that myth and actuality and truth and error are inextricably mixed in modern nationalism. . . . Nationalism, then, becomes a concept so complex and changing that it defies short, logical definition. (7)

Our discussion so far has centred on the relevance of nationalism to the creation or maintenance of a nation-state based on a single nation or nationality. But what of a state incorporating more than one nation? Akzin (1964) has suggested that very few states in the world today could be called mono-ethnic states in any real sense:

> Under modern conditions the purely mono-ethnic state has become an anachronism, and an almost vanished one at that. The transportation of frontiers following the meanderings of political history on the one hand, and the increased mobility of mankind due to the development of com-

merce and communications on the other, have transformed practically every state . . . into a poly-ethnic one. There are, however, states in which the dominant ethnic group is so well integrated and occupies so overwhelming a position in respect to numbers and status, and in which the secondary ethnic groups are relatively so insignificant, that the latter may be ignored for most practical purposes. States of this kind (e.g., Sweden, Norway, Denmark, the Netherlands, postwar Poland, Hungary, Bulgaria, and perhaps France, Britain, and Greece, etc.) face the problem of poly-ethnicity to a minor extent only, as a largely transitional issue pending the full integration of any hetero-ethnic groups. (49-50)

Given this increasing scarcity of mono-ethnic states, we must be careful how we employ the term nationalism, for if nationalism refers to nation-states, as Kohn (1955) and other writers have suggested, and if a nation-state is essentially a mono-ethnic state, then presumably nationalism may apply more to an ethnic minority (or majority) *within* a poly-ethnic or multi-national state than to the state's citizenry as a whole.

Thus Akzin (1964: 51-52) has pointed out that if any state cohesion does in fact prevail, attachment to the *state*, i.e., *patriotism*, tends to be emphasized, while attachment to a dominant *nationality* within the state, i.e., *nationalism*, is less conspicuous. However, poly-ethnic states are by no means necessarily politically cohesive as wholes. According to Furnivall (1939), nationalism within a plural society is itself a disruptive force, tending to shatter and not to consolidate the social order. And in Akzin's words (1964: 49), "the assumed identity between the political and the ethnic community is shaken by the appearance of hetero-ethnic elements within the state."

Akzin's (1964) elaboration of this idea seems especially relevant to the Canadian situation. He has written:

in [some] states . . . poly-ethnicity is a central rather than a lateral issue. Such a case may be due to the yet incomplete ethnic integration of the main mass of the inhabitants, to the larger numerical proportion of non-dominant ethnic groups . . . [e.g., the French and the "New"Canadians] ". . . in relation to the total population, to a strong concentration of a non-dominant ethnic group in part of the state's territory. . . ." [e.g., the French Canadians in Quebec] . . . The problems posed by poly-ethnicity in such cases are of a durable character, and their solution . . . may seriously affect the structure and social climate of the state involved, in extreme cases even its territorial integrity or its existence. . . . In these types of poly-ethnic states the issue becomes particularly acute if one or more of the ethnic groups within them have been aroused to present claims of a political nature, bearing on the basic values or organizational structure of the state concerned, and must therefore be regarded as nationalities. . . . (50-51)

In other words, we can note that in certain poly-ethnic states a majority nationalism, or for that matter a general patriotism towards the state as a whole, may be effectively countered by a minority nationalism, a nationalism referring to a nationality *within* the state.

However, when one exhausts the lists of all the various definitions, the end result is summarized by Connor (1978). He points out that a nation is difficult to define because the *essence* of a nation is intangible. This essence is a psychological bond that joins a number of people and differentiates the group, in the subconsciousness of its members, from other people.

Normally, one becomes a citizen of a particular nation-state by being born within a set political boundary. This boundary may change over time as political units emerge and die, grow or decrease in size. Hence, by holding an ascriptive trait, one belongs to a particular national group. However, one can become a national at any point in one's life by applying for such status and fulfilling the necessary requirements established by the particular nation-state (Klass and Hellman, 1971). In fact, in some cases, many people can belong to two nationalities (or not belong to any) at one point in time.

At best one can thus characterize nationality as a quasi-legal term, referring to a status denoting a consciousness of a group of people possibly sharing the following: physical environment, language, customs, history, religion, political entity and a view of the future (Atwater, et al. 1967; Griessman, 1975).

The applicability of the concepts *nationality, nation, nation-state* and *nationalism,* to Canadian society will be discussed in more detail in Chapter 6.

Minority Group

Yetman and Steele (1971) point out that the origin of the concept *minority group* was derived from the European experiences after the emergence of the nation-state concept and the subsequent conceptualization of nationalism. In the European context, the term was used to identify various national and ethnic groups that had (because of changes in political boundaries) become subordinate to other people.

Louis Wirth was perhaps the first social scientist to introduce this concept as an analytical tool. He defined a minority as:

> a group of people who, because of their physical or cultural characteristics, are singled out from others in the society in which they live for differential and unequal treatment and who therefore regard themselves as objects of collective discrimination. (Wirth, 1945: 347)

The general focus of this definition centres on the existence of minorities' subjective feelings and their subordinate status in the society. However, Simpson and Yinger (1958: 22) have cautioned that "minorities are not all alike. They differ in the symbols which set them apart, in the nature of their relationships to the dominant groups and in their reactions to the situation."

The ambiguity apparent in the many usages of this term has been summed up recently by the Theodorsons (1969), who have suggested that a minority group can be:

> any recognizable racial, religious, or ethnic group in a community that suffers some disadvantage due to prejudice or discrimination. ... This term, as commonly used, is not a technical term, and indeed it is often used to refer to categories of people rather than groups, and sometimes to majorities rather than minorities. ... On the other hand, a group which is privileged or not discriminated against but which is a numerical minority would rarely be called a minority group. Thus, as the term is often used, a

minority group need be neither a minority nor a group, so long as it refers to a category of people who can be identified by a sizeable segment of the population as objects for prejudice and discrimination.

Recognizing that the term minority group has not been very explicit, Schermerhorn (1970: 12-13) has stressed that it is imperative to circumscribe the meaning of this term. He therefore restricts its application to a subordinate group which is small in size and power, as opposed to a dominant group signify-ing "that collectivity within a society which has pre-eminent authority to func-tion both as guardians and sustainers of the controlling value system, and as prime allocators of rewards in the society." Yet even Schermerhorn's restric-tion of the term emphasizes, as do the definitions by other writers, a conflict situation which is not necessarily applicable to every ethnic group in Canada.

Wagley and Harris (1964), Schermerhorn (1967), Van der Zander (1972) and Williams (1964) have all suggested that the concept minority group refers to a self-conscious social group into which one is usually born and whose members experience various disabilities as a result of special attributes which they share. Gittler (1956) defines a minority group as a group whose members ex-perience a wide range of discriminatory treatment and frequently are relegated to positions relatively low in the status structure of a society. The term, as used by social scientists, does not have any numerical connotation despite its literal meaning. It would seem, then, that the notion of power becomes central to this concept, i.e., the ability to make decisions in favor of one's membership group. It should be made clear at this time that since the concept is not attached to a specific group, almost any social grouping can be defined in terms of minority status. Today social scientists have begun to use the terms dominant and subor-dinate as synonymous with majority and minority. They argue that this ter-minology represents more accurately the differences in power that differentiate one from the other.

After a careful analysis of the concept, Van Amersfoort (1978) argues that the concept of minority has three constituent properties:

(1) a continuous collectivity within the population of a state,
(2) a numerical position that excludes it from taking effective part in the political process,
(3) an objectively disadvantageous position in the sense that its members do not participate to the same degree as the majority population in the legal system, educational system, labor market and the housing market. (233)

Because of the clarity of the definition provided by Van Amersfoort we feel that it is the most acceptable definition to be used by students. This definition necessarily implies the existence of one dominant group and, any number of minority groups in existence at any one time. The dominant group has the greatest power in the society and has the highest social status of all groups. For those groups labeled "minority," one can theoretically establish a hierarchy (so that some have more power than others) yet it must be understood that each group (individually—and in some instances collectively) has less power than the dominant group. If this ranking is able to be established, then it becomes clear that each social system can have only one dominant group.

While the above definition is clear and useful for social scientists, there are other problems in attempting to establish the characterizing attributes of the concept minority group, in an attempt to empirically establish boundaries of the group one wishes to study. For example, some minority groups are concentrated in one nation, region or geographical location, e.g., Quebec French-Canadians. Or, it may be the case that they are interspersed throughout the political unit of which they are a part, e.g., the poor, or native people. Hence, it may be that in one region of the nation-state they are dominant while in other areas they hold minority status.

REFERENCES

Akzin, B. *State and Nation*. Garden City, NY: Anchor/Doubleday, 1964.

Albig, *Modern Public Opinion*. New York: McGraw Hill, 1956.

Atwater, E. K. Fouster and J. Prybyla. *World Tensions*. New York: Appleton Century Crofts, 1967.

Banton, M. *Race Relations*. London: Tavistock, 1967.

Barker, Sir E. *National Character and the Factors in its Formation*. New York: Harper, 1927.

Bastide, Roger. "Color, Racism and Christianity, " *Daedalus*, 96 (Spring 1967): 312-328.

Bauer, O. *Die Nationalitätenfrage und die Sozialdemokratie*. Vienna: Brand, 1924.

Birren, F. *Colour in Your World*. London: Collier-Macmillan Ltd., 1962.

Blumer, H. "What is Wrong with Social Theory," *American Sociological Review*, (19 February 1955): 3-10.

Bruner, J., J. Goodnow and G. A. Austin. *A Study of Thinking*. New York: John Wiley and Sons, 1956.

Burke, E. Speech, "On the State of Representation of the Commons in Parliament," 1782 in *Works* (1925-30), Col. 3.

Carr, E. H. *Nationalism and After*. London: Macmillan, 1945.

Connor, Walker. "A Nation is a Nation, is a State, is an Ethnic Group," *Ethnic and Racial Studies*, Vol. 1, (October 1978): 379-400.

Coon, C. *The Origin of Races*. New York: Knopf, 1962.

Davis, A. K. "Urban Indians in Western Canada: Implications for Social Theory and Social Policy," *Transactions of the Royal Society of Canada*, Vol. 6 (June 1968): 217-228.

Deutsch, K. W. *Nationalism and Social Communication*. Cambridge, Mass: MIT Press, 1953.

Dingwall, E. J. *Racial Pride and Prejudice*. London: Watts Publishing, 1946.

Disraeli, B. 1836, Cited in *Lord Beaconsfield, The Spirit of Whiggism*.

Furnivall, J. S. *Netherlands India*. Cambridge University Press, 1939.

Gittler, J. *Understanding Minority Groups*. New York: John Wiley & Sons, 1956.

Gosset, T. *Race: The History of an Idea in America*. Dallas: SMU Press, 1968.

Griessman, B. *Minorities*. Hinsdale, Ill: Dryden, 1975.

Hertz, F. *Nationality in History and Politics*. New York: Oxford, 1944.

Huxley, J. S. and A. C. Haddon. *We Europeans*. Oxford, 1940.

Klass, M. and H. Hellman. *The Kinds of Mankind*. New York: J. B. Lippincott, 1971.

Kohn, H. *Nationalism: Its Meaning and History*. New York: Van Nostrand, 1955.

Lamprecht, Moderne Geschichtswissenschaft, Freiburg, 1905 (cited in A. Cobban, *National Self-Determination*. London: Oxford, 1945, pp. 52-53).

Livingstone, F. "On the Non-Existence of Human Races," *Current Anthropology*, 3 (1962): 279-281.

McAllister, R. *The Sociological Use and Misuse of Ethnicity*, Mimeo. Riverside: University of California, 1975.

Madge, C. *Society in the Mind*. New York: Free Press, 1964.

Mannheim *Ideology and Utopia*. New York: Harcourt and Brace, 1936.

Marshall, G. "Racial Classifications: Popular and Scientific," in M. Mead, T. Dobzhansky, E. Tobach and R. Lights (eds.), *Science and the Concept of Race*. New York: Columbia University Press, 1968.

Meinecke, F. *Weltbürgertum und Nationalstaat*. Leipzig: Koehler & Amelang, 1908.

Mill, J. S. *Essay on Representative Government*, 1861.

Molnar, S. *Races, Types and Ethnic Groups*. Englewood Cliffs, NJ: Prentice Hall, 1975.

Montagu, A. "The Concept of Race," *American Anthropologist*, 64 (1962): 919-928.

Moore, W. H. *The Clash: A Study in Nationalities*. Toronto: J. M. Dent, 1918.

Nash, "The Ideology of Race," *Current Anthropologist*, 2 (1962): 285-289.

Osborne, *The Biological and Social Meaning of Race*. San Francisco: W. H. Freeman and Co., 1971.

Osgood, C., G. Suci and P. Tannenbaum. *The Measurement of Meaning*. Urbana, Ill: University of Illinois, 1957.

Park, R. "Human Migration and the Marginal Man," *American Journal of Sociology*, 3 (1928): 113-128.

Parsons, T. *Social Structure and Personality*. New York: Free Press, 1964.

Renan, E. "Qu-est-ce qu'une nation," in *Discours et conferences*, 2nd ed., Paris: Calmann-Levy, 1887, pp. 277-310.

Sargent, W. *The Enjoyment and Use of Color*. New York: Scribner's Sons, 1923.

Schermerhorn, R. "Polarity in the Approach to Comparative Research in Ethnic Relations," *Sociology and Social Research*, 51, January (1967): 235-240.

Schermerhorn, R. *Comparative Ethnic Relations*. New York: Random House, 1970.

Shafer, B. *Nationalism: Myth and Reality*. New York: Harcourt Brace, 1955.

Simpson, G. and J. Yinger. *Racial and Cultural Minorities*. New York: Harper and Row, 1958.

Slobodin, *Metis of the Mackenzie District*. Ottawa: St. Paul University, 1966.

Snyder, L. *The Idea of Racialism*. New York: Van Nostrand, 1962.

Spengler, O. *Gedanken*. Munich: C. H. Beck, 1941.

Stalin, Joseph. *Marxism and the National Question*. Moscow, 1914.

Steward, J. H. *Theory of Cultural Change*. Urbana, Ill: University of Illinois, 1955.

Don Sturzo, Luigi. *Nationalism and Internationalism*. New York: Roy, 1946.

Theordorson, G. A. and A. *Modern Dictionary of Sociology*. New York: T. Y. Crowell, 1969.

Tolman, E. "A Psychological Model" in Parsons and Shils (eds.), *Toward a General Theory of Action*. Cambridge: Harvard University Press, 1951.

Van Amersfoort, H. " 'Minority' as a Sociological Concept," *Ethnic and Racial Studies*, 1, 2, (1978): 218-234.

Van den Berghe, P. L. *Race and Racism: A Comparative Perspective.* New York: John Wiley, 1967.

Van den Berghe, P. L. "Race and Ethnicity: A Sociological Perspective," *Ethnic and Racial Studies*, Vol. 1, 4, (October 1978): 401-411.

Van der Zander, J. *American Minority Relations: The Sociology of Race and Ethnic Groups.* New York: Ronald Press, 1972.

Wagley, C. (ed.) *Race and Class in Rural Brazil.* Paris: UNESCO, 1952.

Wagley, C. and M. Harris. *Minorities in the New World.* New York: Columbia University Press, 1964.

Weber, M. *Economy and Society, Vol. 1.* New York: Bedminster Press, 1968.

Williams, R. *Strangers Next Door: Ethnic Relations in American Communities.* Englewood Cliffs, NJ: Prentice Hall, 1964.

Wirth, Louis "Types of Nationalism," *American Journal of Sociology*, Vol. XLI, (May 1936.)

Wirth, Louis "The Problem of Minority Groups," in R. Linton (ed.), *The Science of Man in the World Crisis.* New York: Columbia Univ. Press, 1945.

Yetman, D. and C. Steele. *Majority and Minority: The Dynamics of Racial and Ethnic Relations.* Boston: Allyn & Bacon, 1971.

Chapter 3

Ethnicity: Objective Criteria

If the concepts *race, culture* and *subculture, nation* and *nationality,* and *minority group* have continually been redefined in the literature of the social sciences, so have the more recent concepts of *ethnic group* and *ethnicity.* In one of the earliest attempts at a definition, Ware (1931) considered ethnic communities to be "groups bound together by common ties of race, nationality, or culture, living together in an alien civilization but remaining culturally distinct." She added, "purely religious communities do not fall under the term although they are in many respects similar to the groups here discussed." But if "purely" religious communities could not be considered as ethnic communities, C. A. Dawson (1936), writing on the development of ethnic bloc settlements in the Canadian Prairies, did include ethno-religious groups, e.g., Hutterites, Mennonites, Doukhobors, French- and German-Catholics, in an essay on ethnic communities. Warner and Srole (1945) rather ambiguously commented that "the term ethnic refers to any individual who considers himself, or is considered, to be a member of a group with a foreign culture and who participates in the activities of the group. Ethnics may be either of foreign or native birth." Francis (1976) pointed out that an ethnic group is not a race, if race refers to physical characteristics, nor is it a nation, if a nation is an aggregation of people united by political ties as well as other factors. French writers, particularly Delos, tended to interchange these terms; however Francis did borrow the idea of a *we-feeling* (la communauté de conscience de nous) from them, commenting that "the catalyst, or principal factor, which brings about such an extension of we-feeling is a mental process based on abstraction and hypostatical transposition of characteristics from the primary to the secondary groups." Francis stated flatly that we cannot define the ethnic group as a plurality pattern characterized by distinct language, culture, territory, folkways and mores, religion, attitudes and standards, descent, history, common government, etc. But, in keeping with Dawson and perhaps Ware, he did recognize that "sectarian groups . . . show all the traits and typical behavior of ethnic groups. . . . "

More recent writers have generally enumerated various factors as possible components of ethnic identity. Thus Berry (1958: 54) suggested the possibility of an ethnic group possessing ties of cultural homogeneity; a high degree of loyalty and adherence to certain basic institutions such as family patterns, religion, and language; distinctive folkways and mores; customs of dress, art, and ornamentation; moral codes and value systems; patterns of recreation; some sort of object to which the group manifests allegiance, such as a monarch, a religion, a language, or a territory; a consciousness of kind, a we-feeling; common descent (perhaps racial), real or imagined; and a political unit. However, out of this bewildering variety, which factors are the most significant? Akzin (1964: 36) has limited the term ethnic to "those characteristics which, being prevalent within the group and distinguishing it from other groups, lead us to consider it a people apart." Among the significant factors in his view—and in the view of such contemporary sociologists as Gordon (1964), Tumin (1965), the Theodorsons (1969), and Schermerhorn (1970)—are, first and foremost, a common cultural tradition and a sense of identity as a traditionally distinct subgroup within a larger society; and possibly possession of their own language, religion, and distinctive customs.

Thus ethnic groups may usually be minorities, though they can be dominant or national groups. They can be racial groups, though often this is not the case. They may be called subcultures, as defined by Steward (1955), determined in conjunction with social class (ethnicity and class may be combined to form *ethclass*), rural or urban residence, and regionalism, as explained by Gordon (1964: 38, 47-53). Objectively defined, an ethnic group may be little more than a population category, merely an aggregate of people sharing a given ethnicity or ethnic identity. Ethnicity may be ascribed to or assumed by persons. Ethnic consciousness is not an automatic subjective correlate of the objective ethnic category (Vallee, 1975).

Moreover, the term ethnic has often been used interchangeably with one or the other of the significant identificational factors. Certain traits may be emphasized more than others, depending on the group concerned. And the salience or significance of ethnicity in general varies with the historical situation and with the particular group (Tumin, 1965).

Principal Components of Ethnic Identity

We have noted that an ethnic group exhibits—or is believed to exhibit—a complex of traits, the sum of which identify the group. Consolidating the many identificational factors enumerated by sociologists, we may consider an objective definition of ethnic identity to be based primarily on the following four factors:

(1) *ethnic origin*, largely determined—according to Canadian census specifications—by the mother tongue spoken by an individual or his patrilinear predecessor upon immigration to North America; or referring to patrilinear descent from a forefather claiming membership in a certain ethnic group in a region from which he emigrated (not necessarily in the mother country), with this descent represented in a family name typical of the group (unless changed, e.g., Anglicized);

(2) *mother tongue*, i.e., a language traditionally spoken by members of a particular ethnic group;

(3) *ethnic-oriented religion*, i.e., participation or membership in a religious affiliation recognized as the traditional religion of a particular ethnic group;

(4) *folkways*, i.e., the practice of certain customs unique to the group.

In short, ideally the typical tradition bound ethnic group member may (a) value his ethnic origin, (b) fluently and primarily speak his traditional mother tongue, (c) attend an ethnic-oriented church as regularly as possible, and (d) follow various customs particular to his group. Conversely, ethnic identity change may refer not only to (a) de-emphasis of an ethnic origin, but also to (b) loss of mother tongue, (c) conversion from or loss of interest in an ethnic-oriented religion, and (d) failure to practise various folkways.

While language, religion, and folkways may be treated more or less as objective factors, ethnic origin will be discussed primarily from a subjective standpoint, otherwise it could be considered simply as a demographic statistic with little functional significance to sociologists and other social scientists. In other words, besides mentioning some complications arising out of the definition of their ethnic origin by members in certain ethnic groups, we will also be concerned with the *attitude* which the members have toward the preservation of their group identity, and with their orientation toward traditionalism.

A problem in utilizing those objective criteria is that, to put it succinctly, different ethnic groups have emphasized different criteria at different times for different reasons. Not all members of an ethnic group take a subjective interest in their ethnicity, genealogy, or group's history. Some ethnic groups have stressed retention of their traditional language, in which case they may be termed *ethno-linguistic* groups, while others have not. Some ethnic groups may be defined primarily by their unique religious beliefs and organization, in which case they could be called *ethno-religious* groups (e.g., Hutterites, Doukhobors, and possibly Mennonites and Jews); but in some ethnic groups religion may be regarded as not being vital to group membership. Lastly, the term folkways admittedly covers a wide variety of usages, arts, and practices. Thus certain folkways, such as preparing distinctive foods, may be characteristic of one group, while other folkways, for example performing folk music or folk dancing, may be a prominent tradition for another group. In fact, a given ethnic group might well be defined primarily neither in terms of an emphasis on common descent, nor language, religion, or folkways, but in terms of looking or behaving differently (from the rest of society); ethnic identity may be *supposed* and *imposed*.

As Anderson has explained (1980: 67-8), the variable significance of language, religion, and diverse customs as factors relating to ethnic consciousness can be very complex. To mention some specific Canadian examples, the Hutterites, essentially an ethno-religious group, have completely maintained use of their unique Austro-German dialect as well as distinctive dress, food, values and socialization practices, and communal organization. Whereas other ethno-religious groups, such as some progressive Mennonites (another Anabaptist group) and Reform Jews, have chosen to identify primarily in religious rather than ethno-linguistic terms.

Some ethnic groups may be internally divided by religious affiliations, and may place little emphasis on maintenance of a traditional mother tongue, while retaining a considerable degree of ethnic consciousness. For example, two of the numerically most significant ethnic categories in Canada, the Canadians of Scottish and Irish origin (together forming at least one–fifth of the total Canadian population), have little familiarity with Celtic languages (except perhaps, Scots in Nova Scotia), yet exhibit many folk traditions. Of course, this particular situation does not represent linguistic assimilation in Canada as much as it reflects the fact that only a small minority of Scots in Scotland (except in several remote areas in the Highlands and the Hebrides) or a larger minority of Irish in Ireland (except in the *Gaeltacht*) are fluent in Scottish or Irish Gaelic, despite attempts at Celtic linguistic revival in both of these countries (and more successfully in Wales).

The Ukrainian minority in Canada merits mention; this minority is particularly significant in the Prairie provinces and is also prevalent in the larger central Canadian cities. The Ukrainian Orthodox Church of Canada, in contrast to the Russian Orthodox Church (but largely similar to the eastern-rite Ukrainian Catholic Church), has with few exceptions steadfastly refused to adopt English as the principal language of the liturgy. Yet it should be pointed out that little more than half of the people claiming Ukrainian origin in Canada are still Orthodox or eastern-rite Catholic in religious affiliation, and little more than half can still speak Ukrainian. At the same time, a fairly high degree of ethnic consciousness prevails among Ukrainian-Canadians, who exhibit a rich tradition of folk music, dancing, and arts.

French-Canadians (the largest single ethnic group in Canada, forming about 28% of the total population) have traditionally stressed the survival (la survivance) of both their Roman Catholic religion and French language, as represented in their slogan "notre foi, notre langue." Yet the Roman Catholic Church has recently lost much of its once strong influence in French-speaking Quebec. Church attendance has declined dramatically during the past couple of decades, from an estimated 70% in 1957 down to only 30% in 1975 of Montreal's 1.5 million Catholics (*Associated Press*, Dec. 8, 1977). Clearly, then, it seems possible to identify as a French-Canadian without being a practising or even nominal Catholic. Moreover, separatists in Quebec have often tended to conveniently dismiss *les assimilés*, the more than half a million French-Canadians who cannot speak French out of 1.4 million French-Canadians outside Quebec, as no longer being truly French.

It is obvious that many Canadians take considerable interest in their ethnic background without speaking the traditional language, participating in a traditional religious affiliation to which most of their co-ethnics belong, or following certain folkways. One can be a Canadian of Scottish origin without speaking Gaelic, being a staunch Presbyterian, or parading around in a kilt. But it is viewed as more problematic whether one can claim to be Hutterite, Doukhobor, or Jewish without participating, at least nominally, in these religions. Or Ukrainian-Canadian unless one speaks Ukrainian and is at least a nominal member of a specifically Ukrainian church. Or French-Canadian unless one can speak French (presumably it is no longer considered so necessary to be Catholic as well).

Whatever pitfalls may be encountered in attempting an objective definition of ethnicity, clearly most ethnic collectivities in Canada have tended to stress one or more of these identificational criteria. So let us now probe further into the possible significance of language, religion, and folkways as factors serving to bolster ethnic consciousness.

Language and Ethnic Identity

Sociolinguists, sociologists and other social scientists have devoted much attention to the relationship between languages and ethnic consciousness (Anderson, 1980, Fishman, 1965); in fact many have stressed that language is the most important component of ethnic identity. For example, Freeman (1958: 34) has referred to language as "the rough practical test of nationality"; Shibutani and

Kwan (1965: 59, 75, 479) as "an essential part of culture and at the same time the instrument through which other aspects of culture are organized," as well as—with Bram (1955: 19, 23)—"a symbol of group identity" through socialization; Park (1950: 262) as the keynote to a "common community of purpose"; and Handlin (1951: 187) as the main focus of immigrant group identity in North America rather than place of origin. However, Fishman (1965) and others (e.g., Bram, 1955: chaps. 5-6; Potter, 1960: chap. 2; Trudgill, 1974: chaps. 3, 6) have pointed out the difficulty which sociologists have had in defining ethnicity (as distinct from nationality, race, religion), while linguists have found it no simple task to precisely delimit languages (as distinct from dialects, patois and argots).

Moreover, if the linguistic factor is *usually* important for most ethnic groups, it is not *always* an important, much less the *only*, component of ethnic identity (Anderson, 1980: 67). It is quite possible, then, for an ethnic group to lose its traditional mother tongue without losing its sense of identity, as Borrie (1959: 285) and others have cautioned. Ethnic consciousness is not necessarily dependent on maintenance of a unique traditional language, although linguistic change in an ethnic group may be to some extent an indication of acculturation and assimilation. The degree to which an ethnic group feels that its identity is being eroded is related to the emphasis which the group traditionally places on language, religion, and folkways as the keynote to group identity. In other words, if an ethnic group has tended to emphasize maintenance of its own traditional language, loss of that language will be equated largely with loss of group identity. Language, religion, and folkways, tend to be important components of ethnic identity and culture for most ethnic groups. Which aspects of ethnic identity are dispensible in situations of change is not so easy to determine, however.

Suffice it to say at this point in our discussion that analysing linguistic change as an integral part of ethnic identity change can be very complicated, for several reasons (Anderson, 1980: 78).

First, we have stressed that language can be an important criterion of ethnic identity. But, while retention of a traditional ethnic language is usually the most significant identifying criterion for ethnic groups (i.e., most ethnic groups could be defined as ethno-linguistic groups), it is not the only criterion, nor is it necessarily the most significant for all ethnic groups (e.g., some ethnic groups could more readily be defined as ethno-religious groups than as ethno-linguistic groups).

Second, if an ethnic group largely or completely loses its traditional mother tongue, it does not necessarily cease to exist as an identifiable entity. Criteria other than language may become emphasized as a key to ethnic consciousness (Gans, 1979).

Third, a wide variety of factors may serve to determine the survival potential of ethno-linguistic minorities (including subjective awareness of ethnicity by ethnic group members, the greater strength of trans-ethnic nationalism than of minority intra- or sub-nationalism, demographic/ecological considerations, institutionalization of ethnic communities, and ethnic relations).

Fourth, ethno-linguistic minorities (with some notable exceptions) particularly immigrant groups, tend to eventually lose their traditional languages, for a variety of reasons. But these minorities differ in their tendency and capability to resist linguistic assimilation.

Fifth, the ability of minority group members to speak a traditional ethnic language may differ significantly from their desire (or possibly even freedom) to speak that language.

Sixth, linguistic change among ethno-linguistic minorites may assume the form of linguistic assimilation (implying loss of a traditional mother tongue) or of linguistic accommodation (implying change or compromise but not necessarily loss). Perhaps the former is more typical of immigrant groups in North America, the latter of ethno-linguistic minorites in Europe (where many examples of remarkable longevity of minority languages can be noted, such as among Basques, Bretons, Sorbs or Wends). Linguistic accommodation may include bilingualism and multiculturalism, as well as partial linguistic change reflected in neologisms, dialects and argots.

Religion and Ethnic Identity

Religion has frequently been used to bolster ethnic consciousness and perhaps language maintenance (e.g., Fishman, 1965: 66-9; Bram, 1955: 46-7; Shibutani and Kwan, 1965: 76, 413; Gordon, 1964: 35-7; Yinger, 1963: 89-113). Many of the functions of religion are oriented toward the preservation of ethnic identity. As various social scientists have pointed out, religion contributes to a sense of identity in an age of depersonalization; it may be a nationalistic force and assume the role of the protector of ethnic identity; it promotes social integration; it attempts to validate a people's customs and values; it inculcates values through socialization; it affirms the dignity of ethnic group members who might be considered by non-members as having low status; it tends to be a pillar of conservatism; and it often encourages conscious social isolation from outsiders (Yinger, 1963: 95, 104; Nottingham, 1954; Shibutani and Kwan, 1965: 413; Park, 1950: 366). Allport (1954) has commented:

> The chief reason why religion becomes the focus of prejudice is that it usually stands for more than faith—it is the pivot of the cultural tradition of a group. . . . The clergy of a church may, often do, become defenders of a culture. . . . In defending the absolutes of their faith, they tend to defend their in-group as a whole, finding in the absolutes of their faith justification for the secular practices of their in-group. Not infrequently they justify and sweeten ethnic prejudices with religious sanctions. . . . Piety may thus be a convenient mask for prejudices which intrinsically have nothing to do with religion. . . . We have argued that whereas realistic conflicts between religions may occasionally occur, most of what is called religious bigotry is in fact the result of a confusion between ethnocentric self-interest and religion, with the latter called upon to rationalize and justify the former. . . . In its institutional organization, therefore, religion is divisive. . . . The divisions that exist make it easy to contaminate the universalistic creeds of religion with irrelevant considerations of . . . national origin, cultural differences, and race. (415-418)

To Allport's comments we can add that a religious denomination or sect may be primarily universalistic or ethnocentric in its orientation; it may be a universal or folk religion (Schneider, 1970: 73-78). Moreover, we may constructively distinguish between (a) ethnic parishes of general (inter- or trans-ethnic) denominations (e.g., French, Polish, or German Roman Catholic parishes); (b) autonomous ethnic sub-denominations (e.g., Ukrainian Catholics); (c) independent ethnic denominations (e.g., Ukrainian Orthodox). We may further distinguish between juridical and non-juridical ethnic parishes, the former being parishes officially designated as serving the interests of a particular ethnic group (Harte, 1951). In addition to these distinctions, one must realize that some religious organizations represent divisions of formerly united denominations, while others are inclusive of several sects or subdivisions, and still others are related to various similar churches and sects which might be offshoots from the parent organization. To a considerable extent the proliferation of church schisms and sectarianism can best be explained by the variation in values and practices in an ethnically heterogeneous society, rather than simply by theological influences (Niebuhr, 1929; Yinger, 1963: 100).

In discussing religious change vis-a-vis ethnic identity change, several alternatives may be discerned. Religion may *cause* social change; or religious change may *result* from social change. For example, possibly there has been a move away from any form of religion, i.e., a general secularization. Contemporary sociologists have related the secularization of ethnic groups to the migration and mobility processes, assimilation in the schools, and the preoccupation of ethnic-oriented religious groups with secular concerns (Yinger, 1957, 1963; Schneider, 1970).

Besides secularization in the sense of a complete loss of any religious affiliation, conversion to a different religious affiliation is another type of religious change. For example, in Canada substantial proportions of Mennonites, German and Scandinavian Lutherans, Ukrainian Orthodox and Catholics, have converted to ethnic-oriented or non-ethnic evangelistic sects. In fact, a high proportion of members of certain ethnic groups in Canada are no longer members of the relevant traditional religious affiliations to which their predecessors belonged (see Chapter 11).

By considering the religious factor an important component of group identity, we must beware of prematurely concluding that the ethnic-religious link is indissoluble. But is the trend from folk to universal religion inevitably unidirectional? Will religion persist when an emphasis on ethnicity has declined, as Herberg (1955: 23, 32-4) and Yinger (1963: 93-104) have argued? Or can religion be lost while ethnic identity persists, as Tumin (1965) has suggested? According to Price (1959: 285-6), group settlements based on traditional religious beliefs tend to survive the forces of assimilation far more effectively than group settlements which are essentially ethnic in character, especially if religious forces reinforce separateness.

Folkways and Ethnic Identity

One anthropologist has commented that the sum total of the customs of similar individuals in a group or minority is their culture or subculture (Taylor, 1969: 30). To be more specific, we are equating customs with certain folkways contributing to the uniqueness of each ethnic group's identity. Among these folkways may be included ethnic foods, crafts, clothing, interior home decor, external architecture, rural village or urban neighborhood organization, recreational and leisure activities, kin gatherings, folk arts and music, taboos, family and socialization practices.

Discerning the significance of ethnic food is no simple task in North America, considering that we are all familiar with Italian pizza and spaghetti; French fried potatoes, French-Canadian style pea soup, and filet mignon; German frankfurters, pumpernickel bread and sauerkraut; Eastern European borscht and cabbage rolls; and Scandinavian (or Chinese) smorgasbords. However, many Canadian ethnic groups prepare and consume a wide variety of traditional foods little known to Canadians as a whole. Just to mention a few examples, Hutterites eat many varieties of dumplings, such as *kartoffelknödel* (potato), *fleischkrapfen* (meat), *nukelen* (egg), *schuttenkrapfen* (cheese), and *schnitzkrapfen* (apple). The Russian Doukhobors have their own version of *borscht* (beef or cabbage soup), *perohi* (dumplings), *blinzi* (milk and egg pancakes), *kapusniak* (sauerkraut and buckwheat boiled together), poppy-seed bread, and *holubutzi* (cabbage rolls). The Ukrainians and Poles may be familiar with some of these dishes, as well as with *kasha* (grain pudding), *kulesha* or *mamalyga* (Podcarpathian cornflour bread), and on special holidays such dishes as *paska* (Easter bread), and *kutia* (hulled wheat grains and honey for Christmas time). Some Scandinavian Canadians still prepare such traditional pastries as rosette cookies and *krumkake*; yet other traditional dishes, such as *rømmegrøt* or *fløtegrøt* (cream porridge), *lefsa* (bread), and *lutefisk* (fish in lye), are seldom still prepared at home; whereas *flatbrod* (flat-bread), *gjetost* (goat cheese), and fish balls, sardines and herring are readily available in Canadian supermarkets and therefore are eaten quite regularly in Canada, not just by people of Scandinavian origin. Some sausages, cheeses, and breads similar to ones in Germany are made in German communities in Canada and are also widely consumed beyond the immediate ethnic clientele.

Some families in certain ethnic groups still produce traditional crafts at home. There is a revival among Ukrainian Canadians in the arts of *pysanka* (Easter egg decorating), and in wearing *kylymy* (rugs or tapestries). Such work was particularly common among Bukovinian immigrants in the Prairie bloc settlements. The conservative Hutterites, Doukhobors, Mennonites and Amish were rather independent, making much of their own furniture and clothing in traditional style. Some Mennonite women still make quilts, embroidery, and needlework. Scandinavian crafts include needlework as tapestries or pillow-covers.

Wearing traditional clothing may be related to home craftsmanship. But unique clothing providing immediate ethnic or religious identification is worn on a day-to-day basis by very few groups in Canada today, except conservative ethno-religious groups (Hutterites, Old Order Mennonites and Amish, Hassidic Jews, and the most conservative Doukhobors). The Ukrainian women's embroidered smocks, ribbon headdresses, *obhortkas* (thick wool petticoats), embroidered white linen blouses, long billowing skirts, and leather boots, once common, were rapidly exchanged for typical Canadian clothing, though it is not at all unusual to find elderly women still wearing *babushkas* (long head scarves), and men wearing brimmed tweed caps. The once typical Ukrainian dress for men—coarse wool trousers, embroidered, bulky shirts, leather boots and heavy sheepskin coats—was also soon abandoned. The important consideration concerning traditional dress as a custom contributing to ethnic identity is that it is the only one readily visible to the general public for Whites, therefore it is an emphatic declaration of unique identity (Shibutani and Kwan, 1965: 80, 218).

Also related to crafts is interior home decor; at this point some comments on exterior design (ethnic architecture) would also seem to be in order. The Ukrainian houses in rural Prairie villages have been particularly distinctive. Yet there are few examples of the original style dwellings left; thatched roofs were for the most part replaced by shingled ones within a few years after immigration, and sod or log walls were replaced by white-washed clay ones, then frame ones. Up to the present day, however, religious icons and embroidery are quite common in Ukrainian-Canadian homes, both in rural and urban areas. Traditional conservative Mennonite homes, and present-day Hutterite homes, tend to be very simple, clean and fresh-painted, generally lacking adornments, with the absolute minimum of furniture. Mennonite settlers in Western Canada retained the Dutch custom of connecting homes with barns into one long building. Scandinavian homes in Canada often feature Scandinavian furniture, table runners, needlework, and miniature flags.

Even the layout of rural villages may constitute a folkway. For example, the Metis communities of Batoche and St. Laurent in Saskatchewan are semi-nucleated line or *rang* villages, with farmhouses on the road, paralleling the river, and fields extending away from the road and river; such a pattern is typically French-Canadian, found also in the old Manitoba river settlements and originally along the St. Lawrence in Quebec. Although in the Prairies the collective or nucleated Doukhobor villages have long been eradicated, they are still found where the more conservative Doukhobors resettled in interior British Columbia. Other villages of this type are the Old Colony Mennonite *bruderhofs*, still found in Manitoba and Saskatchewan, with residences lined up along a wide main street and a common pasture under the direction of the *herdschult*. The organization of Hutterite colonies is somewhat different: everyone eats in a central dining hall, there is a common kitchen and laundry as well as common farm buildings, and every building is set at right angles to the others in strict conformity with the Hutterite view of an ordered environment.

Recreational and leisure-time activities with an ethnic orientation might include, for example, fairs and festivals, bazaars, religious processions, community picnics, sports events, indoor and outdoor concerts, and plays. Some groups (e.g., Ukrainians, Jews, Italians) stress elaborate weddings, sometimes lasting several days. Mennonites have held building-bees, hog-slaughters, quilting bees, and *freundschaft* (extended family) gatherings (similar to the *Landsmannschaften* meetings among Eastern European Jews, or the *grande famille* tradition among French-Canadians).

Many immigrant groups in Canada brought with them cultures rich in folk arts, music and dancing. Pipe bands and Highland dancing, lavishly decorated Eastern Orthodox churches and Ukrainian folkdances have all become a common feature of the Canadian scene along with a vast range of artistic and musical contributions to Canadian culture from a diversity of ethnic groups. Doubtless this creativity is the most obvious feature of the heterogeneous Canadian mosaic (which we will discuss further in Chapter 6). Yet it should be pointed out that some groups (e.g., the Ukrainians) have tended to emphasize these folk arts more than others; certain groups in Canada (e.g., the Scandinavians) have revealed less of an inclination toward performing ethnic dances, singing or music. This is not necessarily a universal trait among different ethnic cultures.

Again, certain groups in Canadian society, notably the most conservative ethno-religious groups, have stressed taboos to ensure fairly rigid social control which could keep members within the fold. For example, among the Mennonite and Amish people in the Kitchener-Waterloo region in Ontario, the most conservative (Old Order) sects will not use electricity, any mechanized farm machinery, or drive cars or trucks (instead they use horses and buggies). But less conservative Mennonites and Amish in the same region may drive their cars completely painted black (including any chrome), or partly black (excluding chrome), or looking not too flashy (but not necessarily black), depending on degrees of conservatism or liberalism. In contrast, conservative Old Colony and *Bergthaler* Mennonites in the Prairies did not dress distinctively yet long frowned upon contacts with the outside world or even with more liberal Mennonites. And Hutterites still dress uniquely, and live segregated from the general society but allow for uncontrolled use of electricity, powered machinery and vehicles, and are among the most modernized and productive farmers in the West (Anderson and Driedger, 1980).

Finally, it should be mentioned that a variety of folkways relate to family traditions. In addition to extended family gatherings (mentioned above), particular ethnic groups may reveal differences in family size and structure, socialization techniques, propensity toward intermarriage, attitudes toward punishment of children, fertility or family planning behavior and attitudes toward sex roles (e.g., the role or place of women in the family or society) (Ishwaran, 1980). In concluding this section on folkways, it seems appropriate to quote a comment by Price (1959):

> It is plain that chain migration tends to strengthen in the group settlement the customs which prevail in the particular ideology or locality of Europe from which the migrants come. . . . A group may adopt the dress, the diet and the economic habits of the host society—as have numerous ethnic . . . settlements in . . . Canada. . . . But this does not necessarily mean that the groups concerned are becoming assimilated into the host society, or even becoming integrated with it. . . . Provided there continues a hard core of ideas or customs the group settlement persists as a separate entity, no matter how similar its economic behavior, or its habit of diet or dress, may be to that of the host society. (280, 286)

Overemphasis of Ethnicity

Ethnicity has been carelessly overemphasized in the literature of sociology and other social sciences, as exemplified in frequent mention of the term *ethnic groups*, and in frequent citing of census data referring to ethnic, linguistic, and religious populations.

First, can we legitimately talk about the "ethnic group"? Or are we actually referring to collectivities of ethnic-minded individuals? (Breton, 1978). But do ethnic minded individuals necessarily represent *group* interests? What proportion of the claimed members of a given ethnic group are actually aware of, interested in, or readily identifiable by their ethnic identity?

Burnet (1975: 7) has pointed out that "only a portion, and probably a small portion, of Canadians have participated in a complete, living folk culture; only a portion have learned folk customs and folk arts in their homeland; (and) those who have learned parts of their ancestral folk culture in Canada have sometimes been informed by guardians of its purity that what their grandparents taught them was debased or distorted."

Elaborating on Breton's point that the ethnic community in its organizational aspect is not likely to represent all segments of a collectivity of a certain ethnic origin, Stasiulis (1979) has continued to explain that in fact, it may systematically exclude certain sections of the ethnic population and articulate the interests of only a limited number of elements within the total ethnic population, as defined by social class, ideology, region, religion, or other criteria.

Second, it has often been reiterated—but apparently not often enough—that census definitions of ethnic origin are highly unreliable. The census counts in its ethnic origin category only those who claim the ethnic origin of the original *male* immigrant or predecessor to Canada. Thus, on the one hand, census data for some ethnic groups are underestimated; if we were to also count female predecessors or immigrants, and consider a person to be in an ethnic category by virtue of either male or female predecessors, some ethnic collectivities would be considerably larger. On the other hand, census data exaggerate the size of ethnic groups, or at least give us a very misleading impression, because of high proportions of intermarriage. In other words, census data on ethnic origin do not refer as much to homogeneous ethnic groups as to mixed populations. As we have already noted in discussing intermarriage vis-a-vis ethnic identity change, only a relatively small proportion, a minority, of several significant Canadian ethnic groups are in any sense homogeneous. *Most* Canadians, as counted in the census, of German, Dutch, Scandinavian, Italian, Ukrainian, Russian, Polish, Hungarian, or etc. ethnic origin are in fact only *partially* members of each relevant ethnic "group." This crucial fact is more often than not glossed-over in Canadian social science literature.

The concepts *social category* and *social aggregate* have often been used interchangeably with the concept ethnic group. A *social category* designates a number of individuals who possess some common characteristics. These social categories are statistical groupings which may or may not correspond with an actual social group (Hughes and Kallen, 1974; Francis, 1976; McKay and Lewins, 1978). The sociological importance of social categories is that they are often related to social behavior.

A second basis that is used for classifying a social context is physical proximity. Any time a number of individuals are in geographical proximity one can identify them as a *social aggregate*. The relevance and import of this concept lies in the fact that proximity is often a significant factor in determining social behavior and relationships.

These classification systems, then, are not the same as a group. To be sure, they can become social groups, but necessary changes must first take place. A group is a concept used to designate any set of individuals who take each other into account in their interaction patterns. The distinguishing attribute between a social group and a social aggregate or social category is interaction. This then, is the one characteristic that all groups have in common. To be sure, groups vary in size, stability, purpose and homogeneity of the members but the central and characterizing attribute of this concept is interaction.

Hence, when one discusses ethnic groups, we are referring to an actual social group (which may have emerged from a social category). For example, in precontact time (with Whites), Indian people considered themselves Cree, Ojibwa, Crow, etc. and identified themselves as such. However, when White contact took place, Europeans began to categorize each of these groups into a statistical category now referred to as *Indian*. Indians, then, should be considered a social category, not a social or associational group. However, recently the emergence of Pan-Indianism has begun to have an impact on Indian people and perhaps is slowly transforming them from a social category to an ethnic group. Why are we concerned about making a distinction between these terms? The answer is simply that knowing whether a set of individuals is a group, category or aggregate will give us differential predictive powers. This distinction is particularly important when one is using secondary data. For example, if you were told that you had information about one hundred members of a particular ethnic background, you would want to know if these one hundred people were a category, aggregate or a real group before you began to make predictions about their present or future behaviors. Unfortunately, many ethnic researchers do not distinguish between these concepts.

Most authors who use the term ethnic group do not attempt to give a clear, unambiguous definition of the concept. Its general usage refers to the cultural attributes of a number of people. As we interpret this meaning, this would include the sociological component of culture (patterns of interaction); technological (artifacts of the culture) and the ideological component (ideas and belief system of a group of people). As Connor (1978) points out, if this definition is used, it makes the concept ethnic group synonymous with minority group. And, he goes on, this is what has happened in the United States. The result has been the creation of a problem which has gone unresolved.

Manyoni (1978: 277) argues that the concept of ethnic group "does not define a specific social entity distinguishable from other aggregates by exclusive attributes." He goes on to argue that the term "appears to cover a multitudinous variety of socio-cultural units, some of which cannot be broken down into ethnic groups by the criteria assumed to define ethnicity."

Four Perspectives in Defining an Ethnic Group

Upon closer examination of the definition of *ethnic group* we find four distant perspectives with regard to how academics have defined an ethnic group. First of all are the "objectivists." These individuals argue that an ethnic group is a number of people who actually have common cultural attributes and possibly also physiological (e.g., racial) attributes. One simply has to identify the components and count them. This perspective is implicit in emphasizing language, religion, and folkways as criteria in defining ethnicity.

A second school of thought uses a "subjective" framework. Gordon (1964), Barth (1969), Glazer and Moynihan (1963), and Weber (1968) are perhaps the best known proponents of this perspective. They discuss the "shared feelings" of a group of people; the "self ascription," or "ascription by others" as the central characterizing attributes of ethnic groups.

A third manner of defining the concept ethnic group is that of integrating the above two positions (Berry, 1958; Shibutani and Kwan, 1965; Sinka, 1968). These individuals define ethnic groups not only in terms of objective criteria, but add to it the subjective dimension: thus an ethnic group is a hereditary group within a society which is *defined by its members and by others as a separate people*. Biologically and culturally, it need not be distinguishable in objective fact by any unique complex of traits.

A fourth position has been outlined by a number of sociologists (Williams, 1947; Schermerhorn, 1970; Greeley, 1974; Vallee, 1975), who have argued that the crucial characterizing concept is that of descent. Only those groups which have a distinct lifestyle and have passed this on for at least three generations can legitimately be considered an ethnic group.

It should also be pointed out that the definition of ethnic group as usually defined in North America is somewhat at variance with the definition used in Europe. European usage usually refers to ethnic groups as either coterminous with a national society, a nation or nationality, or folk (e.g., German Volk). However, as pointed out previously, in North America this concept, as well as the concept of race, has a very different meaning, at least in English-language social science. The Canadian Royal Commission on Bilingualism and Biculturalism utilized a subjective definition of ethnic groups, while its terms of reference referred to "les deux races fondatrices du Canada," literally—and quite inappropriately—translated into English as "the two founding *races* of Canada." (In anglophone sociology Canadians of British and French origin are founding peoples or ethnic groups, perhaps, but certainly not races, although in deference to native peoples the adjective "founding" is also rather inappropriate). The meaning attached to the concept of ethnic group generally assumes both a subjective and objective definition in contemporary Canadian sociology. For example, Isajiw (1974: 122) characterizes an ethnic group as "an involuntary group of people who share the same culture or descendents of such people who identify themselves and/or are identified by others as belonging to the same involuntary group."

Thus, an ethnic group is like any other social group in society. And social groups have characteristics that cannot be explained in psychological terms. In a sense, then, a group has its own reality. What are these characteristics? First of all, the membership may change as people are born and die or as people move in and out of the group. Still the group retains its reality.

A second dimension of groups centres on the fact that the group has a determining effect on the individual attitudes of the members. Through a process of socialization, new members are able to take on the norms, values and beliefs of current and past members (Burkey, 1978).

Hence, when we talk about an ethnic group we are referring to a social group (which may have emerged out of a social category) with an added ethnic component. This ethnic component refers to a diffuse sense of ancestry, a labeling of individuals as ethnics on the basis of a contrast of culture, language and/or phenotype and a community of interacting members.

One additional dimension related to the idea of ethnic group is that the concept is usually viewed from the perspective of traditional culture. However, as Isajiw (1974: 121) has so clearly pointed out, ethnicity may depend more on the "rediscovery" of ethnic patterns, i.e., "persons from any consecutive ethnic generation who have been socialized into the culture of the general society but who develop a symbolic relation to the culture of their ancestors." In the above process, there is selective retention/rediscovery of specific items from the cultural past which will achieve some sort of relevance for today's society.

In relating the difference between ethnic categories and groups, we wish to use a distinction set forth by Stymeist (1975). He points out that the idea of ethnic groups represents a high level of abstraction in the "ethnic system." He goes on to say:

> Although in some cases there is a direct transition from the base to the apex, in others there is not. That is, in some cases, differences in culture, as for example the difference in culture between different regions of a host country, do not fit into appropriate ethnic categories. (17)

FIGURE 1

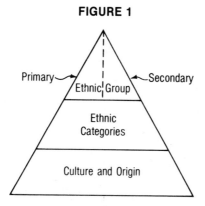

The maintenance or the disintegration of an ethnic group is a result of both internal pressures (within the group) and external pressures (from outside the group). However, as pointed out in Figure 1, we noted that there are two different types of ethnic groups that may result in the differential impacts of specific internal and external factors. The dichotomy set forth by Francis (1954), will be used to elucidate the differences.

Primary and Secondary Ethnic Groups

While we wish to point out the differences of these groups, it is also important to identify the similar attributes. Both groups come into existence when people are transferred from one society to another. A second similarity of the two groups is that there will be a difference between the transferees and the host society. The difference may be objective in nature or subjectively and arbitrarily defined. However, the difference is noticeable enough so that the transferred population can be readily identified with the parent rather than the host society.[1] Here is where the similarity ends.

Primary ethnics are less affected by an unfamiliar environment than those of a secondary type. After moving to a new area, a primary ethnic group still remains firmly embedded, at least on a subsocietal level, in a web of familiar social relationships. These relationships are more important for the satisfaction of ordinary social needs than are relationships with society at large, which are mainly confined to the political and economic sphere and, moreover, touch directly upon the interest of only some of the groups (Francis, 1976: 169). This is very characteristic of groups such as Italians and more recently, Portuguese. The recent work by Anderson and Higgs (1976) clearly demonstrates the intra-interaction patterns of this group (Portuguese) almost to the total exclusion of interacting with other ethnic groups. Breton's notion of *institutional completeness* (Chapter 6) is most applicable to this group.

Ethnics of the secondary type enter the new social system as isolated individuals or as small aggregates of migrants. They depend entirely on the host society for the satisfaction of almost all basic needs. As a result, they are at once forced to adjust to an unfamiliar social setting, to acquire a large number of new social skills, and to submit to the usually painful process of acculturation in order to function properly and to find their niche in the host society (Francis, 1976: 169). For example, when Ugandans or Vietnamese came to Canada, there was little opportunity for them to establish intragroup networks, and as a result they are dispersed throughout Canadian society. However, because of their predominant settlement patterns within urban centres, some networks are now being established. This is, of course, a result of the fact that physical proximity allows for easy social interaction patterns.

Primary, unlike secondary ethnic groups, are characterized by their ability to maintain their original identity and solidarity, to preserve their particular social structure and institutions, and to continue functioning in the host society in much the same way as they did in the parent society. This is so because their members are not compelled to rely entirely on the co-operation with the host society in order to satisfy their most pressing economic and social needs (Francis, 1976: 170). Primary ethnic groups are most likely to emerge when an agrarian population is being transferred into an industrial society.

Ethnics, who in their quest for economic satisfaction, are confronted not only with the problem of an unfamiliar social setting, but also with the resistance of the established (or charter) groups, are inclined to seek the support of people with a familiar background and similiar experience. In addition, they feel the need for more intimate social relationships, which, as a rule, are denied to them, at least on equal terms, by the host society. The need for mutual aid and the desire for intimate social relations and a familiar social environment are likely to lead to an association with individuals of a similar ethnic or national background and consequently to the formation of a primary ethnic group.

Francis has pointed out that primary ethnic groups will emerge when several structural conditions arise within a social system. First of all, there must be op-

---

[1] Native people, it would seem, would not be an ethnic group given this conceptualization. However, upon further consideration one realizes that Natives were continually forced to move or to be what Francis calls "Transferees."

portunities to communicate between dispersed ethnics as well as sufficient freedom of movement for the ethnics, so as to produce a relatively large concentration of them in one locality. This also means that the economy and institutional framework of the host society must be sufficiently elastic so as to accommodate large numbers of ethnics within one area and to permit them to function as a segmental subgroup of the host society.

A second structural condition is that communication with the parent society must be restricted and the chance of returning home limited. The restrictions regarding returning home may be political or economic. The important fact is that the ethnics can find satisfaction of their basic needs only within the host society.

The Complexity of Reality

We would be remiss if we did not address some problematic issues involved in using the concept of ethnic group. First of all, an ethnic group is not necessarily tied to minority status (McAllister, 1975). Secondly, ethnicity is not the same as an ethnic group. It is usually used to suggest a psychological focus, i.e., ethnic identity (Manyoni, 1978). Third, the concept of ethnic group must be viewed as a variable. That is, ethnic groups can emerge and dissipate, depending upon the nature and intensity of the external and internal pressures. In fact, Yancey, et al. (1976) and Burgess (1978) have focused their research on "emergent ethnicity." They argue that:

> The behavior of immigrants and their descendants will vary significantly on whether they have lived under conditions which generated and /or reinforced an 'ethnic community'. . . . ⁻
>
> The contrasting view of ethnicity here is that rather than an ascribed constant or a temporary persistent variable, ethnicity and ethnically based ascription are emergent phenomena. Rather than viewing ethnicity as ascribed status generally as being inevitably doomed by the process of modernization, we suggest that ethnic groups have been produced by structural conditions which are intimately linked to the changing technology of industrial production and transportation. (392)

A fourth problematic aspect of the concept returns to the question of when an ethnic group comes into existence. Students generally note that Americans are not considered an ethnic group in the U.S.A. or that Canadians are not listed as an ethnic group in Canada. Given the criteria that have been provided to identify a particular ethnic group, our conclusion is that almost by any criteria, they can be considered an ethnic group. Why, then, are they not? Our only answer is that by convention or tradition Canadians, or for that matter Americans, are not considered ethnics. Conversely, Anglo-Rhodesians, or British or Afrikaaner populations in South Africa are never called Africans, although they are clearly ethnic groups.

The explication of various concepts discussed above points out to the reader that many labels can be applied to aggregates, categories, or groups. The final decision will depend upon the focus of study. The following figure illustrates that there are a number of different ways in which to identify subsegments of the society. It also shows that there is a complex interweaving of these segments. The result is that one must be careful in delineating the boundaries of the segment one wants to study. Only by carefully specifying the nature and boundaries of the segment will the investigator be able to identify and explain intergroup processes.

Perhaps clarification of our argument could be augmented by presenting an example. First of all, the reader is asked to identify the boundaries of the area surrounding the letter "X" in the two-dimensional matrix. This will represent, for our purposes, the boundaries of a particular segment of society.

FIGURE 2   INTERRELATIONSHIPS OF DIFFERENT GROUP BOUNDARIES

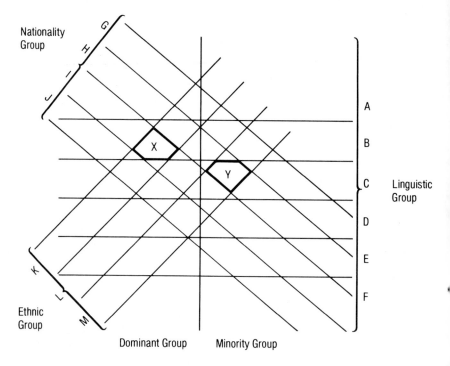

Members of this group would exhibit "I" nationality, "B" linguistic structure, dominant status, and "K" ethnicity. On the other hand, individuals who would fall within the boundaries of the area designated by "Y" would have minority status, "C" linguistic structure, be a member of "H" nationality, and "M" ethnicity.

To more specifically illustrate our model, the reader is asked to conceptualize an individual living in Canada who is a Canadian citizen, has black skin pigmentation, speaks only French and lives in a cultural style closely associated with the West Indies. This example serves to make the point that each individual may occupy positions in several segments of society concurrently. To make matters even more complex, each of the dimensions discussed can vary over time, thus suggesting that one may be a member of one segment of society at a specific time and then change membership at some future time. For example, some individuals are more "ethnic" than others; one may identify more with an ethnic group than someone else even though they both technically belong to the same ethnic group. On the one hand, we find those individuals whose entire self concept is dependent upon the collective definitions made by the group or imposed upon the group by others. For this type of individual, then, the group to which he defines himself as belonging becomes his reference group. It provides the individual with a stable social anchorage which the individual can utilize for all choices that must be made.

A second type of individual is at the other end of the continuum. This person, while nominally belonging to a particular ethnic group, does not utilize it as a comparison or reference group. While this individual may be labeled as belonging to a particular ethnic group for political or statistical purposes, the individual does not view him/herself from this perspective.

Table 1

TYPES OF ETHNIC IDENTIFICATION AND STRUCTURATION

Type of ethnic identification	Ethnic awareness	Ethnic consciousness
Individual level of analysis	An individual knows (s)he possesses an ethnic trait(s) which is no more meaningful than his or her other cultural, physical, social or territorial characteristics; e.g., Brazilian Negroes, Polish Americans.	An individual possesses an ethnic trait(s) which has considerable importance vis-a-vis other personal characteristics to the extent that ethnic identification can be the mode of identification; e.g., participants in a Scottish clan festival.

Type of structuration	Ethnic category	Ethnic group
	A certain number of people can be classified into a specific category because they possess an ethnic trait(s). However, there is no sense of belonging among these people, as this common attribute is not perceived as the basis for any sort of meaningful social interaction. Such aggregates may be called ethnic categories in themselves; e.g., Basque sheepherders, French-Canadians in Toronto.	A certain number of people meaningfully interact on the basis of a similar ethnic trait(s) which they share. There is a consciousness of kind and a sense of belonging present. Such social entities may be called ethnic groups for themselves; e.g., FLQ members, Hassidic Jews.

Source: McKay & Lewins, 1978: 418.

The third type of individuals are those who vacillate between the above positions. These are the individuals who, at various times in their lives, identify strongly with their reference ethnic group, while at other times do not. Their ethnic identity or ethnic allegiance may be said to be situationally bound. Depending upon the situational context in which these individuals are acting within, they will identify with the group.

McKay and Lewins (1978) have developed a typology which illustrates the relationship between ethnic identification and structuration. This model points out that the individual unit of analysis must be kept separate from the group unit of analysis (Van den Berghe, 1967). The central argument put forth in this typology is that a high level of individual identification or consciousness does not mean that this entails group formation. Or, conversely, that just because an ethnic group exists, all individuals within that group will have high ethnic identification or consciousness.

As will be pointed out in Chapters 6 and 7, one can clearly see that our Canadian society consists of diverse ethnic, national, linguistic, and religious origins. In some cases a great deal of the home country cultural baggage has been brought to Canada. While some of this baggage has been discarded over time, each group shows differential rates in retention of these cultural elements.

The question now posed is how do people utilize these symbols and react to them? We must now look at the symbols as listed and attempt to show how people categorize others so that some appropriate response is forthcoming. To get us out of this seemingly complex maze, we wish to invoke the notion of what we will call the Perceived Appearance Group (PAG).

REFERENCES

Akzin, B. *State and Nation*. Garden City, N.Y.: Anchor/Doubleday, 1964.

Allport, G. W. *The Nature of Prejudice*. Garden City, N.Y.: Anchor/Doubleday, 1954.

Anderson, G. and Higgs, D. *A Future to Inherit: The Portuguese Communities of Canada*. Ottawa: McClelland and Stewart and Dept. of Sec. of State of Canada, 1976.

Anderson, A. B. "The Survival of Ethno-linguistic Minorities: Canadian and Comparative Research," in H. Giles and B. St.-Jacques (eds.), *Language and Ethnic Interaction*. London: Pergamon, 1980.

Anderson, A. B. and Driedger, L. "The Mennonite Family: Culture and Kin in Rural Saskatchewan," in K. Ishwaren (ed.) *Canadian Families: Ethnic Variations*. Toronto: McGraw-Hill Ryerson, 1980.

Barth, F. *Ethnic Groups and Boundaries*. London: George Allen and Unwin, 1969.

Berry, B. *Race and Ethnic Relations*. Boston: Houghton-Mifflin, 1958.

Bierstedt, R. *The Social Order*. New York: McGraw-Hill, 1963.

Borrie, W. D. (ed.), *The Cultural Integration of Immigrants*. Paris: UNESCO, 1959.

Bram, J. *Language and Society*. N.Y.: Random House, 1955.

Breton, R. "The Structure of Relationships Between Ethnic Collectives," in Leo Driedger (ed.), *The Canadian Ethnic Mosaic*. Toronto: McClelland & Stewart, 1978. pp. 55-73.

Burgess, M. "The Resurgence of Ethnicity: Myth or Reality?" *Ethnic and Racial Studies*, 1(3) (1978): 265-285.

Burkey, R. *Ethnic and Racial Groups*. London: Cummings Publishing Co, 1978.

Burnet, J. "The Definition of Multiculturalism in a Bilingual Framework," paper presented at the Conference on Multiculturalism and Third World Immigrants in Canada, Univ. of Alberta, Edmonton, 1975.

Connor, W. "A Nation is a Nation, is a State, is an Ethnic Group," *Ethnic and Racial Studies*, Vol. 1 (October 1978): 379-400.

Dawson, C. A. "Group Settlement: Ethnic Communities in Western Canada," Vol. VII, in W. A. Mackintosh and W. L. G. Joerg (eds.), *Canadian Frontiers of Settlement Series*, Toronto: Macmillan, 1936.

Fishman, J. A. "Varieties of Ethnicity and Varieties of Language Consciousness," in J. A. Fishman, *Language and Sociocultural Change*. Stanford, California: Stanford University Press, 1965.

Fishman, J. A. "Language Maintenance in a Supra-Ethnic Age," in op. cit. (1972).

Francis, E. K. "Variables in the Formation of So-Called 'Minority Groups' ", *American Journal of Sociology*, LIX (1954): 6-14.

Francis, E. K. *Interethnic Relations*. New York: Elsevier, 1976.

Freeman, E. A. "Language as a Basis of Racial Classification," in E. T. Thompson & E. C. Hughes (eds.) *Race: Individual and Collective Behavior*. Glencoe, Ill.: Free Press, 1958.

Gans, H. "Symbolic Ethnicity: The Future of Ethnic Groups and Cultures in America," *Ethnic and Racial Studies*, 2, 1 (1979): 1-20.

Glazer, N. and D. P. Moynihan. *Beyond the Melting Pot*. Cambridge Mass.: M.I.T. Press, 1963.

Gordon, M. *Assimilation in American Life*. New York: Oxford Press, 1964.

Greeley, A. *Ethnicity in the United States: A Preliminary Reconnaissance*. New York: Wiley, 1974.

Handlin, O. *The Uprooted*. New York: Grosset & Dunlap, 1951.

Harte, T. J. "Racial and National Parishes in the United States," in T. J. Harte and C. J. Nuesse (eds.), *The Sociology of the Parish*. Milwaukee: Bruce Publishing, 1951.

Herberg, W. *Protestant, Catholic, Jew*. Garden City, N.Y.: Doubleday, 1955.

Hughes, D. and Kallen, E. *The Anatomy of Racism: Canadian Dimensions*. Montreal: Harvest House, 1974.

Isajiw, W. "Definitions of Ethnicity." *Ethnicity* 1 (1974): 111-124.

Ishwaran, K. (ed.), *Canadian Families: Ethnic Variations*. Scarborough: McGraw-Hill Ryerson, 1980.

Manyoni, J. "Ethnics and Non-Ethnics: Facts and Fads in the Study of Intergroup Relations," in M. L. Kovacs, *Ethnic Canadians Culture and Education*. Regina: Canadian Plains Research Centre, 1978.

McAllister, R. *The Sociological Use and Misuse of Ethnicity*. Mimeo. Riverside: University of California, 1975.

McKay, J. and F. Lewins. "Ethnicity and the Ethnic Group: A Conceptual Analysis and Reformulation," *Ethnic and Racial Studies*, 1(4) (October 1978): 412-427.

Niebuhr, R. *The Social Sources of Denominationalism.* New York: Henry Holt & Co., 1929.

Nottingham, E. *Religion and Society.* New York: Random House, 1954.

Park, R. *Race and Culture.* Glencoe, Ill.: Free Press, 1950.

Potter, S. *Language in the Modern World.* Harmondsworth, U.K.: Penguin, 1960.

Price, C. A. "Immigration and Group Settlement," in W. D. Borrie, (ed.), *The Cultural Integration of Immigrants.* Paris: UNESCO, 1959.

Schneider, L. *Sociological Approach to Religion.* New York: John Wiley, 1970.

Schermerhorn, R. *Comparative Ethnic Relations.* New York: Random House, 1970.

Shibutani, T. and Kwan, K. M. *Ethnic Stratification: A Comparative Approach.* N.Y.: Macmillan, 1965.

Sinha, S. "Caste in India: Its Essential Pattern of Socio-Cultural Integration," in A. deReuck and J. Knight (eds.), *Caste and Race.* London: J. and A. Churchill Ltd., 1968.

Stasiulis, D. K. "The Representation and Regulation of Ethnic Group Interests Within the Canadian State," paper presented at the annual meetings of the CSSA, Univ. of Saskatchewan, Saskatoon, June 1-4, 1979.

Steward, J. H. *Theory of Cultural Change.* Urbana, Ill.: University of Illinois, 1955.

Stymeist, D. *Ethnics and Indians.* Toronto: Peter Martin, 1975.

Taylor, R. B. *Cultural Ways.* Boston: Allyn and Bacon, 1969.

Theodorson, G. A. and A. *Modern Dictionary of Sociology.* New York: T. Y. Crowell, 1969.

Trudgill, P. *Sociolinguistics: An Introduction.* Harmondsworth: Penguin, U.K., 1974.

Tumin, M. in Gould, T. and Kolb, (eds.), *Dictionary of the Social Sciences,* 1965.

Vallee, F. "Multi Ethnic Societies: The Issues of Identity and Inequality," in D. Forcese and S. Richer (eds.), *Issues in Canadian Society.* Scarborough: Prentice-Hall of Canada, 1975.

Van den Berghe, P. *Race and Racism: A Comparative Perspective.* New York: John Wiley, 1967.

Ware, C. "Ethnic Communities", *Encyclopaedia of the Social Sciences,* Vol. V, New York: Macmillan, 1931, pp. 607-13.

Warner, W. L. and Srole, L. *The Social Systems of American Ethnic Groups.* New Haven: Yale University Press, 1945.

Weber, M. *Economy and Society, Vol. 1.* New York: Bedminster Press, 1968.

Williams, R. *The Reduction of Inter Group Tensions.* N.Y.: The Social Science Research Council, 1947.

Yancy, W. E., Erickson and R. Juliani. "Emergent Ethnicity: A Review and Reformulation." *American Sociological Review,* Vol. 41 (June 1976): 319-403.

Yinger, J. M. (ed.), *Religion, Society and the Individual.* New York: Macmillan, 1957.

Yinger, J. M. *Sociology Looks at Religion.* New York: Macmillan, 1963.

Chapter 4

Ethnicity: Subjective Perception and Stereotyping

The Variability of Subjective Interest in Ethnicity

We have asked, in the preceding chapter, how ethnicity is perceived by ethnic group members, and who exactly is a member in the first place. In a recent paper, Breton (1978: 55) has appropriately commented: "In a way, our ethnic origin is always with us, but it is not always operative in determining social behavior and in shaping social organization."

Ethnic identity may be objectively defined in terms of certain criteria (language, religion, folkways). However, as we have noted in the preceding chapter, the identifying criteria may vary from group to group and may change from generation to generation. Moreover, *subjective* awareness of ethnicity is highly variable; not all ethnic group members choose to emphasize (in some manner or another) their ethnicity. Of course, it may be emphasized *for* the member (as in visible racial minorities). But, with reference to the principal objective cultural criteria of ethnicity, a given ethnic group member may choose not to speak or use a traditional mother tongue, not to be a member of a traditional religious affiliation, nor to follow certain customs. Moreover, in terms of ethnic group behavior, the individual member may choose not to participate in certain associations or institutions of the ethnic group. Indeed, within several of the larger established Canadian ethnic minorities a *majority* of members have already lost contact with these ethnic criteria (Chapter 6). It would hardly come as a surprise, then, to find that many, probably an increasing number, of ethnic group members do not really feel very "ethnic." Yet one must be wary of jumping to that conclusion because a new ethnicity among the third generation may assume the form of a keen interest in one's genealogical and ethnic history, regardless of one's ability to speak the mother tongue or one's religious inclinations (Gans, 1979).

Perceived Appearance Group

When individuals use the concept *ethnic group*, they generally do not have any information as to whether or not the segment of society constitutes a group or not. Yet they are willing to assume that it is a group and on that basis make predictions about the emergence, persistence or disappearance of a segment of society, about the emergence of conflict and about rates of assimilation. Needless to say, this lack of conceptual clarity has led various researchers in the area to make contradictory predictions.

An alternative (and preferred) strategy that can be utilized by social scientists is to view subsegments of society in social terms. What is important in the analysis of human behavior for the social scientist is the fact that man utilizes symbols. He ascribes meaning to symbols and reacts to them. How he reacts to these symbols is evidenced by the evaluative component placed on each symbol. Clearly, then, it is not the attributes or characteristics themselves which people react towards or against, but underlying assumptions about these attributes and the meanings attached to them.

For example, stereotypes have built up around ethno-racial labels (which are generally confused with nationality and linguistic labels) but nevertheless are socially important. The images that have been built up over time give individuals information as to how to act toward others. Clearly, if you are talking with an individual who has a "Jewish sounding" name, or is perceived as "Jewish-looking," you would not tell the anti-Semitic joke you had planned to tell but rather substitute it with, say, an Irish joke. The label one attaches to oneself (or has attached to oneself by someone else) provides a cue as to how one can act and how others can react, or vice versa. Skin pigmentation, ethnicity, and nationality are all cues for us. The salience of any one (or a combination) of these cues will vary in time and context. It provides us with information as to how to act when in the presence of that individual or group (Gardner and Taylor, 1968a). Over time, we have built up collective images about various subsegments of society. Whether they are true or not is of little importance, the important point is that they exist. We also know that these images change over time. While the traditional stereotype of French-Canadians (held by English-Canadians) was one of the Catholic *habitant* living in a rural area, today it is changing to one of the agnostic, urban nationalist (wanting separation from Confederation).

Therefore, we are introducing the concept of *perceived appearance group* (PAG): an aggregate, category or group of people who are perceived as being distinguishable from a total population because of a certain unique characteristic or a set of characteristics which have high social import for that system.

The Conceptualization of Stereotypes

One of the most basic ways in which individuals can categorize individuals is through the use of stereotypes. As Zirkel (1971) pointed out, by typing individuals in accordance with the culturally prescribed social categories, they are assigned their social identities. Williams (1964) goes on to suggest that the process of stereotyping provides a means of securing high predictability as well as economy of attention and effort in any social interaction. To this we would add that, to an extent, group stereotypes reflect the established relations of PAGs in our society.

As Canada becomes more and more industrialized (and concurrent movement occurs from primary to secondary groups) the necessity of social categorizing increases. This means then, that we must examine the origins, maintenance and changes of stereotypes. However, stereotyping may focus on attributes of individuals other than racial characteristics. Stereotypes are an "adjunct to the human activity of categorizing," which "lead us to minimize certain differences between people who are members of the same group, and to exaggerate the same difference between those people and others who belong to another group" (Tajfel, 1963).

The lines of demarcation between groups of people become, after long periods of time, matters of customary usage. But what are these lines of demarcation? Generally they will be stigmas (used in the most general sense) that have been attached to certain groups of people. We generally refer to these as stereotypes. The concept *stereotype* was originally established by Lippman (1922) and was defined as a "picture in the head." Even though its usage has been refined since that time, most research still operates with this definition in mind. For example Secord and Backman (1964) define a stereotype as "the categorization of persons, a consensus of attributed traits and a discrepancy between attributed traits and actual traits." Kretch, et al. (1962), agree with the definition given by Secord and Backman with the proviso that it has a quality of "rigidity." Simpson and Yinger (1965) elaborate and characterize the concept in the following manner.

(1) It gives a highly exaggerated picture of the importance of some few characteristics—whether they be favorable or unfavorable.

(2) It invents supposed traits out of whole cloth, making them seem reasonable by association with other tendencies that may have a kernel of truth.

(3) (In negative stereotypes), personality tendencies that are favorable, that would have to be mentioned to give a complete picture, are either omitted or insufficiently stressed.

(4) It fails to show how the majority, or other groups, share the same tendencies or have other undesirable characteristics.

(5) It fails to give any attention to the cause of the tendencies of the majority group—particularly to the place of the majority itself, and its stereotypes, in creating the very characteristics being condemned. They are thought of rather as intrinsic or even self-willed traits of the minority.

(6) It leaves little room for change.

(7) It leaves no room for individual variation. (119-120)

The above definitions raise two crucially important points: first, myth versus reality and second, the evaluative content of the stereotypes.

The first question is whether or not these pictures in our head are really what exist in our society, or are they simply cognitions we want to impose upon the world? This is a difficult question to answer because many of the stereotypes are statements difficult to measure. For example, the stereotype that "Indians are poor" is quite common in our society. How does one go about operationalizing the concept "poor" and then bring data to bear upon the question? In many cases this will not be possible; however, in some cases we will be able to objectively evaluate these stereotypes.

The second issue of evaluativeness makes assessment of stereotypes even more difficult. One commonly hears that "Ukrainians (or Newfoundlanders) are stupid." Most Ukrainian or "Newfie" jokes are focused on this particular attribute. However, we find that the evaluative nature of the concept poses problems for the serious student so as to be able to evaluate a subjective concept such as "stupid."

Let us begin by alluding to a general discussion of the theoretical status, the formation of stereotypes, then to their continuance and finally, a discussion of how emotional evaluation is attached to stereotypes. We must point out that the tendency to adopt stereotypes is *independent* of the attitude the individual may hold toward that same group. As Gardner, et al. (1968b) state:

> This conclusion (attitude independence of stereotype) is not unwarranted on the basis of previous research even though it is generally accepted that a stereotype does reflect an attitudinal reaction. Studies purporting to show a relationship between stereotypes and attitudes do so by indicating the presence of negative content in the stereotype of unfavourable groups. They have not, however, demonstrated a relationship between an individual's attitude and his willingness to ascribe stereotyped traits to an ethnic group. Factor II indicates that individual differences in the extent to which the stereotype is adopted are independent of attitudes. . . . (41-42)

Following Ackerman and Jahoda (1950) we may also distinguish between prejudice (an attitude) and stereotypy:

> Prejudice . . . is a term applied to categorical generations based on inadequate data and without sufficient regard for individual differences. . . . But inherent in the process of forming pre-judgments is the danger of stereotyped thinking. The stereotype is distinguished from the prejudgment only by a greater degree of rigidity. Prejudgment occurs where facts are not available. But stereotypy is a process which shows little concern for facts even when they are available.
>   Prejudice in its narrowest sense is distinct from prejudgment and stereotypy. It is a sub-category of prejudgment and it uses stereotypy but it is not identical with either. (3-4)

Their results also suggest that a "number of images are evoked by [an] ethnic group label." If this is true, then it makes little sense to think of an ethnic stereotype as "a single relatively organized construct." Their conclusion is that "there appears to be a number of 'stereotypes' associated with an ethnic group label, and each stereotype seems to involve a hierarchy of assumed attributes" (p. 43).

The above statements should not lead the reader to feel that no disagreement is evident in the field. Such is not the case. Ehrlich (1962) describes stereotypes as "the language of prejudice" and Katz and Braly (1935) define prejudices as "a set of stereotypes." However, more recent research in Canada (e.g., Mackie, 1974; White and Frideres, 1977) has generally shown that the two concepts are independent.

What evidence exists in Canadian society that stereotypes are used by people? To answer this question we will present a short review of some of the existing literature which addresses this question. Lambert, Hodgson, Gardner and Fillenbaum (1960) asked two groups of adults (English and French) to rate various personality characteristics of five bilingual speakers. Their results showed that both English and French-Canadian groups rated the speakers in their English guise much more favorably than in their French guise. Anisfeld, Bogo and Lambert (1962), utilizing a similar approach to the Lambert, et al. study above, compared Jewish and Gentile university students, rating personality characteristics of eight voices—some speaking in flawless English, the other in English with a distinctive, although not exaggerated, Jewish accent. The results revealed that the accented language was devalued on three personality traits—height, good looks and leadership, by both Jewish and Gentile subjects. The Gentile group did not give the accent better evaluations than the pure English voice although Jews did more favorably evaluate the accent voice in terms of sense of humor, ability to entertain, and kindness. In this study, it is clear that the minority group (Jews) did not accept the majority group stereotype about them as did the Gentiles.

Anisfeld and Lambert (1964) compared children and adult French-Canadian (monolingual and bilingual) evaluative reactions to English and French-Canadian youngsters. The attempt was, like the studies above, to ascertain how well one can evaluate personalities on the basis of voice alone. The subjects rated each voice (France-French, French-Canadian French and Canadian English) on 15 bipolar traits, i.e., tall-short, nice-evil, wise-foolish, etc. In general, they found that French-Canadian children rated the personalities of voices in French significantly more favorably than English voices. When comparing monolingual versus bilingual French-Canadian children's ratings of voices, the authors found that monolinguals found greater favorable personality traits of French voices than English, whereas the bilingual children perceived few differences between the voices. While the above research is the obverse of that reported by Lambert, et al. (1960), the explanation is that through socialization processes, a reversal of the positive self-evaluation occurs between childhood and adulthood. In essence, French-Canadian children tend to internalize the relatively low status definition placed upon them in Canadian society. Further support for the Lambert, et al. (1960) study is presented by Larimer (1970).

Gardner and Taylor (1969) ask subjects to associate words with three stimuli words: English-Canadian, French-Canadian and Canadian Indian. The responses provide a clear indication of the image evoked by the label. For English-Canadians, the associations were Ontario, cultural bonds with England and positions of political and economic power. They are also identified as White, conservative and Protestant. French-Canadian is likewise regionally associated with Quebec, and with having cultural links with the motherland—France. The other two attributes that seem to characterize French-Canadians are bilingual and Catholic. Canadian Indians on the other hand do not show any geographical location other than "reserve." Other words used to characterize this group centred about traditional cultural artifacts: teepees, canoes, feathers and arrows.

Rather than artificially eliciting responses to various groups in our society, Paton and Deverell (1974) content-analysed existing material. Their work has been patterned closely to the seminal work in this area by McDiarmid and Pratt (1971). After identifying the social studies textbooks most commonly used in the Saskatchewan school system, each text was analysed with regard to the stereotypes utilized in describing a particular group. The following table indicates the manner in which several groups were identified. Their research clearly indicated a marked differential treatment of the target groups identified in their texts. Generally they found that Indians were treated most unfavorably. Clearly half of the assertions made in the texts were negative. They also found that textbooks consistently depersonalized Blacks.

Table 1

**EVALUATIVE WORDS (AND THE DIRECTION) ASSOCIATED WITH
SELECTED GROUPS IN CANADA**

Evaluative Word	Value
Christians	
great	+ 1.5
faithful	+ 1.5
educated	+ 1.1
famous	+ 1.5
successful	+ 1.5
loving	+ 1.5
	Total + 8.6
Negro	
fierce	−1.5
primitive	−1.5
skillful	+ 1.5
uneducated	−1.5
clever	+ 1.5
dreaded	−1.5
	Total −3.0
Indian	
skillful	+ 1.5
savage	−1.9
hostile	−1.5
beauty	+ 1.5
massacre	−1.9
murderer	−1.9
Total	Total −4.2

Source: Paton & Deverell, 1974.

The more recent work by Indra (1979) illustrates how the press has portrayed South Asians in Vancouver. She found that the press associated South Asians with dirt, disease and abhorrent cultural practices while at the same time "confirming the validity of a press image of those with British backgrounds which had none of these attributes" (p. 171). Overall, she found that the British were associated with positive attributes while South Asians by negative (or devalued) characteristics. Indra found that in comparing stereotypes of South Asians for nearly three-quarters of a century (1905-1975), a strong similarity exists, e.g., crime and violence still remains a stereotype of South Asians.

Stereotyping as Symbolic Interaction

We will begin discussing the most elementary aspects of thought patterns: categorization and conceptualization. We will consider some aspects of the formation of racial and ethnic categories and their consequences. Following that, we will discuss thought systems at the more complex level of ideologies and present some examples of racial and ethnic ideologies that have existed in Canadian society.

One of the clearest results of comparative studies of ethnic group relations is that ethnic labels and categories vary tremendously between societies, even when the same groups are present. In Canada, any person that is legally registered in Ottawa is an Indian, even though it may be impossible for a stranger to perceive his Indian characteristics. Persons of East Indian origin, who may be as dark as those with Negroid characteristics are not conventionally regarded as Blacks. In Britain the general category of "colored" is used to refer to former colonials of both African and East Indian origin. Whereas in South Africa the "Coloreds" are neither Blacks nor East Indians but are a mixed population of Malay and a variety of other origins. Within each society reactions to those who are classed alike tend to be similar.

These facts point to the first issue we wish to consider in our discussion of thought patterns—the formation of thought categories and the association of words with these. We will first discuss this process of conceptualization in general terms and then analyse selected examples of ethnic conceptualization in Canada.

Man cannot respond in a fresh and unique way to every object or event he encounters. He lumps different things into categories and responds in a similar way to all members of a given category. Bruner, et al. (1956) put this succinctly:

> The resolution of this seeming paradox—the existence of discrimination capacities which, if fully used, would make us slaves to the particular—is achieved by man's capacity to categorize. *To categorize is to render discriminably different things equivalent, to group the objects and events and people around us into classes, and to respond to them in terms of their class membership rather than their uniqueness.* (1)

There are few aspects of society where the tendency to ignore individual characteristics and respond to persons on the basis of category membership are more clear than in the realm of race and ethnic relations. Behavior in this realm also illustrates another fundamental point: categories do not exist naturally in the world. In our everyday life and in our scientific activities we invent ways of grouping phenomena. There exist a near infinitude of ways of grouping events in terms of discriminable properties, and we avail ourselves of only a few of these. There are many readily recognizable characteristics of people which could serve as bases for categorizing which are either completely ignored or do not acquire a generally shared meaning or elicit common responses. Even an apparently clear-cut characteristic like skin pigmentation turns out to have very complex imposed criteria. Skin pigmented to a dark brown by prolonged voluntary exposure to the sun denotes a different categorization from skin pigmented as a result of genetic factors. The imposed nature of categories is further illustrated by the fact, mentioned above, that the same range of physical racial characteristics is divided differently in different societies.

An important guide to the nature of the categories used by people in a given society is language. While we agree there is not a *perfect* fit between social experience and language, the lexical systems *primarily* reflect and are guided by social systems.

Brown (1965) maintains that a word and a set of meanings and responses are associated with a category of objects or persons.

> The semantic utterance /word/ is only one variety of socially functional attributes. All sorts of discriminating responses are such attributes for the person who does not yet possess a concept but is concerned with learning it from the behavior of others and from the environment in which they behave. . . . Our kin are distinguised by more than kinship terminology. Categories are marked out in all cases by speech. (284)

Two important messages emerge from this discussion of language and categories. First, by studying the terms used in referring to groups of people within a society we can detect, at least in a general way, how people in that society categorize each other. Second, as Madge (1964) suggests, we can expect the categories to be both cognitive (ideas concerning the nature of the objects) and evaluative (ideas concerning the goodness or badness of the objects).

We began this discussion with references to cognitive maps and pictures of society which exist in the minds of people. Brown (1965) connects these ideas to the discussion of language when he argues that we may assume that speech has less intrinsic importance than nonlinguistic reality, and therefore it is acceptable to describe speech as a map and the rest of the world as the region mapped. In our focus on thought patterns and ethnic relations the region to be mapped consists of all of the people in a society (or in contact with the society). The map maker does not consider everything in the landscape as important enough to indicate on his map. Rather, certain general types of features such as elevation, waterways, routes of travel, and type of vegetation are selected. One does not portray these features in all of their detail but rather categorizes them and develops symbols to indicate each category—for example, railways, highways, hiking trails. Members of a society do not consider all recognizable differences between people as important. We wish to ask to what extent do ethnic or racial aspects of humanity appear as aspects of humanity, and also what are the dimensions along which important differences occur, how are people categorized, and what kinds of beliefs and values are associated with each identifiable category. We will rely heavily on language as the indicator of the maps that people do carry in their heads.

The child, or other new member of a society, learns both the language and the expected responses in the process of socialization. According to Brown (1965), the first-language learning is also the process of cognitive socialization, i.e., as the individual learns the language he comes to think of the world in essentially the same categories as his tutors and to have the same kinds of emotional and behavioral reactions to the members of a given category. While the child is learning to "correctly" label the social and physical world he is also learning whether he should react to the objects with warmth and affection or fear and hostility.

Once a language has basically been learned, however, it is possible for an individual to associate new meanings or reactions with a word and the category it represents simply by hearing others talk—without any direct contact with the objects being referred to. This process permits individuals to develop feelings and responses toward ethnic categories without ever coming into direct contact with representatives of those categories.

As Shibutani and Kwan point out, to facilitate references to these categories, each is given a label. Words are names that designate categories. Symbols allow man to begin to order his experience and clearly one can see the usefulness of such a strategy. "It saves time, it helps in the ordering of the social environment" (Tajfel, 1963: 3). However, more to the point is the question of how we come to perceive the world the way we do. Tajfel claims that when we meet individuals, and are unsure as to how to interact with them, we guess.

> What, if any, are the rules of guessing? There is very little doubt that guessing is NOT random; it is strongly influenced by past experience, motivation, interests, needs, purposes. In a more formal way, expectancies are developed through previous experience which leads us to extrapolate from uncertainty to relatively stable relationships previously encountered. (Tajfel, 1963: 5)

This, of course, is not to say that the ordering of the selected attributes (of the group, person, object) is not arbitrary or conventional. Any symbol (clue, cue) can be selected as a feature for organization of man's behavior. In our society, eye color, size of ears or length of toes are not utilized as attributes to organize society. However, language, skin pigmentation and physical features are utilized. These, then, identify the boundaries of the groups. It should not surprise us, however, to find that the attributes will vary as we move from culture to culture.

> Whether physical or personal (or cultural) characteristics are concerned, stereotypes lead us to minimize certain differences between people who are members of the same group, and to exaggerate the same differences between those people and others who belong to another group.
>   Stereotypes can, therefore, be considered as an escapable adjunct to the human activity of categorizing. As such it is neither bad nor good, it is there, and presumably it serves some purpose in our continuous efforts to simplify the world around us. (Tajfel, 1963: 7-8)

We now turn to the question as to why certain features of groups are categorized for differentiating groups. Again, we will argue that the initial categorizing of attributes is nothing more than an easy way to carry on daily interaction patterns. Individuals and groups attempt to differentiate between various individuals or social types in our system. Initially, the stereotypes may have had a factual basis so that the differentiating of groups of people was simply reflecting reality. In order to maintain the establishment of social types (which have great importance to power maintenance, life styles, and life chances), certain symbols (usually easily distinguishable) are invoked. Several different kinds of symbols can be utilized to identify a social type for which a stereotype exists.

Language

Ehrlich (1973: 21) argues that to study stereotype assignments is to study the language of prejudice. He goes on to point out that the language of prejudice, "like any special language, has a small dictionary which consists of unique terms (ethnophaulisms) and terms of the natural language which are given a special usage."

The language of a society is utilized by individuals wishing to make distinctions between groups of people. Two aspects of language, style and phonic structure, can be used for differentiating peoples into distinct groups. Let us begin with a discussion of *style*. The argument here is that people listen to the style (both semantic and syntax) of the language. Words such as "eh" versus "huh" differentiate Americans from Canadians; "bloody" versus "damn" distinguish British versus American; "zed" versus "zee" distinguish between Canadian or British and American. "Cabin" versus "cottage," and "bag" versus "sack" are other differences which allow Canadians to place individuals into specific categories of national origin. Pronunciation of words is also another symbol that is utilized. Words such as process, schedule and garage can all take on different pronunciations which will allow the observer to identify and place the speaker's ethnic, national, or regional background. Beyond the words themselves (in the same language—English), phrases are also indicative of one's membership in a PAG. The omissions of articles in a sentence also provide the listener with clues as to the national or ethnic origin of the speaker. For example, the sentence "I am going to hospital" versus "I am going to the hospital" may allow the observer to categorize the speaker into some ethno/national category.

A more obvious symbol that can be used to differentiate group membership is the actual use of a different language (francophone versus anglophone). Lambert, et al. (1960) ascertained the degree of stereotyping that went on when people listened to the languages that were being spoken. They recorded French and English voices (which were those of bilingual Canadians) reading a short philosophical text. Two groups of subjects (French and English) were then asked to rate each speaker (in reality the same person) on a number of personality traits. Results showed that definite stereotypes did in fact emerge. The stereotype scale included traits such as excitable, talkative, proud, impulsive, emotional, colorful, artistic, active, religious, sensitive, tenacious and short. They found that English subjects evaluated English-speaking people more favorably on several personality traits than did the French speaking students. Their results showed that having more skill (e.g., being bilingual) with the other group's language (which presumably would permit more intimate interaction) did not lead to a decrease in favorable responses of the speakers.

Religion

This symbol may not be initially utilized by people because of its inaccessibility. However, once the religion is divulged, severe social consequences can follow. However, one's religion is often reflected in one's language. The individual going to mass versus church versus synagogue will have emitted different symbols which will place him into totally different social categories. These words are, of course, taken as indicators of the individual's actual religious beliefs and at least as an indication of one's ethnic affiliation.

Customs

This, of course, refers to the unique (or supposedly unique) patterns of interaction (or action) that are endemic to a particular social group. Celebrating Christmas on January 6th, wearing a skull cap, not eating milk and meat together, or holding a knife in the right hand and a fork in the left hand while you eat are all symbols that are emitted and defined as being part of the culture that make up a particular social group.

Hereditary Traits

The factors to be included under this category are those related to genetics. While these factors are embedded in the genetic structure of man, we do recognize the role of the social and physical environment as interrelating with these factors. For example, while height may be dependent upon the individual's parents' genetic make up, this can be affected by the environment in which the individual exists. There are, of course, a great number of racial and physical factors that could be included under this heading.

Skin pigmentation, for example, is one of the most widely used symbols to differentiate between groups or categories of people. Its widespread use emanates from the fact that it is easily perceivable and requires no social interaction in order to make a social judgement and subsequent placement into a particular group/category.

A wide variety of symbols have to do with the structure, build, and appearance of the body. This would not only include such features of the individual as short or tall, fat or skinny; it would also include such symbols as hair color and type, whether or not the epicanthic fold is present, as well as a host of other physical features (racial traits listed in Chapter 2).

One can use these symbols without having to formally or publicly acknowledge their existence. These symbols, at one level, are considered irrelevant as we live in a society that stresses achieved attributes. Thus, one can privately use ascriptive attributes but publicly one can always claim one is not using them. Because of the lack of validation, the use of these symbols can become problematic for the user and can lead to misperception and eventual misplacement of an individual into a particular PAG.

Names

Surnames are also one of the more widely used symbols to differentiate individuals and make quick placement into groups and categories. Names are symbols used by society in the assignment of statuses and roles to individuals and groups. For example, in an early study by Wax (1948), letters were sent to approximately 100 hotels in the Toronto area. Each hotel was sent two letters, each asking for hotel accommodations on the same day. The only difference between the two letters was that one was signed Mr. Greenberg (a Jewish surname), the other Mr. Lockwood (an English surname). Only half of the hotels responded to the letter signed Mr. Greenberg and of those responding, only one-third offered Mr. Greenberg accommodation. On the other hand, 93% confirmed in writing the reservation for Mr. Lockwood.

A more novel study on the sociological significance of names was conducted by the Canadian Institute of Cultural Research in 1965. They interviewed individuals in the Toronto area who applied for formal name changes. They found that members of racially identifiable groups make little use of name changes since the other (visible) symbols would seem incongruous with the Anglo-Saxon name. On the other hand, they found that those groups most like the dominant group (physically and culturally) also did not change their names. Their results show that a change in name occurs among those groups which are similar enough with the dominant group (Anglo-Saxon), that the new Anglo name would not seem completely incongruous with physical and cultural characteristics, yet are different enough that they would feel that the change was to their advantage. Thus, a person with a name like Wa Cha Yong would not change his name to Joseph Smith; but a Ukrainian with the name Joseph Yakuchuk might consider Joseph Smith, or in moving from francophone Quebec to anglophone Canada or the United States, a Jean-Baptiste de la Rivière might feel obliged to anglicize his name to John B. Rivers.

In yet another more recent study, Labovitz (1974) asked students to evaluate name types that represented selected ethnic groups. His subjects evaluated names that represented British ethnic affiliation (Edward Blake), Canadian Indians (Joseph Walking Bear), and French-Canadians (Marcel Fournier). He found that his respondents (Western Canadian university students) gave a clear rank order of preference for names. The most highly evaluated name was the British, followed by Canadian Indian, with the lowest evaluation being French-Canadian. He also found that while a great degree of variation was evident when subjects evaluated the British and Canadian Indian names, there was a high agreement (low variation) in ranking the French-Canadian names least favorable.

Frideres (1979), in one study, obtained a list of names of individuals published in the local city newspaper applying for name changes. In this initial exploratory study, he has found that about one-quarter of the name changes are because of attempts to change their ethnic affiliation. However, a majority of the changes seem to be for other socially relevant reasons.

Auxiliary Symbols

By giving the title "auxiliary," we do not mean to suggest that any of the previous symbols are any less arbitrary or manmade than the following ones. It simply means that above and beyond the symbols discussed, man has attempted to make even further distinctions. Examples of these symbols would be the Jews (during World War II) having to wear the Star of David. In Canada, when the West was being settled, Metis were easily distinguishable from Indians (and other trappers) by the relative positioning of the belt. Metis wore their belts inside of their capotes, while Indians and White trappers wore them outside. ID cards, such as those utilized in South Africa (stating on the card which particular race you belong to) and, more recently, suggested in Quebec (during the FLQ crisis) are other examples. Clothing, such as the wearing of turbans, skull caps, and saris are all symbols (that sometimes coincide with other symbols) that have meaning for individuals.

Bodily gestures might be additional symbols that are used in deciding which PAG an individual is to be placed in. Research by a number of people shows that various groups use various parts of their anatomy differently when talking or listening, e.g., facial expressions and hand movement.

We have identified single elements of specific behavior that can be used to categorize individuals as part of a group or to differentiate one PAG from another. Each of us uses symbols to direct our behavior toward others. In some cases, we may use only one linguistic symbol because it seems to have a consistency and consensus that increases the probability of correctly categorizing a person. In other cases, we may have to utilize several symbols, trying to place them together into some integrated whole before we can correctly categorize people.

Let us reiterate the fact that these stereotypes (abstractions placing together some conspicuous attributes of a group) may or may not be correct. As Nettler (1970) points out, little research has attempted to ascertain whether or not the stereotype is reflecting reality or not. Mackie (1973) empirically demonstrated the stereotypes held by Western Canadians toward three groups; Indian, Hutterite, and Ukrainian. Her results show that the following stereotype traits emerged.

Table 2

SOCIAL ATTRIBUTES ASSOCIATED WITH SPECIFIC ETHNIC GROUPS IN CANADA

	Indian	Hutterite	Ukrainian
Poor	× 29%[a]		
Uneducated	× 29%		
Oppressed by others	× 20%		
Lazy	× 30%		
Dirty	× 28%		
Drink excessively	× 21%		
Religious	— [b]	× 24%	
Hardworking	—	× 21%	× 29%
Old Fashioned	—	× 22%	
Cliquish	—	× 42%	
Retention of Culture	—		× 29%

[a] percentage of respondents that used a particular symbol.
[b] less than 20% listed this attribute.
Source: Mackie: 1974.

After Mackie collected the above data, she then went on to examine empirically the assumption that these images are fallacious. Using public records, government documents, sociological studies, and other objective data, she found that most seem to be factual. At this point it is not assumed that they do or do not. We argue that if we define stereotypes as mental images of the mind then it really doesn't make any difference. If the members of one group have a particular image of another group then their behavior towards each other will parallel the image. However, it should be pointed out that two outcomes are resultant of the creation of stereotypes:

(1) They do not allow groups to correct (or to attempt to check out) the image with reality and,

(2) They can take on negative (or positive) emotive evaluation.

The existence and use of stereotypes has been clearly pointed out by scholars focusing on conflict between segments of a social system. While this is not the sole import of the concept, its relevance becomes clear in the process of conflict. Preceding the actual conflict, various segments of the population must develop contrast conceptions of a bipolar nature. This means that each segment of society must think in terms of "we, the good guys" and "they, the bad guys."

This means that individuals must be readily identifiable (by whatever means) as to whether or not they belong to a particular PAG. Part of the conflict between French-Canadians and English-Canadians rests on the stereotypes that French have about English and vice versa. French-Canadians hold the view (rightly or wrongly) that English Canada is out to destroy their culture in the form of federal political intervention (erosion of provincial jurisdiction) and language rights (thus the passing of Bill 101 by Quebec). Bill 101 (The Official Language Act) established French as the official language of the Province of Quebec. The Act itself outlines certain provisions and regulations of the Act as well as defining the functions of various committees. As Trudel and Jain (1967) and Richert (1974) point out in the analysis of French and English history books in Canada, French texts reserve their praise largely for French-Canadians and English texts largely for English-Canadians. It is important, then, to remember that stereotypes are used by all groups, no matter what their power status in society.

While no formal list of ethnic/national group descriptive words have been published, Ehrlich (1973) has developed a tentative listing of major stereotype terms for America's ethnic groups. In addition, he has tried to structure a dictionary for the classification of ethnic stereotypes. For example, two categories in his dictionary are positive and negative relational qualities. The words coded in these two categories denote the target group's positive and negative interpersonal qualities. Examples of the positive types are courteous, kind, conventional; while those reflecting the negative type are: arrogant, bitter, rude and strange.

Dimensions of Stereotyping

Shibutani and Kwan (1965) point out that stereotypes can vary among several dimensions—clarity, intensity, degree of complexity, degree of stability, extent to which people are consciously aware of them, extent to which they enjoy consensus, and the manner in which they are evaluated. Let us take each in turn and discuss the elements of these dimensions.

Clarity

This refers to the extent to which attributes used in classifying specific groups do not overlap with each other. For example, if one asks the characterizing attributes of Indians, certain factors such as uneducated, lazy, drunk, and residing on reserves would be chosen. Each of these attributes are relatively independent from each other and would suffice in characterizing individuals as belonging in a particular group. On the other hand, attributes used to characterize groups such as the Scots do not have clarity. The single most important attribute—penny pinching—(an attribute Scots are said to hold in common with Jews) is not clearly delineated from other more complimentary attributes such as frugality, saving, thrifty, etc.

Degree of Complexity

This refers to the extent to which attributes used to characterize a group in one context may not be used in a different context. For example, Jews may be characterized as clannish-cliquish in one context (as one discusses "Jews in general") but also referred to as aggressive in another context. The following hypothetical exchange between the anti-Semite and the academic illustrates this dimension:

A. Jews are good members of the community.

B. That is because they are trying to take over.

A. But they really don't have "powerful" positions in Canadian society.

B. That's because they are only interested in money.

A. But data will show that they do not control the economic structures of Canadian society.

B. See, they are not really good citizens.

One can easily see how the strategic attributes of Jews change as the context in which they are being discussed changes. Hence, a group which has many different contextual attributes is obviously easier to stereotype.

Stability

This refers to the length of time the stereotype has been in use. Ehrlich (1973) argues that stereotypes about ethnic groups appear as a part of the social heritage of that society. Because the transmission of these attributes is a result of socialization, most people growing up in our society know them. Two reasons seem to account for this stability: (1) they can handle negative evidence and, (2) they become social tools for groups to maintain the moral order. It follows, then, that most stereotypes are relatively stable. For example, Ukrainians still are considered by some as poor and ignorant, which would seem to carry over from the days of Sifton when he labeled them the "men in sheepskin coats." However, it is important to point out that stereotypes do change. For example, recent research has suggested that stereotypes of French-Canadians are changing. (See Moif, 1976; Maxwell, 1977; Stein, 1977). The old stereotype of French-Canadians as being Catholic, having large families, and being *habitants* is slowly changing by virtue of published material in both the academic and business community. Business magazines (both emanating from Quebec and directed toward potential investors in Quebec) are portraying a new image of Quebec. Publications such as *Perspective on Quebec, 1973* (published by *The Financial Times of Canada*) portray Quebec as a society in which the "old ways are dying," and as an industrialized, dynamic innovator in the industrial and financial sectors of Canadian society.

Jews as a group also provide an illustration of changing stereotypes. Historically, one of the stereotypes of Jews was that they had horns and tails. Obviously this is a stereotype that we chuckle at today. However, when this criterion was in vogue, people were not willing to view it in such humor. Portrayal of (and information about) Canadian Indians has also changed quite drastically in the past ten years. They are now taking on new as well as losing some old attributes of the stereotypes. For example, they are beginning to become stereotyped as militant—an attribute never before used in characterizing Indians. They also seem to be losing some attributes such as "reserve" and "shy."

Consensus

This attribute refers to the extent to which members of a society agree upon the attributes which are to be used in characterizing the particular group. For example, Mackie (1976) asked individuals to characterize Hutterites. She found varying degrees of consensus in the attributes chosen. For some (like cliquish, religious, old fashioned, hard working, communal social organization, and shy), there was very high agreement. However, on the other hand, she found many traits used by individuals to characterize Hutterites which did not enjoy consensus in the general population. (See Table 2)

Intensity

The intensity of stereotypes can be defined as the degree of acceptance-agreement or rejection-disagreement with a particular stereotype. Each stereotype about a particular group can be organized along an intensity dimension (Ehrlich, 1973). For example, textbooks in elementary and secondary school systems set the stereotypes of groups as well as legitimize them for the young student. In 1969, the Department of Indian Affairs conducted its own study of textbooks used in federal schools and concluded (as a number of other independent studies had) that there was a systematic lack of information on Indian contributions to Canadian culture, the presence of derogatory terms to describe Indians, stereotyping, and inappropriate illustration. The study by McDiarmid and Pratt (1971) investigated Ontario history books and reviewed the treatment of a variety of racial, political, and religious groups in Canada.

Surprisingly, they found that (using a ratio of favorable to unfavorable evaluative terms) approximately four out of five evaluative terms referring to French-Canadians were favorable, while only one out of three was favorable when the group was Indian or Black. This may also suggest that the old stereotypes are changing.

Evaluation

The last factor which can vary in a stereotype is the evaluation that is given to a particular PAG. Shibutani and Kwan point out that a group can be viewed as: inferior, valuable, frustrating, dangerous, or useful objects. The manner in which any one particular group will be evaluated is dependent upon such factors as economic and political condition of the nation-state, stability of the social order, power differences between groups, and the degree to which one group can exploit (profitably) another group. Other factors such as visibility or spatial concentration may also be important factors that affect the evaluation dimension.

Groups such as Indians and Inuits are clearly viewed as inferior and frustrating (Cardinal, 1970) and, according to one internal RCMP evaluation one of the most dangerous, whereas groups such as British are viewed as valuable (Indra, 1979). These evaluations can change over time. For example, Hutterites at the turn of the century were viewed as useful (agriculturalization of the West); then, as time progressed, they were viewed as dangerous, and are presently defined as frustrating (Hostetler and Huntington, 1967). Other groups, such as Finns, were once viewed as dangerous, then later as being useful (as our society made use of them in tapping natural resources).

We have provided examples which illustrate the types of labels attached and the changes of those labels. It is our argument that each group that has come to Canada (and still remains) has been (and is) evaluated by all other groups. In some cases, a great deal of consensus by other groups exists while in other cases "other" groups will disagree as to how the target group will be evaluated.

Campbell (1967), in attempting to assess the determinants of stereotype assignments, focuses on the origin of intergroup relations. He suggests that when there are real differences between groups in terms of culture, custom, or physiological traits, the more likely it is that one (or more) features will appear in the stereotyped imagery each group has of the other.

However, we do not wish to suggest that change does not occur. Generally, we find that when there are periods of organizational change in a society, stereotypes will also change. Changes in the structure may place individuals in different regions, ethno-classes, and roles and thus change their perception (visibility) and relations with the group. In addition, if the change is of high social import, new social categories may be established by law, e.g., immigration policies.

The above dimensions have been presented as analytically separate, so as to illustrate the complexity of stereotypes. Thus, it should be apparent that any stereotype can vary on each dimension discussed. But it should be remembered that a change in one dimension may have implications for other dimensions.

Processes in Stereotyping

As pointed out previously, stereotypes tend to remain stable over long periods of time. How is this possible? What are the conditions that keep various stereotypes intact over a period of time? The answer seems to lie in the fact that stereotypes are learned and reinforced. The learning process (socialization) begins at a very early stage of an individual's life and continues throughout the life of the socializee. Reinforcement of specific actions, beliefs, and values taken by the individual are provided for by the social structure. Some of the reinforcement is intentional while a great deal of behavior is reinforced in contexts that have little or nothing to do with ethnic identity (Shibutani and Kwan, 1967).

Simpson and Yinger (1965) point out that stereotypes are categorized judgements that are part of the overall stream of culture. These judgements (stereotypes) are transferred from one generation to the next through the socialization process. They go on to point out that "they are not dormant traditional items but active ingredients in human interaction, helping to shape experience, to colour observation and finally . . . to create the very tendencies with which they were in the first instance justified" (p. 121).

The ability to place people (on the basis of various kinds of symbols) into particular PAGs or the understanding of how to act toward specific individuals belonging to particular groups is not an inherent ability of man. This behavior, like all other human behavior, is learned. Our general argument is that as children grow up, they come to learn the appropriate attributes that are to be grouped together and form a stereotype. Research by Goodman (1952), Moreland (1958), Eugene and Horowitz (1938), and Bloom (1971) has given adequate demonstration and documentation to this point.

However, besides the family as the agent of socialization (transmission), almost all other societal institutions play an active role in promoting and sustaining the stereotypes evident in that society. The mass media including both radio and television have been very influential in sustaining these images. As pointed out previously, even academic works are not immune to creating and, in some cases, sustaining stereotypes. Other institutions such as education, recreation, and the economy also play an important role in sustaining the existing stereotypes.

The second point made above was that formal intentional socialization processes are not usually invoked in the teaching of the proper stereotype. Parents, kin, teachers, and peers do not formally attempt to educate children (or re-educate adults) as to the appropriate stereotypes except in a country with a high degree of institutionalized racism, such as South Africa. In Canada the attributes are learned incidentally through many different contexts such as epithets, discipline, selective perception, and communicative acts.

Perhaps the following illustration will clarify the issue under discussion. Parents of small children are sometimes faced with dealing with their misbehavior in public places. The concern then is to develop a strategy for coping or stopping the undesired behavior. There are a variety of strategies that could be used—spanking, yelling, ignoring, talking, etc.—to deal with the situation of bringing the child under control. One way that is used to bring the child under control is to threaten the child that if the undesired behavior is continued, you will give them to a policeman. Stated with an appropriate tone and inflection, the child imagines that an encounter with a policeman will be extremely negative. The result is that the child may begin to associate a sense of un-pleasantness with the category of policeman. While the above is a simplistic example, it serves to point out the fact that an association between unpleasant-ness and police can take place without the parent intending such an association to take place.

Let us look at each of the processes involved in sustaining stereotyping:

Epithets

These are statements about PAGs which have high negative (or positive) emotive meaning. People discussing a monetary transaction claim that they were "able to jew him down"; parents discussing the activities of their children will commonly state that "they acted like wild Indians." Other statements such as, "free, White, and 21," "you haven't got a Chinaman's chance in hell," "that was White of you," and a host of others are all reinforcing agents for stereotypes about particular PAGs. The important fact to remember is that in making these statements the communicator was not speaking directly about a specific ethnic group or attempting to characterize a particular group.

Ethnophaulisms

While this concept was coined by Roback in 1944, its systematic role in research has not been widespread nor current. However, their import lies in the fact that they provide us with a linguistic indicator of the past and present relationships between the target group and those individuals or groups using the ethnophaulism. Examples would be Frog or Peasouper (French-Canadian), Limey Brit (British), Camel Jock, Raghead, or Paki (East Indian, Sikh, or Pakistani), Nigger (Negro), Bohunk (East European or Ukrainian), Kraut (German), Kike or Yid (Jew), Polack (Pole), Spic (Spanish-American), Dago/Wop (Italian), Chink (Chinese) as well as a number of other ethnophaulisms that in reasonable taste need not be reprinted in this book.

Jokes

Jokes are told because they are funny. They are not necessarily calculated to reflect or to inform the recipient of the joke that the teller has a prejudicial attitude toward a specific group. It is equally important to point out that the joke is funny because one accepts the underlying premises and assumptions about the ethnic group for which the joke makes reference. For example, Barron (1950) in a content analysis of jokes, found that in comparing three groups (Jews, Irish, Negroes), almost all of the jokes centred around one of the stereotypes of that group. For Blacks, the most pervasive themes were religion, music (dancing), and poor use of the English language. For Jews, themes (directly and indirectly) centred on money, while for Irish jokes the themes were drinking and religion (Roman Catholic). One does not have to look very far into one's repertoire of jokes to see the evidence of this claim. Jokes about Newfoundlanders, Poles, and Ukrainians almost always have a "dumb" theme, while the new set of "Paki" jokes now abundant centre on the "sub-human" character of this group.

Stories

Books, magazines, and short stories all portray characters. How these portrayals are carried off often determines the image that will be held by the reader or listener. We would again argue that the writer probably has no conscious forethought to malign a particular group of people or desire to stereotype any particular group. The only desire of the author is to get across to the reader or listener the "character of the plot." If the desire is to portray a "Mafia underworld murderer" then what better way than to characterize him in traditional stereotyped "Italian" attributes.

The end result is that stereotypes are sustained and carried on even though the writer has no direct intention to do so. The nature of these stories, then, tends to perpetuate the myth of the "real" Canadian (White, Anglo-Saxon, Protestant) by differentiating (subtly and consistently) between Canadians and "other" groups. The consistent denigration of the various minority groups in stories serves to activate the predispositions of a hostile or indifferent audience.

Mass Media

The mass media present similar stories in a different format. In a little known report by Elkin (1971) submitted to the Ontario Human Rights Commission concerning minority groups in mass media advertising, he found that out of a total of over 500 advertisements (in all forms of mass media), only two utilized non-White models.

The Kitchener-Waterloo religious society of Friends also monitored newspapers in the area for two months and reported that out of well over 1,000 identifiable faces used in ads, fewer than 20 were of a visible racial/ethnic group. In the cases where visible group members were used in the ads, they were usually used in a pejorative fashion, e.g., a fat, ugly Indian sitting next to his broken down car (a car advertisement). However, as Belson (1967) pointed out in his study of the impact of British television on racial attitudes of young people, the effect is limited and must be interpreted within the young person's situational and experience-related activities.

Stereotypes, then, reflect the process of social classification of people into specific categories. It has also been pointed out that this process is not always a rational, conscious attempt to denigrate the specific group. The stereotypes can represent classifications that are based on distinctive, easily recognized criteria that are shared (presently and/or historically) by other members of the society.

This process involves minimizing the individual differences and maximizing the categorical properties. This is sometimes known as the *minimax* or *chunking* principle; an easy way to store and recall information. However, even though the categorization process allows for a narrowing of the amount of information one must have before taking action, it also expands the scope of information about an object (Ehrlich, 1973). For example, you need little information to decide whether or not a person is Indian or not, but once you have typed him into that category, you then know (because of stereotypes) a lot about the individual.

Conclusion

The process of using social categories and placing individuals within these categories involves minimizing the individual differences of individuals within the category as well as maximizing the categorical properties. As Ehrlich (1973) points out:

> to categorize a social object implies that the criterial similarities are more important for that object and like objects than any differences among them. This minimax operation makes it easier to store knowledge and to recall it. The use of social categories narrows the amount of information that a person needs to have about someone in order to act. (38)

The end result is that one needs very little information to categorize an individual, but once this placement is made, one is then able to claim a great deal of knowledge about the individual or the group (the truth or falsity of the knowledge becomes a separate issue).

It should be clear now that the utility of stereotypes is great and their use pervasive in our society. They are economical and allow us to carry on interaction patterns with other individuals and groups in a regularized and normative fashion. No matter how hard we may try to eradicate stereotypes, they will continue to be with us and will guide our relations with other people and groups over time.

REFERENCES

Ackerman, N. and M. Jahode. *Anti-Semitism and Emotional Disorder.* New York: Harper & Row, 1950.

Anisfeld, E., N. Bogo and W. Lambert, "Evaluation Reactions to Accented English Speech," *Journal of Abnormal and Social Psychology,* 65 (1960): 223-231

Anisfeld, E. and W. Lambert. "Evaluation Reactions of Bilingual and Monolingual Children to Spoken Languages," *Journal of Abnormal and Social Psychology,* 69(1) (1964): 89-97.

Barron, M. "A Content Analysis of Intergroup Humor," *American Sociological Review,* 15 (1950): 88-94.

Belson, W. The Impact of Television. London: Crosby Lockwood & Son, 1967.

Bloom, L. The Social Psychology of Race Relations. London: George Allen and Unwin Ltd., 1971.

Breton, R. "The Structure of Relationships Between Ethnic Collectivities," in Leo Driedger (ed.), The Canadian Ethnic Mosaic. Toronto: McClelland & Stewart, 1978.

Brown, R. Social Psychology. New York: Free Press, 1965.

Bruner, J., J. Goodnow and G. A. Austin. A Study of Thinking. New York: John Wiley and Sons, 1956.

Campbell, T. "Stereotypes and the Perception of Group Differences," American Psychology, 22 (1967): 817-830.

Canadian Institute of Cultural Research. Ethnic Change of Name: Ontario Pilot Study. Report Series A-1. Toronto, Mimeo, 1965.

Cardinal, H. The Unjust Society. Edmonton: M. G. Hurtig, 1970.

Elkin, F. "The Employment of Visible Minority Groups in Mass Media Advertising." A report submitted to the Ontario Human Rights Commission, 1971.

Ehrlich, H. "Stereotyping and Negro-Jewish Stereotypes," Social Forces, 41 (1962): 171-176.

Ehrlich, H. "The Swastika Epidemic of 1959-1960: Anti-Semitism and Community Relations," Social Problems, Vol. 21, (1973): 264-280.

Eugene, L. and R. Horowitz. "Development of Social Attitudes in Children," Sociometry, I, (1938): 301-308.

Frideres, J. The Invisible Ethnic. Unpublished manuscript, University of Calgary, 1979.

Gans, H. "Symbolic Ethnicity: The Future of Ethnic Groups and Cultures in America," Ethnic and Racial Studies, 2, 1 (1979): 1-20.

Gardner, R. and D. Taylor. "Ethnic Stereotypes: Their Effects on Person Perception," Canadian Journal of Psychology, 22(1) (1968a): 267-276.

Gardner, R., E. Wonnacott and D. Taylor. "Ethnic Stereotypes: A Factor Analytic Investigation," Canadian Journal of Psychology, 22(1) (1968b): 35-44.

Gardner, R. and D. Taylor. "Ethnic Stereotypes: Meaningfulness in Ethnic Group Labels," Canadian Journal of Behavioural Sciences, 1(3) (1969): 182-192.

Goodman, M. Race Awareness in Young Children. Cambridge, Mass.: Addison-Wesley, 1952.

Hostetler, J. and G. Huntington. The Hutterites in North America. New York: Holt, Rinehart & Winston, 1967.

Indra, Doreen. "South Asian Stereotypes in the Vancouver Press," Ethnic and Racial Studies, 2(2) (1979): 166-189.

Katz, D. and K. Braly. "Racial Prejudice and Racial Stereotypes," Journal of Abnormal and Social Psychology, 30 (1935): 175-193.

Kretch, D., R. Crutchfield and E. Ballachey. Individual in Society. New York: McGraw-Hill, 1962.

Labovitz, S. "Some Evidence of Canadian Ethnic, Racial and Sexual Antagonism," Canadian Review of Sociology and Anthropology, 11(3) (1974): 247-254.

Lambert, W., R. Hodgson, R. Gardner and S. Fillenbaum. "Evaluation Reaction to Spoken Languages, " Journal of Abnormal and Social Psychology, 60 (1960): 44-51.

Larimer, G. "Indirect Assessment of Intercultural Prejudices," *International Journal of Psychology*, 5 (1970): 189-195.

Lippman, W. *Public Opinion*. New York: Macmillan, 1922.

Mackie, M. "Arriving at 'Truth' by Definition: The Case of Stereotype Inaccuracy," *Social Problems*, 20(4) (1973): 431-447.

Mackie, M. "Ethnic Stereotypes and Prejudice—Alberta Indians, Hutterites and Ukrainians," *Canadian Ethnic Studies*, 6 (1974): 39-53.

Mackie, M. "Ethnic Stereotypes, Prejudicial Attitudes and Education," *The Alberta Journal of Educational Research*, December, 20 (1974b): 279-292.

Mackie, M. "Outsiders' Perception of the Hutterites," *Mennonite Quarterly Review*, Vol. 50, No. 3, (1976): 58-65.

Maxwell, Thomas. *The Invisible French*. Waterloo, Ontario: Wilfred Laurier Press, 1977.

McDiarmid, M. and D. Pratt. *Teaching Prejudice*. Toronto: Ontario Institute for Studies in Education, 1971.

Moif, Gustav. "Ethnic Groups and Developmental Models: The Case of Quebec," in A. Said and L. R. Simmons (eds.), *Ethnicity in an International Context*. New Brunswick, NJ: Transaction Books, 1976.

Moreland, J. "Racial Recognition by Nursery School Children in Lynchburg, Virginia," *Social Forces*, 37 (1958): 132-137.

Nettler, G. *Explanations*. New York: McGraw-Hill, 1970.

Paton, L. and J. Deverell. *Prejudice in Social Studies Textbooks*. Saskatchewan Human Rights Commission, Saskatoon, 1974.

Richert, J. P. "The Impact of Ethnicity on the Perception of Heroes and Historical Symbols," *The Canadian Review of Sociology and Anthropology*, 11(2) (1974): 156-163.

Roback, A. *A Dictionary of International Slurs*. Cambridge, Mass.: Sci-Art, 1944.

Secord, P. and C. Backman. *Social Psychology*. New York: McGraw-Hill, 1964.

Shibutani, T. and K. M. Kwan. *Ethnic Stratification: A Comparative Approach*. New York: Macmillan, 1965.

Simpson, G. and J. Yinger. *Racial and Cultural Minorities*. New York: Harper and Row, 1965.

Stein, Michael. "The Dynamics of Contemporary Party Movements in Quebec: Some Comparative Aspects of Creditism and Independentism," in Wsevolod Isajiw (ed.), *Identities*. Toronto: Peter Martin, 1977.

Tajfel "Stereotypy," *Race*, Vol. 5 (1963): 3-14.

Trudel, M. and G. Jain. "Etude de la Conception de l'histoire Canadienne," *Report for Royal Commission on Bilingualism and Biculturalism*. Ottawa: Queen's Printer, 1967.

Wax, M. "A Survey of Restrictive Advertising and Discrimination by Summer Resorts in the Province of Ontario," *Information and Comment*, 7 (1948): 10-13.

Williams, R. *Strangers Next Door: Ethnic Relations in American Communities*. Englewood Cliffs, N.J.: Prentice-Hall, 1964.

White, J. and J. Frideres. "Race Prejudice and Racism: A Distinction," *Canadian Review of Sociology and Anthropology*, 14(1) (1977): 81-90.

Zirkel, P. "Self Concept and the Disadvantages of Ethnic Group Membership and Mixture," *Review of Educational Research*, 41 (1971) 211-225.

Part II

Ethnicity in a Changing Canada

The second part of this book introduces the reader to the place of ethnicity in a changing Canada. Where do ethnic minorities fit into Canadian society? Through the sixties Canada was referred to as officially bilingual (in English and French) and bicultural (with the British-origin and French-origin populations regarded as charter groups or founding races). This is not to suggest, however, that it was in fact bilingual or bicultural. These next chapters emphasize that French/English bilingualism has always been limited to a small proportion of Canadians, and that Canadian society at the regional level has tended to appear more unicultural and multicultural than bicultural.

Chapter 5 discusses Anglo/French biculturalism in historical and contemporary perspective. First we raise the question of whether a clear pan-Canadian identity has ever really existed, applying the criteria for nationhood, nation-state, and nationalism (which were discussed in Chapter 2) to Canada as a whole. British traditionalism in Canada is then described in the context of social change. The chapter attempts to clarify that French Quebec fulfills the above criteria, and provides an account of the development of a variety of nationalist and separatist movements in Quebec, particularly during the "Quiet Revolution" of the sixties, the period of FLQ terrorism culminating in the "October Crisis" of 1970, the radicalization of the Bourassa Liberal regime during the early seventies, and most recently the policies of the separatist Parti Quebecois culminating in the referendum on sovereignty-association in May 1980. The "bourgeois" arguments accounting for Quebecois nationalism and separatism in terms of ethnocentrism and parochialism rather than structural or political-economic conditions are summarized, but our discussion of Quebec contrasts the federalist position advocating constitutional reform or maintenance of the status quo, with the separatist position utilizing the national self-determination concept to push for sovereignty-association, if not complete independence. The chapter also discusses the changing situation of French minorities in the other provinces, and concludes with a reassessment of biculturalism.

In 1971 Canada was officially redefined by the federal government as being bilingual (English/French) yet multicultural. Chapter 6 provides an introduction to Canadian multiculturalism. It first emphasizes that "multiculturalism" is a rather novel—and awkward—term in social science literature. The question is raised as to whether in fact Canada does represent a "cultural mosaic," and the chapter describes the romanticization of ethnic history. Any realistic sociological evaluation of a cultural mosaic necessarily must offset the argument for ethnic persistence with the argument for ethnic change. The chapter therefore presents both arguments at some length, taking into consideration data on trends in language use, intermarriage, and the institutionalization of ethnic communities.

Chapter 7 describes the close relationship between immigration and ethnicity in Canada. First a brief historical account of Canadian immigration is presented, then the chapter focuses more specifically on the changing ethno-cultural composition of Canadian society, including the shift in recent years to immigration from non-traditional (Third World) sources. This shift is related in turn to the growth and distribution of non-White ethnic collectivities in Canada. The chapter then provides data pertaining to the question of regional disparities in immigrant distribution in general, as well as the urban concentration of immigrants in particular. Immigrant characteristics—differential fertility, age, education, and occuption—will be described. Finally, the chapter concludes with a brief critique of current policies aimed at the distribution of immigrants.

Chapter 5

Biculturalism

The Question of a Pan-Canadian Identity

With the foregoing definitions in mind, to what extent can we realistically speak of a Canadian nation, nationality, nation-state, and nationalism? We could, perhaps, describe Canadians as a "historically evolved, stable community of people," to use Stalin's words. But our country is relatively young (a sovereign state for a little over a century, though perhaps more in theory than in fact, in certain respects), and some Canadian citizens (e.g., Quebecois) have been reluctant to claim a strong sense of national Canadian identity and a common Canadian heritage, In general, Canadians seem to be very mindful of their various (chiefly European) heritages and of the contribution these cultures have made to Canadian society as a whole, but as yet there seems to be little feeling of a traditional, uniquely Canadian culture held in common by all, or even most, Canadians. There are Canadians who undoubtedly feel that "Canada as a whole would fare far better if it could operate without any hindrance whatsoever as a melting pot, absorbing all ethnic and cultural shades within the predominant Anglo-Saxon element as was done, for instance, in the United States," according to Leon Dion (1961); "still, willingly or not, we must accept the present situation as representing the verdict of our history and to that verdict we must all adjust ourselves some way or another. . . . " Canadian history has so far been one of unity in diversity, with the accent on the latter. And this is hardly surprising, considering that a high proportion of Canadians cannot trace their Canadian descent beyond three or four generations; more than 15% of Canadians were born outside Canada.

As we shall see in further detail in the next chapter, there is no common race in Canada, nor a common language, nor a common religion (criteria for nationhood mentioned in Chapter 2). Every ethnic category in the country is a statistical minority. As for other supposed criteria of nationhood, it could be readily argued that Canadians do occupy a common territory; but this territory is not defined by natural frontiers (n.b. Renan's definition of the nation), and it is so vast (in area Canada is the second largest country in the world) that it includes many regional variations and therefore considerable economic diversity rather than a "common economic life" (n.b. the definitions by Stalin, Deutsch, Moore, Shafer, etc.). Canadian society as a whole can hardly be said to possess a "common psychological make up" (Stalin), a "national mind" (Disraeli), a "common stock of thoughts and feelings" (Baker), or a "national character" (Bauer), though certain writers have claimed the latter for Canadians; nor is there a Canadian nationality as a whole which could realistically be termed a "spiritual unity" (Spengler), a "social soul" (Lamprecht), a "mental community" (Meinecke), or a "collective personality" (Don Sturzo). If Canadian society is a nation or nationality, it is then an admirable exemplification of Carr's statement that a "nation is not a definable and clearly recognizable entity."

Strictly speaking, it goes without saying that one cannot refer to Canadian nationalism unless Canada is already—or is striving to become—a nation-state, and that we cannot have a Canadian nation-state without a Canadian nation. In fact Canadians as a whole could be considered a nation only if we accept the popular yet misleading and oversimplified definitions of the nation as "a people united under a single independent government," and of nationality as "the fact of belonging to a particular state by virtue of birth or allegiance." This would lead us to confuse patriotism with nationalism, as Akzin has suggested, when in a poly-ethnic state like Canada what would be nationalism in a nation-state is actually replaced by patriotism towards the state as a whole and nationalism towards the ethnic minorities within the state. But in the case of Canada, perhaps we can question not only the application of the terms nationalism and nation-state to the country *as a whole*, but also whether there is in *general* (i.e., for *all* Canadians) a significant patriotism towards the Canadian state.

Let us examine in some detail whether this generalization seems justified. Canada lacks cohesion in many respects. Canadians have repeatedly criticized the governmental structure of their country. The primarily French-speaking people of Quebec have felt estranged from primarily English-speaking Canada as a whole. Native people in Canada have occasionally expressed their solidarity with Native people in the United States. Canadians in the Atlantic Coast provinces are geographically closer to the British Isles (from which most of them came) and to the United States (to which many of them have emigrated) than to their compatriots on the West Coast. Urban Canadians have revealed a different outlook on many issues than that of rural Canadians. Canadians in the Prairie provinces, largely of so-called New Canadian ethnic origins, have not been sympathetic towards a British-French biculturalism. The immense attraction of the affluent United States has long pulled Canadians into a series of north to south axes instead of into an east-west union. Canada has long been economically and culturally intimately tied to the United States. Many Canadian social organizations, especially economic enterprises and labor unions, are in fact branches, with varying degrees of independence, of American parent organizations. During the late sixties a rapidly increasing proportion of professors in Canadian universities were Americans. And Canada has been inundated with American mass media: popular magazines, radio, television.

Moreover, Canada has had what could only be considered a weak constitution, traditionally embodied in the British North America Act. On the one hand, the federal government in Ottawa has been weak in certain respects, whereas the provincial governments were comparatively strong; thus the paradox of Canadian politics has been that the whole is not equal to the sum of its parts. But on the other hand, Quebec has long claimed—with increasing vigor—that it does not have enough autonomous control. Even the sovereignty of Canada as a whole could be seriously questioned, for though the BNA Act was the closest thing Canada could claim to a written constitution, it was a statute of the British

Parliament, and any alterations had to be made by this foreign government. Thus Canada was for a long time a supposedly ex-colonial, sovereign state unable to amend its own constitution.

Yet the Canadian state does cohere in certain respects; there is something of a *raison d'etre* for Canada, something of a Canadian pride and sense of identity, and a resulting Canadian nationalism may have been increasing in recent years in response to the campaign of the Committee for an Independent Canada, the platform of the New Democratic Party, and not the least the threat of Quebec separatism.

If the country's British-French biculturalism (*la dualité Canadienne*) and ethnic heterogeneity due to massive and continuing immigration have divided Canadian society as a whole, they have also served to set Canada apart from the American melting pot philosophy and from British colonialism. Canadians have apparently taken considerable pride in being able to retain Old World ties without being subjected to a central assimilationist policy (but this is not to suggest that such a policy was not attempted by Anglo-Canadians). A. R. M. Lower, an eminent Canadian historian, has called Canada "a youthful goddess ranging herself alongside those older and tougher matrons Britannia, Gallia, and America" (1958: 438-9). Canadian patriotism was, then, pride in being Canadian and *not* British, French, or American, though Canada's very strong ties with these countries is appreciated, together with a pride in Canada's own affluence and success. Lower put it rather bluntly: "How sad and sorry Canada must remain as long as it continues to be a pale imitation of the United States" (1958: 442).

Many Canadians would, nonetheless, have reservations about calling their country a closely united state in the sense of a real nation-state. Yet this is not meant to deny the possibility that a Canadian nationalism could in time continue to develop with a reduction of, or in response to, the many serious divisions within the country. Back in 1952 Lower wrote:

> Few would deny today that a nation is being created. At present it is incomplete and there is no doubt about the existence of two nationalities within the one country, English and French. But every day sees new bridges being built between these two peoples and in addition, some progress, though nothing impressive, is made at winning back the country from American private ownership. Today most Canadians would agree (at long last) that they are citizens of a nation-state. (41)

Lower's enthusiasm may well have influenced a Canadian nationalism; yet a more cautious comment was provided the next year by Miriam Chapin (1959) an American writer, who nonetheless still referred to Canadians as a nation:

> National unity in Canada has always been something to be sought, not taken for granted. The bonds that hold Canada together are all man-made. Its very existence is a notable demonstration that history is not inevitable, that men who act with sense and courage can, given a fair chance, control their destiny. The question that now faces Canadians is whether they can still exercise this control, or whether the disruption from within and the pressure from without will bring about their dissolution as a nation. (6-7)

British Traditionalism in Canada

We have seen that, on the one hand, a Canadian identity can be considered relatively weak for many Canadians, especially for many French in Quebec; on the other hand, most French-Canadians have a strong sense of French-Canadian, or perhaps more specifically Quebecois identity, together with a nationalism aimed at maintaining or strengthening Quebec as a nation-state, either within the Canadian state or perhaps outside Canada in the form of an independent state. But a plurality, in fact almost a majority, of Canadians are of British descent; so the question of a British-Canadian identity (similar to the French-Canadian one) must be discussed.

The fact that Canadians of British origin speak the same language as Americans means that they are not likely to feel the same sort of sense of identity as the isolated French-Canadians who are eager to preserve their language and culture. Moreover, British-Canadians, while largely Protestant, belong to a wide variety of religious affiliations; not only are they not united in terms of religion, but also the sheer variety of these affiliations make English-speaking Canada comparable to America. In 1963 Gerard Pelletier, then editor of *La Presse* (a leading French-language daily newspaper in Montreal), mentioned that the loyalty of some British-Canadians in Ontario to Britain is no longer understandable in the Prairie provinces. Moreover, British-Canadians, perhaps brought together to some extent simply by anti-French sentiments, must face the problem of now being a cultural group which, since the disintegration of much of the British Empire, has lost its identity and has been attempting to avoid turning to the United States. This has become an even more vital question with the possibility or probability of Quebec gaining complete independence. Western Canadian separatism has been gaining momentum by capitalizing on Western impatience over the Quebec issue and longstanding distrust of central Canadian (i.e., Ontario) control. A recent development has been the formation of a Unionist Party by a couple of renegade Progressive Conservative MLAs (notably including the former provincial PC leader) in Saskatchewan; this new party has proclaimed its principal aim to be the union of Western Canada with the United States.

In sum, the British-Canadians are too widespread geographically, too similar to Americans, too diversified in terms of religion, and above all too unsure of how much or how little to emphasize their British heritage, to be a nation as the French-Canadians are. But if the British-Canadians do not exhibit a nationalism aimed at some sort of British-Canadian nation-state, just where have they actually fitted into Canadian society? We may say that they have tended to interpret Canadian identity and a form of Canadian nationalism in their own terms. Trudeau once suggested (1962) that the nation-state concept which spurred the political thinking of the British themselves in turn affected British-Canadian thought, so that the Canadian state has been identified with British Canada to the greatest extent possible. Canada itself, not just part of Canada, was to be British in certain respects. Wade (1964) has written,

> the persistent concept of a wholly English Canada, in which the French would be absorbed, did not die at Confederation. ... Its survival was fostered on the one hand by steady British immigration, by growing Anglo-

American dominance in the industrial world which developed in Canada during the second half of the nineteenth century, and by the emergence of the British Empire and the United States as leading world powers; and on the other by depletion of French-Canadian stock through migration to the United States in numbers which reduced French-Canadian population by one-third, and by the fact that the prestige of France never recovered from the crushing blows of 1870-1. (44)

There are innumerable examples of British traditions retained in Canada. It was not until 1965, two years before the centennial of supposed independence from Britain, that a version of the traditional British colonial flag (the Red Ensign) was finally replaced by a distinct Canadian flag, although the Red Ensign, with the Ontario coat of arms replacing the Canadian, could still be flown in Ontario; and the Union Jack, the national flag of the United Kingdom could still be flown in Canada to represent Canada's Commonwealth membership and in Newfoundland until very recently as the provincial flag. The British queen is still head of state in Canada, and is represented by a Governor-General nationally and by Lieutenant-Governors provincially. The national anthem of the United Kingdom, "God Save the Queen," is still played on occasion in Canada as if it were the Canadian national anthem. A variety of Canadian institutions still bear the designation "royal." Canadian armed forces still wear distinctly British uniforms on occasion. The federal and provincial governments are modelled after the British Parliament (although the government of Quebec prefers to refer to itself as the National Assembly). Courts include the Queen's Bench (although Quebec has a distinct law code). Teas are still being given by the Imperial Order of the Daughters of the Empire. The Orange Order and Monarchist League are still active in various locations in Canada.

Yet we would be remiss to concentrate inordinantly on the retention of British traditionalism in Canada, as there has been a steady erosion of this British character in recent years. Lower has suggested that even as early as the turn of the century British imperialism in Canada was already undergoing transformation from the narrow colonialism of former days into a more cautious pro-Canadian (yet still quite British) sentiment:

The closer one was, by denomination or association, to the traditional ruling class, the more likely one was to be an "imperialist." To such people, the word "imperialism" meant the unity of the English-speaking world under the Crown plus a society with a prominent place for the "chosen few" . . . Canadian "imperialism" has never been simple; it can at one and the same time be bitterly contemptuous of "Englishmen" and warmly welcome "the British connection" . . . Canadian nationalists had no desire to part from Great Britain in bad blood, but they did not wish to be committed automatically by the "parent state" to its decisions and they did not want to see its social system transported artificially to the new world. (1958: 348-9)

British traditionalism, notably the monarchy, has increasingly come into question in Canada. Many pertinent questions have been raised in the Canadian press and widely circulating periodicals, for example, June Callwood's description of the 1973 Royal Tour, somewhat irreverently titled "Liz Windsor

Superstar" (*Maclean's*, Sept. 1973). Or Allan Fotheringham's columns titled: "She's a Good Queen. In Fact She's a Great Queen. But She's Somebody Else's." (*Maclean's*, June 27, 1977), and "God Save Us from our Gracious Queen" (*Maclean's* April 14, 1980). Or Gordon Peckover's article on "The Decline and Fall of the Canadian Monarchy" (*Opinion*, Sept. 1978). We would suggest that most Anglo-Canadians certainly do not regard themselves as very British; for most the British connection at best could be described as vague. In this regard it could be noted that two Gallup Polls released August 6 and October 11, 1980 revealed that only a minority of Canadians sampled (47% and 49% respectively) believed the British Queen should be retained as head of state in Canada.

French-Canadians: Within Quebec

While it is questionable whether we can consider the *entire* Canadian population to be a nation (in the narrower sense of the term), there can be little doubt that the French in Quebec constitute a nation (according to most definitions of this term). The Franco-Quebecois are by almost any measure a very cohesive group. They are in general the non-indigenous ethnic group with the longest residence in Canada; many of them can trace their Canadian descent back as far as ten or more generations. Not only can they claim a common heritage derived from French history but also a longstanding variety of French culture developed during three and a half centuries of residence in Canada. About 90% of the French-Canadians in Canada speak French as their mother tongue, as do 98% of the French-Canadians in Quebec. The vast majority (about 77%) of French-Canadians live in Quebec; approximately 96% of them live in that province and in the neighbouring provinces of New Brunswick and Ontario.

Moreover, French-Canadians are extremely cohesive in terms of religion. In 1961, 96% of them were nominally Roman Catholics. The Roman Catholic Church in Quebec long exercised a profound influence on French-Canadian social and political life; the Church controlled the education of French-Canadians, particularly at the primary and secondary levels and to a lesser extent even at the university level. Unfortunately, a clerical ideal of a patriarchal, primarily rural society, defended long after such a society had become a thing of the past, retarded industrial and technological development in French Canada. Yet the Church did a great deal to encourage a sense of French-Canadian nationalism. The extreme wing of a clerical movement to crystallize and encourage nationalism (as a means of warding off social unrest in Quebec which could turn anti-clerical) openly advocated separatism from the Canadian state in favor of setting up a sovereign French Catholic state. Since the nineteenth century, an *ultranationalism* (to use Ward's term) has attempted to use religion for political ends and at other times politics for religious ends. This has repeatedly aroused the antipathy of English-speaking Canadians, the majority of whom are Protestants, and who have a tradition of the separation of church and state. As Wade (1964: 46) has explained, "this antipathy in turn strengthens the French-Canadians' minority complex, which arises from the acute consciousness that politically speaking they represent only 30% of the population of Canada, and, culturally speaking, less than 1% of the surrounding Anglo-American group. The inferiority complex in a national group, as in individuals, produces arrogant and aggressive attitudes, which only intensify the conflict."

There would seem to be ample reason for calling Quebec a nation-state, even though it is not precisely coterminous with Canada's French population. It is ethnically very homogeneous, despite the cosmopolitan nature of Montreal; 81% of the province's population are of French origin and 87% are French-speaking. Lower (1958) has admitted:

> French Canada, fortified behind its language and its faith, has something that English Canada did not possess: a way of life of its own, and a way of life that by mid-century was fast developing its cultural expressions. French-Canadians were a people. It still was doubtful whether English-Canadians were, especially in that the immigration policy of the administration of the day appeared designed to upset whatever social homogeneity they had previously attained. (441-42)

Marcel Chaput, a leading *separatiste* during the sixties, has done much to persuade French-Canadians to recognize the fact that they are a nation and Quebec is their nation-state, and to convince them that Canada does not deserve their allegiance:

> There is no Canadian nation. . . . There is a Canadian state. . . . The Canadian state is a purely political and artificial entity. . . . On the contrary, the French-Canadian nation is a natural entity whose bonds are those of culture, flesh, and blood. . . . We feel that French-Canadians must be in control somewhere, in a country of their own, specifically in Quebec. . . . Quebec is not a province like the others; it is the national state of the French-Canadians. (1961: 4-5)

Chaput has argued that French-Canadians feel a perpetual conflict between their status as Canadian citizens and as members of a French-Canadian nation:

> In this dilemma which is always with us, there is only one possible choice for French-Canadians—we must be French-Canadians first, before being Canadians, because our French-Canadian status is based on the fact that we form a natural ethnic family, whereas our Canadian status is based on purely artificial political ties. (53)

René Levesque, writing in 1963, when he was the Quebec minister of natural resources, similarly had this to say:

> French Canada is a true nation. It has all the elements essential to national life; it possesses unity, as well as human and material resources, including equipment and personnel, which are as good or better than those of a large number of the peoples of the world. . . . [But] politically we are not a sovereign people. For the moment, the point is not whether we might or might not be sovereign; the point is simply that we *are* not. Thus, we are a true nation, but a nation unattended by sovereignty. . . . This nation possesses its national state, Quebec. . . . Those who talk to us about that legal entity, the "Canadian nation," generally forget that a more fundamental and profound reality lies in the human, cultural, and social entity, embodied in the French-Canadian nation. (*Le Devoir*, July 5, 1963)

In a speech that same year to Canadians outside Quebec, Jean Lesage, then *Premier ministre* of Quebec, stated that:

the French-speaking Canadians are particularly worried about the place that they occupy in Confederation as it exists today. In Quebec, especially, the ideas expressed on this subject are many and varied, but rarely do we find one of these ideas that does not show dissatisfaction to a more or less marked degree. Because. . . .the French-Canadians do not have the feeling that they belong to Canada to the same extent that their English-speaking countrymen do. After all, the feeling of belonging, and from there, interested cooperation, is one of the original aims of a successful federal regime. And on this particular point, as Premier of Quebec and as representative of the French-Canadians, I cannot say that Confederation is a success. . . . (from a speech at Charlottetown, P.E.I., 1963)

When Canada was itself theoretically becoming a sovereign state more than a century ago, the most prominent spokesman for the French-Canadians was Cartier. He did not envisage a Canada which was to be simply a federation of British North American provinces in which the will of the majority should prevail. Rather he emphasized bilingualism and biculturalism, and the equal right of the British and French groups to preserve their own cultures. In fact, he remarked, "some have regretted that we have a distinction of races, and have expressed the hope that, in time, this diversity will disappear; the idea of a fusion of the races in one is utopian; it is an impossibility." Today the continuing French-Quebecois insistence upon provincial autonomy (if not complete independence) and a reduction of federal centralization are based on Cartier's interpretation. Because Cartier's optimism has been discredited by developments during this past century, French-Canadians naturally are indignant that outside of Quebec the bicultural and bilingual character of Canada is only grudgingly recognized if it is accepted at all. They have resented the fact that while a third of the French-Canadians are bilingual, some 96% of the English-speaking Canadians not of French origin cannot speak French. And French-Canadians have resented being regarded as virtual foreigners by other Canadians. However, Cartier's optimism and contemporary French-Canadian resentment aside, it seemed unlikely that the predominance of a different ethnic group in one province, with a long history of particularism, would be considered by the other provinces an adequate reason for Quebec's being granted wider freedom and more autonomy within Canadian federalism. Yet since the election of the avowedly separatist Parti Quebecois in 1976, under the leadership of René Levesque, who then became the provincial *Premier ministre*, English Canada has been found to take the demands of Quebec more seriously.

It has not been surprising to find, therefore, a strong contemporary French-Canadian nationalism aimed primarily at preserving French identity and serving, in varying degrees, as an alternative to Canadian patriotism. But if French-Canadian nationalism was "the natural aspiration of a people who believe in themselves and who are determined to survive with their language, their traditions, and their religion" (Scott, 1939: 73-4), when this nationalism became translated more specifically into separatism, it was criticized in far less sympathetic terms by many writers, who closely related it to what they conceived to be a problem of French-Canadian introversion. For example, Chapin (1959) wrote that:

The reason why French-Canadians as a group and in much of their individual action feel so much uneasiness is that they fear for the survival of their own community, and, with it, the excuse for their ingrown nationalism. Quebec is interested in ordinary political and social issues. . . . only to the extent to which they affect the province's preoccupation with the preservation of a Catholic, French-speaking nation in North America. Prospect of war breaks through the mists of language and prejudice to become a genuine concern because then the bugbear of conscription threatens. Otherwise French-Canadians in Quebec trouble their heads little about affairs outside their own bailiwick. Their intellectuals argue over whether Quebec should stand alone or unite with the rest of Canada to resist American domination. Year in and year out, what concerns Quebec is its own resistance movement—resistance to interference from Ottawa, which it distrusts as an instrument of English-Canadian rule, even when the Prime Minister comes from the heart of Quebec; resistance to the flood of American money and products which are changing the habits and loyalties of its youth. Never was a community more fond of being let alone, more wary of the new, less outgoing in its affections. (12-13)

Leon Dion, a well known political scientist at Laval University, remarked in 1961 that French Canadian nationalism should not be considered "a sort of museum piece to be looked at as a queer product of an introverted people"; for it is in fact a very living phenomenon. This nationalism is not only part of a French-Canadian collective mentality but also a fact confronting all Canadians in decisions they must make on a great variety of issues. Moreover, Dion argued that almost every politically conscious French-Canadian in Quebec today would call himself a nationalist; he suggested that, depending on one's definition of nationalism, it could be conceivable that one could come to the conclusion that all French-Canadians must by necessity be de facto nationalists. But he added that many commentators on the Quebec scene had failed to differentiate between ethnocentrism and doctrinaire nationalism. According to Dion, there is, in fact, no real unity in French-Canadian nationalism except for one attitude common to virtually all French-Canadians, namely, a pride in being French-Canadian; yet Dion has emphasized repeatedly and at length that this pride can assume the form of a marked ethnocentrism resulting from the minority status of the French-Canadians in Canada and their majority status in Quebec. Thus, whatever the political ideology of a certain French-Canadian, there seems to be a point where he tends to feel and act in an ethnocentric manner. Dion attributed the variety and constancy of French-Canadian nationalism to the fact that this nationalism feeds upon the permanent fact of a collective minority status and consciousness (Dion, 1961).

Would separatism result in a renaissance of French culture in North America? Some prominent writers on French Canada vehemently criticized this suggestion. Pierre Elliott Trudeau, for example, wrote in 1962 that:

[W]e (French Canadians) have expended a great deal of time and energy proclaiming the rights due to our nationality, invoking our celestial mission, bewailing our misfortunes, denouncing our enemies, and avowing our independence, and for all that not one of our workmen is the more skilled, nor a civil servant the more efficient, a financeer the richer, a doctor the more advanced, a bishop the more learned, nor a single solitary politician the less ignorant. . . . In truth, it is the very concept of sovereignty which must be surmounted, and those who proclaim it for the nation of French Canada are not only reactionary, they are preposterous. . . . The ultimate tragedy would be in not realizing that French Canada is too culturally anaemic, too economically destitute, too intellectually retarded, too spiritually ossified, to be able to survive more than a couple of decades of stagnation, emptying herself of all her vitality into nothing but a cesspit, the mirror of her nationalistic vanity and "dignity". . . . (Cité Libre, April 1962)

To these strong words Mason Wade (1964: 78) added that the special tragedy of Quebec is that its desire to be left to itself is probably stronger than ever before, at a time when it is becoming impossible for any portion of the world to go its own way regardless of the rest of mankind. Again, this author argued that the great mass of the French-Canadians are underprivileged economically and intellectually, pointing out that their standard of living is well below the North American norm.

In Quebec during the Quiet Revolution the term nationalism comprised a gamut of opinions ranging from the terrorism of the FLQ (Front de Liberation Quebecois) through the militant separatism of the RIN (Rassemblement pour l'Indépendance Nationale), and the legal separatism of the Parti Republicain du Quebec, to the strong anti-separatism of the nationalists working for a wider recognition of the French fact in Confederation. In turn these movements were the heirs to the earlier clerical, conservative nationalist movement led by Abbé Groulx, and the socialistic and anti-clerical views of vocal young artists and intellectuals who, alongside l'Alliance Laurentienne, Les Jeunes-Canada, and quite a few members of other traditional nationalistic movements, had proclaimed the right and desirability of political self-determination for French-Canadians living in the Province of Quebec (Dion, 1961).

In view of the plethora of nationalist and separatist movements in Quebec prior to their consolidation into the comprehensive Parti Quebecois, what was the support for separatism during the sixties? According to a questionnaire-based survey of separatism carried out in 1963 by Montreal's Groupe de Récherche Sociale and published in Maclean's magazine, an estimated 13% of French-Canadians were actual separatists and another 23% were undecided about separation from Canada. This survey reported that at the time most separatists were fairly young, most were students or white collar workers, and most had already completed or were having a university education or some sort of special training beyond high school. Nearly 60% of them were estimated to have joined the separatist movement within the last couple of years (before the survey). Many of them did not believe that separation would have a negative effect on Quebec's economy. Their contact with English-speaking Canadians had been infrequent, on the whole, and practically non-existent at home on an intimate social level. But extremely few separatists responded favorably to the FLQ's dramatic call to arms:

QUEBEC PATRIOTS, TO ARMS! THE HOUR OF NATIONAL REVOLUTION HAS STRUCK! INDEPENDENCE OR DEATH!

In fact, an estimated one-third of the French Quebecois interviewed apparently thought that some of their fellow nationals had joined the separatist cause only because it was currently à la mode, or "the thing to do." Of the separatists themselves, an estimated 42% favored separatist candidates in a legal provincial election; and another 39% favored holding a referendum; only 7% were in favor of staging a *coup d'etat*.

Clearly the support for legal separatism grew among French Quebecois during the seventies. The decade began, however, with the most attention being directed at illegal terrorism: during the October Crisis, the kidnapping of James Cross, British diplomat, was soon followed by the assassination of Pierre Laporte, the Quebec Minister of Labour, on October 17, 1970. FLQ cells claimed responsibility for both acts. The following day the War Measures Act was applied to Quebec, calling for military occupation of Montreal. In January, 1972 three major Quebec labour unions with a combined membership of over half a million members—the Quebec Federation of Labour (QFL), the Confederation of National Trade Unions (CNTU), and the Quebec Teacher's Federation (QEC)—issued manifestos to their members, the aim of which was to put a "radical socialist party" in power at the next provincial election. But the Liberal Party was returned to power under Premier Robert Bourassa in 1973. Although it won only six seats in the National Assembly, the Parti Quebecois gained 30% of the popular vote (an increase from 23% in 1970), perhaps most of the French Quebecois vote, and ran second in seventy-eight ridings (effectively eliminating the Union Nationale, which had been an important force and in power for several years under Daniel Johnson during the Quiet Revolution of the sixties.

Under mounting pressure to take a stronger, more nationalistic stand for French Quebec, Bourassa's Liberals introduced a provincial language policy through Bill 22 in February, 1974 (passed in the National Assembly June 30, 1974), which aimed at encouraging the children of the new immigrants to attend French-language schools rather than English-language ones. The 1971 census data had revealed that out of over six million people in Quebec, about 79% were of French origin, 11% of British origin, and 10% of other origins. But out of 2.7 million in Montreal, 64% were French, 16% British, and 20% of other origins (twice the proportion of "others" in Montreal as in the province as a whole). There were more than 542,000 non-British, non-French people in Montreal, most of them recent immigrants. They included over 161,000 Italians, 114,000 Jews, 42,000 Ukrainians, Poles and Russians, 40,000 Greeks, 38,000 Germans, 16,000 Portuguese, 10,000 Blacks and West Indians, as well as Chinese and Vietnamese, Syrians and Lebanese, and many other ethnic groups. The vast majority of these immigrants were speaking little or no French. Exceptions were 108,000 Italians, 54,000 Jews (including francophone immigrants from Morocco), and such groups as Haitians, Vietnamese, Syrians and Lebanese who may have learned French prior to immigration.

The Parti Quebecois, led by René Levesque, was swept to power by a considerable majority in the fall of 1976, promising to hold a referendum on separation from Canada "within a couple of years." On April 1, 1977 the PQ unveiled an even more far-reaching language policy in the form of a White Paper on a French-Language Charter, which would force all newcomers (not just foreign immigrants) to send their children to French schools and would require all commercial enterprises (from corporations and companies to stores) to use French only in signs and to increase a French presence in their staffs or be fined. This policy of *francization* boldly asserted that "there will no longer be any question of a bilingual Quebec." In early November 1979 the PQ released its White Paper on Sovereignty-Association, which outlined at great length details of a policy aimed at political independence from Canada yet economic (including monetary) union with Canada. The opposition Liberals under Claude Ryan wasted little time in making public on January 9, 1980 a "Beige Paper" on constitutional reform, advocating extensive—even radical—changes in the position Quebec occupies in confederation, but stressing that an autonomous Quebec could still remain politically a part of Canada.

Since the Parti Quebecois came to power, a bewildering variety of public opinion polls have been inflicted on Quebecois with conflicting results. For example, a Gallup Poll sponsored by *The Canadian* magazine reported on April 9, 1977 that 66.9% of French-Canadians interviewed felt that the federal government of Canada should try to negotiate special political and economic arrangements with Quebec to try to *prevent* separation. The Canadian Institute of Public Opinion (Gallup Poll) found in February 1977 that 22% of Quebecois favored separatism (up from 11% in 1968), and by April 1977 that this had declined to 20%. But another survey, also conducted in April 1977, for the CBC by SORECOM, reported that 32.4% had said they would vote in favor of an "independent Quebec economically associated with the rest of Canada" (i.e., sovereignty-association) if the PQ government was successful in negotiating such an arrangement. Another CBC poll in March 1979 indicated that a majority (51%) of Quebecois would give the PQ a mandate to negotiate sovereignty-association. Yet in the next month the Institut Quebecois d'Opinion Publique (IQOP) concluded that 58.7% of those polled believed Quebec would remain in confederation. With Parti Quebecois publication in December 1979 of the two-part, carefully qualified question asking for approval of a mandate to negotiate sovereignty-association with the federal government, the great referendum debate began in earnest, climaxing in the actual referendum on May 20, 1980. In the meantime numerous polls were conducted, generally indicating that a slight minority (40% +) of the Quebec electorate supported a "oui" (yes) vote for negotiation but an approximately equal proportion would vote "non" (no). This still left a considerable proportion (as much as 20%) undecided.

In the final test, the referendum itself on May 20, these undecided voters seem to have supported the "non" vote, as 59.5% (approximately 2.2 million) of the electorate voted against sovereignty-association, whereas only 40.5% (1.5 million) voted in favor of it.

Analysis of the referendum results is instructive; a slight majority (52%) of francophones voted "oui," whereas virtually all (96%) of non-francophones voted "non." In polling areas where the majority of voters were anglophone a high proportion (well over 80%) expressed their opposition to sovereignty-association. The only exceptions to this pattern, in fact, were in areas which have strongly supported the Parti Quebecois in recent elections, but even in the constituency with the strongest *Péquiste* support, situated in East Montreal, the "oui" forces won little more than 60% of the vote.

The implications of the referendum for Canada are considerable. The Parti Quebecois's inexorable increase in popular support (if not a corresponding exodus of Anglo-Canadians and their businesses from Montreal) slowed down—but for how long and how completely remains to be seen. What became quite clear is that a sizable majority of Quebecois—and not just the English-speaking minority of the province—still support federalism. But it is not so clear that they would support a retreat back to the Quebec of former Liberal or Union Nationale governments. Rather the implication of the referendum is that a cautious support of a renewed federalism, i.e., for thorough constitutional change, has been registered. And one would do well to bear in mind that a very significant minority of all voters, in fact just over half of the francophone ones, did vote in favor of the provincial government negotiating sovereignty-association.

The final qualification is that, despite the fact that Claude Ryan, the Liberal Party leader, who also served as leader of the "non" forces, gained a fairly impressive majority, this result by no means signifies the demise of the Parti Quebecois under René Levesque (as recent polls have indicated widespread support for many of the changes initiated by the latter party as the provincial government).

French-Canadians: Outside Quebec

So far in this chapter we have concentrated on the French within Quebec. But what about French minorities in the other provinces? Almost one out of every four French-Canadians lives outside Quebec; about a million and a half Canadians of French descent are found in the other provinces. Approximately half are in Ontario, a quarter in the Atlantic Provinces, and a quarter in the West.

The original Quebecois emigrated, for the most part, from Normandy and other French provinces; whereas the Acadians in the Atlantic Provinces originally came from the region known as la Vendée in western France and spoke a different dialect. The Quebec French became British subjects in 1759, the Acadians several decades earlier, in 1713. At the first Acadian National Conference at Memramcook, New Brunswick, in 1881, an Acadian National Society was founded and a patron saint and national feast-day were chosen apart from the Quebec ones. At a second conference at Tignish, Prince Edward Island (Ile Saint-Jean), two years later, an Acadian national flag and national anthem were selected. M. A. Savoie (1961) has commented:

> thus the Acadians proclaimed in no uncertain terms that they considered themselves a cultural group, distinct from all others in the land, and expressed their determination to remain so and furthermore to maintain and develop all the cultural values which were particular to their group. . . . I believe that we had here the beginning of a small nation. . . .

But however distinct the Acadians feel themselves to be, they are essentially a variety of French-Canadians; they are, in other words, very much a part of the French-Canadian nation, in terms of language, ethnic origin, religion, etc. What they are *not* (yet) part of is the French-Canadian nation-state, if the Province of Quebec can be considered such a nation-state.

Almost all of the Franco-Ontarians are ultimately of Quebecois origin (but most have lived in Ontario/Upper Canada for generations), as are a substantial proportion of French-Canadians out west. However, the western French also came from a complex variety of other sources: they included not only migrants direct from Quebec, but also francophone Metis (French-Indian mixed people), settlers from the American Midwest and New England, Acadians and Franco-Ontarians, and immigrants from a wide variety of regions in France as well as from Belgium and Switzerland (Anderson, 1978).

The French fact in Western Canada should hardly be underestimated. There are more than a third of a million French-Canadians in the western provinces (in 1971, 86,515 in Manitoba, 56,200 in Saskatchewan, 94,665 in Alberta, and 96,550 in British Columbia); forty-seven distinct French rural bloc settlements in the Prairies (ten in Manitoba, thirty in Saskatchewan, and seven in Alberta); a hundred and fifty-eight largely French communities, excluding urban neighborhoods (fifty-five in Manitoba, sixty in Saskatchewan, and forty-three in Alberta); plus numerous French-language parishes (Anderson, 1974). But linguistic assimilation has clearly taken a heavy toll among French minorities not in the region of Ontario and New Brunswick adjacent to Quebec.

Table 1

USE OF THE FRENCH LANGUAGE BY FRENCH-CANADIAN MINORITIES OUTSIDE QUEBEC, BY REGION, IN 1971

Province/ Region	French Canadians	French mother tongue	%	French-speaking at Home	%	Speak only French	%
Saskatchewan	56,200	31,605	56.2	15,935	28.4	1,825	3.3
Manitoba	86,515	60,550	70.0	39,600	45.8	5,020	5.8
Alberta	94,665	46,500	49.1	22,695	24.0	3,305	3.5
Total Prairies	237,380	138,655	58.4	78,230	33.0	10,150	4.3
B.C.	96,550	38,035	39.4	11,510	11.9	1,775	1.8
Total West	333,930	176,690	52.9	89,740	26.9	11,925	3.6
Northern Ont. (5 eastern counties)*	195,065	162,345	83.3	135,575	69.5	37,675	19.3
Windsor & Co. Essex	58,850	26,155	44.4	11,920	20.3	1,600	2.7
Toronto	71,885	37,250	51.8	17,320	24.1	4,715	6.6
Eastern Ont. (5 counties)*	190,695	162,900	85.4	142,870	74.9	41,095	21.6
Total Ontario	737,360	482,045	65.4	352,460	47.8	92,845	12.6
New Brunswick	235,025	215,725	91.8	199,085	84.7	100,985	43.0
Other Atlantic Provinces	110,950	50,335	45.4	33,920	30.6	5,375	4.8
Total Atlantic	345,975	266,060	76.9	233,005	67.3	105,340	30.4
Total French Canadians Outside Quebec	1,417,265	924,795	65.3	675,205	47.6	210,110	14.8

*Note: The five counties of the eastern portion of northern Ontario are Cochrane, Algoma, Sudbury, Temiskaming, and Nipissing. The five counties of eastern Ontario are Stormont, Glengarry, Prescott, Russell, and the Regional Municipality of Ottawa-Carleton.
Source: Calculated from Statistics Canada, 1971 Census of Canada, Catalogue 92-736, Vol. 1, part 4, Bulletin 1.4-8, "Population: Language by Ethnic Groups."

It is understandable, perhaps, why several of the provincial French associations, such as the ACFC (Association Culturelle Franco-Canadienne) in Saskatchewan, and a significant radical group within the FFHQ (Fédération des Francophones hors Québec/the Federation of Francophones Outside Quebec), took a stand supporting a "oui" vote for the referendum on sovereignty-association. It is their intention to push for further rights owed to them by the non-French majority by capitalizing on the increasing politicization of the French in Quebec. Ultimately, however, this policy could spell cultural suicide, as many French outside Quebec fear (not without ample reason) that concessions to French minorities would be rapidly abandoned if and when Quebec separates. Thus, French minorities outside Quebec are caught in a dilemma as to how exactly they are to relate to the political alternatives/options for Quebec: complete separation/independence, sovereignty-association, constitutional reform/autonomy, or maintenance of the status quo.

Biculturalism Re-examined

In many respects Canadian bilingualism and biculturalism are myths. On the one hand, Canada has long been officially bilingual at the national level. On the other hand, in fact only 13.4% of Canadians (not quite one out of every eight Canadians) were bilingual in English and French in 1971, and most of these bilingual Canadians were French; very few Anglo-Canadians were at all conversant in French. Of at least a million and a half French-Canadians outside Quebec, about a third no longer recognized French as their mother tongue and more than half of them did not speak French as their primary language at home. In fact, in every province outside Quebec except New Brunswick, the majority of the French-origin population were not using French primarily at home.

Table 2

USE OF FRENCH LANGUAGE BY FRENCH POPULATION AT HOME, IN PROVINCES OUTSIDE QUEBEC, 1971

Province	Canadian-born French-origin Population	Number Speaking French as Primary Language at Home	Proportion not Speaking French as Primary Language at Home
Newfoundland	15,140	1,930	87.3%
Prince Edward Island	15,140	4,185	72.4%
Nova Scotia	78,555	25,355	67.7%
New Brunswick	232,370	189,930	18.3%
Ontario	719,190	324,045	54.9%
Manitoba	83,680	35,415	57.7%
Saskatchewan	53,690	13,750	74.4%
Alberta	89,860	19,525	78.3%
British Columbia	89,985	8,270	90.8%

Source: Calculated from Statistics Canada, 1971 Census of Canada, Catalogue 92-736, Vol. 1, part 4, Bulletin 1.4-8, "Population: Language by Ethnic Groups."

One might also note, in passing, that within Quebec there were over 23,000 Canadian born French-origin people who could not speak French. In Canada as a whole, 275,795 Canadians not claiming French origin nonetheless considered French to be their mother-tongue, 204,265 of them residents of Quebec. Within Quebec a unilingual francization policy is likely to increase this number of non-French-origin francophones, of course.

It should be emphasized that to most French-Canadians (i.e., particularly Quebecois) nationalism and separatism, of one variety or another, are far more significant than patriotism toward the Canadian state. As Dion (1961) has commented, "Canadianism, in so far at least as its impact upon French-Canadians is concerned, while it has offered great schemes of cultural and social betterment for the collectivity, is nevertheless a failure as a popular movement, because it has underestimated the importance and the sensitivity of the basic French-Canadian ethnocentrism." On the other hand, as numerous writers have agreed, French-Canadian nationalism has played an extremely significant role not only in Quebec politics but also in Canadian politics in general; it is, in short, of vital concern to French-Canadians as well as to all Canadians.

For their part, British-Canadians have not been very enthusiastic about any bilingualism or biculturalism in Canada. Even thirty years before independence Lord Durham criticized a British-Canadian superiority complex, or ethnocentrism, and a British contempt for the French in Canada. How, then, can a Canadian patriotism, a French-Canadian nationalism, and a British-Canadian interpretation of Canadian nationalism coexist? On the one hand, a limited ethnic pluralism in the form of biculturalism serves as a *theoretical* foundation for Canadian identity. On the other hand, as Akzin (1964: 113) has suggested, the very presence of the two major entities within one country gives rise to inter-ethnic tension, which is typical for the multinational states of Europe and which makes it impossible to ignore the distinction between the community of citizens and the national group, and to confuse the state and its over-all population with the nation.

Many writers in past decades have emphasized that Canadian unity at a national level depends on bettering the relations between the French and British Canadians. According to Saunders (1946),

> what "la bonne entente" finally sums up to is a recognition that Canada must of necessity, and in justice to all, build its true unity and its future greatness upon the basis of a dual culture. Nothing but a willing acceptance of this principle will ever effect a healing of the breach between French and English in this country. On no other foundation can a greater Canada be securely built. (16)

Patriotic as such writings may sound, they were always realistically conditional; acceptance of biculturalism by Canadians has been slow. Almost prayerfully, the Franco-Ontarian Sanouillet warned in 1962 that:

> if English-speaking Canada believes the effort (to accept biculturalism) is not worth their while, and that is, after all, quite possible, then it should not be surprised if, one day, French Canada, with its wealth, its history, its immense economic and cultural potential, slips away. Hopefully we must therefore make it a duty to wish that the traditional political sagacity of

the Anglo-Saxons meets up with the true French vocation, which is to rise above narrow nationalism. May they both help Canada to triumphantly pass over the obstacles accumulated by two centuries of incomprehension, misunderstandings, and injustices. (28)

Like Sanouillet, P. E. Trudeau, long recognized as a most fervent and outspoken federalist, encouraged French-Canadians to rise above narrow nationalism. He has pointed out that, since the French-Canadians have declined assimilation and Anglo-Canadians have looked upon Quebec as a backwater or ghetto, French-Canadians have had two choices in responding to this situation. He has suggested (in 1962) that French-Canadians (in Quebec) could "respond to the vision of an overbearing Anglo-Canadian nation-state with a rival vision of a hived-off French-Canadian nation-state"; on the other hand, they could "scrap the very idea of nation-state once and for all and lead the way toward making Canada a multicultural state." Trudeau believed that the first choice was, and is, that of the separatists or advocates of independence (in his view an emotional and prejudiced choice). Addressing French-Canadians, he has asked, "Why are we so afraid to face these Anglo-Canadians in the bosom of a pluralistic state and why are we prepared to renounce our right to consider Canada our home 'a mari usque ad mare' ?" Trudeau has encouraged Quebecois to abandon "the bellicose and self-destructive idea of nation-state in favor of the more civilized goal of poly-ethnic pluralism."

But if Trudeau, who not so incidentally has gained most of his Liberal seats in Quebec in federal elections, was so vehemently opposed to separatism, he was by no means opposed to French-Canadian nationalism. Two decades ago (1962), he wrote that "Anglo-Canadians have been strong only by virtue of our own (French-Canadian) weakness." Moreover, he stated that Anglo-Canadians will have to retire to their proper place, instead of interpreting Canadian identity in their own British terms for all Canadians.

The great question is whether Canadians will heed such suggestions. Will they in fact be able to emphasize their common Canadian identity rather than their identity as British-Canadians, French-Canadians, etc.? Can Canadians of British origin show a genuine interest in, or at least tolerate, French Canada? How long will French and New Canadians be obliged to accept British traditions as national symbols in a country which has supposedly been sovereign for a century and whose people are predominantly not of British origin? The British and French factors in Canadian society will not soon (if ever) become closely united in terms of assimilation, but this does not mean that British and French-Canadians cannot tolerate and understand each other. Canada may never possess a strong nationalism directed towards a single Canadian nation-state, strictly speaking, but this does not mean that there cannot be a Canadian pride in a poly-ethnic state incorporating an autonomous Quebec. Yet this problem of Canadian unity is actually only one case of what is really a global challenge, namely, how the peoples of the world can learn to coexist despite their differences, to be equal, in other words, without being identical.

Of course, this still leaves unresolved the question of Quebec. The federalists, notably Trudeau and Ryan, would have us believe that the only courageous course for Quebec is to stay within confederation. But these two principal proponents admittedly differ on the question of just how much constitutional reform might be necessary for Quebec to gain some appropriate measure of autonomy. Whereas the separatists would have us believe that the only truly humanitarian course for Quebec is the realization of the basic human right of national self-determination. But separatists clearly differ on the question of what the goal of this self-determination will be—sovereignty-association or complete independence—not to mention the question of how socialist the new government should be.

REFERENCES

Akzin, B. State and Nation. Garden City, New York: Anchor/Doubleday, 1964.

Anderson, A. B. "Ethnic Identity Retention in French-Canadian Communities in Saskatchewan," paper presented at the annual meeting of the Canadian Sociology and Anthropology Association, University of Toronto, 1974.

Anderson, A. B. "French Settlements in Saskatchewan: Historical and Sociological Perspectives," paper presented at the Tenth Annual Meeting of the Saskatchewan Genealogical Society, Saskatoon, October 20-21, 1978.

Chapin, M. Contemporary Canada. New York: Oxford University Press, 1959.

Chaput, M. Why I am a Separatist. Toronto: Ryerson Press, 1961.

Dion, L. "Varieties of Nationalism: Trends in Quebec," in C. F. Macrae (ed.) French Canada Today: Report of the Mount Allison Summer Institute, 1961.

Lesage, J. Speech at Charlottetown, Feb. 2, 1963, in F. Scott and M. Oliver (eds.) Quebec States Her Case. Toronto: Macmillan, 1964.

Levesque, R. From le Devoir, July 5, 1963 (in Scott and Oliver).

Lower, A. R. M. Canada: Nation and Neighbour. Toronto: Ryerson Press, 1952.

Lower, A. R. M. Canadians in the Making. Toronto: Macmillan, 1958.

Maclean's magazine. Special issues: "Separatism" (Nov. 2, 1963) and "Portrait of a Nation at the Bargaining Table" (Feb. 8, 1964).

Pelletier, X. G. From la Presse, August 1, 1963 (Scott and Oliver).

Sanouillet, M. Le Séparatisme Québécois et Nous. Toronto: Editions Nouvelles Francaises, 1962.

Saunders, R. M. "The French Canadian Outlook". Canadian Modern Language Review, 1946.

Savoie, C. "La Véritable Histoire du F.L.Q." in Scott and Oliver, Quebec States Her Case. Toronto: Macmillan, 1964.

Savoie, M. A. "Varieties of Nationalism: The Acadians, a Dynamic Minority" (in C. F. Macrae, (ed.) French Canada Today: Report of the Mount Allison Summer Institute, 1961.

Scott, F. R. Canada Today. Toronto: Oxford University Press, 1939.

Scott, F. R. and M. Oliver, (eds.) Quebec States Her Case. Toronto: Macmillan, 1964.

Trudeau, P. E. "The Conflict of Nationalisms in Canada," in Cité Libre, April, 1962 (in Scott and Oliver).

Wade, M. (ed.) La Dualite Canadienne (Canadian Dualism) Toronto: University of Toronto Press, and Quebec: Les Presses se l'Université Laval, 1960.

Wade, M. The French Canadian Outlook. Toronto: McClelland and Stewart, 1964.

Chapter 6

Multiculturalism*

Multiculturalism: A Novel Concept

The term *multiculturalism* is relatively novel in social science literature, perhaps even more recent an invention than the term *ethnicity* (Burnet 1975: 1). In fact, *multiculturalism* has not been declared an official federal policy in Canada until the present decade, when it took precedence over the longstanding Canadian emphasis on *biculturalism* (a term presumably first used in the 1920s). Yet this is not to suggest, of course, that multiculturalism as a sociological phenomenon or even as a policy is new to the Canadian scene.

Multiculturalism is a rather awkward term in a number of respects (Burnet 1975: 13-16). In view of the actual situation of Canadian ethnic minorities (nationally *every* ethnic group in Canada is a minority), and considering the intended government policies affecting ethnic minorities, a different term might have seemed more appropriate to use, such as ethnic diversity, ethnic pluralism, multi-ethnic, poly-ethnic, or some such term as used in other ethnically complex societies. However, the term ethnic, alone or accompanied by its prefixes and suffixes, may have implied a somewhat derogatory status, at least in the minds of some Canadians during the sixties. Members of the two Canadian charter groups (as they were fond of calling themselves), the Anglos and the French, did not appreciate being equated with the ethnics, who included recent immigrants, the so-called New Canadians, DPs and the like. Moreover, these charter Canadians and other Canadians were becoming loath to proclaim their ethnic identity; ethnicity was for new arrivals who were not yet fully integrated into Canadian society, i.e., who were not true Canadians. However, frequent use of the term ethnic, and perhaps increasing disapproval of the term culture, in the most recent social science literature would seem to add to recognition of multiculturalism as an awkward or misleading term. After all, are we actually referring to the variety of *cultures* in Canadian society (difficult to define) or to the heterogeneity of the Canadian population?

Isajiw (1975: 1) has appropriately suggested that "one has to distinguish between multiculturalism as an ideology, a social policy, and as a feature of the structure of our society. The three meanings are, of course, interdependent. An analysis of the structure of society may indicate a certain ideology as the most appropriate one to follow. On the other hand, an ideology applied into policy systematically pursued over a longer period of time may contribute to the development of one or another feature of the social structure."

---

* Portions of this chapter constitute excerpts from A. B. Anderson & D. K. Stasiulis (1980)

The Question of a Cultural Mosaic

In attempting to assess the extent to which Canadian multiculturalism is fact (sociological reality), fancy (ideology), or policy, first one should question whether multiculturalism in Canada is in fact empirically observable. Is Canadian society really a cultural mosaic compared to an American melting pot? Does recent sociological research and research in other disciplines support this notion? To what extent, and how rapidly, are Canadian ethnic minorities losing their traditional cultures, languages, and religious identifications? Is intermarriage increasingly undermining a cohesive sense of ethnicity? Secondly, should multiculturalism (a novel term in social science literature) be viewed as a fanciful retreat or preoccupation of selected (not all) ethnic group members? We have already raised the question (in Chapters 3 and 4) of how ethnicity is perceived by ethnic group members (and for that matter, who exactly is a member?). Do "professional" ethnic group members (with vested interests in maintaining ethnic group solidarity) tend to romanticize their ethnic history, and to perpetuate certain myths of multiculturalism (loosely defined)?

Our initial question must be whether multiculturalism in Canada is in fact empirically observable; whether recent research in sociology and related disciplines supports the notion of Canadian society as a cultural mosaic. One doesn't have to look very far to find ample evidence of multiculturalism in Canada. Each year hundreds of thousands of Canadians attend ethnic gatherings across Canada, including Scottish Highland Games in most provinces, Caribana and Caravan in Toronto, Mosaic in Regina, Folklorama in Winnipeg, "Our Heritage"—a multicultural festival in Saskatoon, a Greek street festival in Vancouver, an annual Icelandic celebration in Manitoba—not to forget the "Frog Follies" in a French community in Manitoba, to mention but a few.

Indeed, the notion of a Canadian mosaic is hardly new. As Burnet (1979) has written,

> It is true that from the 1920s on . . . there was much talk of the Canadian mosaic. Speakers and writers indefatigably praised the situation in which ethnic groups could retain their distinctiveness and yet be Canadian, in contrast to the American melting pot as they conceived it. They vied with each other in proposing visual and gustatory metaphors, such as flower garden, salad and stew, for the Canadian situation. In 1965 John Porter could say that the mosaic was the country's most cherished value. (2-3)

During the seventies there remained many prominent advocates of a mosaic supported by federal policy. At the first Canadian Conference on Multiculturalism, held in Ottawa in October, 1973, Stanley Haidasz, the first and only (short-lived) Canadian minister of state for multiculturalism, commented (*Toronto Star*, October 20, 1973) that "multiculturalism is here to stay . . . because it is an essential element in the government determination to promote unity and protect national identity"; while George Ignatieff repeated the often heard warning that Canadians will lose their identity to Americanization unless ethnic groups preserve their cultural heritage. (There is relatively little evidence, incidentally, to support the notion that the United States is a melting pot while Canada is a mosaic.) Haidasz was not concerned about the perils of creating or maintaining a hyphenated Canadianism, commenting that "we are first and foremost Canadians and multiculturalism is really a policy for all Canadians." He asserted that a flexible universal multicultural policy can serve to break down prejudices that Canadians might have toward ethnic minorities, thus Canada will become more, not less, unified. Senator Paul Yuzyk (1975) has waxed even more eloquently on the subject:

> Present-day Canada is a pluralistic society, a country of numerous minorities with two dominant cultures. During the past one hundred years she has been gradually evolving into a multicultural nation. The concept of a "bilingual, multicultural Canadian nation" is realistic and the very essence of a dynamic Canadianism. It is fortunate that Canadian governments have rejected the "melting pot" theory with its colorless uniformity and have promoted a "mosaic-type" of Canadian culture based on the voluntary integration of the best elements of the cultures of the component ethnic groups. The development of a composite Canadian culture, rich in variety, beauty and harmony, reflects the principle of "unity in continuing diversity" and the democratic spirit of compromise inherent in the Canadian Confederation. (5)

At a recent Ukrainian fund-raising dinner in Saskatoon one speaker told the audience that:

> "Canada's unique characteristic and strength is multiculturalism," but that "a government cannot create a multicultural society by legislation. Only the people can do it." He said that "Canadians have abandoned the futile evangelism of patriotic nationalism. Instead, every Canadian can enjoy the joy and pride of his cultural roots, recognized, respected and accepted as a worthwhile contribution to Canadian society." (*Saskatoon Star Phoenix*, October 23, 1978)

If there are strong advocates of multiculturalism, there are also more cautious spokesmen for ethnic associations. For example, at the 1973 Ottawa Conference, Robert Kadoguchi, then executive-director of the Japanese-Canadian Cultural Centre in Toronto, cautioned that there is a danger in stressing ethnicity too much, lest ethnic group members neglect to regard themselves as Canadians first. At the very least, opinion varies, even among ethnic minority spokesmen, as to how much ethnicity should be stressed.

Moreover, an elementary consideration, too often overlooked in generalizations about Canada as a whole, is that the extent of ethnic diversity varies greatly from region to region. Given the proportions which people of British, French, native, or other origins form of the regional population, it seems likely that Anglo-conformity will prevail in the Atlantic provinces (with the possible exception of New Brunswick, which still has a British-origin majority but a large and increasing French minority); biculturalism tends to gain most support from French minorities *outside* Quebec or British *within* Quebec; francization has increasingly become the policy of Quebec, supported by a substantial French majority; leaving multiculturalism largely restricted to the ethnically diverse western provinces and larger cities.

The Romanticization of Ethnic Identity and Ethnic History

We have suggested that multiculturalism may be more of a new concept than a time-honored institution. Nonetheless, Canadian writers and speech-makers have been fond of telling us that immigrants have brought with them to Canada a rich variety of world cultures. Indeed they have. But there can be little doubt that ethnicity—and for that matter, multiculturalism—is often romanticized. Pertinent questions might be:

First, which aspects and how much of ethnic cultures were actually invented in the New World rather than the Old World? For example, such Chinese dishes as chow-mein and chop-suey were reportedly developed on the North American West Coast in Chinese restaurants serving non-Chinese clientele. Some letters in the Ukrainian alphabet, as well as certain Ukrainian words, were first used by Ukrainian immigrants in Canada.

Do immigrants necessarily see themselves as contributors to a Canadian cultural mosaic, or do some—perhaps political refugees or political return migrants—view their stay in Canada as only temporary? For example, activist Chilean refugees may be less interested in integrating into Canadian society than in returning to a liberated Chile. A considerable proportion (averaging approximately one-third) of immigrants into Canada may leave the country, usually to return home. One recent survey conducted among West Indians in a Toronto neighborhood revealed that almost half of the respondents intended to return to the Carribean sooner or later (Anderson, 1975).

Have historians tended to romanticize or distort the Old World background of Canadian ethnic groups? For example, Anderson (1973) has described the romantic tradition among Scottish-Canadians:

> When the Scots came to Canada they brought with them a rather romanticized view of their history and identity. For the Scot has always been something of a romantic, quite in spite of some rather obvious inconsistencies in Scottish traditionalism. He would readily refer to the "glorious" clans of the Highlands, when in fact clanship was at best an anachronistic feudal system which forced clansmen, too often destitute and undernourished, to fight in bloody battles verging on genocide. Clans, tartans, pipe bands, the Black Watch were all an important part of Highland if not Scottish tradition. Here we again encounter some degree of romanticization, though, for these most Scottish of traditions all seem to be rather recent innovations in the context of the great length of Scottish history.
>
> Yet Scottish romanticism has continued, if not increased, among the descendants of Scottish immigrants to Canada. Clan rivalries were keenly pursued in Canada, and in general Scottish-Canadians revealed a great interest in genealogy (some clan histories have been written in Canada rather than Scotland). Without doubt an interest in clans was stimulated in Canada by the fact that several clans emigrated "en masse" to Canada.
>
> Indeed, had not so many Scottish emigrants been forced to leave Scotland, perhaps it would be safe to assume that they would not have been so nostalgic; they came to Canada sadly as exiles. Those who came during the colonial period had been faced with disastrous defeat at Culloden Moor in 1746; the destruction of the hereditary power of the clan chiefs; the replacement of clanship as the traditional social organization in the Highlands; the emigration of entire clans with their chiefs; the

replacement of clan chiefs with non-Highland lairds who charged exorbitant rents and plundered private property; the eradication of semi-nomadic bands of fighting clansmen; the construction of military roads (leading to government centralization and control by Lowlanders and the English); extreme destitution, malnutrition, and the general inadequacy of limited agricultural resources; overpopulation due to a decreasing death rate (with the introduction of inoculations); the Highland Clearances and rising prices in the wool market; the collapse of the kelp industry (providing alkali) in the Western Isles with the introduction of barilla from abroad; the persecution of Catholics (many Highlanders were still Catholics, unaffected by the Reformation). And those Scots who emigrated more recently have been faced with living conditions and wages generally far below Canadian standards. If a certain degree of nostalgia is explicable, nonetheless one can only wonder if some of the romanticism of the Scottish-Canadian (towards things Scottish) is not itself an exaggerated tradition, given the circumstances back "home" in Scotland. (38-39)

In recent years a number of sociologists (e.g., Clark, 1976; Burnet, 1979) have commented on some of the myths of multiculturalism. We have already dismissed the myth that Canadian society is a cultural mosaic while American society is a melting pot. We are tempted to note in passing that Anglo-conformity is not restricted to the Canadian dominant society; it has been mentioned by many American sociologists as well; and at any rate it may well be outdated, historically anachronistic, and sociologically insignificant today in either country. We have also stressed that to call Canada bilingual and bicultural can be rather misleading. But to mention a few more myths:

—North America was not discovered by the English, nor Spanish, French, Vikings, Basques or any other Europeans (as historians would still have us believe). It was first settled, and therefore presumably discovered, by Native people (this should hardly come as a great revelation).

—Several Canadian ethnic groups—not only obvious ones, like the English and French, but also Scandinavians, Portuguese, Celtic Irish, and Highland Scots—are fond of claiming a long history of settlement in Canada. These claims too often border on mythology; at best they are exaggerations.

—Some ethnic groups have also revealed a propensity to exaggerate the proportion they form out of the total Canadian population. Coupled with this tendency is the not infrequent statement that the *third force* (non-British, non-French) has grown to be about a third of the Canadian population. But if French-Canadians also form a third, as is often claimed, then Canadians of British origin make up the remaining third. Not so—in point of fact "British" Canadians make up about 45% of the population and have even increased their proportion slightly between the 1961 and 1971 censuses. The "others" make up about a quarter, the French a little more, but neither a third.

—French-Canadians do not "breed like rabbits"; they are not largely a priest-ridden peasantry. In fact Quebec has had, for the past decade, the lowest birth rate for any province in the country. A high proportion of Quebecois are urban residents; a low proportion attend church regularly; and the leadership of at least four major labor unions is avowedly Marxist.

Table 1

CHANGING PROPORTION WHICH CANADIANS OF BRITISH, FRENCH, NATIVE, AND OTHER ORIGINS FORMED OUT OF TOTAL CANADIAN POPULATION 1921-1971*

	1920	1931	1941	1951	1961	1971
British	55.4	51.9	49.7	47.9	43.8	44.6
French	27.9	28.2	30.3	30.8	30.4	28.7
Native*	1.3	1.2	1.1	1.2	1.2	1.4
Other	15.4	18.7	18.9	20.1	24.6	25.3

*probably excluding large numbers of Metis, especially in 1941.
Source: Calculated from Statistics Canada, Census of Canada, 1921, 1931, 1941, 1951, 1961, 1971.

—There is also what Burnet (1979) has called the myth of common bonds among the members of the "other" ethnic groups, or sometimes common bonds among all the minorities. She has lucidly questioned:

> whether common bonds exist. The other ethnic groups vary in many respects, among them numbers; region of concentration; time of arrival; occupational, income and educational distribution; physical characteristics; relations with their homeland; degree of ethnic awareness, and capacity for collective action. Moreover, there are among them memories of old wars and antagonisms. Indeed, even the members of a single ethnic group are usually highly differentiated, especially if some of them have lived in Canada for a long time. As for the French-Canadians, they seem unaware of many of the ethnic distinctions that exist among those that they lump together as English-Canadians, and of any comparison between their claims and those of other ethnic groups. Likewise, the native peoples are convinced of the uniqueness of their situation and their rights. Hence, while temporary coalitions of ethnic groups concerning specific issues, such as immigration policy, may occur, no Third Force is likely to emerge. (14)

—Burnet (1979: 15-22) has also pointed out that a current vogue is the replacement of the myth of British benevolence with yet another myth, that of British villainy, the unremitting oppression of other ethnic groups by those of British origin; this latter myth holds that racial and ethnic prejudice and discrimination are peculiarly Anglo-Saxon or Anglo-Celtic, in short, WASP-ish (never mind the formality that approximately half of the British-origin population of Canada are of Scottish, Irish, and Welsh origin, hence hardly Anglo-Saxon, or that a significant proportion of these British-origin Canadians are Catholics rather than Protestants). Burnet has argued that "it is important to question the myth of oppression by those of British origin because denigration of Canadians of British origin is no firmer basis for multiculturalism than denigration of other Canadians. If we are to understand one another, we must forego the pleasure of regarding some ethnic groups as more virtuous than others. . . . " However, the present authors would not agree that Anglo-Canadian oppression of ethnic minorities has been *entirely* mythical; unfortunately there has been far too much evidence to the contrary.

Ethnic Persistence Versus Change: The Argument for Persistence

W. W. Isajiw (1975), a sociologist at the University of Toronto, has developed a carefully qualified theory of ethnic persistence:

> The phenomenon of what has been called "new ethnicity" is widespread enough both in Canada and in the United States to warrant the conclusion that there must be some factors within the present state of the structure of our society as a whole which contribute to the retention or "rediscovery" of ethnic identity among the established ethnic groups. . . . The dynamics of ethnic pluralism as a current social phenomenon involving the established ethnic groups, regardless of ethnic economic differentiation, have to be sought in the structure and processes in our society as a whole, rather than simply in the structures of the ethnic enclaves themselves. . . . To understand the process of ethnic persistence from one generation to another, one should focus on the question of retention of ethnic identity, rather than simply on retention or perpetuation of ethnic culture or ethnic institutions. . . . Intellectually the most fruitful way—if not the only way—to assess continuity between ethnic generations is in terms of the social psychological concept of ethnic identity; purely sociological concepts are not enough. . . . But this is not to say that cultural patterns are not involved in the persistence of ethnicity across generations. Retention of any identity always requires some symbolic expression. Yet it would be unrealistic and contrary to the available data to assume that what ethnically conscious members of the third generation are trying to do is to simply contain and retain all ossified traditions of their ancestors. The contrary appears to be true, if they want to retain any traditions, they are those which are most meaningful to their own life in society as a whole. The consecutive generations are to a high degree culturally assimilated into the total society. They, nevertheless, have the ability to turn to their ancestral past and pick from it those cultural patterns in which they may find meaning. But the meaning which they do find in them is different from that which these patterns had had for their ancestors. Hence the continuity between generations is provided not by the patterns themselves, but by the feeling of identity with the people who have also attached meanings to the patterns, even if the meanings themselves are different or contradictory. (9-11)

Thus, Isajiw has pointed out that ethnic identity of the third generation should not be assumed to be the same phenomenon as that of the first generation. Some forms of ethnic identity may disappear with one generation, while others may emerge and be perpetuated with consecutive generations.

In a later paper with an imaginative title, "Olga in Wonderland: Ethnicity in a Technological Society," Isajiw (1978: 29-30) further explains that his basic concern is "not the introduction of technology into traditional ethnic societies, but the reverse, that is, the process by which ethnic groups are introduced into, and remain part of, technological societies." He contends "that on the one hand technology and the technological culture bring ethnic groups together, yet on the other hand, and in an indirect way, they contribute to the persistence and perpetuation of ethnicity in North American societies."

The first point that Isajiw makes is a good one. Namely, that the persistence of ethnicity should be sought in the larger structures and processes of the society as a whole. However, his extrapolation from this premise is not a necessary nor, we feel, a fruitful one in understanding the persistence of ethnicity (i.e., his view that one should focus on the question of retention of ethnic *identity*). The more logical extension of his argument would be that one should focus on the objective structural factors which bring into being ethnic-based phenomena such as ethnic *institutions* and then trace the process whereby these structural factors make salient ethnic identity and the impetus to organize along ethnic lines, etc. Focusing on the study of ethnic identity *per se* could limit one's understanding to the manifestations of certain subjective states among ethnic members. What one would like to understand are the reasons for, and the nature of, the process of *generation* of these subjective states.

At least five basic considerations may be related to the argument for the persistence of ethnic heterogeneity in Canadian society and for the longevity of multiculturalism:

First, some ethnic minorities in Canada are *visible*, that is to say, racially distinct from the bulk of the population. As the vast majority of Canadians are White, in the Canadian case the visible ethnic minorities are non-White groups, such as South Asians, West Indians and Blacks, Chinese and Japanese, Native peoples, etc. To a considerable extent ethnic identity has been, and may continue to be, imposed on these racial minorities (directly or indirectly) because they are easily identifiable through visibility. Ethnic consciousness is perhaps more likely to arise as visible minority members group together in defensive solidarity, in defensive reaction to perceived or actual discrimination and exploitation. Moreover, racial amalgamation tends to proceed more slowly than cultural exchange or assimilation, at least in North America. Non-White Canadians have been subjected to deportation, segregation, economic exclusion, harassment and discriminatory immigration practices, although a larger proportion of recent immigrants into Canada have been non-White. Therefore, it seems that generalizations about assimilation, integration and the like which may be applied to Canadian ethnic minorities distinguished by their different cultures more than by physical appearance, do not necessarily hold for visible minorities.

Second, even for White ethnic minorities, ethnic identity is likely to persist where certain basic criteria for ethnic identification tend to be stressed by many or most members of an ethnic collectivity. These members may exhibit a capacity to clearly define their group, if they are aware of their collective uniqueness as a category. They may reveal a strong sense of survival for their unique culture and place strong emphasis on ethnic identity to the extent that they regard it as immoral not to stress ethnic traditions, as in the case of refugees. Many Canadian activist ethnic or ethno-religious minorities already have a longstanding tradition as a minority, and a long history of survival (possibly a long history of being persecuted). Moreover, ethnic consciousness may be supported by an ability to speak and probably be literate in a traditional language (usually unique to a particular ethnic group); and this language may be stressed as key to group survival. And religion often plays a significant role in defining the group; affiliation to a particular religious denomination can supplement an emphasis on ethnicity *per se* (many Canadian ethnic groups are in fact ethno-religious groups). Finally, a wide range of folkways could add to an awareness of group identity or culture.

Third, ethnic relations may have a lot to do with ethnic persistence. For example, if an ethnic or ethno-religious minority withdraws (or is obliged to withdraw) to the extent that it avoids many or most forms of contact with the general society ethnic persistence is likely. This behavior is, however, atypical for most Canadian ethnic minorities and is restricted to such subgroups as Hassidic Jews, Hutterites, Old Order/Old Colony Mennonites/Amish, and the Sons of Freedom/Zealots sect of Doukhobors. What is quite common is minority avoidance of ethnic marital assimilation, if group norms expect ethnic (and possibly religious) endogamy. Or the members of an ethnic minority may have a strong sense of cultural superiority with relation to other ethnic minorities or the majority, or vice versa. More specifically, the members of an ethnic minority may tend to be xenophobic in their reaction to other ethnic minorities or the majority; conversely the minority's chance for survival may be limited if the majority tends towards xenophobia, as the latter may result in forced assimilation. Finally, it is important to recognize that ethnic persistence may be enhanced if the members of one ethnic group are in latent or overt conflict with other ethnic groups. Thus conflict in a local community shared by two well-defined ethnic groups may enhance a sense of survival.

Fourth, ethnic identity is likely to persist if conceptualization of *national* identity (i.e., Canadian identity) is relatively weak or confusing compared to subnational (regional and ethnic) identities. As Gordon has suggested, the members of an ethnic minority may resist identificational assimilation (loss of traditional ethnic identity through the development of a sense of identity/peoplehood based exclusively on the host society) and acculturation (exchanging most or virtually all of their own cultural patterns for those of the host society, i.e., the process of Canadianization). Ethnic persistence has doubtless been encouraged in Canada by a general (if new) emphasis or toleration of multiculturalism as an ideology or goal. In other words, in a majority-minority situation, ethnic persistence will be enhanced if the majority does in fact accept the minority's right to distinctiveness.

Fifth, numerous historians, sociologists and other commentators writing about the Canadian ethnic mosaic have suggested that the durability of ethnic diversity in this country owes much to the Anglo-French bilingual-bicultural framework. After all, so this argument goes, bilingualism and biculturalism have served as an important bulwark against Americanization, and have contributed to an emphasis on ethnicity within Canadian society, contrasting to an American emphasis on the melting pot. However, this line of thinking is rather simplistic. The United States is in point of fact not a melting pot; not only does that country include large concentrations of Blacks and Spanish-speaking populations (in some respects comparable to the concentration of French population within Canada), but also innumerable examples of urban ethnic neighbourhoods and rural ethnic settlements (comparable to the Canadian ethnic mosaic). Moreover, Canadian society is not uniformly multicultural, nor bicultural; as we have noted above, *multi*culturalism, *bi*culturalism, or *uni*culturalism (represented in Anglo-conformity or francization) may prevail in one province, region or area.

Sixth, the ability of an ethnic minority in Canada to maintain its separate identity may be highly dependent upon replenishment through continued immigration. As Richmond has commented (*Toronto Star,* January 19, 1974), "the reason we have such ethnic awareness today is because we still have a stream of immigration. The future situation will depend on how big the immigration flow is and how much money is allocated to multiculturalism programmes." The recency of immigration accounts for much of the multicultural character of the larger cities. Ethnic identity change is more in evidence, we would contend, outside these cities (with the obvious exception of French in Quebec, virtually a state within a state, and of conservative ethno-religious groups, such as the Hutterites, and of the Native peoples segregated on reserves). The vast majority of the most recent immigrants, a large proportion of them non-White, have concentrated in the larger cities, particularly Toronto, although the federal government's latest immigration policy may induce prospective immigrants to disperse (this point will be pursued further in the next chapter).

A distinction should be drawn, then, between ethnic minorities consisting primarily of relatively recent (first-generation) immigrants (e.g., Greeks, Portuguese, Chileans and Spanish-speakers, Vietnamese, West Indians, East Indians), on the one hand, and ethnic minorities longer settled in Canada (e.g., including not only the so-called charter groups—British and French—who may be conceived as less concerned with the persistence of their ethnicity than with the aggrandizement of their collective economic and political power, but also including such Euro-Canadian groups as Ukrainians, Germans, Scandinavians). These two basic types, immigrant/concentrated and established/dispersed, are of course interrelated, but the primarily immigrant minorities are more concerned with problems of *adjustment*, whereas the primarily established minorities tend to be concerned with *persistence* (Isajiw, 1975: 2), implying, in turn, two basic types of multicultural policies aimed at these differing concerns.

Seventh, the persistence of ethnicity may relate closely to demographic/ecological conditions. For example, ethnic identity is likely to persist if an ethnic minority has geographical proximity to a national centre of that group, or maintains close connections (e.g., exchanges) with the mother country. Or if the ethnic minority is sufficiently numerous, politically significant, and relatively concentrated (a) within Canada as a whole, (b) within a particular province, or (c) within an intra-provincial region. An ethnic minority may have established rural settlements or become concentrated in urban neighbourhoods of considerable size and extent. In fact, a larger proportion of ethnic group members may reside within a local area in which they predominate than those residing in ethnically heterogeneous areas. Moreover, the persistence of ethnicity may be enhanced if (a) the local community in which ethnic group members reside is large and institutionally diversified; (b) if ethnic group members constitute a high proportion of the total population of the local community in which they reside; (c) if the local community in which ethnic group members reside is relatively isolated from contact with people of other ethnic origins; (d) if the local community is relatively stable, i.e., not undergoing fairly rapid demographic changes (e.g., rural depopulation) which might have a negative effect on ethnic identity preservation; and finally (e) if the local ethnic community has revealed considerable durability over a period of time (e.g., the shifting location of ethnic quarters in Canadian cities; a most interesting example of this process is the relocation of Chinatown in Toronto).

Eighth, several other demographic factors in the form of population characteristics could serve as intervening variables pertaining to an analysis of ethnic persistence. These factors might include age, generation, sex, occupation, class, education, mobility, etc. One might hypothesize, for example:

(a) That older ethnic group members will be more likely than younger members to emphasize ethnicity.

(b) That the longer the period of residence in Canada since immigration, the less will be the emphasis placed on ethnicity.

(c) That female ethnic group members will emphasize their ethnic identity more than males because they do not participate in the workforce to the extent that males do, or have as many contacts with the outside world (they tend to stay at home).

(d) That ethnic group members in certain occupations (where a vested interest in the preservation of ethnic identity is expected, or where contacts with people of the same ethnic background are promoted) are likely to emphasize their ethnicity.

(e) That ethnic group members not divided from each other by class distinctions will stress ethnic group identity.

(f) That ethnic group members with a higher (or conversely with a limited?) education may reveal the most interest in their ethnicity.

(g) That a low degree of upward social mobility could enhance ethnic consciousness.

It is, of course, important to understand that these are not conclusions we are drawing but only working hypotheses remaining to be tested in specific surveys.

Ninth, the degree of institutional completeness and enclosure of ethnic minorities may bear on ethnic persistence. According to the concept of institutional completeness, first applied by Breton (1964) to immigrant communities in Montreal, "some of the most critical factors bearing on the absorption of immigrants would be found in the social organization of the communities which the immigrant contacts in the receiving country. . . . the community of his ethnicity, the native (receiving) community, and the other ethnic communities." Breton felt that the integration of the immigrant should not be seen from a purely assimilationist point of view in which integration is said to have taken place when the immigrant is absorbed in the receiving society. Integration was rather conceived of as taking place in any one of the communities mentioned above or in two or three directions at the same time. That is, an immigrant can establish a network of social affiliations extending beyond the boundaries of any one community. Finally, it is also possible for the immigrant to be unintegrated. Breton argued that "the direction of the immigrant's integration will to a large extent result from the forces of attraction (positive or negative) stemming from the various communities." He examined "the extent to which institutional completeness of the ethnic community is related to its capacity to attract the immigrant within its social boundaries." Breton pointed out that "ethnic communities can vary enormously in their social organization. . . . Institutional completeness would be at its extreme whenever the ethnic community could perform all the services required by its members." But Breton has admitted that "of course, in contemporary North American cities very few, if any, ethnic communities showing full institutional completeness can be found." In other words, according to the concept of institutional completeness, ethnic identity is likely to persist if the members of an ethnic minority successfully resist structural assimilation (large-scale entrance into the institutions of the host society); if there is a high degree of organizational/institutional interdependence within the institutional framework of an ethnic community; and if certain institutional foci within an ethnic community tend to be multi-functional (e.g., an ethnic-oriented parish involved in ethnic-oriented voluntary associations, schools, etc.). The local ethnic community may have a church (or equivalent religious establishment) specifically oriented toward the maintenance of ethnic consciousness. The ethnic group may control the education (at as many levels as possible) of its members, and more generally control the institutions responsible for the socialization of group members into an awareness of group identity. Ethnic identification may be reinforced if a wide variety of ethno-oriented voluntary associations are available to the members of an ethnic group, and if the members participate as regularly as possible in these associations; also if these voluntary associations can satisfactorily adjust to changing conditions (e.g., changing interpretations of ethnic identity; a shift from an emphasis on the mother country to an emphasis on Canadian integration; de-politicization, etc.) through alteration of the original functions and purposes of the associations.

Another important point is whether the ethnic group has access to mass media (television and radio stations or programmes, newspapers, etc.) in the traditional language of the group, or at least catering to the group's interests. In fact, many sociologists have emphasized that a significant indicator of boundary maintenance is the extent and nature of ethnic involvement in the media. Tables 2 and 3 reveal the number of radio and television stations by language of broadcast. While these data simply report the number of stations, Table 4 reveals the number of newspapers and periodicals published in a language other than French or English. When comparisons are made between the rank order relation of radio broadcast time per week with the number of newspapers and periodicals, we find little correspondence. In other words, those ethnic minorities which use radio broadcast time do not rely heavily on newspapers or periodicals. This suggests that ethnic minorities rely upon techniques that are suited to existing local social and technological conditions. It also suggests that other techniques such as voluntary associations are used to retain the ethnicity of the members. Table 5 provides further data alluding to the issue of news media, language and ethnic retention. It shows the number of community newspapers that are published in one or the other or both official languages.

The model provided by Breton has generated much discussion in Canadian ethnic studies. For example, Vallee (1969: 23-24) essentially supported Breton in reiterating the need for the organization of ethnic group structures and institutions which influence socialization and ethnic community decision-making. The concepts of institutional completeness and residential segregation have been combined by Driedger and Church (1974) in their research on Winnipeg. Similarly, institutional completeness was taken into consideration in a study of ethnic enclosure among West Indian immigrants in a Toronto neighborhood (Anderson 1975). Following Van den Berghe (1965: 78-9), Schermerhorn (1970: 127) had explained: "social or structural pluralism varies from maximal to minimal forms which can be conceptualized as degrees of enclosure with indicators like endogamy, ecological concentration, institutional duplication, associational clustering, rigidity and clarity of group definition, segmentary relations of members with outsiders, etc."

Table 2

TELEVISION STATIONS[1] BY LANGUAGE AND PROVINCE, MARCH 1976

	English	French
Newfoundland	67	3
Prince Edward Island	2	—
Nova Scotia	23	5
New Brunswick	11	7
Quebec[2]	12	79
Ontario	71	16
Manitoba	42	7
Saskatchewan	55	1
Alberta	70	3
British Columbia[3]	233	—
Yukon	10	—
Northwest Territories	24	—
Canada	620	121

[1] Includes originating stations and rebroadcasters.
[2] Excludes one station which is classified as multilingual.
[3] Since the survey was taken a French station has begun operating in British Columbia.
Source: *Perspective Canada II*, Statistics Canada, Printing and Publishing, Supply and Services, Ottawa, 1977, p. 275.

Table 3

RADIO STATIONS[1] BY LANGUAGE AND PROVINCE, MARCH 1976

	English	French	Other[2]
Newfoundland	48	3	1
Prince Edward Island	5	—	—
Nova Scotia	35	13	—
New Brunswick	24	10	—
Quebec	35	130	1
Ontario	171	34	4
Manitoba	36	6	3
Saskatchewan	26	4	1
Alberta	57	3	—
British Columbia	174	4	1
Yukon	15	—	—
Northwest Territories	20	—	10
Canada	646	207	21

[1] Includes AM and FM originating stations and rebroadcasters.
[2] Includes languages other than English and French.
Source: *Perspective Canada II*, Statistics Canada, Printing and Publishing, Supply and Services, Ottawa, 1977, p. 276.

Table 4

FOREIGN LANGUAGE MEDIA

	Newspapers and periodicals[1]	Radio broadcast time per week[2]
	number	hours and minutes
Arabic	2	2:27
Armenian	—	1:30
Belgian	—	:55
Bulgarian	—	2:05
Byelorussian	1	—
Chinese	4	9:15
Croatian, Serbian, Slovenian and Yugoslavian	7	23:20
Czech and Slovak	4	1:54
Danish	1	:59
Dutch	7	15:30
Estonian	2	:57
Finnish	2	4:24
German	10	55:31
Greek	6	65:33
Hindi	—	10:22
Hungarian	8	5:38
Icelandic	1	—
Italian	19	156:05
Japanese	2	1:00
Jewish	4	—
Korean	—	:30
Latvian	1	—
Lithuanian	3	2:00
Macedonian	—	4:30
Maltese	—	:30
Norwegian	1	1:30
Pakistani	1	1:35
Polish	4	13:45
Portuguese	6	23:27
Russian	—	5:40
Spanish	3	1:00
Swedish	2	:58
Ukrainian	22	42:52

[1] As at February 1974.
[2] As at August 1972.
Source: *Perspective Canada*, Statistics Canada, Information Canada, Ottawa, 1974, p. 283.

Table 5

COMMUNITY NEWSPAPERS BY LANGUAGE AND PROVINCE

	1971	1972	1973
Newfoundland:			
English	6	8	11
French	—	—	—
Bilingual	—	—	—
Prince Edward Island:			
English	—	2	2
French	—	—	—
Bilingual	—	—	—
Nova Scotia:			
English	31	30	33
French	1	1	1
Bilingual	—	—	—
New Brunswick:			
English	15	14	13
French	1	1	3
Bilingual	2	3	2
Quebec:			
English	21	17	20
French	111	117	99
Bilingual	50	55	55
Ontario:			
English	285	292	299
French	3	2	4
Bilingual	3	1	1
Manitoba:			
English	63	63	61
French	1	1	1
Bilingual	1	1	1
Saskatchewan:			
English	94	97	100
French	2	2	2
Bilingual	4	4	1
Alberta:			
English	103	122	119
French	1	1	1
Bilingual	—	—	—
British Columbia:			
English	101	107	117
French	1	1	1
Bilingual	—	—	—

Source: *Perspective Canada II*, Statistics Canada, Printing and Publishing, Supply and Services, Ottawa, 1977, p. 274.

Interesting as these various Canadian studies may be, in focusing primarily or exclusively on *endogenous* factors, they are restricted, by and large, to a level of analysis which is empirical *rapportage*. They describe situations of ethnic community organization; but do not go very far in taking into consideration the *exogenous* structural context, and therefore contribute relatively little to a comprehensive theory of ethnic persistence or change. Breton has at least moved away from emphasizing institutional completeness *per se* toward emphasizing ethnic collectivities' organizational capacity for collective action (Breton, 1974). Thus, an ethnic community, conceptualized in terms of the organizational aspect of ethnic group behavior rather than in terms of such elements as culture or ethnic identity, may be said to consist of congeries of organizations and associations holding different types and degrees of relations to each other. Empirically, an ethnic community can range from a multidimensional matrix of institutions that interact with each other, covering a wide range of communal concerns, to a large number of autonomous organizations with little interaction among them, serving often duplicative functions. Most recently Breton (1978: 55) has argued that, while there has been ample research on the degree of inequality and the occurrence of conflict among Canadian ethnic collectivities, relatively little has been done toward developing conceptual frameworks for analysing the various types of ethnic collectivities found in Canadian society, or how such variations affect the ways these collectivities relate to each other. Breton has suggested that we know little about the conditions under which people establish relationships and form groups on an ethnic basis, or about variations in institutional arrangements which may or may not emerge to accommodate existing cultural diversity, or about particular forms of institutional accommodations.

Tenth, structural constraints may serve to prolong ethnic diversity. Where do ethnic groups, particularly recent immigrants and non-Whites (increasingly one and the same) fit into the capitalist socio-economic structure? We have already noted above Isajiw's (1975: 9) position that the dynamics of ethnic pluralism have to be sought in the structure and processes of society as a whole, rather than simply the structures of the ethnic enclaves themselves. In other words previous research accounting for variations in the extent and type of organizational activity across communities, ethnic or otherwise, has focused on factors endogenous to the organizations or interorganizational field (e.g., leadership structure, mass-elite relationships, organizational resources, etc.) or to the ethnic community as a whole (e.g., cultural heritage); while exogenous variables (such as the political and economic context in which organizations are located) have heretofore played a peripheral role in most analyses of community activity (Stasiulis 1979: 1). Yet it is precisely these exogenous factors which account for selectivity in immigration policy (Li and Bolaria, 1979), entry into the labor force, distribution of immigrants, etc. Structural analysis is vital to an in-depth understanding not only of ethnic persistence versus change but also multicultural policies.

Specifically, in considering the structural (economic/political) context for ethnic persistence, one might question:

—whether the ethnic minority is exploited (economically or politically) by the majority;

—whether an ethnic minority operates its own economic institutions (stores, co-operatives, etc.) avoiding (at least to some extent) economic integration with the dominant society;

—whether the members of an ethnic minority tend to vote along ethnic lines, i.e., vote for candidates of the relevant ethnic background or who espouse the interests of the group;

—whether the group effectively controls their decision-making processes in the community which could affect their ability to preserve their unique identity;

—whether there is effective leadership of the ethnic minority or ethnic community (from the national to the local level); and whether the ethnic elite values ethnic identity preservation.

Ethnic Persistence Versus Change: The Argument for Change

During the past decade a number of Canadian sociologists (Anderson, 1972, 1977; Driedger, 1975; Isajiw, 1975, 1978) have pointed out that the measure of ethnic identification may vary according to the criteria used to measure it. If considerable attention has been devoted by sociologists to the persistence of ethnicity in Canadian society, perhaps they have devoted even more attention to ethnic identity change. A myriad of recent studies have indicated clearly that ethnic identity—whether revealed in, for example, retention of traditional language, religious affiliation, certain customs or an institutional infrastructure—is steadily changing from generation to generation, particularly among the established, longer-settled Euro-Canadian minorities (this generalization becomes less true, however, for recent immigrants, particularly non-Whites, as noted above). For example, extensive research has been conducted on the rates, causes, and consequences of ethnic identity change by Driedger in Manitoba and Anderson in Saskatchewan. These authors have focused on cross-ethnic research on specific topics, such as institutional completeness (Driedger, 1973 and Church, 1974), cultural identity factors (Driedger, 1975; Anderson, 1977), language trends (Anderson, 1978a) and intermarriage attitudes and trends (Anderson, 1974b); or they have focused on various aspects of identity change in specific ethnic groups such as Mennonites (e.g., numerous publications by Driedger and a joint chapter by both authors, Anderson and Driedger, 1980), French (Driedger, 1976; Anderson, 1974a, 1978b, 1979: Appendix), and Ukrainians (Driedger, 1978, 1979; Anderson, 1979). An earlier, more general theoretical statement on intergenerational changes in ethnic identification was made by Nahirny and Fishman (1965).

To briefly illustrate the probable erosion of ethnicity across Canada, at least among the established Euro-Canadian groups, let us examine census data on two principal cultural criteria in the objective definition of ethnicity: language and religion, excluding subjective considerations for now as well as biophysical criteria, while bearing in mind that census data are neither as accurate nor as informative as more detailed survey data.

Language

While Canada is formally committed to a policy of bilingualism (producing no end to the problems over language use and maintenance), we find the issue made even more complex by virtue of the fact that other languages are still used and in many instances have semi-official recognition. Much of the data on language use and retention emanates from Statistics Canada and is measured in terms of mother tongue. This refers to the question "what language did you first learn and are still able to speak?" The data in Table 6 show the changes in linguistic patterns from 1941 to 1971. We find a steady increase in the amount of English (anglophones) with a concurrent decrease in French (francophones). The "other language" groups also reflect a slight decrease.

Table 6

POPULATION BY MOTHER TONGUE

	1941		1951		1961		1971	
	number	%	number	%	number	%	number	%
English	6,488,190	56	8,280,809	59	10,660,534	58	12,973,810	60
French	3,354,753	29	4,068,850	29	5,123,151	28	5,793,650	27
Other	1,663,712	15	1,659,770	12	2,454,562	14	2,800,850	13
TOTALS	11,506,655	100	14,009,429	100	18,238,247	100	21,568,310	100

Source: *Perspective Canada*, Statistics Canada, Information Canada, Ottawa, 1974, p. 259.

Table 7 shows the actual distribution of languages other than English or French since 1941. Much of the data in Table 7 shows that non-official languages are, on the whole, decreasing. However, small increases are evident for some groups. The most noticeable increases are for the languages of Italian and Portuguese, although smaller increases are evident for Chinese, Indo-Pakistani and Serbo-Croatian. In some cases the increases are due to the fact that greater numbers of immigrants are arriving in Canada and a second generation phase-out has not yet occurred.

The actual distribution of official languages by provinces is presented in Table 8. This table shows changes from 1961 to 1971 for each province as well as illustrating the extent of monolingualism and bilingualism in Canada. While some small changes in language patterns are evident, a consistent pattern seems to emerge. First of all we find an increase in nonofficial languages with a subsequent decrease in the official languages. Secondly, the use of French only has had the greatest decline, although the overall percentage of bilingualism is increasing. However, we know that most of the bilingual population will be French.

Perhaps a clearer picture of language use can be assessed from Table 9. This shows the ability of specific ethnic groups to converse in one or both (or neither) of the official languages. It is clear that Italians and Asians are by far the largest groups or categories unable to speak one of the official languages. Conversely, we find that nearly one-third of the French are able to speak in either of the official languages. The general picture shows that almost all ethnic groups can speak English. Only those groups residing in Quebec are only able to speak in French. This includes both French-Canadians as well as other ethnic groups, e.g., Italians. It is easy for the student to understand Quebec's concern regarding French culture, of which language is an important component. If

Table 7
MOTHER TONGUE OTHER THAN ENGLISH OR FRENCH

Language group	1941	1951	1961	1971
		%		
Arabic	0.5	0.3	0.5	1.0
Chinese	2.0	1.7	2.0	3.4
Czech and Slovak	2.3	2.7	2.1	1.6
Dutch	3.2	5.3	6.9	5.2
Finnish	2.3	1.9	1.8	1.3
German	19.4	19.8	23.0	20.0
Greek	0.5	0.5	1.7	3.7
Indian and Inuit	7.9	8.7	6.8	6.4
Indo-Pakistani	—	0.1	0.2	1.2
Italian	4.8	5.6	13.8	19.2
Japanese	1.4	1.1	0.7	0.6
Magyar (Hungarian)	2.8	2.6	3.5	3.1
Polish	7.7	7.8	6.6	4.8
Portuguese	—	—	0.7	3.1
Russian	3.2	2.4	1.7	1.1
Scandinavian[1]	8.7	6.4	4.4	3.0
Serbo-Croatian	0.9	0.7	1.2	2.7
Ukrainian	18.8	21.2	14.7	11.1
Yiddish	7.8	6.2	3.4	1.8
Other	5.8	5.0	4.3	5.7
TOTAL OF LANGUAGES OTHER THAN ENGLISH OR FRENCH	100.0	100.0	100.0	100.0
Number	1,663,712	1,659,770	2,454,562	2,800,850

[1] Scandinavian includes Norwegian, Swedish, Danish and Icelandic.
Source: *Perspective Canada*, Statistics Canada, Information Canada, 1974, p. 259.

language is an important element of French-Canadian culture and recent immigrants to Quebec are not adopting this language, the import of French becomes less and less. Hence French-Canadian culture will be lost. It makes sense, then, for the Quebec government to force recent immigrants to send their children to French language schools.

Thus far we have presented data with regard to mother tongue. However, we also have data available which specify the extent of linguistic use in the home. Table 10 shows the provincial distributions by languages spoken at home. Again, with the exception of Quebec and New Brunswick, we find Engish the overwhelming language spoken at home. The low rate of English and French spoken in the NWT simply reflects the large proportion of Native people in the area. This also explains, in part, the basis of the conflict between Native and non-Native peoples.

Tables 11 and 12 show the interrelationship between mother tongue and language of the home. They show that only use of English both as a mother

Table 8
POPULATION BY OFFICIAL LANGUAGES

	English Only 1961	English Only 1971	French Only 1961	French Only 1971	Both English and French 1961	Both English and French 1971	Neither English nor French 1961	Neither English nor French 1971
				%				
Newfoundland	98.5	98.0	0.1	0.1	1.2	1.8	0.2	0.1
Prince Edward Island	91.1	91.2	1.2	0.6	7.6	8.2	0.2	—
Nova Scotia	92.9	92.6	0.8	0.5	6.1	6.7	0.2	0.2
New Brunswick	62.0	62.5	8.7	15.9	19.0	21.5	0.2	0.1
Quebec	11.6	10.5	61.9	60.9	25.5	27.6	1.1	1.0
Ontario	89.0	87.3	1.5	1.2	7.9	9.3	1.6	2.2
Manitoba	89.6	89.2	0.9	0.5	7.4	8.2	2.1	2.1
Saskatchewan	93.6	93.6	0.4	0.2	4.5	5.0	1.5	1.2
Alberta	94.1	93.7	0.4	0.2	4.3	5.0	1.2	1.1
British Columbia	95.3	94.1	0.2	0.1	3.5	4.6	1.0	1.2
Yukon	93.5	93.2	0.3	0.1	5.6	6.6	0.6	0.1
Northwest Territories	58.9	73.3	0.5	0.3	7.0	6.1	33.6	20.3
CANADA	67.4	67.1	19.1	18.0	12.2	13.4	1.3	1.5

Source: *Perspective Canada*, Statistics Canada, Information Canada, Ottawa, 1974, p. 225.

tongue and as a language spoken at home has increased. These data suggest that while individuals are able to speak and understand a language other than English, few utilize the language in the home.

According to 1971 census data, most Canadians of German, Jewish, Dutch, Polish, Ukrainian, Russian, Czechoslovakian, Scandinavian, or Japanese origin no longer recognized their group's traditional language as their mother tongue. The majority of people in these groups, as well as those of Finnish, Hungarian, or native origin, did not speak primarily the traditional ethnic language at home.

This, of course, reflects the fact that children are continually exposed to English as the working language. Thus parents must speak English to their children. Concurrently the children are re-educating the parents to speak English. As a result, the children are steadily losing the linguistic abilities of their parents. Nonuse of a mother tongue will result in total loss if left long enough. This argument seems to be substantiated from the data in Table 13. This Table shows that as the age cohort gets older (and in particular in the working age group), among French-Canadians use of English at home increases while French declines.

Anderson's research on language retention in Saskatchewan (1978a) similarly indicates that while a high proportion of respondents (N = 1,000) in rural ethnic settlements could speak a non-English mother tongue, in some groups (German Catholics, Scandinavians) a relatively low proportion actually did use

Table 9

OFFICIAL LANGUAGE OF SPECIFIED ETHNIC GROUPS

	Converse in neither English nor French		Converse in English Only		Converse in French Only		Converse in both English and French		Total
	1961	1971	1961	1971	1961	1971	1961	1971	
					%				
British	0.1	—	95.5	94.1	0.4	0.6	4.0	5.3	100.0
French	0.2	—	8.6	8.2	61.2	60.1	30.1	31.7	100.0
German	1.3	11.2	95.7	94.0	0.5	0.8	2.6	4.0	100.0
Italian	17.4	16.6	65.2	63.3	6.8	6.0	10.6	14.1	100.0
Jewish	1.3	0.9	79.9	74.3	0.5	1.4	18.4	23.4	100.0
Netherlands	1.6	0.7	95.3	94.6	0.2	0.3	2.9	4.4	100.0
Polish	2.5	2.6	91.3	89.6	0.7	0.7	5.5	7.1	100.0
Russian	2.7	3.8	90.3	89.3	0.5	0.6	6.5	6.3	100.0
Scandinavian	0.2	0.2	97.4	96.6	0.3	0.3	2.1	2.9	100.0
Ukrainian	2.5	2.0	94.6	93.6	0.2	0.2	2.6	4.2	100.0
Other European	4.9	9.2	85.4	79.8	2.0	2.2	7.7	8.8	100.0
Asiatic	11.2	12.0	80.9	78.3	1.3	1.6	6.6	8.1	100.0
TOTALS	1.3	1.5	67.4	67.1	19.1	18.0	12.2	13.4	100.0

Source: *Perspective Canada*, Statistics Canada, Information Canada, Ottawa, 1974, p. 228.

Table 10

LANGUAGE MOST OFTEN SPOKEN AT HOME, 1971

	English	French	Other	Total
			%	
CANADA	67.1	25.7	7.2	100.0
Newfoundland	99.1	0.4	0.5	100.0
Prince Edward Island	95.7	3.9	0.4	100.0
Nova Scotia	95.5	3.5	1.0	100.0
New Brunswick	67.9	31.4	0.7	100.0
Quebec	14.7	80.8	4.5	100.0
Ontario	85.1	4.6	10.3	100.0
Manitoba	82.6	4.0	13.4	100.0
Saskatchewan	89.9	1.7	8.4	100.0
Alberta	90.8	1.4	7.8	100.0
British Columbia	92.8	0.5	6.7	100.0
Yukon	95.0	0.7	4.3	100.0
Northwest Territories	58.1	1.7	40.2	100.0

Source: *Perspective Canada*, Statistics Canada, Information Canada, Ottawa 1974, p. 224.

Table 11

MOTHER TONGUE AND LANGUAGE SPOKEN IN THE HOME, 1971

	Mother tongue (1)	Language of the home (2)	Percentage change from (1) to (2)
English	12,973,810	14,446,235	+ 11.3
French	5,793,650	5,546,025	−4.3
German	561,085	213,350	−62.0
Italian	538,360	425,235	−21.0
Ukrainian	309,855	144,760	−53.3
Native Indian	164,525	122,205	−25.7
Netherlands	144,925	36,170	−75.0
Polish	134,780	70,960	−47.4
Greek	104,455	86,830	−16.9
Chinese	94,855	77,890	−17.9
Portuguese	86,925	74,765	−14.0
Magyar (Hungarian)	86,835	50,670	−41.6
Serbo-Croatian	74,190	29,310	−60.5
Yiddish	49,890	26,330	−47.2
Other	41,835	31,900	−23.8
Finnish	36,725	18,280	−50.2
Indo-Pakistani	32,555	23,110	−29.0
Russian	31,745	12,590	−60.3
Arabic	28,550	15,260	−46.5
Czech	27,780	15,090	−45.7
Norwegian	27,405	2,160	−92.1
Danish	27,395	4,690	−82.9
Spanish	23,815	17,710	−25.6
Swedish	21,680	2,210	−89.8
Gaelic	21,200	1,175	−94.5
Slovak	17,370	9,465	−45.5
Japanese	16,890	10,500	−37.8
Inuit	15,295	15,080	−1.4
Lithuanian	14,725	9,985	−32.2
Estonian	14,520	10,110	−30.4
Flemish	14,240	3,190	−77.6
Lettish	14,140	9,250	−34.6
Romanian	11,300	4,455	−60.6
Icelandic	7,860	995	−87.3
Welsh	3,160	370	−88.3
TOTALS	21,568,310	21,568,310	

Source: *Perspective Canada*, Statistics Canada, Information Canada, Ottawa, 1974, p. 260.

Table 12

PROPORTION OF PEOPLE OF SELECTED ETHNIC ORIGINS RECOGNIZING ETHNIC MOTHER TONGUE AND USING IT AS A PRIMARY LANGUAGE AT HOME, 1971

Ethnic Group	Proportion Recognizing Traditional Mother Tongue	Proportion Using It as Primary Language at Home
Jewish	16.6	8.5
Scandinavian	20.0	2.1
Dutch	32.4	7.7
German	35.9	13.9
Russian	37.0	16.0
Polish	38.4	19.9
Japanese	42.3	24.5
Czechoslovakian	48.4	26.0
Ukrainian	48.9	22.8
Hungarian	53.7	30.2
Native Groups	53.9	42.0
Finnish	56.0	28.0
Italian	70.4	57.2
Chinese	76.5	62.4
Greek	78.3	65.6
Portuguese	82.8	72.3

Source: Calculated from Statistics Canada, 1971 Census of Canada, Catalogue 92-736, Vol. 1, Part 4, Bulletin 1.4-8 "Population: Language by Ethnic Groups."

these languages (Tables 14 and 15). A decline in use of the traditional mother tongue from older to younger age cohorts was apparent for all groups surveyed except the Hutterites (Table 16).

Summarizing his findings, Anderson (1978a) has concluded:

A central question must be whether the ability to speak a traditional mother tongue is necessary for the maintenance of ethnic identity. There can be little doubt that the infrastructure of certain ethno-religious collectivities in Saskatchewan stresses the interdependence of ethnicity and language. On the other hand, it was noted that some ethnic groups retain strong advocates of ethnic traditionalism who cannot speak the erstwhile tongue. In fact, by 1971, out of twenty-nine ethnic categories in Saskatchewan in only nine did a majority still speak the traditional mother tongue; there is very little use of the mother tongue at home among the younger generation in almost every group. This clearly means that in the foreseeable future there will be virtually no use—or extremely little use—of a traditional mother tongue for most ethnic groups in Saskatchewan. But does this necessarily also mean that ethnic distinctiveness—and for that matter multiculturalism—will cease to be stressed? At the very least, the criteria for ethnic identity will progressively become reinterpreted. However, the survey data equally clearly suggest that an

Table 13
LANGUAGE RETENTION BY AGE, 1971

Age and mother tongue	Language in Home			
	English	French	Other	Total
		%		
0-4 years:				
English	98.4	0.4	1.2	100.0
French	2.5	97.3	0.2	100.0
5-9 years:				
English	98.7	0.4	0.9	100.0
French	3.1	96.8	0.1	100.0
10-14 years:				
English	99.0	0.4	0.7	100.0
French	3.3	96.6	0.1	100.0
15-19 years:				
English	99.0	0.4	0.6	100.0
French	4.1	95.8	0.1	100.0
20-24 years:				
English	98.8	0.6	0.5	100.0
French	6.6	93.2	0.2	100.0
25-44 years:				
English	98.7	0.7	0.6	100.0
French	8.3	91.5	0.2	100.0
45 + years:				
English	98.9	0.6	0.5	100.0
French	7.8	92.0	0.2	100.0

Source: *Perspective Canada*, Statistics Canada, Information Canada, Ottawa, 1974, p. 224.

astonishingly high proportion of residents in rural ethno-religious bloc settlements are still able to converse in their traditional languages, even in the Scandinavian and German Catholic settlements, although use of English is increasingly preferred. But the survey data also indicated that age and generation differences in language use are increasingly becoming evident. Thus, even in the relatively conservative bloc settlement context, linguistic assimilation would seem to be inevitable, if proceeding at a slower pace than in urban and mixed areas.

In sum, even in the rural bloc settlements, the traditional bastions of ethnic cultures, despite a recent re-emphasis of multiculturalism (be it as a national or provincial government policy or as romanticization), many processes of social change doubtless will continue to decrease any use of traditional mother tongues in particular and probably also any emphasis on ethnicity in general. Five principal processes seem particularly worthy of note:

First, widespread intermarriage between people of different ethnic origins.

Table 14

LANGUAGE PREFERENCE OF RESPONDENTS (PERCENTAGES)

Group	Category (1)	(2)	(3)	(4)	(5)	Total
French	9.9	48.0	20.3	20.8	1.0	100 (N = 202)
German Catholic	—	13.7	15.3	64.2	6.8	100 (N = 190)
Mennonite	1.6	52.5	14.8	28.3	2.9	100 (N = 244)
Hutterite	—	100.0	—	—	—	100 (N = 6)
Ukrainian Orthodox	6.0	33.7	22.9	37.3	—	100 (N = 83)
Ukrainian Catholic	3.2	44.2	21.4	29.9	1.3	100 (N = 154)
Polish Catholic	6.7	33.3	46.7	13.3	—	100 (N = 15)
Doukhobor	5.0	25.0	40.0	25.0	5.0	100 (N = 20)
Scandinavian	—	25.6	11.6	52.3	10.5	100 (N = 86)
Total Sample	3.6	38.5	18.3	36.2	3.4	100 (N = 1000)

(1) Speak only traditional mother tongue, no English.
(2) Bilingual (in mother tongue and English), but speak primarily mother tongue both at home and in community.
(3) Bilingual; but speak primarily mother tongue at home, English in community.
(4) Bilingual, but speak primarily English at home and in community.
(5) Speak only English, not bilingual.
Source: A. B. Anderson, 1972: 144; 1977: 204-205; 1978a: 71.

Table 15

LANGUAGE PREFERENCE OF RESPONDENTS (CONSOLIDATED)

Group	speak only mother tongue	use mother tongue at least fairly often	can speak mother tongue
French	9.9	78.2	99.0
German Catholic	—	29.0	93.2
Mennonite	1.6	68.9	97.2
Hutterite	—	100.0	100.0
Ukrainian Orthodox	6.0	62.6	100.0
Ukrainian Catholic	3.2	68.8	98.7
Polish Catholic	6.7	86.7	100.0
Doukhobor	5.0	70.0	95.0
Scandinavian	—	37.2	89.5
Total Sample	3.6	60.4	96.6

Source: A. B. Anderson, 1972: 145; 1977: 204; 1980a: 71.

Second, several decades of discriminatory provincial legislation against use of "foreign" languages in school instruction, a conscious policy of using schools as assimilatory agents to ensure conformity to the dominant Anglo-Canadian mode.

Third, the breakdown of the institutional completeness and segregation of ethnic communities, largely through the consolidation of formerly highly localized and ethnically homogeneous schools and other focal points of local community activity into more heterogeneous units.

Table 16

PROPORTION OF RESPONDENTS IN EACH AGE CATEGORY SPEAKING ENGLISH (PRIMARILY OR EXCLUSIVELY), PER GROUP

Group	13-19	20-29	30-49	50-69	70 & Over
French	46.7	31.6	22.2	11.1	7.4
German Catholic	90.9	86.7	92.3	63.6	44.4
Mennonite	39.3	50.0	44.6	30.8	0.0
Hutterite	0.0	0.0	0.0	0.0	0.0
Ukrainian Orthodox	57.1	66.7	47.1	31.0	0.0
Ukrainian Catholic	50.0	55.6	42.4	18.6	0.0
Polish Catholic	—	—	50.0	0.0	0.0
Doukhobor	100.0	—	44.4	0.0	0.0
Scandinavian	100.0	100.0	96.6	44.4	0.0

Source: A. B. Anderson, 1972: 226; 1978a: 76.

Fourth, a steady process of secularization together with a progressive de-emphasis of the one-time close link between ethnicity, language, and religion.
Fifth, very large-scale rural depopulation and the decline of smaller communities, concurrent with rapid urbanization. (83-84)

With regard to "other" language retention, we know that, on the whole, their loss is quite high. As pointed out by O'Bryan, et al. (1976), seven in ten immigrants self-reported full fluency in their "other" language. However, when assessing the second generation's language fluency, they discovered only one in ten were fluent and by the third generation, virtually all "other" language fluency was lost. As O'Bryan, et al. acknowledge, there are group differences in language loss as well as regional differences. Large and recent ethnic concentrations in major urban centres are most likely to maintain some fluency in their language but even this qualification does not seem relevant when Western urban centres are analysed and compared with rural settlements.

What seems to be most important in terms of language retention is the fact that most (if not all) nonofficial language use takes place in the context of family, kin, and perhaps peers and friends. Beyond this fairly limited circle of interaction, use of the nonofficial language is very limited. Nonusage of any language will result in continued loss of the language; linguistic assimilation can be slowed, but whether it can—or will—be halted completely is questionable.

Census and survey data have provided ample evidence of a declining interest in ethnicity if one measures the strength of ethnicity in terms of such criteria as language, religion, and endogamy. But some ethnic groups have not emphasized maintenance of a unique mother tongue (Scots, Irish, Jews, etc.) while other ethnic groups were already anglophone (West Indians, East Indians, etc.) or francophone (Haitians, and perhaps Lebanese, Sephardic and Moroccan Jews, Vietnamese) before immigrating. At any rate, loss of ability to converse in an ethnic mother tongue does not *necessarily* imply complete loss of ethnic identity, i.e., assimilation; it may indicate a reinterpretation of the criteria considered vital to that identity.

Religion

Religion, like language, has often been stressed by sociologists as bolstering ethnic identity. Yet in Canada census data inform us that in fact more and more ethnic groups have been moving away from their traditional religious affiliation through the processes of conversion, secularization, and particularly intermarriage. To cite some examples, by 1971 only a third (33.4%) of Canadians of Scandinavian origin were still Lutherans (although among those of Finnish descent almost double that proportion—60.3%—were Lutherans). Half (52.2%) of Ukrainian-Canadians were neither Ukrainian Orthodox or Catholic. Almost a third (29.1%) of Polish-Canadians (excluding Jews) were no longer Roman Catholics. Little more than half (about 55%) of the Canadians claiming Dutch descent were Catholics, Reformed, or Mennonites. A third (33.1%) of Czechoslovakian-Canadians were neither Catholic nor Lutheran. Over a third of a million (368,660) French-Canadians and 50,910 Italian-Canadians were not Catholics. And thousands of Greeks in Canada are no longer Greek Orthodox, Hungarians are neither Catholic nor Lutherans, Portuguese not Catholic, Russians neither Doukhobors nor Russian Orthodox, etc.

Intermarriage

Intermarriage between Canadians of different ethnic origins has doubtless served to weaken the solidarity of many ethnic groups and has probably brought about a general de-emphasis of ethnicity. By 1971 the majority of Canadian-born family heads in several large ethnic groups were intermarried: Scandinavian 80.9%, Polish 75.9%, Hungarian 74.2%, Dutch 73.1%, Italian 69.9%, German 61.7%, Russian 59.0%, Ukrainian 55.0%. Yet the majority of Canadian-born family heads in the British, French, Jewish, and Asian ethnic groups were still endogamous.

The rate of intermarriage for various ethnic categories is shown in Table 17. The data show that members of ethnic groups tend to marry spouses of the same ethnic affiliation—that is, in-group marriages can best characterize the Canadian population in terms of marriage patterns. This is not to suggest that all groups reflect a high rate of in-group marriages because other factors will certainly influence the process of mate selection. For example, if a group makes up a relatively small proportion of a given population in a specific urban center, one will find they generally exhibit a high out-group marriage pattern. One of the reasons is simply the fact that there are not enough marriageable partners available. However, the data reported in Table 17 show that while a high in-group marriage rate is evident, some variations are displayed. Jews, for example, have by far the highest rate while Germans have the lowest rate. It is clear then, that other processes are at work. Social networks must be established and maintained so that eligible marriage partners can be brought together even though physical proximity is not evident. Sending children to specific summer camps, attending specific academic and social institutions and affiliating with particular religious institutions all allow for an intensive social network to be created and maintained. This, to a certain extent, reflects boundary maintenance and indirectly, the importance of ethnic identity for these ethnic members.

Table 17

RATE[1] OF MALE AND FEMALE ENDOGAMY AND EXOGAMY
—CANADA, 1961

Ethnic origin of males	Ethnic origin of females					
	British	French	German	Italian	Jewish	Ukrainian
British	8,126	580	405	51	4	91
French	849	8,831	85	34	1	27
German	3,072	450	5,203	49	5	175
Italian	1,083	650	145	7,669	5	80
Jewish	356	113	48	12	9,114	24
Ukrainian	1,464	331	442	68	4	6,181
	Ethnic origin of males					
British	8,154	492	410	67	8	88
French	972	8,506	101	68	4	34
German	2,989	365	5,095	66	8	198
Italian	885	343	113	8,226	5	71
Jewish	192	37	31	13	9,297	10
Ukrainian	1,476	252	376	81	9	6,059

Source: Henripin, Charbonneau, and Mertens, "Études des aspects démographiques problèmes ethniques et linguistiques du Canada," and Census of Canada, 1961, Cat. 93-520.
[1] Proportion expressed on a base of 10,000.

In considering intermarriage as an indicator of ethnic identity change, we would do well to heed Isajiw's (1975: 11) caution that "partners of ethnically mixed marriages often retain their respective identities." Nonetheless, our point is that when an ethnic group has unsuccessfully attempted to maintain its identity through preservation of these criteria, then ethnicity must be redefined and ethnic diversity or multiculturalism may come into question. A case in point might be Ukrainian-Canadians, some of whom are ardent advocates and supporters of multiculturalism; in point of fact, we have noted that a majority can no longer speak Ukrainian, nor are they members of principal Ukrainian churches, nor are their spouses and families homogeneous Ukrainian.

So at least to an appreciable extent, as Smith (1970) has appropriately commented:

> The mosaic concept is also an idealization of reality. A greater degree of behavioural assimilation has taken place in Canada than that concept would appear to allow for. The majority of second generation German-Canadians, Icelandic-Canadians, and even Ukrainian-Canadians speak English and not their parents' native tongue. Their Old World culture, when it is retained, is regarded as something to be brought out and dusted off, rather self-consciously, on special occasions. It does not form a central part of Canada's cultural life, and when it is brought to the attention of Canadians at large, the tendency is to regard it as an imported exotic. (250)

REFERENCES

Anderson, Alan B. "Assimilation in the Bloc Settlements of North-Central Saskatchewan: A Comparative Study of Identity Change Among Seven Ethno-Religious Groups in a Canadian Prairie Region." Ph.D. thesis in sociology, University of Saskatchewan, Saskatoon, (1972)

Anderson, Alan B. "The Scottish Tradition in Canada: Its Rise and Fall," in A. H. Brodie (ed.), *Scottish Colloquim Proceedings*, Vol. 6/7, (1973): 35-47.

Anderson, Alan B. "Ethnic Identity Retention in French Canadian Communities in Saskatchewan," paper presented at the annual meetings of the Canadian Sociology and Anthropology Association (CSAA), University of Toronto, August 1974a.

Anderson, Alan B. "Intermarriage in Ethnic Bloc Settlements in Saskatchewan: A Cross-Cultural Survey of Trends and Attitudes," paper presented at the annual meetings of the Western Assoc. of Sociology and Anthropology, Banff, Dec. 1974b.

Anderson, Alan B. "Ethnic Enclosure and Discrimination in a West Indian Community in Toronto," paper presented at the Conference on Multiculturalism and Third World Immigrants in Canada, Univ. of Alberta, Edmonton, Sept. 3-6, 1975.

Anderson, Alan B. "Ethnic Identity in Saskatchewan Bloc Settlements: A Sociological Appraisal," in Howard Palmer (ed.), *The Settlement of the West*. Calgary: Univ. of Calgary/Comprint Publishing, 1977.

Anderson Alan, B. "Linguistic Trends Among Saskatchewan Ethnic Groups," in M. L. Kovacs (ed.), *Ethnic Canadians: Culture and Education*. Regina: Canadian Plains Research Centre, 1978a, Chap. 6, pp. 63-86.

Anderson, Alan B. "French Settlements in Saskatchewan: Historical and Sociological Perspectives," paper presented at the Tenth Annual Meeting of the Saskatchewan Genealogical Society, Saskatoon, Oct. 20-21, 1978b.

Anderson, Alan B. "Ukrainian Ethnicity: Generations and Change in Rural Saskatchewan," and Appendix: "French Ethnicity in North-Central Saskatchewan," in J. L. Elliott (ed.), *Two Nations, Many Cultures: Ethnic Groups in Canada*. Scarborough, Ont.: Prentice-Hall of Canada, 1979.

Anderson, A. B. and L. Driedger "The Mennonite Family: Culture and Kin in Rural Saskatchewan," in K. Ishwaran (ed.), *Canadian Families: Ethnic Variations*. Scarborough, Ont.: McGraw-Hill Ryerson, 1980.

Anderson, A. B. and D. K. Stasiulis "Canadian Multiculturalism: A Critique." Paper presented at the Conference on "Ethnicity, Power, and Politics," the biennial meetings of the Canadian Ethnic Studies Association, Vancouver, Oct. 11-13, 1980.

Breton, Raymond. "Institutional Completeness of Ethnic Communities and the Personal Relations of Immigrants," *American Journal of Sociology*, LXX, No. 2, Sept. 1964, pp. 193-205.

Breton, Raymond. "Types of Ethnic Diversity in Canadian Society", paper presented at the Eighth World Congress of Sociology, Univ. of Toronto, August 23, 1974.

Breton, Raymond. "The Structure of Relationships Between Ethnic Collectivities," in Leo Driedger (ed.), *The Canadian Ethnic Mosaic*. Toronto: McClelland & Stewart, pp. 55-73.

Burnet, Jean. "The Definition of Multiculturalism in a Bilingual Framework," paper presented at the Conference on Multiculturalism and Third World Immigrants in Canada, Univ. of Alberta, Edmonton, Sept. 3-6, 1975.

Burnet, Jean. "Myths and Multiculturalism," paper presented at the annual meetings of the Canadian Society for the Study of Education, Univ. of Saskatchewan, Saskatoon, June 6, 1979.

Clark, S. D. "The Canadian Society and the Issue of Multiculturalism," published lecture given at the Univ. of Saskatchewan, Saskatoon, Jan. 27,1976.

Driedger, Leo. "Impelled Group Migration: Minority Struggle to Maintain Institutional Completeness," *International Migration Review*, Vol. 7, No. 3 (1973).

Driedger, Leo. "In Search of Cultural Identity Factors: A Comparison of Ethnic Students in Manitoba," *Canadian Review of Sociology and Anthropology*, Vol. 12, pp. 150-162, 1975.

Driedger, Leo. "Maintenance of Urban Ethnic Boundaries: The French in St-Boniface," paper presented at the annual meetings of the CSAA, Laval University, Quebec, May 26-29, 1976.

Driedger, Leo. "Ukrainian Identity in Winnipeg," in M. L. Kovacs (ed.), *Ethnic Canadians: Culture and Education*. Regina: Canadian Plains Research Centre 1978. Chap. 12, pp. 147-165.

Driedger, Leo. "Ukrainian Identity in Canada: Evidence of Encroaching Assimilation," paper presented at the annual meetings of the CSAA, Univ. of Saskatchewan, Saskatoon, June 1-4, 1979.

Driedger, L. and G. Church. "Residential Segregation and Institutional Completeness: A Comparison of Ethnic Minorities" *Canadian Review of Sociology and Anthropology*, Vol. 11, No. 1, Feb. 1974, pp. 30-52.

Isajiw, Wsevolod W. "Immigration and Multiculturalism—Old and New Approaches," paper presented at the Conference on Multiculturalism and Third World Immigrants in Canada, Univ. of Alberta, Edmonton, Sept. 3-5, 1975.

Isajiw, Wsevolod W. "Olga in Wonderland: Ethnicity in a Technological Society," in Leo Driedger (ed.), *The Canadian Ethnic Mosaic*. Toronto: McClelland & Stewart, 1978, pp. 29-39.

Li, Peter and B. S. Bolaria. "Canadian Immigration Policy and Assimilation Theories," in John Fry (ed.), *Economy, Class and Social Reality*. Toronto: Butterworths, 1979.

Nahirny, V. and J. A. Fishman. "American Immigrant Groups: Ethnic Identification and the Problem of Generations," *Sociological Review*, 13, (1965): 311-26.

O'Bryan, J. Reitz and O. Kyplowska. *Non-Official Language: A Study in Canadian Multiculturalism*. Ottawa: Information Canada, 1976.

Schermerhorn, R. R. *Comparative Ethnic Relations: A Framework for Theory and Research*. New York: Random House, 1970.

Smith, A. "Metaphor and Nationalism in North America," *Canadian Historical Review*, Vol. LI, 1970.

Stasiulis, Daiva K. "The Representation and Regulation of Ethnic Group Interests Within the Canadian State," paper presented at the annual meetings of the CSAA, Univ. of Saskatchewan, Saskatoon, June 1-4, 1979.

Vallee, F. G. "Regionalism and Ethnicity: The French-Canadian Case," in B. Y. Card et al. (eds.), *Perspectives on Regions and Regionalism.* University of Alberta, Edmonton, 1969.

Van den Berghe, Pierre L. (ed.) *Africa: Social Problems of Change and Conflict.* San Francisco: Chandler, 1965.

Yuzyk, Paul. "Canada as a Multicultural Society," paper presented at the Conference on Multiculturalism and Third World Immigrants, Univ. of Alberta, Edmonton, Sept. 3-6, 1975.

Chapter 7

Immigration: A Socio-Demographic Profile

History of Canadian Immigration

It is clear, upon analysis of the data, that the ethnic make-up of Canada has changed over time. However, it is not the task of this chapter to present an in-depth analysis, but rather a brief review, of historical trends. Only those trends that have theoretical or practical import for understanding contemporary ethnic relations in Canada will be included. Any understanding of the changing ethnic composition of Canadian society presupposes some acquaintance with immigration history.

With the exception of Native people, today's entire Canadian population consists of immigrants and their direct descendants. To a large extent, our population consists primarily of the descendants of immigrants from France and the British Isles. Canada's immigration policy has fluctuated from very restrictive measures to curtail immigration to one of very active involvement in recruiting immigrants. For example, during certain periods of Canadian history, restrictions on Americans owning land in Canada (and thus entering Canada) effectively eliminated any large-scale movement into the country. On the other hand, immigrants from Italy (during the 1950s) were very actively recruited. Immigration has always been an important social fact in Canada. Canada has received about 10 million immigrants since Confederation and the percentage of foreign-born living in Canada has ranged over time from 15 to 22% of the total population. It is currently about 15% of the total population.

In the immediate decade after Confederation (1871 to 1881), over 300,000 immigrants entered Canada. During the second decade of the 19th century, this number had increased to well over one million and during the 1950s, the number increased to one and a half million. From 1966 to 1971, the rate remained about the same as during the 1951 to 1961 period—836,000. Thus, as stated previously, immigration has always accounted for a substantial component in the growth of the Canadian population, and it is estimated that immigration will continue to represent a sizable proportion of the growth of Canada. For example, in 1975 Canada increased its total population by 354,000. Of this total growth, nearly 50% was due to immigration. The rate of immigration at present is about 8.2 per 1,000 of the population.

Early in the 17th century, France, because of a colonial ideology (coupled with a mercantilistic economic structure), began to settle and exploit New France (what we now call Canada). By Confederation (nearly 300 years later), the population of Canada had risen to over three million. This population in-

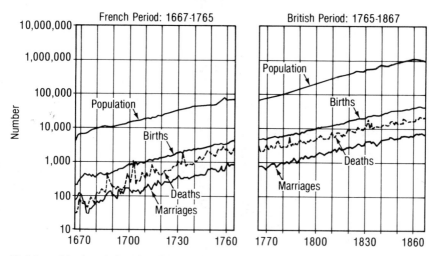

FIGURE 1 DETERMINANTS OF POPULATION GROWTH
BRITISH AND FRENCH REGIMES
PROVINCE OF QUEBEC, CANADA: 1667-1867

All data on this chart derived from D.B.S. Publications

Source: W. Kalbach and W. McVey, *The Demographic Bases of Canadian Society*
(2nd ed.), McGraw-Hill Ryerson, Toronto, p. 22, 1979.

crease was generally due to immigration. However, the increase in the French population itself had been due almost entirely to natural increases. Figure 1 shows the growth rate of the French and English population from 1670 to Confederation.

The size of the Native population took an opposite direction. It has been estimated that nearly 200,000 Native people inhabited what is now called Canada at the time of French settlement. However, by 1867 less than 100,000 Native people remained. Since this period of time, through isolation and cultural and physical genocide, Native people have been relegated to playing a minor part in shaping Canadian society.

Since we are arguing that a substantial proportion of the population increase in Canada has resulted from immigration, it suggests that we should find a variety of ethnic, linguistic, and religious groups settling in Canada. The arrival of these various groups into Canada can be followed through five phases.

The first phase was the French era. Until the British conquest, large numbers of French nationals migrated to Canada to attempt a new life. This era came to a close at the time of Confederation, with British economic and political domination. From this time on, British nationals have immigrated to Canada in greater numbers than any other national group, and this pattern lasted until the beginning of the 20th century. The number of immigrants coming to Canada each year from Confederation until 1902 (phase II) reached 100,000 per year only three times (1882-1884). All other years the number fell well below this number. From 1903 to the beginning of World War I, the third phase in Canada's development took place. During this phase nearly 200,000 people per year

Table 1

POPULATION GROWTH IN BRITISH NORTH AMERICA 1765-1871

Year	Quebec	Ontario	Nova Scotia	New Brunswick	P.E.I.	Manitoba	Terr.	British Columbia	New-foundland
1765	69,810								
1767			11,779	1,196	519				
1784	113,021	10,000							
1790	161,311								
1806		70,700							
1811		77,000							
1814		95,000							
1817			81,351						
1822	427,465								
1824		150,066		74,176					
1825	479,288	157,923							
1827	471,875	177,174	123,630						
1831	553,134	236,720				2,390			

Year										
1834		321,145		119,457		3,356				
1836		374,099								75,094
1838		399,422	202,575	156,162		3,966				
1840		432,159				4,704				
1841					47,042					
1842		487,053								
1843						5,143				
1844	697,084									
1845										
1846						4,871				52,064
1848		725,879			62,678					
1849						5,391				
1851	890,261	952,004	276,854	193,800						
1857							5,700	55,000		
1861	1,111,566	1,396,091	330,857	252,047	80,857		6,691	51,524	124,288	
1869							48,000			
1871	1,191,516	1,620,851	387,800	285,594	94,021	25,228		36,247	146,536	

Source: W. Kalbach and W. McVey, *The Demographic Bases of Canadian Society* (2nd ed.), McGraw-Hill Ryerson, Toronto, 1979, p. 24-25.

entered Canada. The major *pull* factor for attracting immigrants to Canada during this phase was a result of the Canadian government's aggressive policy to develop the agricultural potential in the West. In addition, *push* factors from the immigrating countries came as a result of poor homeland economic conditions. The two factors merged and the result was one of the largest migrations ever recorded in history.

However, as McLeod (1969) points out, most immigrants were poorly educated, and had little knowledge of French or English. Because they did have some agricultural skills, their settlement resulted in initial concentrations of specific nationalities within a geographical area. While these bloc settlements made the transaction from the homeland to the new country easier, it also produced an unanticipated consequence. The geographical concentration allowed for the continuance and maintenance of traditional linguistic and cultural patterns. After the social and political consequences of this bloc settlement became apparent, the Canadian government attempted (with some degree of success) to stop further bloc settlement. However, as Anderson (1977) has pointed out in his writings on ethnic identity retention in Saskatchewan bloc settlements, identity (both behaviorial and attitudinal) still remains high. The majority of the settlers in the West during this period consisted of five principal types of ethnic collectivities: British (English, Scottish, and Irish from Eastern Canada as well as the British Isles, and some Welsh who arrived in Saskatchewan from Wales via Argentina); French (from Quebec, France and Belgium); German-speaking groups (mostly from German, Mennonite, and Hutterite colonies in Russia); Slavic groups (Ukrainians, Poles, Russian Doukhobors, etc.); and Scandinavian groups.

A short fourth phase came after World War I but ended when the economic depression reduced the immigration flow to a small trickle. During this period of immigration, new laws were introduced to control the flow of specific groups. As O'Bryan, Reitz and Kuplowska (1976) point out, immigrants from enemy countries, those who used an enemy language or those who were defined by the Canadian government as not easily assimilable were refused entry. While eventually these rigid restrictions were removed, a general attitude emerged among dominant group Canadians and was sustained with regard to certain groups' abilities to assimilate into the Canadian way of life.

However, unlike the pre-World War I immigrants, these immigrants were better educated and had some technical skills, and as a result, tended to settle in urban rather than rural areas. Woycenko (1967) makes this point when referring to the migrating Ukrainians:

> The war and technological progress had equipped them with more knowledge and skills. They were inclined to urban living and only a small number settled permanently on farms. Many looked on agricultural work as a temporary occupation for the transitional period until jobs in the city were available. (13)

The final phase of immigration did not begin until after World War II when once again immigration figures seldom fell below 100,000 per year. Table 2 illustrates the flow since the mid 19th century. The last phase of immigration (the post-war migration) has involved a greater number of immigrants as well as a greater diversity of national origins. These immigrants (like those of the previous period, only more so) were educated and held skills useful for current

Canadian technology. They also tended to take up residence in urban areas. However, with some notable exceptions (Italians) these new groups have not formed closed enclaves within the urban setting. The absorptive capacity of Canadian society during this last wave has been high and, as a result, adjustment for these recent immigrants has been much easier than those entering in preceding times.

In summary, the data in Table 2 show that for nearly thirty years (1851-1881), immigration made up a small percentage of the total population growth. However, from 1881 to 1931, immigration consistently contributed to at least 10% of the total growth. After this time, one clearly sees that immigration has not contributed disproportionately to the overall growth. It should be noted, however, that while the percentage has decreased, the actual number of immigrants has been substantial.

Table 2

IMMIGRATION IN THE CONTEXT OF CANADIAN POPULATION GROWTH

	Population at end of decade[1]	Growth in population	Immigration	Emigration[2]	Gross immigration as a percentage of total population[3]	IMMIGRATION AS A PERCENTAGE OF POPULATION GROWTH	
						Gross	Net
	thousands					%	
1851-61	3,230	793	209	85	6.5	26.4	15.5
1861-71	3,689	459	183	379	5.1	40.7	−41.7
1871-81	4,325	636	353	440	8.2	55.5	−13.7
1881-91	4,833	508	903	1,109	23.0	177.8	−40.6
1891-01	5,371	538	326	506	9.4	60.6	−33.4
1901-11	7,207	1,836	1,759	1,043	24.4	95.8	38.0
1911-21	8,788	1,581	1,612	1,381	18.3	101.9	14.6
1921-31	10,377	1,589	1,203	974	11.6	75.7	14.4
1931-41	11,507	1,130	150	242	1.3	13.2	−8.1
1941-51	14,009	2,502	548	379	3.9	21.9	6.7
1951-61	18,238	4,229	1,543	462	8.4	36.4	25.5
1961-71	21,568	3,330	1,429	702	6.8	43.8	22.8

[1] As at June.
[2] Estimated.
[3] Calculated at end of decade.
Note: From 1941, figures for Newfoundland are included for population and population growth but not for immigration and emigration.
Source: *Perspective Canada*, Statistics Canada, Information Canada Ottawa, 1974, p. 274.

The Changing Ethnic Composition of Canada: Historical Perspective

Table 3 illustrates the changing ethnic composition of Canada during the past century.

Table 3
ETHNIC ORIGIN OF THE CANADIAN POPULATION, 1871-1971[1]

	1871	1881	1901	1911	1921	1931	1941	1951	1961	1971
Total[2]	3,485,761	4,324,810	5,371,315	7,206,643	8,787,949	10,376,786	11,506,655	14,009,429	18,238,247	21,568,310
British	2,110,502	2,548,514	3,063,195	3,999,081	4,868,738	5,381,071	5,715,904	6,709,685	7,996,669	9,624,115
French	1,082,940	1,298,929	1,649,371	2,061,719	2,452,743	2,927,990	3,483,038	4,319,167	5,540,346	6,180,120
Dutch	29,662	30,412	33,845	55,961	117,505	148,962	212,863	264,267	429,679	425,945
German	202,991	254,319	310,501	403,417	294,635	473,544	464,682	619,995	1,049,599	1,317,200
Italian	1,035	1,849	10,834	45,963	66,769	98,173	112,625	152,245	450,351	730,820
Jewish	125	667	16,131	76,199	126,196	156,726	170,241	181,670	173,344	296,945
Polish			6,285	33,652	53,403	145,503	167,485	219,845	323,517	316,430
Russian	607	1,227	19,825	44,376	100,064	88,148	83,708	91,279	119,168	64,475
Scandinavian	1,623	5,223	31,042	112,682	167,359	228,049	244,603	283,024	386,534	384,795
Ukrainian			5,682	75,432	106,721	225,113	305,929	395,043	473,337	580,660
Other European	3,830	5,760	23,811	97,101	214,451	261,034	281,790	346,354	711,320	876,860
Asiatic	4	4,383	23,731	43,213	65,914	84,548	74,064	72,827	121,753	285,540
Indian and Eskimo	23,037	108,547	127,941	105,611	113,724	128,890	125,521	165,607	220,121	312,760
Others and not stated	29,405	64,980	49,121	52,236	39,727	29,035	64,202	188,421	242,509	171,645

ETHNIC ORIGIN OF THE CANADIAN POPULATION (PERCENTAGES), 1871-1971

	1871	1881	1901	1911	1921	1931	1941	1951	1961	1971
Total	100.00	100.00	100.00	100.00	100.00	100.00	100.00	100.00	100.00	100.00
British	60.55	58.93	57.04	55.49	55.41	51.86	49.68	47.89	43.85	44.60
French	31.07	30.03	30.71	28.61	27.91	28.22	30.27	30.83	30.38	28.70
Dutch	0.85	0.70	0.63	0.78	1.34	1.44	1.85	1.89	2.36	2.00
German	5.82	5.88	5.78	5.60	3.35	4.56	4.04	4.43	5.75	6.10
Italian	0.03	0.04	0.20	0.64	0.76	0.95	0.98	1.09	2.47	3.40
Jewish	*	0.02	0.30	1.06	1.44	1.51	1.48	1.30	0.95	1.40
Polish			0.12	0.47	0.61	1.40	1.45	1.57	1.77	1.50
Russian	0.02	0.03	0.37	0.61	1.14	0.85	0.73	0.65	0.65	0.30
Scandinavian	0.05	0.12	0.58	1.56	1.90	2.20	2.12	2.02	2.12	1.80
Ukrainian			0.10	1.05	1.21	2.17	2.66	2.82	2.59	2.70
Other European	0.11	0.13	0.44	1.35	2.44	2.51	2.45	2.47	3.90	3.90
Asiatic	*	0.10	0.44	0.60	0.75	0.81	0.64	0.52	0.67	1.30
Indian and Eskimo	0.66	2.51	2.38	1.46	1.29	1.24	1.09	1.18	1.21	1.40
Others and not stated	0.84	1.51	0.91	0.72	0.45	0.28	0.56	1.34	1.33	1.00

Source: Statistics Canada, Census of Canada.
[1] Data for 1871 and 1881 are incomplete, particularly in the treatment of small numbers of those from central Europe, 1891 is omitted because of insufficient data.
[2] For 1871 includes the population of the four original provinces of Canada only: Nova Scotia, New Brunswick, Quebec, and Ontario. Newfoundland is excluded until 1951.
*Percentage lower than 0.01.

The data in this table show that immediately after Confederation, the population of Canada was basically French and English, making up well over 90% of the total population. The only other ethnic segment that contributed significant numbers were the Germans and, as one looks at the table, it is clear that they have maintained their relative proportion for the past one hundred years.

A second significant fact demonstrated in the data is that the French have consistently maintained their significant presence in Canada. About one-third of the total population have been French-Canadians, although recently this has been decreasing. Simultaneously, the population of British ethnic affiliation has been decreasing proportionately, but at a much faster rate. In 1871, they made up over 60% of the population, but one hundred years later they only made up 44%. The British became a statistical minority within Canada in 1941, according to these census data.

With the reduction of these two charter groups and the concurrent increases in immigration from other countries, a third force has emerged. While individually these groups usually make up less than 5% of the total population, collectively they now make up over 20% of the total population. As we have already noted earlier, the proportion of non-British and non-French on the Prairies is much higher, thus adding to their potential impact of the mosaic for this region.

Data calculated for the ethnic origins of immigrants between 1900 and 1965 (see Table 4) reveal several different migration patterns. The influence of German and Dutch migration has clearly been evident since Confederation. As pointed out previously, in 1871 less than 8% of the total population consisted of ethnic origins other than British and French. And of that 8%, over 70% were German while an additional 10% were reported being Dutch. Only during wartime did the immigration pattern of these groups cease from steadily increasing. Several other groups, however, have begun to immigrate to Canada within the past decade in increasing numbers, notably Chinese, South Asians, Greeks, West Indians, Portuguese, Spanish, and Yugoslavs.

Chart 1 shows the actual birthplace of the foreign-born population for the past century. As pointed out above, it clearly demonstrates the substantial decreasing input by immigrants for the United Kingdom. It also shows a decrease in immigrants born in the U.S.A. since the turn of the century. The changing ethnic immigration patterns have been the result of both economic and political conditions for both Canada and the homeland of these immigrants. Depressed economic conditions in the homeland have long been a primary reason for individuals leaving their homeland and seeking a better life elsewhere. In addition, immigration policies established by the Canadian government have promoted or retarded the migration of specific types of immigrants into Canada. By superimposing our five-phase population development of Canada onto the groups coming into Canada we can best explain the above.

During the first phase of population growth, the French were in political and economic control of Canada. Their attempts to control the fur trade and extract primary resources from Canada led to a continued relatively high migration rate of French nationals. However, because Roman Catholicism as a religious ideology was important for these immigrants, a high birth rate was evidenced. As a result, until very recent times, they have maintained a stable percentage in Canada's population without any sizable number of new French immigrants.

CHART 1   BIRTHPLACE OF FOREIGN BORN POPULATION

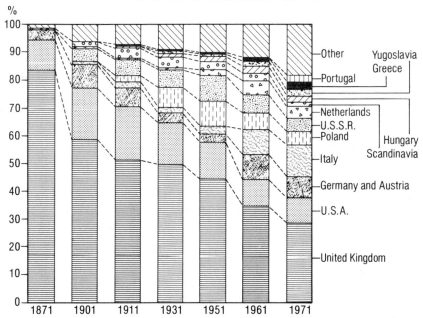

Source: *Perspective Canada,* Statistics Canada, Information Canada, Ottawa, 1974, p. 270.

With Confederation came a new political structure along with greater industrialization. Coupled with this, England was concerned about establishing a stable population base in Canada to thwart American and French influence. While greater numbers of British subjects immigrated to Canada, other groups also came because they desired economic and political security in the new state of Canada, and the new government was willing to provide these securities. As a result, the relative percentage of British ethnics in Canada has steadily decreased. It is clear, then, that the overall increase in Canada's population has come from "other" (non-British, non-French) immigrants.

The result of these immigration patterns has been the creation of a structure usually referred to as a mosaic, but a closer look shows that this mosaic has maintained a distinct white color.

Table 5 shows the ethnic composition by province (and Canada as a whole) for 1971. It illustrates the differential distribution of ethnic collectivities throughout Canada. For example, Germans make up between 12.5-19.4% of the total population in the three western provinces. Asians are concentrated in B.C. with extremely low numbers in other provinces. Italians, on the other hand, are concentrated in Ontario and Quebec. While the data in Table 5 show the proportion of the ethnic collectivities relative to the total population, another way of looking at the proportion is to ask what proportion does it constitute when the two charter groups are removed. In other words, we know that 45% and 29% of the total population are British and French respectively. Hence we could ask, what is the relative proportion of various other ethnic categories for the remaining 26%?

Table 4
ETHNIC ORIGIN OF IMMIGRANTS—CANADA, 1900-1965[1]

Ethnic origin	1900-1901	1901-1902	1902-1903	1903-1904	1904-1905	1905-1906	1906-1907	1907-1908
Total	49,149	67,379	128,364	125,899	142,853	184,064	122,165	257,309
Albanian								
Arab[2]	98	70	46	58	48	19	31	50
Armenian	62	112	113	81	78	82	208	563
Austrian[3]	228	320	781	516	837	1,324	562	1,899
Belgian	132	223	303	858	796	1,106	650	1,214
British[4]	11,813	17,275	42,198	51,029	65,887	87,741	57,099	123,940
Bulgarian		1	7	14	2	71	179	2,529
Chinese	7	2				18	92	1,884
Czech and Slovak								
Danish	88	163	308	417	461	474	297	290
Dutch	25	35	223	169	281	389	394	1,212
Egyptian	1	3	1	3	2	18	10	8
Estonian								
Finnish	682	1,292	1,734	845	1,323	1,103	1,049	1,212
French	360	431	937	1,534	1,743	1,648	1,314	2,671
German	984	1,048	1,887	2,985	2,759	1,796	1,889	2,363
Greek	81	161	193	191	98	254	545	1,053
Hungarian	546	1,048	2,074	1,091	981	739	499	1,307
Icelandic	912	260	917	396	413	168	46	97
Indian[5]					45	387	2,124	2,623
Iranian		1	40	5	8	7	31	7
Italian	4,710	3,828	3,371	4,445	3,473	7,959	5,114	11,212
Japanese	6				354	1,922	2,042	7,601

Ethnic origin								
Jewish	2,765	1,015	2,066	3,727	7,715	7,127	6,584	7,712
Latvian								
Lebanese[6]								
Lithuanian								
Luxemburger								
Maltese			2					
Mexican								
Negro[7]	265				5	42	108	136
Norwegian	4,702	1,015	1,746	1,239	1,397	1,415	876	1,554
Polish		6,550	8,656	8,398	7,671	6,381	2,685	15,861
Portuguese				2	2	8	7	3
Roumanian	152	551	438	619	270	396	431	949
Russian	1,044	2,479	5,505	1,955	1,911	3,152	1,927	6,281
Spanish	14	1	7	5	10	12	29	61
Swedish	485	1,013	2,477	2,151	1,847	1,802	1,077	2,132
Swiss	30	17	73	128	150	172	112	195
Syrian	464	1,066	847	369	630	336	277	732
Turkish	37	17	43	29	30	357	232	489
Ukrainian					3	266	303	912
Yugoslav[8]	23	1,761	1,761	1,588	1,130	1,374	233	2,193
Others	446	994	137	313	563	1,203	870	1,079
From the United States[9]	17,987	26,388	49,473	40,739	39,930	52,796	32,239	53,285

Source: Division of Immigration, Department of Manpower and Immigration.

[1] Fiscal years from 1900-1901 to 1907-1908, calendar years from 1908 to 1965.

[2] Excludes those of Egyptian, Syrian, and Lebanese origin.

[3] Included with those of German origin from 1926 to 1952.

[4] Includes those of English, Irish, Welsh, and Scottish origin, immigrants from Newfoundland (before 1949), Bermuda, and the British West Indies (Jamaica, Trinidad, Barbados, etc.).

(Table 4—cont'd)

Ethnic origin	1908	1909	1910	1911	1912	1913	1914	1915
Total	143,326	173,694	286,839	331,288	375,756	400,870	150,484	36,665
Albanian						1	6	
Arab[2]	7	13	7	1	11	12	4	
Armenian	111	76	20	44	109	137	57	
Austrian[3]	1,758	3,337	8,523	4,987	1,231	3,232	626	14
Belgian	775	894	1,305	1,705	1,669	2,766	1,495	224
British[4]	58,512	56,148	115,855	147,770	147,619	158,398	50,755	9,907
Bulgarian	63	495	985	1,664	6,388	1,270	4,512	1
Chinese	2,163	1,883	4,657	6,644	6,992	6,298	1,600	82
Czech and Slovak	58	123	217	282	352	447	172	
Danish	146	254	476	602	848	868	419	163
Dutch	480	570	1,036	1,080	1,359	1,710	735	182
Egyptian	2	2			7	2	3	
Estonian								
Finnish	453	1,348	2,262	1,637	2,135	3,508	637	91
French	1,944	1,633	1,980	2,169	2,673	2,668	1,568	191
German	1,386	1,405	2,440	4,297	5,025	5,710	3,006	34
Greek	174	461	784	584	1,523	898	1,506	124
Hungarian	453	692	992	703	1,210	2,113	562	
Icelandic	33	85	244	219	215	306	150	15
Indian[5]	296	5	14	3	5	88		1
Iranian	5	5		19	24	19	8	
Italian	4,006	6,919	8,181	7,218	14,265	27,704	7,365	365
Japanese	858	244	420	727	675	886	681	380
Jewish	2,504	2,779	5,060	5,044	6,885	11,574	4,279	73

Latvian								
Lebanese[6]								
Lithuanian								
Luxemburger								
Maltese					46	483	20	1
Mexican					12	9		
Negro[7]	76	7	70	138	211	264	200	36
Norwegian	654	1,285	2,019	1,829	1,798	1,698	967	196
Polish	7,346	4,092	5,454	6,028	10,077	13,339	2,373	7
Portuguese	2	5	25	8	8	62	14	
Roumanian	368	307	442	761	1,136	1,530	442	5
Russian	3,415	4,131	6,736	8,030	15,843	28,758	6,606	43
Spanish	38	33	170	222	239	1,181	781	9
Swedish	1,015	1,905	3,065	2,589	2,330	2,671	1,086	152
Swiss	122	165	304	235	221	291	240	49
Syrian	173	213	98	146	208	299	94	6
Turkish	149	458	600	415	993	169	60	
Ukrainian	234	274	2,874	10,631	19,222	18,907	6,504	
Yugoslav[8]	1,708	860	886	664	1,981	2,747	657	4
Others	89	179	338	165	116	135	81	13
From the United States[9]	51,750	80,409	108,300	112,028	120,095	97,712	50,213	24,297

5 Includes immigrants from India, Pakistan, and Ceylon.
6 Included with those of Syrian origin until 1955.
7 Except from the United States.
8 Includes those of Croatian, Macedonian, Serbian, and Slovene origin.
9 Not divided by ethnic origin.

(Table 4—cont'd)

Ethnic origin	1916	1917	1918	1919	1920	1921	1922	1923
Total	55,914	72,910	41,845	107,698	138,824	91,728	64,224	133,729
Albanian					2	6	1	6
Arab[2]					6	11	4	
Armenian	3	2		7	50	79	43	404
Austrian[3]	1			3	25	12	20	61
Belgian	84	65	29	885	2,191	578	300	1,368
British[4]	10,140	4,114	5,396	57,929	77,160	44,367	32,604	75,501
Bulgarian				1	4	26	15	163
Chinese	313	547	2,988	2,085	1,329	2,732	810	811
Czech and Slovak					276	155	123	1,934
Danish	165	71	38	189	478	603	297	1,025
Dutch	166	76	68	120	575	240	118	798
Egyptian					9	7		3
Estonian							12	33
Finnish	276	129	15	25	1,198	460	654	324
French	192	130	136	1,486	984	364	289	1,258
German	17	1		11	112	195	177	294
Greek	274	59	5	31	297	195	187	162
Hungarian					23	41	26	26
Icelandic	10	3	10	10	50	22	33	26
Indian[5]	3				9	11	22	30
Iranian			2	2	1	9	1	5
Italian	713	327	60	717	3,927	2,508	2,030	6,062
Japanese	553	887	1,036	892	525	481	395	404
Jewish	137	38	25	74	1,335	8,731	3,385	9,494

Origin								
Latvian								18
Lebanese[6]					16		119	204
Lithuanian							7	45
Luxemburger								151
Maltese	92	164	2	16	154	1	50	
Mexican		1	22	391	1	61	47	1
Negro[7]		38	71	3	142	41		40
Norwegian	95	230	2	59	412	489	448	1,670
Polish	359			176	3,544	2,853	2,758	4,157
Portuguese	15	2		24	4	952	2	965
Roumanian	4			3	702	420	440	
Russian	26	32	45	10	963	9	168	2,852
Spanish	68	38	12	44	202	509	20	39
Swedish	360	166	96	19	645	205	666	3,295
Swiss	29	14	9	188	211	153	114	1,527
Syrian	2	10		86	395		88	235
Turkish	5			9	9		5	10
Ukrainian	1				478	93	38	816
Yugoslav[8]	5		1	11	72	151	137	714
Others	27	29	8	63	120	70	37	108
From the United States[9]	41,779	65,739	31,769	42,129	40,188	23,888	17,534	16,716

Source: Division of Immigration, Department of Manpower and Immigration.

[1] Fiscal years from 1900-1901 to 1907-1908, calendar years from 1908 to 1965.
[2] Excludes those of Egyptian, Syrian, and Lebanese origin.
[3] Included with those of German origin from 1926 to 1952.
[4] Includes those of English, Irish, Welsh, and Scottish origin, immigrants from Newfoundland (before 1949), Bermuda and the British West Indies (Jamaica, Trinidad, Barbados, etc.).

(Table 4—cont'd)

Ethnic origin	1932	1933	1934	1935	1936	1937	1938	1939
Total	20,591	14,382	12,476	11,277	11,643	15,101	17,244	16,994
Albanian			4	1	4	8	10	4
Arab[2]	2		1			3	3	2
Armenian	1	7		3	5	4	4	2
Austrian[3]								
Belgian	40	26	62	80	85	98	177	153
British[4]	3,327	2,304	2,166	2,103	2,197	2,859	3,389	3,544
Bulgarian	12	12	5	12	21	31	25	23
Chinese	1	1	1			1		
Czech and Slovak	332	452	656	512	684	35	1,684	967
Danish	49	46	23	22	22	1,348	45	78
Dutch	30	25	49	73	115	108	200	306
Egyptian								
Estonian		1	2	3	5	2	9	6
Finnish	32	45	63	38	50	73	67	63
French	90	76	79	90	136	128	139	159
German	562	389	304	230	315	541	588	1,071
Greek	34	29	39	49	73	97	121	128
Hungarian	311	484	427	319	320	555	596	360
Icelandic	1			7		3		
Indian[5]	61	35	33	26	12	11	9	19
Iranian	1				1	2		
Italian	280	253	320	333	298	416	367	202
Japanese	119	106	125	70	103	146	57	44
Jewish	313	420	577	560	449	317	456	1,467
Latvian	3	3	1	2	3	9	6	1

Latvian	20	23	54	74	74	77	33	1
Lebanese[6]	155	87	779	880	1,783	934	612	59
Lithuanian	70	5						
Luxemburger	29	13	34	37	25	40	16	5
Maltese			1					
Mexican								
Negro[7]	34	57	50	89	92	186	136	14
Norwegian	3,216	841	2,607	5,102	2,241	2,549	1,049	66
Polish	2,908	1,952	5,359	8,248	8,319	6,197	4,968	560
Portuguese	3	2	15	5	13	14	5	28
Roumanian	2,471	338	317	221	283	344	245	71
Russian	5,545	881	1,074	1,092	957	674	1,017	11
Spanish	3	60	32	28	22	29	7	62
Swedish	2,550	1,218	2,324	3,164	3,424	3,073	1,022	37
Swiss	758	277	503	681	473	510	257	15
Syrian	253	127	221	101	41	55	67	1
Turkish	43	21	4	8	2	6	8	
Ukrainian	49	2,196	9,468	10,836	16,039	10,973	8,045	503
Yugoslav[8]	2,183	2,132	4,182	3,149	4,377	2,038	1,285	212
Others	130	4	1					
From the United States[9]	16,042	17,717	20,944	23,818	29,933	31,852	25,632	15,195

5 Includes immigrants from India, Pakistan, and Ceylon.
6 Included with those of Syrian origin until 1955.
7 Except from the United States.
8 Includes those of Croatian, Macedonian, Serbian, and Slovene origin.
9 Not divided by ethnic origin.

(Table 4—cont'd)

Ethnic origin	1924	1925	1926	1927	1928	1929	1930	1931
Total	124,164	84,907	135,982	158,886	166,783	164,993	104,806	27,530
Albanian	2	11	11	35	31	21	32	5
Arab[2]		5	8	7		4	5	1
Armenian	338	152	66	55	11	16	27	5
Austrian[3]	97	56						
Belgian	1,504	965	1,842	2,369	1,261	862	329	54
British[4]	59,680	35,457	48,819	52,940	55,848	66,801	31,709	7,678
Bulgarian	170		87	240	265	301	353	14
Chinese	7			2	1	1		
Czech and Slovak	2,872	1,908	4,826	5,010	5,534	3,046	2,857	407
Danish	2,066	983	1,467	3,778	3,732	2,852	1,184	65
Dutch	1,821	1,020	1,643	2,066	1,569	1,252	1,110	38
Egyptian	3							
Estonian	65	27	77	110	107	98	83	8
Finnish	6,123	1,561	4,721	5,054	3,674	4,614	2,749	100
French	351	457	521	875	675	775	424	94
German	2,560	6,560	10,943	12,689	14,089	13,907	10,602	797
Greek	215	214	274	557	685	684	530	23
Hungarian	1,107	2,741	5,182	5,781	6,265	5,375	3,279	493
Icelandic	48	50	31	28	26	8	25	
Indian[5]	49	57	68	56	55	49	80	52
Iranian	10	19	4	6	1	1	1	1
Italian	2,676	1,652	2,539	4,440	849	1,243	1,104	467
Japanese	510	424	443	511	535	179	217	174
Jewish	5,428	2,637	4,441	4,744	3,532	3,353	3,702	214

Origin								
Lebanese[6]	43	42	43	19	41	41	39	51
Lithuanian								
Luxemburger	2							
Maltese					4	2	1	
Mexican					6	1	2	
Negro[7]	9	16	9	3	4	9	5	10
Norwegian	54	29	34	27	35	22	28	38
Polish	379	360	392	405	378	632	570	381
Portuguese	2	1	3	3	2	3	1	1
Roumanian	31	27	40	38	59	82	109	23
Russian	74	63	47	84	73	125	151	129
Spanish	7	11	8	6	10	17	7	1
Swedish	34	13	15	26	15	44	18	14
Swiss	17	21	15	38	44	92	50	75
Syrian	20	13	13	26	19	12	22	14
Turkish		2			1	1		
Ukrainian	438	378	563	476	801	1,206	1,880	1,753
Yugoslav[8]	171	192	286	302	377	462	576	256
Others								
From the United States[9]	13,709	8,500	6,071	5,291	4,876	5,555	5,833	5,649

Source: Division of Immigration, Department of Manpower and Immigration.
[1] Fiscal years from 1900-1901 to 1907-1908, calendar years from 1908 to 1965.
[2] Excludes those of Egyptian, Syrian, and Lebanese origin.
[3] Included with those of German origin from 1926 to 1952.
[4] Includes those of English, Irish, Welsh, and Scottish origin, immigrants from Newfoundland (before 1949), Bermuda, and the British West Indies (Jamaica, Trinidad, Barbados, etc.).

(Table 4—cont'd)

Ethnic origin	1940	1941	1942	1943	1944	1945	1946	1947
Total	11,324	9,329	7,576	8,504	12,801	22,722	71,719	64,127
Albanian								2
Arab[2]								1
Armenian	3		1			3	11	8
Austrian[3]								
Belgian	32	13		6	10	15	724	843
British[4]	3,021	2,300	2,259	3,834	7,713	14,677	51,408	38,747
Bulgarian	1							6
Chinese							8	20
Czech and Slovak	79	17	12	7	12	44	206	261
Danish	21	7	5	6	13	21	83	195
Dutch	67	18	7	10	21	60	2,146	3,192
Egyptian	1	1	1	2	1	7	8	282
Estonian	3	1			1	6	22	43
Finnish	119	116	67	129	234	454	1,767	523
French	53	21	13	11	42	98	449	300
German	49	3	1	1	3	18	61	659
Greek	77	6		2	15	16	83	96
Hungarian			1		2	2	15	8
Icelandic	6	1	3			1	4	116
Indian[5]	1				1		2	5
Iranian								
Italian	93	2		3	15	43	145	139
Japanese	43	4					1	

Jewish	329	132	41	44	74	347		
Latvian	3			2		2	5	448
Lebanese[6]								
Lithuanian	8		1	2	4	3	19	1,273
Luxemburger								
Maltese		1		1	1	5	12	16
Mexican			4		1	2	2	3
Negro[7]	29	29	25	3	18	50	125	94
Norwegian	24	8	5	6	15	69	269	178
Polish	19	16	3	6	32	249	565	2,610
Portuguese	4	5		2	6	8	38	25
Roumanian	8	2		2	3	3	19	29
Russian	10	12	7	5	8	40	154	234
Spanish	28	8	7	8	14	22	57	46
Swedish	8	2	5	3	5	21	86	63
Swiss	12	8	9	5	9	10	72	148
Syrian	1	2		1	6	12	11	25
Turkish				1			6	1
Ukrainian	3				8	12	114	2,044
Yugoslav[8]	35		1	1	3	8	26	146
Others					2		10	2
From the United States[9]	7,134	6,594	5,098	4,401	4,509	6,394	11,469	9,440

[5] Includes immigrants from India, Pakistan, and Ceylon.
[6] Included with those of Syrian origin until 1955.
[7] Except from the United States.
[8] Includes those of Croatian, Macedonian, Serbian, and Slovene origin.
[9] Not divided by ethnic origin.

(Table 4—cont'd)

Ethnic origin	1948	1949	1950	1951	1952	1953	1954	1955	1956
Total	125,414	95,217	73,912	194,391	164,498	168,868	154,227	109,946	164,857
Albanian	20	51	28	54	16	14	25	21	5
Arab[2]	5	25	28	52	69	17	14	56	86
Armenian	10	7	35	80	71	70	68	131	181
Austrian[3]						3,574	3,841	1,779	2,948
Belgian	1,071	714	457	2,638	1,349	1,431	1,328	988	2,127
British[4]	46,057	22,201	13,427	31,370	42,675	47,077	44,593	30,150	51,319
Bulgarian	68	78	85	360	109	54	48	39	30
Chinese	74	797	1,741	2,697	2,313	1,929	1,950	2,575	2,093
Czech and Slovak	1,433	2,076	1,441	3,142	949	543	295	252	297
Danish	616	863	905	4,613	2,056	1,562	1,399	1,393	3,642
Dutch	10,169	7,782	7,404	19,130	21,213	20,472	16,340	6,929	7,956
Egyptian								17	10
Estonian	1,903	2,945	1,949	4,573	934	451	290	186	162
Finnish	200	236	483	4,130	2,293	1,232	697	632	1,094
French	1,074	1,021	1,188	6,193	4,212	3,136	2,813	2,225	3,106
German	3,051	5,988	5,825	32,395	28,257	35,015	29,845	18,082	26,457
Greek	712	719	866	2,885	1,691	2,059	2,892	3,014	5,236
Hungarian	1,130	1,633	1,577	4,376	1,435	858	502	427	4,274
Icelandic	3	14	13	18	35	53	39	19	41
Indian[5]	67	51	77	97	168	139	175	245	330
Iranian	1	2	2	7	10	18	10	13	10
Italian	3,202	7,742	9,059	24,351	21,383	24,293	24,595	20,247	29,806
Japanese	5	11	11	3	6	46	71	97	120
Jewish									1,632
Latvian	3,073	2,847	1,767	2,789	1,437	550	456	340	334

Lebanese[6]	4,336	2,248	960	1,330	762	278	246	206	408
Lithuanian								158	190
Luxemburger								37	153
Maltese	715	240	840	1,600	692	745	935	349	378
Mexican	4		2	12	6	6	4	6	23
Negro[7]	125	132	90	91	105	167	167	310	504
Norwegian	355	355	237	896	1,209	939	993	709	842
Polish	13,799	12,233	6,612	12,938	5,485	3,176	2,274	1,886	2,269
Portuguese	51	66	87	157	256	555	1,324	1,427	1,971
Roumanian	534	391	392	995	388	269	214	93	137
Russian	1,406	885	604	2,273	1,072	485	355	241	234
Spanish	70	51	67	671	312	257	207	289	532
Swedish	137	172	139	798	503	435	306	271	387
Swiss	281	294	409	1,061	1,274	826	961	597	1,044
Syrian	31	72	86	208	209	190	233	95	67
Turkish	3	1	9	19	18	35	25	18	48
Ukrainian	10,011	6,570	3,769	6,894	2,821	908	692	516	540
Yugoslav[8]	2,845	1,460	1,013	4,144	2,176	1,999	1,541	1,375	1,993
Others		1		20	46	43	20	30	64
From the United States[9]	7,381	7,744	7,799	7,732	9,306	9,379	10,110	10,392	9,777

Source: Division of Immigration, Department of Manpower and Immigration.

1 Fiscal years from 1900-1901 to 1907-1908, calendar years from 1908-1965.
2 Excludes those of Egyptian, Syrian, and Lebanese origin.
3 Included with those of German origin from 1926 to 1952.
4 Includes those of English, Irish, Welsh, and Scottish origin, immigrants from Newfoundland (before 1949), Bermuda, and the British West Indies (Jamaica, Trinidad, Barbados, etc.).

(Table 4—cont'd)

Ethnic origin	1957	1958	1959	1960	1961	1962	1963	1964	1965
Total	282,164	124,851	106,928	104,111	71,689	74,586	93,151	112,606	146,758
Albanian	22	13	18	33	43	27	51	20	24
Arab[2]	87	69	60	81	58	65	153	205	260
Armenian	272	189	231	143	176	769	899	841	871
Austrian[3]	2,293	905	748	953	583	445	538	671	766
Belgian	2,786	1,000	814	739	707	516	509	674	650
British[4]	112,828	26,622	19,361	20,853	13,295	16,635	25,256	29,928	39,523
Bulgarian	59	15	44	42	25	17	23	32	73
Chinese	1,662	2,615	2,561	1,370	861	826	1,502	3,176	5,182
Czech and Slovak	307	139	112	133	96	81	77	162	207
Danish	7,790	1,799	1,372	1,126	484	606	612	739	895
Dutch	12,310	7,595	5,354	5,598	1,960	1,681	1,812	2,061	2,628
Egyptian	52	19	16	12	7	62	241	379	423
Estonian	221	122	88	134	52	51	63	44	59
Finnish	2,829	1,258	890	993	350	340	285	415	580
French	5,471	2,539	1,797	2,179	1,731	2,109	2,559	3,155	3,367
German	29,564	14,449	10,781	10,792	6,191	5,118	4,906	5,128	7,454
Greek	5,631	5,418	4,965	5,009	3,858	4,164	5,554	5,127	6,630
Hungarian	29,825	2,723	1,044	1,207	734	759	902	987	1,212
Icelandic	56	43	23	12	5	1	12	16	3
Indian[5]	324	451	716	673	744	814	1,301	2,167	3,784
Iranian	24	13	8	13	18	28	41	35	137
Italian	29,443	28,564	26,822	21,308	14,630	14,181	15,887	21,091	28,893
Japanese	178	188	191	159	116	134	174	137	203
Jewish	5,472	2,290	2,686	2,385	1,510	1,349	1,697	2,636	2,269
Latvian	415	186	123	141	98	56	72	48	81

Lebanese[6]	348	244	279	225	200	422	579	624	748
Lithuanian	168	140	87	80	86	34	46	49	54
Luxemburger	124	26	12	12	8	13	21	12	9
Maltese	654	473	422	481	207	364	895	1,191	1,130
Mexican	15	29	21	38	22	18	14	22	38
Negro[7]	634	781	989	1,013	1,020	1,377	2,270	2,470	3,853
Norwegian	1,337	471	354	341	180	208	288	289	346
Polish	2,909	2,996	3,733	3,182	2,753	1,956	1,866	2,399	2,566
Portuguese	4,748	2,177	4,354	5,258	2,976	3,398	4,689	6,090	7,040
Roumanian	206	130	148	174	135	143	153	135	127
Russian	375	196	140	158	109	112	108	132	174
Spanish	1,182	639	531	758	768	739	1,351	1,498	1,792
Swedish	763	282	248	227	111	144	160	213	234
Swiss	1,294	793	612	742	591	584	588	737	1,100
Syrian	76	21	49	19	36	109	80	164	227
Turkish	91	99	82	122	129	130	285	325	521
Ukrainian	494	351	295	298	128	122	164	154	230
Yugoslav[8]	5,725	4,868	2,304	3,517	2,266	1,965	2,383	3,055	3,151
Others	92	65	105	131	116	271	349	608	2,101
From the United States[9]	11,008	10,846	11,338	11,247	11,516	11,643	11,736	12,565	15,143

[5] Includes immigrants from India, Pakistan, and Ceylon.
[6] Included with those of Syrian origin until 1955.
[7] Except from the United States.
[8] Includes those of Croatian, Macedonian, Serbian, and Slovene origin.
[9] Not divided by ethnic origin.

Table 5

POPULATION BY ETHNIC GROUPS, CANADA AND THE PROVINCES 1971

	New-found-land	Prince Edward Island	Nova Scotia	New Bruns-wick	Quebec	Ontario	Mani-toba
				%			
British Isles	93.9	82.7	77.5	57.7	10.8	59.3	41.9
French	3.0	13.8	10.1	37.1	79.1	9.6	8.9
Austrian n.e.s.	—	—	—	—	—	0.2	0.3
Belgian	—	0.1	0.1	0.1	0.1	0.3	0.9
Chinese	0.1	—	0.1	0.1	0.2	0.5	0.3
Czech	—	—	0.1	—	0.1	0.3	0.4
Danish	—	0.1	0.1	0.3	—	0.2	0.4
Dutch	0.1	1.1	1.9	0.8	0.2	2.7	3.6
East Indian	0.1	0.1	0.2	0.1	0.1	0.4	0.3
Estonian	—	—	—	—	—	0.2	—
Finnish	—	—	—	—	—	0.5	0.1
German	0.5	0.9	5.2	1.3	0.9	6.2	12.5
Greek	—	—	0.2	0.1	0.7	0.9	0.2
Hungarian	—	—	0.1	0.1	0.2	0.9	0.5
Icelandic	—	—	—	—	—	—	1.3
Indian (native)	0.2	0.3	0.6	0.6	0.5	0.8	4.4
Inuit	0.2	—	—	—	0.1	—	—
Italian	0.1	0.1	0.5	0.2	2.8	6.0	1.1
Japanese	—	—	—	—	—	0.2	0.1
Jewish	0.1	0.1	0.3	0.2	1.9	1.8	2.0
Latvian	—	—	—	—	—	0.2	0.1
Lithuanian	—	—	—	—	0.1	0.2	0.1
Norwegian	0.1	0.1	0.3	0.2	0.1	0.3	0.8
Polish	0.1	0.1	0.4	0.1	0.4	1.9	4.3
Portuguese	0.1	—	0.1	—	0.3	0.8	0.4
Roumanian	—	—	—	—	—	0.1	0.1
Russian	—	—	—	—	0.1	0.2	0.4
Slovak	—	—	—	—	—	0.2	0.1
Spanish	—	—	0.1	—	0.2	0.1	0.1
Swedish	—	—	0.1	0.1	—	0.2	0.9
Syrian-Lebanese	0.1	0.2	0.3	0.2	0.1	0.1	0.1
Ukrainian	—	0.1	0.3	0.1	0.3	2.1	11.6
West Indian	—	—	0.1	—	0.1	0.3	0.1
Yugoslav	—	—	—	—	0.1	0.9	0.3
Others and unknown	1.3	0.2	1.3	0.6	0.5	1.4	1.3
TOTALS	100.0	100.0	100.0	100.0	100.0	100.0	100.0
Number	522,105	111,645	788,960	634,560	6,027,765	7,703,105	988,245

Source: *Perspective Canada*, Statistics Canada, Information Canada, Ottawa, 1974, p. 264.

Table 5 (cont.)

POPULATION BY ETHNIC GROUPS, CANADA AND THE PROVINCES 1971—
Concluded

	Saskat-chewan	Alberta	British Columbia	Yukon	North-west Terri-tories	Canada
			%			
British Isles	42.1	46.7	57.8	48.5	25.2	44.6
French	6.1	5.8	4.4	6.7	6.5	28.7
Austrian n.e.s.	0.4	0.4	0.5	0.6	0.2	0.2
Belgian	0.4	0.3	0.2	0.3	0.2	0.2
Chinese	0.5	0.8	2.0	0.5	0.3	0.6
Czech	0.5	0.6	0.4	0.4	0.2	0.3
Danish	0.6	1.2	1.0	0.8	0.5	0.4
Dutch	2.1	3.6	3.2	2.8	1.0	2.0
East Indian	0.2	0.3	0.9	0.1	0.2	0.3
Estonian	—	0.1	0.1	0.1	—	0.1
Finnish	0.2	0.2	0.5	0.5	0.1	0.3
German	19.4	14.2	9.0	8.5	3.8	6.1
Greek	0.1	0.2	0.3	0.1	0.1	0.6
Hungarian	1.5	1.0	0.8	1.1	0.3	0.6
Icelandic	0.3	0.2	0.3	0.2	0.2	0.1
Indian (native)	4.4	2.7	2.4	14.0	20.6	1.4
Inuit	—	—	—	0.1	32.8	0.1
Italian	0.3	1.5	2.5	0.9	0.7	3.4
Japanese	—	0.3	0.6	0.2	—	0.2
Jewish	0.2	0.4	0.6	0.2	0.1	1.4
Latvian	—	0.1	0.1	0.1	—	0.1
Lithuanian	0.1	0.1	0.1	0.1	—	0.1
Norwegian	3.9	3.2	2.4	2.6	1.5	0.8
Polish	2.9	2.7	1.4	1.3	0.8	1.5
Portuguese	—	0.1	0.4	0.1	0.1	0.4
Roumanian	0.6	0.3	0.2	0.4	0.1	0.1
Russian	1.1	0.6	1.1	0.4	0.2	0.3
Slovak	0.1	0.2	0.1	—	0.1	0.1
Spanish	—	0.1	0.1	0.1	0.1	0.1
Swedish	1.6	1.5	1.5	1.7	0.5	0.5
Syrian-Lebanese	0.1	0.1	—	—	—	0.1
Ukrainian	9.3	8.3	2.8	3.3	1.8	2.7
West Indian	—	0.1	—	0.1	—	0.1
Yugoslav	0.2	0.5	0.7	0.8	0.3	0.5
Others and unknown	0.8	1.6	1.6	2.4	1.5	1.0
TOTALS	100.0	100.0	100.0	100.0	100.0	100.0
Number	926,245	1,627,875	2,184,620	18,390	34,810	21,568,310

Source: *Perspective Canada*, Statistics Canada, Information Canada, Ottawa, 1974, p. 264.

Tables 6 and 7 show the population and the relative proportion of each "other" ethnic category from 1871 to 1971. One first notices that Germans and Dutch formed over 80% of the other ethnic groups in 1871, but since the arrival of the other groups, their proportion has declined. Although Germans are still the largest non-charter group in Canada, Italians and Ukrainians have also formed a substantial proportion of the noncharter group ethnic population for several decades. Because some geographical concentration exists, it means that within a region or large urban centre, specific ethnic collectivities may make up relatively large proportions of the population.

CHART 2   ETHNIC GROUPS OTHER THAN BRITISH AND FRENCH

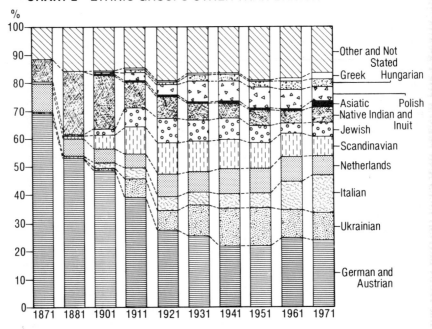

Source: *Perspective Canada,* Statistics Canada, Information Canada, Ottawa, 1974, p. 263.

In sum, we find that the character of Canada's population has been heavily influenced by immigration. It would not be wrong to characterize it as a "nation of immigrants." However, it would be wrong to assume that Canada comprises only "foreigners." Well over 80% of the total population have been born in Canada and thus are Canadian citizens. Only in Ontario and B.C. are there less than 80% native born.

The Changing Ethnic Composition of Canada: Recent Trends

The vast majority (79.7% in 1971) of foreign-born Canadian residents were born in Europe. However, with some liberalization of immigration policies (in 1962 and 1967), during the sixties and particularly the seventies, European countries have been progressively and rapidly de-emphasized as sources for emigrants to Canada. For example, between 1966 and 1973 the proportion of immigrants ar-

POPULATION BY ETHNIC ORIGIN OTHER THAN BRITISH ISLES AND FRENCH FOR CANADA, 1871, 1881, AND 1901-1971

Ethnic Group	1871	1881	1901	1911	1921	1931	1941	1951	1961	1971
					(1,000s)					
Other European	240	299	458	945	1,247	1,825	2,044	2,554	4,117	4,960
Austrian, n.o.s.	—	—	11	44	108	49	38	32	107	42
Belgian	—	—	3	10	20	28	30	35	61	51
Czech-Slovak	—	—	—	—	9	30	43	64	73	82
Finnish[a]	—	—	3	16	21	44	42	44	59	59
German	203	254	311	403	295	474	465	620	1,050	1,317
Greek	—	—	—	4	6	9	12	14	56	124
Hungarian[b]	—	—	2	12	13	41	55	60	126	132
Italian	1	2	11	46	67	98	113	152	450	731
Jewish	—	1	16	76	126	157	170	182	173	297
Lithuanian	—	—	—	—	2	6	8	16	28	25
Netherlands	30	30	34	56	118	149	213	264	430	426
Polish	—	—	6	34	53	146	167	220	324	316
Roumanian[c]	—	—	—	6	13	29	25	24	44	27
Russian[d]	1	1	20	44	100	88	84	91	119	64
Scandinavian	2	5	31	113	167	228	245	283	387	385
Ukrainian	—	—	6	75	107	225	306	395	473	581
Yugoslavic	—	—	—	—	4	16	21	21	69	105
Other	4	6	5	7	18	9	10	36	88	195
Asiatic	—	6	24	43	66	85	74	73	122	286
Chinese	—	4	17	28	40	47	35	33	58	119
Japanese	—	—	5	9	16	23	23	22	29	37
Other	—	—	2	6	10	15	16	19	34	129
Other	52	174	177	158	153	158	190	354	463	519

Statistics Canada, 1971 Census of Canada, Bulletin 1.3-2, Ottawa, Information Canada, 1973, Table 1. Dominion Bureau of Statistics, 1961 Census of Canada, Bulletin 7.1-6, Ottawa, The Queen's Printer, 1966, Table 1.

a Includes Estonian prior to 1951.
b Includes Lithuanian and Moravian in 1901 and 1911.
c Includes Bulgarian in 1901 and 1911.
d Includes Finnish and Polish in 1871 and 1881.

Source: W. Kalbach and W. McVey, The Demographic Bases of Canadian Society, (2nd ed.), McGraw-Hill Ryerson, Toronto, 1979, pp. 198-199.

Table 7

POPULATION BY ETHNIC GROUP

	1871	1911	1921	1931	1951	1961	1971
				%			
Austrian	—	3.8	7.3	2.4	1.1	2.3	0.7
Belgian	—	0.8	1.4	1.3	1.2	1.3	0.9
Czech and Slovak	—	—	0.6	1.5	2.1	1.6	1.4
Dutch	10.1	4.9	8.0	7.2	8.9	9.1	7.4
Finnish	—	1.4	1.5	2.1	1.5	1.3	1.0
German	69.4	35.2	20.1	22.9	20.8	22.3	22.9
Greek	—	0.3	0.4	0.5	0.5	1.2	2.2
Hungarian	—	1.0	0.9	2.0	2.0	2.7	2.3
Italian	0.4	4.0	4.6	4.7	5.1	9.6	12.7
Jewish	—	6.7	8.6	7.6	6.1	3.7	5.2
Lithuanian	—	—	0.1	0.3	0.5	0.6	0.4
Polish	—	2.9	3.6	7.0	7.4	6.9	5.5
Roumanian	—	0.5	0.9	1.4	0.8	0.9	0.5
Russian	0.2	3.9	6.8	4.3	3.1	2.5	1.1
Scandinavian[1]	0.6	9.8	11.4	11.0	9.5	8.2	6.7
Portuguese[2]	—	—	—	—	—	—	1.7
Ukrainian	—	6.6	7.3	10.9	13.2	10.1	10.1
Yugoslav	—	—	0.3	0.8	0.7	1.4	1.8
Other European	1.3	0.6	1.2	0.4	1.2	1.9	1.7
Chinese	—	2.4	2.7	2.3	1.1	1.2	2.1
Japanese	—	0.8	1.1	1.1	0.7	0.6	0.6
Other Asiatic	—	0.6	0.7	0.7	0.6	0.7	2.2
Native Indian and Inuit	7.9	9.2	7.8	6.2	5.6	4.7	5.4
Other and not stated	10.1	4.6	2.7	1.4	6.3	5.2	3.5
TOTALS (other than French and British)	100.0	100.0	100.0	100.0	100.0	100.0	100.0
Number in thousands	293	1,147	1,465	2,068	2,980	4,699	5,764
French	31.1	28.6	27.9	28.2	30.8	30.4	28.7
British	60.5	55.5	55.4	51.9	47.9	43.8	44.6
Other	8.4	15.9	16.7	19.9	21.3	25.8	26.7
TOTALS	100.0	100.0	100.0	100.0	100.0	100.0	100.0
Number in thousands	3,689	7,207	8,788	10,377	14,009	18,238	21,568

[1] Includes Danish, Icelandic, Norwegian and Swedish.
[2] Included with "Other European" prior to 1971.
Source: *Perspective Canada*, Statistics Canada, Information Canada, Ottawa, 1974, p. 262.

riving from European sources declined from 76% to 39%, while arrivals from Asian sources increased from 6% to 23%. Generally all continents and major regions of the Third World (mostly less developed countries) have been increasing their proportion of the immigrant flow into Canada since the fifties, but particularly during the late sixties and seventies, coinciding with a steady and most recently marked decline in the flow from more developed countries in Europe (excluding industrialized Japan, Australia, New Zealand, and the United States).

Table 8

PERCENTAGE DISTRIBUTION OF IMMIGRANTS BY SOURCE AREA, 1950-73

Area	1950-55	1956-61	1962-67	1968-73
Africa	0.4	1.0	2.2	3.3
Asia	2.8	2.7	7.2	16.8
Australasia	0.8	1.4	2.2	2.3
Europe	88.0	84.8	73.5	49.9
North & Central America (except U.S.A.)	0.7	1.0	2.8	8.4
U.S.A.	6.3	7.7	10.4	15.2
South America	0.8	1.3	1.6	3.6
	0.2	0.1	0.1	0.5
	100.0	100.0	100.0	100.0

Source: Calculated from Immigration and Population Statistics. Ottawa: Dept. of Manpower and Immigration, 1975.

It could also be noted that by 1973 the majority (57%) of immigrants from Africa, Asia, and Latin America to Canada had arrived within the past five years, compared to a small proportion (18.7%) of immigrants from Europe, the United States and Australia.

Table 9

PROPORTION OF IMMIGRANTS ARRIVING 1968-73 (OUT OF TOTAL IMMIGRANTS BETWEEN 1946 AND 1973), BY WORLD REGIONS

Region	Number of Immigrants 1946-73	Number of Immigrants 1968-73	% arriving 1968-73
Europe	2,871,173	459,881	16.0
United States	384,137	139,857	36.4
Australia & New Zealand	60,886	21,345	35.1
Total above regions	3,316,196	621,083	18.7
Africa	63,120	30,820	48.8
Latin America & Caribbean	183,093	109,810	60.0
Asia & Oceania	280,554	159,611	56.9
Total Third World	526,767	300,241	57.0
Total Canada	3,842,963	921,324	24.0

Source: Calculated from Immigration and Population Statistics. Ottawa: Dept. of Manpower and Immigration, 1975.

British immigrants have consistently maintained the position of the U.K. as the largest single source of emigrants to Canada. The British proportion of the total immigrant flow declined abruptly from 71.6% in 1947 to 18.2% in 1950, then has fluctuated but has never exceeded 32.5% (1966) or been lower than 12.7% (1971). Although the sheer number of British immigrants has been falling sharply according to the most recent data, up to the time of writing this chapter the British proportion stood at approximately 15%.

The total flows from Third World sources together did not exceed the European flows until 1976. Some recent major influxes have come from European sources, such as an estimated 285,000 immigrants from Britain, 82,000 from Portugal, and 72,000 from Italy during the past decade. However, the most dramatic influx of immigrants has been from the Third World. To cite some examples: First, 40,944 immigrants from India and Pakistan arrived from 1968 to 1973. The proportion of immigrants from these two countries increased steadily from 1.8% in 1965 to 7% by 1974. During the 1969 to 1972 period, over 6,000 a year were arriving; then the flow increased sharply to between 11,000 and 16,000 a year since 1973. India has been ranked the fourth principal supplier of immigrants since 1973 with about 5% of the total immigrant flow. Second, the migration from the non-Latin Caribbean (i.e., the former British, French, and Dutch sphere) has been even more significant; 73,270 English, French, or Dutch-speaking West Indians immigrated directly from the Caribbean and the Guianas during 1968 to 1973 (including 27,792 from Jamaica, 24,866 from Trinidad and Tobago, 13,946 from Guyana, 5,937 from Haiti, and 4,927 from Barbados). The most recent data suggest an influx of at least 13,000 West Indians a year from the Caribbean, the majority from Jamaica (ranked fifth in 1976), Guyana (ranked ninth) and Trinidad. (The problem in accurately estimating East Indian and West Indian immigrant flows will be discussed later in dealing with methodological problems). Third, Hong Kong has been ranked the third major source of Canadian immigrants for the past several years; 45,377 Chinese from Hong Kong alone arrived between 1968 and 1973. The Chinese proportion of the total Canadian immigration fluctuated between about 1% and 3% between 1950 and 1967, then increased steadily to about 8% in 1973. By 1968/69 more than 8,000 Chinese a year were entering Canada as landed immigrants; this number declined slightly to approximately 5-6,000 during the early seventies, then increased markedly to 13-15,000 in 1973/75 and probably over 18,000 by 1976/77 (with 8,821 arriving during the first half of 1976 from Hong Kong alone). The Philippines contributed 23,802 immigrants between 1968 and 1973; by 1976 immigrants from that source were arriving at a rate of about 6,000 a year (with the Philippines ranked seventh). Latin America countries contributed 36,445 immigrants between 1968 and 1973; by 1977 Latin American immigrants were arriving at a rate of almost 9,000 a year.

Immigrants who entered Canada as refugees have contributed substantially to recent flows from Third World countries. In just three months (Sept.-Nov. 1972) 4,420 Ugandan Asians were admitted to Canada; eventually the number of Ugandan refugees in Canada reached at least 7,000. Similarly, in just a two-month period (May-June 1975) 4,580 South Vietnamese and Cambodian refugees were accepted to Canada. Between September 1973 and June 1975, 1,786 Chileans entered officially classified as refugees, while perhaps an equal number had entered by mid-1975 through ordinary immigration processes (Cobus, 1977). Between 1968 and 1973 7,333 Lebanese arrived, but more than that number probably arrived as an immediate result of the civil war in that country in 1976/77 alone. It has been estimated that most of the more than 2,000 immigrants to Saskatchewan in 1976/77 were Chilean and Lebanese refugees who settled in Saskatoon and Regina (Sheila Robertson in *Saskatoon Star-Phoenix*, Sept. 30, 1977).

The Growth and Distribution of Non-White Immigrant Populations in Canada

Longitudinal analysis of destination statistics, referring to the intended destinations of immigrants upon arrival in Canada, reveals that for decades the majority of European immigrants consistently chose Ontario as their preferred destination, whereas immigrants arriving from Third World countries and regions (mostly non-Whites) tended to be more evenly distributed, excepting, perhaps, the most recent influx (D'Costa 1975). For example, between 1956 and 1971 British Columbia received a higher proportion of Third World immigrants than Ontario, as did Quebec between 1962 and 1970. However, by 1971 almost half of the Third World immigrants were found in Ontario, which had more than double the proportion of Quebec and approximately triple the proportion of British Columbia.

Table 10
DISTRIBUTION OF IMMIGRANTS FROM THIRD WORLD COUNTRIES, BY PROVINCE, 1971

Ontario	151,990	48.2%
Quebec	67,885	21.5
British Columbia	52,935	16.8
Alberta	19,165	06.1
Manitoba	11,640	03.7
Saskatchewan	5,340	01.7
Nova Scotia	3,365	01.1
New Brunswick	1,405	00.4
Newfoundland	1,100	00.3
Prince Edward Island	240	00.1
Total Canada	315,390	100%

Source: Calculated from Statistics Canada, 1971 Census of Canada, Catalogue 92-727, Vol. 1, Part 3, Bulletin 1.3-6, "Population: Birthplace."

Moreover, the disproportionate share of Third World immigrants claimed by Toronto has clearly increased since 1971. The vast majority of the approximately 459,000 immigrants from Third World sources who arrived during the next five years after the 1971 census settled in Ontario, particularly in Toronto.

Let us now take a closer look at the population trends and changing distribution of non-White immigrant groups in Canada, specifically the Chinese, Japanese, South Asians, and Blacks and West Indians.

Chinese were among the earliest non-White immigrants to enter Canada.

Perhaps the first influx in considerable numbers was into British Columbia between 1858 and 1866, attracted to Canada with the opening of the Cariboo goldfields after previous experience in the California gold rush of 1849; prior to migrating to North America many of these Chinese had been farm labourers in Kwang-tung. Many of these earliest arrivals left Canada after the late 1860s, while those remaining typically moved into restaurants, laundries, shoemaking, tailoring, gardening, domestic services, etc. The as yet small Chinese population in Canada was augmented between 1881 and 1885 with the importation of thousands of coolies by the Canadian Pacific Railway to work in railway-building gangs, mostly in interior B.C. While some returned to China, many remained in Canada, although further immigration was restricted with the tenfold increase of a head tax from $50 in 1885 to $500 in 1903. Nonetheless, the Chinese minority continued to grow steadily: from 17,312 in 1901 to 27,831 in 1911 and 39,587 in 1921. Finally in 1923 all Chinese were refused entry to Canada, cutting off the supply of females in particular; the Chinese Immigration Act of 1923 was not repealed until 1947. Thus the Chinese population declined from 46,519 in 1931 to 34,627 in 1941, and remained fairly static during the 1940s, by which time half of the Chinese in Canada, mostly men, were still in B.C. With the immigration of families after 1947, the Chinese population grew from 32,528 in 1951 to 58,197 in 1961. Then the rate of Chinese immigration increased rapidly with the gradual liberalization of immigration policies, concomitant with a redistribution of Chinese population. Of 118,815 Chinese counted in the 1971 census, 36,405 (30.6%) were in metro Vancouver (30,640 in the city proper compared to 15,223 in 1961); 26,285 (22.1%) were in metro Toronto (17,755 in the city proper cf. 6,715 in 1961); and 10,655 (9%) were in metro Montreal (7,420 in the city proper cf. 3,330 in 1961). An additional 48,675 immigrants arrived from Hong Kong, China, and Taiwan (almost entirely from Hong Kong) just during 1972 to 1975, and about 18,000 a year in 1976/77. The emergence of Toronto as a major concentration of recent Chinese immigrants became apparent. The Chinese population of that city had been only about 4,000 in 1951; by 1961 it had almost doubled, half living in Chinatown; then by 1971 it tripled, and recent data suggest an estimated 50,000 Chinese in that city by the mid-seventies.

There were only a few hundred Japanese in Canada by 1896, but then male laborers imported their families so that the Japanese population grew rapidly within five years to 4,738 in 1901 and then almost doubled within a decade to 9,067 in 1911. Despite Canadian government limitation of Japanese immigration as early as 1908, when entrants were restricted to family members, the Japanese minority continued to grow, to 15,868 by 1921 and 23,342 by 1931, although a static trend prevailed during the thirties, the Japanese population being only 23,149 in 1941. About 96% of these Japanese in 1941 were residents in British Columbia, especially downtown Vancouver and Steveston in the Fraser Delta, and to a lesser extent in the Okanagan and in Victoria. In 1942 they were classified as enemy aliens due to Japan's aggression in the war, in spite of the fact that the vast majority were Canadian citizens and most were Canadian-born; their property was confiscated and auctioned-off; and they were deported to concentration camps in interior B.C., Alberta, and Northern Ontario. At the end of the war over 11,600 Japanese were in interior B.C., where they remained to form substantial proportions of the population of Greenwood and New Denver, but most eventually left other communities (Slocan, Sandon, Kaslo) and one settlement (Tashme) was completely dissolved. Gradually most of the evacuated Japanese gravitated back to the Vancouver area or resettled in Toronto, although the Lethbridge area in Alberta retained quite a concentration (about 3,000 in 1971). A relatively small number were repatriated back to Japan. The Japanese population in Canada had declined to 21,663 in 1951, then it increased to 29,157 in 1961 and 37,260 in 1971. By the 1960s almost equal numbers of Japanese (about 11,000) were found in B.C. and Ontario. About 70% were Nisei (Canadian-born) as opposed to Issei (born in Japan). By 1971 the Japanese minority in Toronto considerably outnumbered their counterparts in Vancouver. Eleven thousand six hundred and ninety (31.4% of the total Japanese-Canadian population) were in metro Toronto (where they were widely scattered, with only 3,880 in the city proper, down from 4,407 in 1961), compared to 9,050 (24.3%) in metro Vancouver (most of whom, 5,045, were concentrated in the city proper, cf. 3,132 in 1961). Almost another five thousand Japanese immigrants arrived in Canada between 1968 and 1973; the flow during the seventies has been small compared to the large Chinese influx.

While several thousand South Asians (Indians and Pakistanis) settled in Canada three generations back, the vast majority have arrived very recently. In 1905/6 about five thousand settled in the Vancouver area before immigration officials completely stopped immigration from India. The South Asian population in this area had declined to less than half that number by 1911 (Morrow, 1976). In 1961 there were only 1,560 Asians in the city of Vancouver who were not Chinese or Japanese, compared to 7,720 in 1971. The number of Asians in Canada, excluding Chinese and Japanese, increased almost fourfold from 34,399 in 1961 to 129,460 in 1971. Between 1946 and 1975, 84,957 immigrants arrived from India and Pakistan (excluding, of course, Indians and Pakistanis from such sources as Britain, Uganda, South Africa, Malaysia, Fiji, Mauritius, Trinidad, and Guyana. In the 1971 census, 67,925 South Asians were counted of whom 30,920 (45.5%) were in Ontario (the vast majority in Toronto), and 18,795 (27.7%) in B.C. (mostly in Vancouver). Since that enumeration an additional 45,219 immigrants have arrived from India and Pakistan, along with thousands of South Asians from other source countries.

The population trends among Blacks in Canada have been similar to trends among Chinese in so far as both ethnic minorities have been in Canada for a long period of time, both have had static or declining trends and both have recently been growing very rapidly. For many decades the size of the Black minority has on the whole remained static. As early as 1860 there were an estimated 50,000 Blacks in Canada. However, after the American Civil War ended in 1865 many emigrated back to the United States from which they had temporarily fled with the assistance of abolitionists. By the turn of the century Canadian Blacks numbered only 17,437, and by 1911 their number had fallen slightly, to 16,994. Natural growth of the Black population could not balance emigration. However, the Black minority did begin to grow very slowly, despite continued emigration; in 1921 there were 18,291 Blacks in Canada, in 1931 some 19,456, and in 1941 there were 22,174. In four decades the country had gained little more than five thousand Blacks, and then a wartime decline reduced the minority to 18,020 by

1941. Yet the next decade was to radically alter this trend. Better living conditions aided natural population growth while Toronto, one of the fastest growing cities in North America (according to many reports), and Montreal, then the largest city in Canada, were proving attractive to West Indian and American Negro immigrants. The Black population of Montreal stood at 367 in 1951, that of Toronto at 1,541; by 1961 each of these cities had Black and West Indian populations of over 6,000. In ten years the number of Blacks and West Indians in Canada almost doubled to 32,127 in 1961, but this number was still only three-fifths of the size of the Black population a century earlier. That is, during the century following the American Civil War the natural growth of Canada's Black population, together with immigration of West Indian and American Negroes, did not sufficiently counter the loss of Black population through emigration. But the past national decline notwithstanding, recent growth of the Black and West Indian population has been remarkable. During the sixties the Black and West Indian population again doubled. Of 62,470 Blacks and West Indians in 1971, 44.8% were in metro Toronto and 15% in Montreal; 27,960 were in metro Toronto (11,660 in the city proper cf. 3,153 in 1961); 9,380 in metro Montreal (5,575 in the city proper cf. 2,965 in 1961); 2,085 in metro Halifax (only 960 in the city proper, down from 2,038 in 1961); 1,865 in metro Winnipeg (1,070 in the city proper cf. 661 in 1961); and 1,770 in metro Vancouver (930 in the city proper cf. 572 in 1961). With growth of the Black and West Indian population, largely due to the recent heavy influx of immigrants from the Caribbean, a proportionate redistribution has occurred. Back in 1961 Nova Scotia accounted for 37% of the total Black population in Canada, compared to 34.4% in Ontario; whereas in 1971 the proportion in Nova Scotia had declined to only 10%, compared to 60.4% in Ontario. By the mid-seventies estimates of the Black and West Indian population in Toronto alone ranged as high as 65-80,000.

Have recent non-White immigrants tended to hive off into a separate existence in urban ghettoes within Canadian cities, either willingly or due to discrimination from the White majority? Clearly most of the South Asian and Japanese immigrants are widely scattered. Chinatowns have become increasingly prominent fixtures of the urban scene in Vancouver and most notably Toronto; but probably most Chinese do not live in Chinatown (for example, in 1971 only 4,800 Asians were living within the census tracts including Chinatown out of 26,285 Chinese in Toronto). While at least three major concentrations of West Indians may be discerned in Toronto, it is equally true that many recent immigrants from the Caribbean have not settled in these compact areas. One recent study of the largest of these West Indian neighborhoods (Anderson, 1975) produced some interesting data pertaining to the degree of ethnic enclosure. On the one hand, this study noted the significance of chain migration through kin networks, the proliferation of island associations and clubs, a high emphasis placed by these immigrants on retaining their West Indian identity, a relatively low emphasis on identification with American-origin Blacks, the recency of arrival in Canada in most cases, a limited desire to remain in Canada for long term or to become a Canadian citizen, frequent use of West Indian shops and services in the neighborhood (particularly foodstores and to a lesser extent barbers or hairdressers and restaurants), and finally, a very high proportion of respondents whose friends were also West Indians. On the other hand, this study noted a low proportion of respondents who employed or were employed by other West Indians, a limited awareness of having settled in a West Indian neighborhood on purpose, limited participation in West Indian clubs, associations, or churches, a marked desire to have closer contacts with White Canadians, open-mindedness about interracial intermarriage, and surprisingly little indication of respondents having *personally* experienced discrimination in housing, employment, social interaction, or even immigration processes. The latter finding was particularly interesting, in view of ample evidence of discriminatory treatment in all of these spheres; yet other studies (Ramcharan, 1975; Head, 1975; and other reports discussed in Anderson, 1978); noted higher indices of discrimination.

Regional Disparities in Immigrant Distribution

Central Canada (Ontario and Quebec) has long been a primary destination or region of settlement for immigrants coming to Canada. However, for at least one decade Western Canada (the Prairie provinces and British Columbia) received considerably more immigrants than did Central Canada. Spurred on by the Dominion government's policy during the Laurier regime, subsidized commercial transportation companies, railway settlement schemes, and ethnic colonization societies, if not by dismal conditions back in the mother countries, millions of immigrants sought "the last, best West" around the turn of the century (Anderson, 1977). Laurier had predicted an inflow of fifty million people by mid-20th century, while CPR executive Lord Strathcona (Donald Smith) had predicted at least eighty million by the end of that century; in fact a government pamphlet had gone even further to suggest that there would be room in Canada for one hundred million (Bruce 1978: 1). Between 1896 and 1914, over three million immigrants arrived in Canada; over a thousand a day were entering by 1911, and in 1913 almost 413,000 came in a single year. Well over a million remained in the West (ibid.).

By 1971, approximately the same number of living immigrants who had arrived *before* 1921 were found in the Prairies (33.3% of total pre-1921 immigrants still living) and in Ontario (34.2%); a *majority* (53.7%) of pre-1921 immigrants were living in Western Canada (including British Columbia). Yet the proportion of more recently arrived immigrants remaining in the Prairie provinces steadily declined (but increased slightly for the immigrants arriving during the sixties): 33.3% of the pre-1921 immigrants were prairie residents in 1971, compared to 26.4% of immigrants who arrived during the twenties, 18.1% during the thirties, 16.1% during the forties, 10.6% during the fifties, and slightly up to 11.0% during the sixties. The majority of immigrants who arrived during two recent decades, the fifties and sixties (54.8% and 55.7%) settled in Ontario, as have the majority of immigrants who have arrived during the seventies. Relatively few immigrants elected to settle in Quebec, although this tendency was somewhat less apparent by the sixties (for example, 9.6% of the total pre-1921 immigrants living in 1971, compared to 17.7% of the immigrants who arrived during the sixties).

In 1971 two-thirds (66%) of the foreign-born population were residents of Central Canada (Ontario & Quebec). Contrasting the geographical distribution of the total Canadian population with that of the foreign-born population by regions, we may note that a higher proportion of the foreign-born population

Table 11

IMMIGRANT POPULATION BY PERIODS OF IMMIGRATION (TO 1971), FOR CANADA AND MAJOR RECEIVING REGIONS, WITH PROPORTIONATE DISTRIBUTION

	to 1921	1921-30	1931-40	1941-50	1951-60	1961-70
Canada	772,030	444,969	87,703	336,429	1,539,561	1,055,595
	100.0	100.0	100.0	100.0	100.0	100.0
Ontario	264,366	198,339	41,959	184,234	664,259	587,930
	34.2	44.6	47.8	54.8	43.1	55.7
Quebec	74,476	46,688	14,202	43,773	209,310	186,895
	09.6	10.5	16.2	13.0	13.6	17.7
B.C.	157,808	71,982	11,300	41,794	140,248	138,015
	20.4	16.2	12.9	12.4	09.1	13.1
Prairie provinces	256,966	117,308	15,875	54,312	163,675	115,595
	33.3	26.4	18.1	16.1	10.6	11.0

Source: Calculated from Statistics Canada, 1971 Census of Canada, Catalogue 92-740, Vol. 1, Part 4, Bulletin 1.4-12, "Characteristics of Persons Born Outside Canada."

was found in Central Canada and the West Coast (British Columbia) than would be expected on the basis of the general population distribution, and conversely a lower proportion in the Atlantic region and the North, while in the Prairies the proportion was roughly what would be expected.

Table 12

DISTRIBUTION OF FOREIGN-BORN BY REGIONS (REGIONS RANKED IN ORDER OF SHEER SIZE OF FOREIGN-BORN POPULATION), 1971

	Total regional population	Canadian-born population	Foreign-born population	% of foreign born in Can. living in that region	% the regional pop. forms of the total Cdn. population	% the foreign born in region form of the total regional population
Central Canada	13,730,870	11,554,555	2,176,315	66.0	63.6	15.8
Prairie provinces	3,542,365	2,998,170	544,195	16.6	16.4	15.4
B.C.	2,184,620	1,687,965	496,655	15.1	10.1	22.7
Atlantic provinces	2,057,265	1,983,700	73,565	2.2	9.5	3.4
Northern Territories	53,190	48,405	4,785	0.2	0.3	9.0

Source: Calculated from Statistics Canada, 1971 Census of Canada, Catalogue 92-740, Vol. 1, Part 4, Bulletin 1.4-12, "Characteristics of Persons Born Outside Canada."

POPULATION BY BIRTHPLACE, BY PROVINCE, 1971

	New-found-land	Prince Edward Island	Nova Scotia	New Bruns-wick	Quebec	Ontario	Mani-toba	Saskat-chewan	Alberta	British Colum-bia	Yukon	North-west Terri-tories	Canada
						%							
Canada	98.3	96.7	95.3	96.2	92.2	77.8	84.7	88.1	82.7	77.3	85.9	93.7	84.7
Austria	—	—	—	—	0.1	0.2	0.4	0.4	0.3	0.3	—	—	0.2
China	—	—	0.1	0.1	0.1	0.2	0.2	0.2	0.4	0.9	—	0.3	0.3
Czechoslovakia	—	—	—	—	0.1	0.3	0.2	0.1	0.3	0.2	—	—	0.2
France	—	0.1	0.1	0.1	0.6	0.1	0.2	0.1	0.1	0.1	—	0.3	0.2
Germany	0.1	0.3	0.4	0.3	0.3	1.3	1.2	0.8	1.6	1.6	1.6	0.6	1.0
Greece	—	—	0.1	—	0.4	0.6	0.1	0.1	0.1	0.1	—	—	0.4
Hungary	—	—	—	—	0.2	0.5	0.3	0.3	0.4	0.3	0.5	—	0.3
Italy	—	—	0.1	0.1	1.5	3.3	0.5	0.1	0.7	1.0	0.5	0.3	1.8
Netherlands	—	0.3	0.2	0.1	0.1	1.0	0.5	0.2	1.1	1.0	0.5	0.3	0.6
Poland	—	—	0.1	0.1	0.4	1.0	1.7	0.9	1.3	0.6	0.5	0.3	0.7
Portugal	—	—	—	—	0.2	0.6	0.3	—	0.1	0.3	—	—	0.3
United Kingdom	0.7	1.0	1.8	1.3	1.1	6.7	4.2	3.1	4.3	8.3	3.8	2.0	4.3
United States	0.4	1.2	1.1	1.3	0.8	1.3	1.2	2.6	2.9	2.6	2.2	0.9	1.4
U.S.S.R.	—	—	0.1	—	0.3	0.9	2.1	1.5	1.2	0.8	—	—	0.7
Yugoslavia	—	—	—	—	0.1	0.7	0.2	0.1	0.3	0.4	0.5	0.3	0.4
Other	0.3	0.4	0.6	0.4	1.6	3.2	2.1	1.4	2.3	4.0	2.2	1.1	2.4
TOTALS	100.0	100.0	100.0	100.0	100.0	100.0	100.0	100.0	100.0	100.0	100.0	100.0	100.0
Number in thousands	522	112	789	635	6,028	7,703	988	926	1,628	2,185	18	35	21,568

Source: Perspective Canada, Statistics Canada, Information Canada, Ottawa, 1974, p. 271.

The data by provinces and territories reveal that about half (51.8%) of the foreign-born residents were living in Ontario alone. That province, as well as British Columbia and Alberta, had a disproportionately high foreign-born population, while the Atlantic provinces, Quebec, Saskatchewan, and the Northwest Territories had a relatively low proportion of foreign-born residents. Ontario rivalled British Columbia in claiming to have the highest proportion of foreign-born in any provincial population (22.2% in Ontario compared to 22.7% in B.C.).

Between January and September 1974, 166,401 landed immigrants were admitted into Canada, of whom 91,141 (54.8%) settled in Ontario, 26,306 (15.8%) in B.C., 25,936 (15.6%) in Quebec, and 10,664 (6.4%) in Alberta. During the same period in 1976, 117,511 were admitted (reflecting a 21% drop over the comparable figure for 1975), of whom 56,871 (48.4%) settled in Ontario. Comparing the 1976 data with the data of the previous year, it seemed that the proportion of immigrants going to Ontario was declining. The number of immigrants arriving in Ontario during the first nine months of 1976 was 20,937 less than the number during the same period in 1975; this was the largest drop for any province. Whereas the proportion heading for Quebec was increasing (from 15.2% in 1975 to 19.2% in 1976). But it is likely that discriminatory language legislation in the latter province will deter non-francophone immigrants from settling in that province rather than in anglophone Canada. At any rate, it is important to stress that Ontario has been receiving about three times the number of immigrants as Quebec. Data indicate that 73,735 immigrants were admitted to Canada during the first six months of 1976, compared to 57,983 in the same period in 1977. Of 32,426 immigrants who arrived during the second quarter (April-June) of 1977, about 16,000 (49.3%) settled in Ontario, 5,400 (16.7%) in Quebec, 6,353 (20%) in B.C. and 3,550 (10.9%) in Alberta. The proportion of francophone immigrants to Quebec most recently has been increasing, comparing data for the first six months of 1977 with the same period during the previous year. In January through June 1977, 69.7% of the 10,059 immigrants to Quebec were francophone or non-anglophone, compared to 66.5% of the 12,996 immigrants the previous year. French-speaking immigrants arriving in Quebec in recent years have included immigrants from France, Belgium, Switzerland, St. Pierre et Miquelon, Haiti and the French Caribbean, Lebanon and francophone Africa (including some French-speaking Sephardic Jews from Morocco).

We have already noted that the proportion of immigrants settling in the Prairie region has steadily declined over the past several decades. However, disparities should also be noted *within* this region. Of the three Prairie provinces, Alberta has consistently had the highest proporton of immigrants. In fact, the majority of living Prairie residents (by 1971) who had immigrated during the past four decades (i.e., since 1931) were living in Alberta, whereas a steadily decreasing proportion of Prairie immigrants were found in Saskatchewan: 33.3% of the pre-1921 Prairie immigrants, compared to 26.1% who settled in this province during the twenties, 20% during the thirties, 16.9% during the forties, 12.8% during the fifties, and 11.5% during the sixties.

Immigrants to Saskatchewan during the peak period, the initial couple of decades in this century, accounted for over 15% of the total immigrant flow into

Table 14

DISTRIBUTION OF FOREIGN-BORN POPULATION BY PROVINCES AND TERRITORIES (RANKED IN ORDER OF SHEER SIZE OF FOREIGN-BORN POPULATION) IN 1971

Prov./Terr.	Total regional population	Canadian-born population	Foreign-born population	% of foreign born in Can. living in that region	% regional pop. forms of total Cdn. pop.	% foreign born in region forms of total reg. pop.
Ontario	7,703,105	5,995,715	1,707,390	51.8	35.7	22.2
British Columbia	2,184,620	1,687,965	496,655	15.1	10.1	22.7
Quebec	6,027,765	5,558,840	468,925	14.2	27.9	7.8
Alberta	1,627,875	1,345,615	282,260	8.6	7.5	17.3
Manitoba	988,250	837,000	151,250	4.6	4.6	15.3
Saskatchewan	926,240	815,555	110,685	3.4	4.3	11.9
Nova Scotia	788,960	751,770	37,190	1.1	3.7	4.7
New Brunswick	634,560	610,825	23,735	0.7	2.9	3.7
Newfoundland	522,105	513,170	8,935	0.3	2.4	1.7
P.E.I.	111,640	107,935	3,705	0.1	0.5	3.3
Yukon	18,385	15,845	2,540	0.1	0.1	13.8
N.W.T.	34,805	32,560	2,245	0.1	0.2	6.5

Source: Calculated from Statistics Canada, 1971 Census of Canada.

Table 15

IMMIGRANT POPULATION BY PERIODS OF IMMIGRATION (TO 1971), PRAIRIE PROVINCES, WITH PROPORTIONATE DISTRIBUTION

	to 1921	1921-30	1931-40	1941-50	1951-60	1961-70
Manitoba	70,289	31,469	4,259	17,408	46,573	35,560
	27.4	26.8	26.8	32.1	28.5	30.8
Saskatchewan	85,590	30,602	3,170	9,158	20,869	13,290
	33.3	26.1	20.0	16.9	12.8	11.5
Alberta	101,087	55,237	8,446	27,746	96,233	66,745
	39.3	47.1	53.2	51.1	58.8	57.7
Total	256,966	117,308	15,875	54,312	163,675	115,595

Source: Calculated from Statistics Canada, Census of Canada.

Table 16

IMMIGRANT ARRIVALS IN SASKATCHEWAN, 1906-1920, FROM A REPORT OF THE CANADIAN DEPARTMENT OF THE INTERIOR

Year	Number of Immigrants	% of Total Canadian Immigration
1906	28,728	15.1
1907	15,307	12.2
1908	30,590	11.6
1909	22,146	15.0
1910	29,218	13.1
1911	40,763	13.1
1912	46,158	13.0
1913	45,147	11.2
1914	40,999	10.6
1915	16,173	11.1
1916	6,001	12.3
1917	9,874	13.1
1918	12,382	15.6
1919	8,552	14.8
1920	14,287	12.1

Source: Canadian Dept. of the Interior, "Saskatchewan: Its Development and Opportunities." Ottawa: Natural Resources Intelligence Service, 1925, p. 8.

Canada certain years and never formed less than 10% of the total Canadian immigration.

The massive waves of immigration into Canada in recent years, reportedly forcing the federal government to repeatedly redesign its immigration policies, certainly has had very little effect on the Prairies and virtually no effect on Saskatchewan. The proportion of new immigrant arrivals destined for Saskatchewan has been declining most rapidly in the most recent years. This trend seems to bear little relationship to the province's recurrent profitable or recessive economic cycles (Saskatoon Star-Phoenix, Feb. 4, 1975). During 1973 and 1974, for example, Saskatchewan-bound immigration declined to the lowest point in fifteen years, only 1% of the total Canadian immigration. Yet this was a period of relative agricultural prosperity coupled with an officially declared shortage of various skilled occupations. During the sixties the proportion of immigrants destined for Saskatchewan typically varied between 1.54% and 2.0% of the total Canadian flow, according to Manpower and Immigration data. Between 1970 and 1972, the proportion dropped to 1.16% and 1.24%, then declined to about 1% in 1973 and 1974 (1,866 out of approximately 184,000 immigrants in 1973 and about 2,000 out of 200,000 the next year). Both Manitoba and Alberta have been attracting more of the recent immigrants than Saskatchewan. For example, during the first nine months of 1974, 10,664 new immigrants were destined for Alberta, compared to 5,638 for Manitoba, but only 1,636 for Saskatchewan. Doubtless this was largely due to the more industrialized base of the Alberta and Manitoba economies and the preference of new immigrants for work in industry rather than in mining or agriculture (where employment opportunities are limited anyway). It might also seem pertinent to add at this point that the mid-decade census in 1976 revealed that Saskatchewan was the only province in which the population declined during the 1971 to 1976 period.

The reasons for recent immigrants settling in Central Canada and perhaps British Columbia rather than other regions are complex. Among the more obvious reasons, first one could note that nominated immigrants (about half of the recent immigrants to Canada) are most likely to have been nominated by relatives in places where most recent immigrants have concentrated, and these nominated immigrants are likely to settle near their relatives. Moreover, a significant consideration is the gravitation of immigrants to principal centres of concentration of their ethnic group, thus softening any possible culture shock experienced in the move and adjustment to Canada; perhaps initially new immigrants find it easier to make friends among co-ethnics. Second, apart from such considerations of kinship and ethnicity, economic factors provide considerable incentive for settling in larger cities with rapidly expanding populations, industrialization, and more diversity in job opportunities. Other factors which could affect immigrant distribution are numerous: for example, a depressed regional economy (e.g., Atlantic provinces); travelling distance (e.g., European or Caribbean immigrants to Western Canada); a forbidding winter climate (particularly unattractive to immigrants from warmer climates, especially for the northern territories); agricultural land already occupied (in the case of would-be rural settlers who might otherwise have continued to settle in the Prairies or Atlantic region in larger numbers). On the other hand, housing tends to be cheaper in the less urbanized regions; there is less competition on the job market for certain types of work in these less developed regions; and above all a new immigration policy would encourage immigrants to locate away from the three largest urban centres (providing that job opportunities are available).

Urban Concentration

According to the 1971 census, a considerably higher proportion of foreign-born Canadian residents than of native-born were living in urban centres:

Table 17

URBAN PROPORTIONS AMONG FOREIGN-BORN AND NATIVE-BORN RESIDENTS IN CANADA, 1971

	Foreign-born	Native-born	Total Canada
Urban	87.8% (2,892,170)	74.1% (13,544,680)	76.2% (16,436,850)
Rural Non-Farm	8.7% (287,365)	18.7% (3,423,140)	17.2% (3,710,505)
Rural Farm	3.5% (116,055)	7.1% (1,304,955)	6.6% (1,420,960)
Total	100% (3,295,530)	100% (18,272,780)	100% (21,568,310)

Source: Calculated from Statistics Canada, 1971 Census of Canada, Catalogue 97-727, Vol. 1, Part 3, Bulletin 1.3-6, "Population: Birthplace."

By 1971 almost nine out of every ten Canadian residents who had not been born in Canada were living in urban areas, contrasting with a fairly high proportion of immigrants who settled in rural areas prior to 1921. In fact, by the seventies the majority of immigrants admitted to Canada each year were proceeding to Ontario and more than half that number were settling specifically in Toronto. During the past few years Toronto has been receiving an *annual* inflow of at least 40,000 immigrants, in other words, more now than any other single city in North America (Hawkins, 1972: 64). This immigration reflects one of the highest rates of urbanization due to immigration in the world today.

It is instructive to examine the urban concentration of immigrants in the context of other demographic trends, namely, the progressive urbanization of the total Canadian population, as well as patterns of internal migration within Canada and particularly within the southern Ontario urban region. Two recent research reports provide pertinent data in these two respects. First, in relating immigration to general urbanization, in a 1976 report for the urban affairs department economists Chris Burke and Derek Ireland have outlined urban population trends and regional disparities. The report recommends encouraging the growth of major cities in Quebec and the Atlantic provinces while distributing population more evenly elsewhere. Presumably this could make the less developed provinces more competitive economically with such wealthier provinces as Ontario. But the report has warned that if current trends continue unchecked, by the end of this century Ontario will gain half of Canada's total population increase at the expense of poorer provinces such as Saskatchewan, while the already significant gap between relatively affluent and poor regions will likely widen.

Second, in relating immigration to internal migration, a 1975 report on "Internal Migration and Immigrant Settlement," prepared by research economist Soren Nielsen, points out that both Toronto and Montreal have experienced net outflows of internal or intra-Canadian migrants, yet have continued to grow because of a heavy net inflow of foreign immigrants. An estimated total of 50,000 internal migrants left Toronto for other areas in Ontario during the period between 1966 and 1971; but their place was more than taken by a foreign immigration of about a quarter of a million persons. The study commented that Toronto's inflow was dominanted by foreign immigrants, Montreal's by migrants from other urban areas in Canada. By 1971 Montreal, Toronto, and Vancouver, Canada's three largest cities, together represented about 30% of the total Canadian population (respectively 12.7%, 12.2% and 5%); and these three cities took in approximately 60% of all domestic and foreign migrants. With the influx of immigrants, particularly non-White migrants from Third World countries, increasing or remaining high during the seventies in these cities, the significance of immigration to urbanization would not likely diminish, were it not for the new 1978 immigration policy encouraging (if not forcing) new immigrants to locate elsewhere than in these cities. The possible effect of this new policy will be discussed below (in the next section of this chapter dealing with "Distribution and Immigration Policies").

CHART 3   RURAL-URBAN DISTRIBUTION SELECTED ETHNIC ORIGINS CANADA: 1971

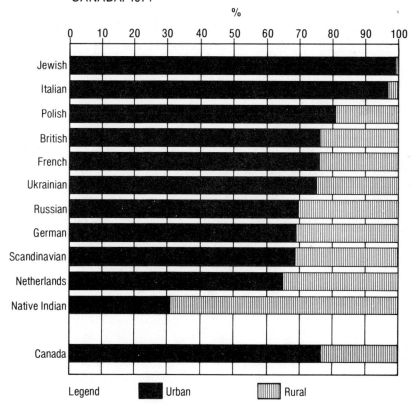

All data derived from Statistics Canada Publications

Source: W. Kalbach and W. McVey, *The Demographic Bases of Canadian Society*, (2nd ed.), McGraw-Hill Ryerson, Toronto, p. 208, 1979.

Chart 3 shows the rural-urban distribution of a select number of ethnic groups as well as Canada as a whole. The data show that Canada has become very urbanized, with over 70% of its population residing in urban areas. Specific ethnic groups, however, do show variations on this overall pattern. Jews, for example, are the most urbanized group with over 95% residing in ur-ban areas, with the majority within Montreal, Toronto, and Winnipeg. Italians are also very urban. At the other end of the continuum we find Native people residing in the rural areas, with only about 20% urban.

Distribution and Immigration Policies

Until very recently Canada's immigration policies have been notable for their lack of attention paid to the question of immigrant distribution. Although there have been occasional schemes designed to encourage immigrants to settle outside central Canada, immigration officials have believed until recently that immigrants must be free to settle where they choose (Hawkins, 1972: 64). In 1974 immigration officials came up with the vague notion of up to ten points (out of a hundred) to be awarded or penalized according to whether or not the prospective immigrant could claim a pre-arranged job or skills to fill positions in work-scarce areas. It was presumed that these areas would not be in central Canada; yet at the same time it was reported that southwest Ontario was one area showing the biggest recent increase in job vacancies (Toronto Star, Oct. 26, 1974).

In February 1975 the "Green Paper on Immigration and Population" was tabled in the House of Commons. Although this voluminous document purported to be an unbiased account, it wasted little time in distinguishing between one type of immigrant and another, between the "traditional" European immigrant and "foreign" immigrants from "certain Asian and Caribbean nations," who were easily recognized by their "distinctive features." Thus the Green Paper raised two different questions: first, how many people would be admitted into Canada, and second, where would these people come from? The paper implied that perhaps it would be in the best interests of Canadians to ensure continued immigration from traditional sources. The paper noted that more and more immigrants were entering Canada from non-traditional sources: Asia, the Caribbean, Latin America. Of course, it was not pointed out that prior to 1962 Canada had admitted extremely few immigrants from non-European sources, excluding the United States, and for decades this country had discriminated, covertly or too often overtly, against would-be Chinese, Japanese, and Black immigrants. Moreover, the Green Paper related problems of overurbanization and escalating unemployment to immigration. The paper complained that "few means exist at present to steer immigrants against prevailing population currents, and these are limited in their effectiveness"; and the paper therefore recommended that "a more dispersed pattern of immigrant settlement" would be advisable to prevent racial strife.

A new immigration policy directly related to immigrant distribution was not long in coming. In September of 1976 the Minister of Manpower and Immigration announced a policy "which will stress the desirability that immigrants settle in other places than Toronto, Montreal and Vancouver." The government would be empowered to direct prospective immigrants toward areas experiencing shortages of people to fill certain occupations. In diverting immigrants from crowded urban areas, the government would require them to settle for at least six months in communities with labor shortages. Initially the new regulations, embodied in Bill C-24, would not apply to immigrants sponsored by relatives already resident in Canada. But the new policy would particularly affect marginal applicants needing additional points, i.e., applicants whose entry would be determined by their willingness to spend at least six months working in regions where employment was readily available. The granting of landed status possibly would be delayed for three months after arrival, and would occur not at the port of entry but at the destination. The designation of prospective labor-short communities would involve careful consultation between various levels of government—federal, provincial, and municipal.

This new policy, which took effect in January 1978, is not without its problems. On the positive side, Hawkins has suggested (Hawkins, 1977) that Bill C-24 has not really changed immigration policy; rather it has "improved the mechanisms for managing immigration to meet both compassionate aims and national goals." Immigration will be directly related to population growth and distribution, and the provinces will become involved (not without some reluctance) in settlement patterns and in policy determining the number of immigrants admitted. In encouraging (better yet, regulating) the distribution of immigrants, the federal government, co-operating with provincial and municipal governments, would designate the communities which could both handle and benefit from immigration. Such communities would be relatively small, have good economic growth potential, room for adequate housing and services. In short, prime immigrant reception areas would not be designated unless they clearly have the capability of handling immigrants.

But on the negative side, it has been pointed out that implementation of such a policy could be subject to wide discretionary judgements on the part of immigration officers. Immigrants might prefer to settle in larger cities, where more diversity in jobs would obviously be available and where they could adjust more easily in the company of their co-ethnics. Immigrants were likely to stay in a specified location for the required six months, then move to a large city. Non-White immigrants tend to be wary of being forced to settle in what might appear to be racial work camps (witness, for example, the development of such camps or urban ghettoes accommodating literally millions of *gastarbeiter*, "guest workers," in industrialized northern European countries).

Perhaps a fairly typical Canadian attitude towards the new (mostly non-White) immigrants, an attitude reflected in the Green Paper, which formed the foundation for the policy changes embodied in Bill C-24, was expressed by Rev. E. M. Howse, onetime moderator of the United Church (*Toronto Star*, April 19, 1975):

> Canada will have first to decide what are the limits of the population it can support without destroying itself, without bloating our cities beyond endurance, and devouring farm land needed for the feeding of the world. Accordingly, while Canada may accept many applicants it would have refused in the past, it will still have to reject many more. And those who are barred will inevitably feel themselves to be the victims of discrimination. And as, with the population balance of the present world, more of those refused will be coloured than white (as perhaps more of those admitted) we shall inevitably suffer the charge of racism. . . . Canadians can have some degree of satisfaction that, in recent years, our immigration policy has been as open and humanitarian as that of any country.

Perhaps it has, in recent years. With the gradual liberalization of Canadian immigration policies, between 1968 and 1973 Canada accepted 526,767 immigrants from Third World sources—Latin America and the Caribbean, Africa,

Asia and Oceania—as well as several hundred thousand immigrants from less developed countries in eastern and southern Europe, including almost half a million Italians (mostly from the poverty-stricken southern provinces of the Mezzogiorno) and over a hundred thousand from Portugal (and Portuguese possessions). Tens of thousands were admitted as refugees, including post-war displaced persons, Hungarians in 1956, and more recently Tibetans, Vietnamese and Cambodians, Ugandan Asians, Chileans and Lebanese.

But that is only one side of the story. In past decades Canadian immigration policy was decidedly hypocritical. Canada never had the strict quota system exemplified in American policy, nor the guest worker designation represented in contemporary West German, Swiss, French, etc. policies, nor the "Whites only need apply" philosophy of South Africa, Rhodesia, or Australia. But Canada certainly did have periodic overt exclusion of Orientals and South Asians and covert exclusion of Blacks. Indeed, it even had the forced redistribution and repatriation of Japanese who were Canadian citizens if not Canadian-born. The Minister of Immigration and Manpower recently commented (*Toronto Star*, Nov. 4, 1974), in reply to charges of discriminatory practices by immigration officers against non-White applicants, that "allegations of discrimination have been made from time to time. In *every* case I have initiated an investigation and in almost every case there proves to be no foundation in fact". Unfortunately it has been in very recent years, during the present decade, that numerous complaints were made over the arbitrary granting of landed status to applicants, as well as the arbitrary reclassification of applicants, by immigration officers. Large-scale deportation of immigrants classified as illegal immigrants occurred, too often without proper investigation, and re-application was prohibited. If Canada has admitted many refugees, it is equally true that many have *not* been admitted, for example numerous highly qualified applicants in European refugee camps, and a substantial proportion of Chileans and Haitians (Anderson and Stewart, 1979).

On the one hand, the new immigration policy is the first policy clearly intended to cope with the difficult question of immigrant distribution and to link it with manpower requirements. On the other hand, the very effectiveness of this policy is fraught with difficulties from the outset. We have noted that there are ample reasons, personal or social as well as economic, for the disproportionate distribution of immigrants. Perhaps it seems pertinent to add that, given the past if not continuing record of negative features of Canadian immigration policies (not denying that there have also been positive features to the credit of Canada), it would hardly be surprising to find new immigrants suspicious of what could be termed forced distribution.

Methodological Considerations in Analysing Immigrant Distribution in Canada

A number of methodological problems are implicit in analysing the distribution of immigrants in Canada. First, it is no easy matter to define precisely the immigrant population. For our purposes in this chapter, an immigrant in Canada could be defined as any Canadian resident who was not born in Canada (excluding short term visitors and Canadian citizens born outside Canada). In 1971 the census counted the total population of Canada at 21,568,310, of whom

84.7% (18,272,780) had been born in Canada and the remaining 15.3% (3,295,530) were foreign-born. All of these foreign-born residents could be considered immigrants, except for the few cases of Canadian citizens born outside Canada (as returning Canadian citizens, the latter never have had to acquire landed immigrant status). But it must quickly be added that the term foreign-born should not necessarily imply that these residents of Canada are foreign in the sense of not being Canadian citizens. The majority, 60.2% (1,983,015) of these foreign-born residents had become (or some already were) Canadian citizens, compared to 39.8% (1,312,515) who still retained their previous citizenship in 1971.

Second, it is difficult to estimate South Asian and West Indian immigrant flows, a substantial portion of recent immigration into Canada. Detailed data on immigration direct from India and Pakistan, and from the Caribbean, are available. But a large proportion of the recent immigrants from Uganda (7,600 during the decade prior to 1973), Fiji (4,919), and Mauritius (760) must have been ethnic South Asians, as were perhaps a substantial proportion from South Africa (7,608) and Malaysia (2,737). Virtually all of the more than 63,000 South Asians in Uganda were deported, and South Asians now constitute about half of the population of Fiji and more than two-thirds of the population of Mauritius. There are over three-quarters of a million South Asians in South Africa, and over a million in Malaysia. Moreover, the vast immigration from England (270,227 from 1963 to 1973) doubtless included a significant number of both South Asians and West Indians, who number well over a million in that country. Finally, in Trinidad (which sent 29,584 emigrants to Canada from 1963 to 1973 and several thousand since 1973) Blacks and Mulattoes form 59% of the total population, South Asians 36%; while in Guyana (which sent 1,776 in 1963 to 1973 but perhaps five or six times that number just since 1973) Blacks form about 36% and South Asians 55%. Thus, to add to the confusion, many immigrants from the latter two sources could be termed "East Indian West Indians" (if we can consider Guyana, actually in South America, to be culturally West Indian).

Third, it should be briefly mentioned that while detailed data exist on the *intended* destinations of landed immigrants, little or no data exist on whether or not these immigrants go to these destinations. But with the introduction of new immigration restrictions which could effectively force non-nominated immigrants to settle in specified locations for several months *prior* to being granted landed status, this distinction may be largely obliterated.

Fourth, very few data are available on the relationship between the possible physical mobility of immigrants and their redistribution. What exactly are the internal migration patterns of immigrants once they have arrived in Canada? What are their intra- and inter-urban and intra- and inter-regional movements? How long do they remain in principal immigrant reception areas, ethnic neighborhoods, or within cities? When and why do they choose to move? It goes without saying that such data would have a profound effect on the interpretation of the rationality and effectivity of the new regulations concerning communities designated to receive immigrants.

Fifth, few data are available on possible return migration. The implication in data on immigration flows from various source countries is that these immigrants have come here to stay. At least the tendency to stay seems to have been increasing recently. For example, the number of Canadians who emigrated between 1971 and 1976 dropped markedly from the previous two five-year periods; but this does not tell us what proportion of these emigrants were returning immigrants. The ratio of immigrants remaining in Canada to immigrants admitted remained quite constant between 1946 and 1968 (about two-thirds remained), but from 1969 to 1971 a considerably lower proportion were estimated to become return migrants. Yet more information on tendencies in certain ethnic populations would clarify the question of return migration. For example, in one study of West Indians in Toronto (Anderson, 1975), little more than half (52.5%) of the sample (N = 200) reported that they intended to remain in Canada permanently; a third (32.5%) intended to stay more than five years but eventually return to the Caribbean, while the remainder intended to stay for a shorter period in Canada (12.5%) or were visiting (2.5%).

Table 18
IMMIGRANTS ADMITTED, RECORDED IN THE CENSUS AND RATIO REMAINING IN THE COUNTRY, 1946-1971
(In Thousands)

	Number of immigrants admitted	Number of immigrants recorded in Census	Ratio of immigrants remaining to immigrants admitted
Total Population of Canada		21,568.3	
Immigrants who arrived:			
prior to 1946		953.6	
1946-55	1,222.3	789.0	64.6
1956-60	782.9	497.3	63.5
1961-65	498.8	347.0	69.6
1966-68	601.6	416.4	69.2
1969-71[1]	357.2	292.2	81.8
Total: all immigrants		3,295.5	
all post-war immigrants	3,462.5	2,341.9	67.6

[1] For 1971, includes first five months of arrival only.
Source: Statistics Canada, Advance Bulletin—*Population by Period of Immigration*, Cat. No. 92-761 (AP-10), September, 1973.
Source: Louis Parai, *The Economic Impact of Immigration*, Canadian Immigration and Population Study, Ottawa: Manpower and Immigration, p. 90.

Demographic Characteristics of Immigrant and Ethnic Populations

Because of the number and diversity of immigrated ethnic populations in Canada, it is beyond the scope of the present book to present a detailed discussion of each one with regard to their various attributes. Rather we will focus on a limited number of collectivities and compare selected social characteristics. These characteristics to be investigated are important factors when studying inter-ethnic (and intra-ethnic) relations. They provide information with regard to life chances for specific individual ethnic group members, the survival of the ethnic culture and potential power base of the members in their relations with members of other ethnic groups. For example, if one finds that educational attainment is low for one group, it suggests that this group might also be placed in a potentially vulnerable position vis-a-vis other ethnic minorities or the dominant society.

Chart 4 shows the overall educational attainment of selected ethnic categories. This table shows that Scandinavians have the highest percentage of any groups having some education. That is, only about 2% have no education in this group. However, if one looks at the extent of secondary educational attainment, we find that the British Isles' categories have the highest rate. At a post-secondary level, we find Jews at the top of the scale. At the bottom of the scale (measured any way) we find Native people. Nearly 80% of all Native people have less than a secondary education. This is closely matched by the Italian

CHART 4   EDUCATIONAL ATTAINMENT SELECTED ETHNIC ORIGINS [1] CANADA: 1971

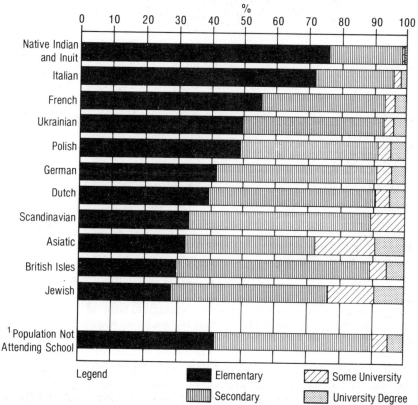

Legend: Elementary   Some University   Secondary   University Degree

[1] Population 25 years of age and over   All data derived from Statistics Canada Publications

Source: W. Kalbach and W. McVey, *The Demographic Bases of Society*, (2nd ed.), McGraw-Hill Ryerson, Toronto, 1979, p. 257.

population (74%). Both ethnic categories also show that fewer than 5% have a university degree. On the other hand, the British have nearly 14% with university degrees and only slightly more than one-quarter (26%) having less than a secondary education.

The relevance of this attribute will reflect the social position attainable by the ethnic members. Having high educational attainments means that ethnics may have high interest group power and thus influence the dominant segment of our society in their decision making processes. Education will be related to occupation as well as income. Table 19 shows the average income of the male non-agricultural labor force by ethnic group. We find that Jews have an income well above the overall Canadian average. The data also show that besides Jews, only the British make above the average income. Germans and Ukrainians make slightly below the average income while the French and Italians fall well below the national average.

Table 19

AVERAGE TOTAL INCOME

Average total income of the male non-agricultural labour force and of the total male labour force, by ethnic origin—Canada, 1961.

Ethnic Origins	Male non-agricultural labour force		Total male labour force
	Dollars	Index	Index
All origins	4,414	100.0	100.0
British	4,852	109.9	109.8
French	3,872	87.7	85.8
German	4,207	95.3	103.1
Italian	3,621	82.0	81.0
Jewish	7,426	168.2	166.9
Ukrainian	4,128	93.5	86.8
Others	4,153	94.1	98.2

Source: A. Raynauld, G. Marion and R. Beland, "La repartition des revenus selon les groupes ethniques au Canada," 1968, A study prepared for the Royal Commission on Bilingualism and Biculturalism.

The age distribution of each ethnic category is an important sociological fact from several respects. First of all, to a certain extent it reflects the reproductive rate of each group. This, of course, will be suggestive in terms of their impact on the total population growth rate. For example, if a group has a high proportion of young people, these young children will fall within the procreative years as they move into the 20-35 age category. The age distribution may also affect the viability of an ethnic group. If most of the ethnic members are old, as they begin to phase themselves out of the social dynamics of the community (and eventually die) the viability of the group may also lessen. Table 20 shows the age distribution for selected ethnic groups.

Two ethnic collectivities are most at variance with the general overall Canadian distribution—Native Indians and Italians. Natives have an extremely high birth rate (with a resultant high proportion of young people) but also a very high

Table 20

AGE BY ETHNIC GROUP, 1971

	0-4	5-9	10-14	15-24	25-44	45 +	Total	Total persons
					%			number
British	8	10	10	19	23	30	100	9,624,120
French	8	11	12	20	26	23	100	6,180,120
German	8	10	10	17	29	26	100	1,317,200
Italian	11	12	10	16	31	20	100	730,820
Ukrainian	7	9	9	17	25	33	100	580,655
Netherlands	9	12	13	18	26	22	100	425,945
Indians and Inuit	16	16	13	20	21	14	100	312,765
Scandinavian	7	9	10	18	26	30	100	384,795
All other	9	9	9	17	29	27	100	2,011,890
Canadian average	8	10	11	19	25	27	100	21,568,310

Source: *Perspective Canada*, Statistics Canada, Information Canada, Ottawa, 1974, p. 278.

death rate which means there are many fewer older (45 +) people. Italians have a higher proportion of young people and a lower proportion of older people. This latter fact is not because of high death rates but rather a function of their recency of immigrating to Canada. Because most have only been in Canada for 20 years (and given the fact that young people tend to immigrate), the resultant figures show that they have simply not been in Canada long enough to have any sizable cohort of old people. The Ukrainians, on the other hand, show an opposite profile. They have a much smaller proportion of their population in the young age category, while at the same time a much greater number in the older category. This seems to be a result of the fact that they have been long-time residents (thereby accounting for the "old" population). Their birth rate currently has been much lower than in the past, suggesting that they are becoming more middle class and are reducing their family size.

It is at once interesting and challenging to attempt an explanation of ethnic and religious considerations in analysing differential fertility rates and family size. Any such attempt is fraught with difficulties. Tables 21 and 22 provide data on differential fertility rates respectively for ethnic and religious categories. From the ethnic data we can note that Native Indians have exceptionally high fertility rates; this information is basic to understanding that they also tend to have large families and why an increasingly high proportion of Native people are moving from the reserves into cities. These data also indicate that French-Canadians have relatively high fertility, but before we jump to conclusions we should bear in mind that Quebec has had the lowest birth rate for any Canadian province in recent years. The Dutch have a fairly high birth rate, but probably this is due to the considerable proportion of Mennonites claiming Dutch origin. Religious data inform us that Mennonites, as well as Hutterites and Mormons, tend to have higher fertility rates than Catholics, although in general predominantly Catholic ethnic and immigrant groups have relatively

Table 21

**CHILDREN BORN PER 1,000 WOMEN EVER MARRIED, 45 YEARS OF AGE
AND OVER, SHOWING ETHNIC ORIGIN, MOTHER TONGUE AND LANGUAGE
MOST OFTEN USED IN THE HOME, CANADA, 1971**

Group or Language	Children Born Per 1,000 Women Ever Married		
	Ethnic Origin	Mother Tongue	Language Most Often Spoken At Home
English	2,846	2,863	2,903
French	4,387	4,428	4,484
German	3,256	3,419	3,642
Indian and Inuit	6,155	6,654	6,784
Italian	3,258	3,380	3,490
Netherlands	3,817	4,124	4,515
Polish	2,910	2,814	2,676
Ukrainian	3,127	3,218	3,482

Source: Statistics Canada, *1971 Census of Canada*, Bulletin 5.1-6, Ottawa: Information Canada, 1976, Tables 5, 6, and 7.

Table 22

**CHILDREN BORN PER 1,000 WOMEN EVER MARRIED BY RELIGIOUS
DENOMINATIONS FOR TOTAL WOMEN, AND WOMEN 45 YEARS OF AGE
AND OVER, CANADA, 1971**

Religious Denomination	Age Group	
	Total 15 Years of Age and Over	45 Years of Age and Over
Anglican	2,475	2,696
Baptist	2,724	3,054
Greek Orthodox	2,436	3,077
Jewish	2,117	2,286
Lutheran	2,444	2,752
Mennonite and Hutterite	3,816	4,890
Pentecostal	3,190	3,805
Presbyterian	2,332	2,507
Roman Catholic	3,137	4,084
Salvation Army	3,303	3,831
Ukrainian Catholic	2,822	3,229
United Church	2,484	2,731
No Religion	2,061	2,566
Other	2,769	3,302

Source: Statistics Canada, *1971 Census of Canada*, Bulletin 5.1-6, Ottawa: Information Canada, 1976, Table 4, p. 39.

high rates. Some Mennonites have an extended family tradition, exemplified in their *freundschaft* gatherings of sometimes several hundred kin. Hutterites probably have the highest birth rate of any ethno-religious group in Canada. And Mormons place a lot of importance on family living. Not infrequently certain qualifications must be taken into consideration, however. Rural/urban differences may be more significant than simply ethnicity or religion *per se*. Subgroup distinctions could be very relevant. For example, Canadian Jews in general have relatively low fertility rates, but Hassidic Jews—an Orthodox subgroup in Montreal—emphasize large families.

Conclusion

This brief profile of the different ethnic groups and categories that make up our society reaffirms the high degree of heterogeneity that exists today. We have shown that the ethnic scene has not been a static profile but rather one which has changed over time and by region, because individuals with different ethnic affiliations have entered Canada at different times and at different rates. Various macro factors have had a great impact upon the settlement pattern of the immigrants, their ethnic maintenance and relationships with the dominant society. In addition, the absorptive capacity of Canadian society has always had a great impact upon the immigrants' integration into Canadian society. When the timing of the immigrant groups' entrance did not match the supposed needs of Canadian society, adjustment patterns were different from those which came when the timing was more carefully matched with the needs.

Because of the different waves of immigration, with each group reacting to different push-pull factors, some ethnic categories do not have a high degree of boundary maintenance. For example, Radecki and Heydenkorn (1976) have clearly demonstrated that different periods of immigration of Poles to Canada have created some internal discord over values, ideology and organizational structures.

This chapter has also provided data with regard to the social profiles exhibited by selected groups in our society. It is clear that some groups exhibit profiles that are more suited to a highly industrialized society, and thus will benefit from Canadian society more than other groups. To be sure, these profiles may have changed over time and will continue to change. Ethnic group members who generally occupied low-status occupations at the turn of the century now occupy some positions that can be considered middle class. However, it is clear that none of the groups has been able to penetrate the elite positions in Canadian society (Porter, 1965; Kelner, 1970; Clement, 1975). However, one trend that has been consistently present for all groups is the urbanization process. This process has affected all groups as our society becomes more industrialized and centralized. How this will affect intergroup behavior remains to be seen, but it is clear that this concentration of different ethnic groups into an urban centre is leading to new and sometimes conflict oriented behavior.

REFERENCES
Anderson, Alan B. "Ethnic Enclosures and Discrimination in a West Indian Community in Toronto," research paper presented at the Conference on

Multiculturalism and Third World Immigrants in Canada, University of Alberta, Sept. 3-6, 1975.

Anderson, Alan B. "Ethnic Identity in Saskatchewan Bloc Settlements: A Sociological Appraisal," in Howard Palmer (ed.), *The Settlement of the West*. Calgary: University of Calgary/Comprint Publishing Co., 1977, Chap. 10.

Anderson, Alan B. "Racism in Toronto," *Canadian Ethnic Studies*, Vol. X, No. 2, 1978.

Anderson, Alan B. and T. Stewart. "Refugee Movements into Canada: 1946-79," paper presented in a joint session of the Canadian Sociology and Anthropology Association and the Canadian Population Society, University of Saskatchewan, June 2, 1979.

Bruce, Jean. *The Last Best West*. Toronto: Fitzhenry & Whiteside, 1978.

Burke, Chris and Ireland, Derek. A report on urban population trends and regional disparities prepared for the Dept. of Urban Affairs, 1976, cited in the *Saskatoon Star-Phoenix*, Nov. 4, 1976.

Clement, W. *The Canadian Corporate Elite*. Carlton Library, McClelland and Stewart, Toronto, 1975.

Cobus, Mona. "A Look Back at Chile: Canada's Attitude Towards Refugees and Immigrants," *Rights and Freedoms*, July-August 1977.

D'Costa, Ronald. "Trends in Recent and Third World Immigration to Canada," research paper presented at the Conference on Multiculturalism and Third World Immigrants in Canada, University of Alberta, Sept. 3-6, 1975.

Hawkins, Freda. *Canada and Immigration: Public Policy and Public Concern*. Montreal and London: McGill-Queen's University Press, 1972.

Hawkins, Freda. Address given at a seminar on "C-24: Canada's New Immigration Bill," Canadian Institute of International Affairs, Saskatoon Branch, April 11, 1977.

Head, Wilson. A report on discrimination against Blacks in Metro Toronto, prepared for the Ontario Human Rights Commission; excerpts in the *Toronto Star*, Sept. 27, 1975.

Kelner, M. "Ethnic Penetrations in Toronto's Elite Structure." *Canadian Review of Sociology and Anthropology*, Vol. 7, No. 2, 1970.

McLeod, N. R. "Need Culture and Curriculum." Toronto: Board of Education, Report 44, 1969.

Morrow, Michael. "The 'Hindoos': Anti-East Indian Tensions in British Columbia," *Last Post*, Feb. 1976.

Nielson, Soren. "Internal Migration and Immigrant Settlement," a report prepard for the federal government, cited in the *Toronto Star*, Sept. 13, 1975.

O'Byran, J. Reitz and O. Kyplowska. *Non Official Language: A Study in Canadian Multiculturalism*. Ottawa, Information Canada, 1976.

Porter, J. *The Vertical Mosaic*. Toronto, University of Toronto Press, 1965.

Radecki, H. and B. Heydenkorn. *A Member of A Distinguished Family: The Polish Group in Canada*. Ottawa: McClelland and Stewart in association with the Secretary of State of Canada. 1976.

Ramcharan, Subhas. "An Analysis of West Indian Migrants' Attitudes to the Canadian Society," research paper presented at the Conference on Multiculturalism and Third World Immigrants in Canada, University of Alberta, Sept. 3-6, 1975.

Woycenko, O. *The Ukrainians in Canada*. Winnipeg: Trident Press, 1967.

Part III

Canadian Ethnic Relations

Theories of intergroup relations in Canada have not been well developed (Morris and Lanphier, 1977). To be sure, a number of writers have specialized in the study of ethnic groups in Canada, but we find that the research is directed to specific case studies, to specific groups in specific areas and limited to a particular time period. It seems surprising to find that in a nation defined as a mosaic or kaleidoscope, that Canadian sociologists have yet to produce a general theory on the subject. Even more interesting is the fact that almost every social scientist in Canada recognizes the importance of ethnicity as a causal or explanatory variable in our society and attempts to introduce the concept in their research, yet they have failed to develop a coherent conceptual framework. This third part of the book, therefore, provides an analytical framework for studying ethnic relations in Canada.

Chapter 8 introduces the reader to conflict theory and its application to the study of ethnic relations. First we attempt to provide an integrated model of conflict theory and ethnic (i.e., perceived appearance group/PAG) relations. The chapter discusses the emergence of conflict, the role of subordinate leadership, and several functions of conflict, then provides an illustration of conflict in Canada: the FLQ development during the sixties in Quebec.

Chapter 9 outlines three levels of racism: individual, institutional, and cultural. Racism is examined in broad comparative and historical perspective, and the bulk of the chapter is devoted to a review of racism in Canadian history and in contemporary Canada.

Chapter 10 develops a model of ethnic relations in Canada. It describes the relationships between ethnic (PAG) interest groups and the dominant (Anglo-Canadian) society. Much of the chapter is devoted to a detailed discussion of dominant social control mechanisms and how these mechanisms have been applied to ethnic minorities in Canada.

Chapter 8

Conflict

Conflict Theory and Ethnic Relations: An Integrated Model

Large-scale conflict in industrial societies has, by and large, been channeled into nonviolent forms.[1] Lenski and Lenski (1978) point out that three factors mediate against the emergence of conflict in industrial societies. First of all, industrial societies have a relatively high standard of living and thus members have a vested interest in political-economic stability. A second reason centres on the acceptance (and acting out) of a democratic ideology which strengthens support of the existing political-economic structure. Finally, they point out that because of the complexity of industrial societies, compromise as a resolution to differences has become an accepted *modus operandi*.

This analysis does have some merit and should be considered in our examination of conflict in Canada. For example, the major overt conflicts (violence) between French and English and English and Native people have generally taken place prior to the industrialization of Canada. Since then the conflict between these groups has generally taken place within the institutional (political) arena.

But the general question still remains. If we posit a model of groups trying to control or not wanting to be controlled, why isn't there more open conflict? Sites (1975) gives some very good answers to this question. First of all, people are generally aware of their relative power and thus equally cognizant of their limitations. Why engage in conflict if you know you cannot win? Secondly, it turns out that almost everyone has something to gain by giving a little to gain more through common effort. A third reason lies in the fact that in group situations, the identification and satisfaction of needs is varied. Because we all have different identities, we may value different things.

When conflict is absent in a social system, it means that either the segments of society have equal amounts of resources (power) or some segments realize they cannot win. In addition, the social system will not necessarily be maintained through coercion but by the mutual internalization of contraints by all segments of the system.

While Canadians claim there are legitimate ways in which dissatisfied groups can air their grievances, a great deal of sporadic conflict has been engaged in during the past two hundred years. Over the history of Canada, a number of ethnic minorities, or perceived appearance groups (PAGs), have challenged the policies and actions of the dominant group (Leslie, 1969). As

---

[1] We agree with Dahrendorf (1959) that conflict can be conceptualized in terms of two dimensions—intensity and violence. Intensity refers to the amount of energy invested into a conflict situation while violence refers to the weapons chosen.

Leslie points out, the decision to challenge the dominant group and to engage in conflict with them is a decision that is not based upon "revolutionary romanticism." Rather, it is based on a sincere belief that institutionalized techniques of influence and social change are ineffectual (Breton and Breton, 1962). This means that groups invent and legitimize their decision to engage in conflict. Deutsch (1967) has identified several rationales that are used by groups when they engage in conflict. The most common rationale is one of "last resort," i.e., every alternative strategy has been used in an attempt to address the group's problem and each has failed. A second rationale is referred to as "necessity." In some cases people define conflict as an "inexorable act of nature" while others define conflict as necessary because of the inherent structure of a social system. Whatever the rationale inherent in the ideology of conflict, there are three major elements: (i) the only effective means for producing change, (ii) justification of violence on moral grounds, and (iii) rejection of nonviolent techniques (Kuper, 1969). In many cases, the only real weapon that an economically impoverished group has is the righteousness of the cause. Gamson (1975) has clearly demonstrated in his analysis of conflict that violence is *not* a product of frustration, desperation, or weakness. His conclusion is that violence is an instrumental act, aimed at furthering the purposes of the group.

Past research on conflict has generally focused on one of the following three perspectives: (i) the issues, (ii) the participants or, (iii) the means used. The result of this research has been a detailed analysis of one of the dimensions in the process of conflict. However, the combined role of all three has not been systematically addressed. Our model integrates all three perspectives in an attempt to provide a more complete and integrated explanation of intergroup conflict.

The overall model to be used in our analysis of conflict has been set forth by Lightbody (1969). Lightbody's model begins with the assumption that in any situation where minority ethnics exist, these groups will seek power and attempt to influence the existing dominant group. Thus, demands of the minority ethnic group and responses of the dominant group are the first ingredients for assessing the emergence and sustaining of conflict.

The following model (Figure 1) illustrates the relationship between demands of various minority ethnics and the responses of the dominant group and its relevance to the emergence of conflict. The continuum OX represents the demands made by various minority ethnic groups. At the end of the continuum (X), the minority ethnic group is demanding an autonomous political identity and authority either within or outside the larger nation-state.

Each minority ethnic group may be placed (at any given time) somewhere on this continuum depending upon the strength and scope of the group's demands. The critical point (B) occurs when these demands of the specific group change in substance. Up until this point, the minority ethnic group's demands are basically directed to gain additional influence with regard to the existing political system. The request for a bilingual educational system would represent this type of action to gain some influence. Beyond this, the demands change their qualitative character, as Lightbody (1969) points out:

> Beyond this political hurdle demands become "nationalist" (one might suggest "separatist"), institutional and insatiable in character: they are

FIGURE 1

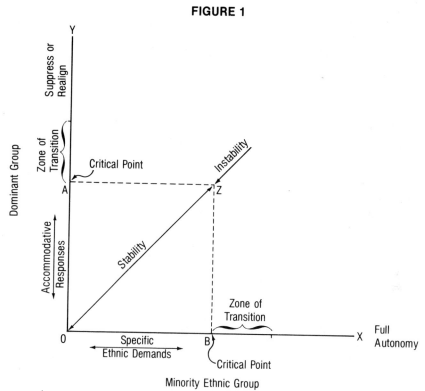

Source: Lightbody, 1969.

made primarily for an ethnically separate institutional vehicle which presumably will be more responsive to the group's demands. (333)

We have only investigated half of the process. In addition to the demands, there are responses made by the dominant group. The OY continuum represents the responses of the dominant group to the demands of the minority ethnic group. These responses may range from informal recognition of a minority ethnic group to more formalized recognition of the group as a legitimate actor in the political arena, which may mean the formal provision of separate institutions. Again as Lightbody (1969) points out, once the responses move beyond the critical point:

the state must realign its institutional structures about a new ethnic configuration by physically attempting to suppress the dissident elements into grudging assimilation into the majority culture. (334)

The model predicts, then, the points at which conflict will take place. Given that the demands and responses of the parties involved fall within the OBZA area, conflict will be absent and stability will result. Once the demands, responses, or both are beyond this area, conflict (instability) will emerge, and violence becomes a distinct possibility.

Max Weber (1947: 132) defined conflict as: "intentionally to carry out the actor's own will against the resistance of the other party or parties." Coser (1956: 232) defines social conflict as "a struggle over values or claims to status, power, and scarce resources, in which the aim of the conflict groups are not only to gain the desired values, but also to neutralize, injure, or eliminate rivals." Oberschall (1973: 38), on the other hand, defines conflict as "the gaining of desired values in which one group may neutralize, injure, or eliminate the other group." Kriesberg (1973: 17) views conflict as a relationship between two or more parties that believe (define) they have incompatible goals. While all of these definitions are worded differently, all agree that differences about something exist for the parties of conflict. And some attempt to resolve these differences (real or imagined) takes place, with each party convinced their's is the correct solution, definition of reality, or appropriate goal.

In all societies we find some positions in the social organization structure are entrusted with the right to exercise control over other positions and to produce compliance (if necessary) with authority by coercion. At any given point in time there exists in society the problem of how scarce resources or goals are to be distributed among various individuals and groups. Social conflict usually results from these opposing interests. However, this should alert us to the fact that not all societies experience the same degree of conflict, and that conflict may vary in intensity over time (Bonacich, 1972).

Bonacich (1972) uses the word "antagonism" to encompass all levels of intergroup conflict. This includes beliefs (prejudice), behaviors (riots, discrimination), and institutional arrangements. Her usage of the term stems from the assumption that the processes leading to and sustaining each of the above are the same. The second rationale emerges from her belief that antagonism does not carry any moralistic overtones; thereby allowing for the possibility that conflict may be a mutual, interaction product. Even though we will continue to use the concept conflict, we are in basic agreement with Bonacich. Conflict can be viewed as a variable; ranging from beliefs to revolutions involving large-scale physical violence.

The emergence of conflict is not always a function of the dispensing of material rewards. In many cases symbolic rewards or potential symbolic rewards will be at the heart of conflict. As Oberschall (1973) points out:

> Social conflict is seldom a simple mechanical reaction to grievances and frustrations experienced in the pursuit and defence of material interests. Interests and dissatisfactions are experienced and interpreted by ways of moral ideas about right and wrong, justice and injustice or conceptions of the social orders as they are expressed in ideals and highly regarded principles. The drive to change existing institutions, whether to reform or revolutionize them, is inspired by unrealized ideals; measured against the ideals that are enshrined in the sacred books, the constitutions, and collective myths, reality falls short. The gap may be wide or narrow; its very existence will justify the effort to close it in the name of legitimate, highly valued and respected principles. (187)

For this reason, conflicts over symbols generally are more intense than non-symbolic conflicts. The question of conflict between groups cannot be analysed apart from questions of group membership and its symbolic representation

(DeVos, 1966). The defence of these symbols, then, is seen as an unselfish action worthy of group support. Again, as Oberschall states: "disrespect for symbols or an attempt to substitute different symbols will be perceived as an attack on the integrity of moral standing, sense of identity and self respect of the entire group."

The nature of the conflict and the form it takes between any two (or more) parties will be contingent upon several structural conditions evident in society. Each of these factors may play an important mediating role in the intensity, direction, and nature of the conflict. First of all the groups in question must be aware (consciousness) that an incompatibility of goals exists. Secondly, the degree to which conflict is regulated and institutionalized will, to a certain extent, determine the nature of the conflict. The rules that regulate conflict generally will differ in content, specification and degree of institutionalization (Kriesberg, 1973). Third, the participants may view the conflict as a zero-sum game, i.e., to what extent a gain of one group is dependent upon the loss of the other. This will determine how calculations are made and goal achievements partially determined. Fourth, to what extent the boundaries of each group are clear (visible) and permeable. Fifth, the structured relations of the groups will affect the process of conflict, e.g., to what extent the groups are organized in terms of role specialization of the various actors in the group. The last factor to be identified is the systemic relations of the groups to each other. Are the units independent of each other or is one part of the other?

Circumstances underlying social conflict can either be of consensus or disconsensus (Aubert, 1963). In the former case, both parties want the same goal but it is viewed as a zero-sum game. In the latter case, each party wants different things and because co-ordination of both groups is required, goal achievement for both groups cannot be attained. Each type may be viewed as analytically separate although in real life elements of both types are evident.

Examples of consensus conflict would be evident in occupational status indices. There are only a certain number of high status jobs and these must go to the most deserving group. All segments of society agree to this goal but fully realize that if the jobs are taken by one sector of society it means that other sectors will not have these jobs. We find, for example, that certain ethnic categories are over represented in certain occupations and under represented in others (Porter, 1965). This characterization of Canadian society has remained constant for well over fifty years. Bonacich (1972) has proposed a model of conflict which is based on the notion of a split labor market. She argues that ethnic conflict will emerge when a society develops a labor market split along ethnic lines. By almost any standard we will find that Jews are on the top of the SES scale, Native people on the bottom. British will closely follow the Jews and Ukrainians, Italians will be well below the average. Francophones will be paid less for doing the same job as anglophones. The comparisons could go on but it is sufficient at this time to note that an ethnic division of labor does exist and is the basis of consensus conflict.

With regard to disconsensus conflict, we find that a number of groups have different values and beliefs. However, if the different values or beliefs are defined as quaint, or if each group is indifferent to the other values, then the conflict will not emerge. On the other hand, when the "other" values and beliefs are viewed as negative, then potential conflict may emerge. This incompatibility arises in areas of education and welfare. Conflict over the use of linguistic patterns has been an issue in Canadian society since its inception. Conflict over value systems has emerged between Doukhobors and non-Doukhobors, Mennonites and non-Mennonites, Hutterites and non-Hutterites, Indians and non-Indians. Issues such as education have produced conflict between groups since well before the beginning of the 20th century. In New Brunswick, the School Act of 1871 was an attempt to create a single, secular educational system. However, the Irish and Acadians refused to accept this goal and refused to apply the law or to pay taxes to support this goal. After a great deal of conflict over a four year period, the application of the Act was severely limited. While the actual overt conflict subsided at this time, low levels of conflict remained for nearly 100 years. Then in 1967 the Acadians, for the first time, were able to force schools to provide all instruction in French. During the time period of 1959 to 1967, after the Acadians presented their petition to the school board with regard to this issue, overt conflict was very evident. In this case, other groups such as the Orange Lodge and the Loyal True Blue Association became involved in the conflict against the Acadians.

Emergence of Conflict

Most intergroup conflicts occur between groups after they have been living together for some time. This means that a moral order and rules of behavior (for all groups) have been established. Conflict will begin to become evident when this moral order is disrupted and subordinate ethnic groups begin to act in non-normative fashions. Shibutani and Kwan (1965) refer to this as the breakdown of the *color line.*

As the color line begins to deteriorate and blur the distinctions between groups, group consciousness will begin to develop. Members of the minority ethnic group will discover that they occupy similar social spaces and develop a consciousness of kind. Kriesberg (1973) suggests that three aspects of awareness are required: (1) Consciousness of kind must exist for the group. A major requisite for this to emerge is the intensity and frequency of communication between members. The greater the frequency and intensity of the interaction, the greater the likelihood that a sense of consciousness of kind will emerge. A bondedness will emerge and common symbols will be defined positively. Hence those groups with extensive cross-national communication vehicles find maintenance of group identity easy. On the other hand, such groups as the Polish, with a limited number of communications (and regional in perspective) have a difficult time in maintaining a collective identity. Others such as Native people are in the process of developing communication networks; (2) ethnic groups must be dissatisfied with their position relative to other ethnic groups; and (3) ethnic groups must think that a reduction of their dissatisfaction can be brought about by the *other* group changing their behavior.

Because of the above processes, group boundaries emerge and become clearly defined. The initial boundaries that emerge may be more or less visible and permeable but, differences in membership are important and as a result, an intensification of ethnocentrism occurs. A "we"-"they" definition emerges, e.g., an adversary is identified. Moral judgements about "we" and "they" result. There is a polarization of participants into "good" and "evil." The existing stereotypes begin to reinforce the social boundaries and the "we" group is viewed as good while the "they" group is transformed into "evil." The "we" participants begin to impute vile motives to the "they" group. Since any act may be interpreted in a number of ways, the "they" actions are interpreted in the least favorable light while the "we" acts are defined as noble. It is important to point out that this process can be viewed as occurring for both groups. Shibutani and Kwan (1965) point out that a remarkable feature of conflict is that the conception of the enemy formed on one side is almost a mirror image of the conception formed on the other (contrast conception).

As the contrast conceptions develop, the boundaries become more and more rigid, and a rigidity of beliefs within each group occurs. First of all, sanctioned communication results. A member of a "we" group can no longer question the actions of his group or suggest a "favorable" interpretation of the "they" group behavior. To do so would encourage others of the "we" group to begin to suspect one of complicity or at least of being duped. The result of this sanctioned and selective communication is that one only says positive things about one's own group and negative things about the other group.

This contrast conception formation also facilitates the maintenance of group solidarity. Since the "other" group is defined as "bad," "we" must combat these evil forces. Hence it is honourable to join the fight against evil. At the same time one is able to obtain some measure of identity by affiliating with a group. Other members of the group reward in group normative behavior. Hence to follow the norms of the in group has substantial material as well as psychic rewards (both potential and real).

The emergence of the contrast conception also allows for the emergence of an ethical dualism. Because in group members view the out group members as the enemy, and thus capable of great brutality and evil doing (something less than human and thus hardly deserving respect or consideration), many actions which would be considered immoral if directed toward in group members would not be so considered when they are directed toward out group members (Gladstone, 1959).

The double standard of morality that develops thus allows each group to act toward the "other" group in ways which would not normally be condoned. All of this is, of course, justified because of the opponent's evil intent. As pointed out previously, actual justification of the conflict may take on different dimensions. For example, one justification for engaging in conflict is the "last resort" rationale. The argument here is that the group has tried all other avenues of resolving the incompatibilities. Other rationales might be the "weakness of man" or the "necessity" justification. What is important to remember is the fact that each group has some over-arching rationale for engaging in conflict.

Subordinate Leadership

The rationale used to engage in conflict is vocalized by the minority ethnic group leaders (Lasswell, 1966). An attempt is made to redefine the position of the minority ethnic group from one of inferior to one of equal or in some cases superior status to that of the dominant group. Initially, the discontent experienced by the minority ethnic members is diffuse and nonfocused but the leadership is eventually able to identify an adversary (the cause of the discontent) and thus allow for directed behaviors toward that group. As the partisan organization develops, the leadership changes. The new leaders are usually not leaders of the past and are not part of the established community. These new leaders are not faced with maintaining their position in the community and do not feel constrained by the existing norms of the community (Coleman, 1957).

The emerging leadership's first role is to increase the readiness of the group to act in a collective fashion. This is accomplished by building a loyalty of a constituency to an organization or to a group of leaders (Guindon, 1964). This means that a sense of legitimization of the new leaders must be established. The legitimizations are generally created by the intellectuals who have joined the organization and who sometimes have become the new leaders. Blain (1962), in analysis of Quebec nationalism, argues that since the end of the Duplessis era, intellectuals have begun to play a very prominent role in generating and sustaining conflict between the French and the English.

The new leaders begin to identify the problems and provide possible solutions. Handling these problems will, the leaders argue, change the position of the subordinate group in the social structure and provide psychic rewards such as a sense of dignity and self respect. For example, in 1956 a group of Black leaders in Toronto forced the Board of Education to remove the book *Little Black Sambo* from school libraries.

The role of the leadership in conflict is a most important factor. Their ability to solve (simultaneously) two problems will generally determine whether or not they retain positions of leadership. First of all, they must keep members committed to the cause, even when they are not actively participating in conflict behaviors. Secondly, control of the various factions within the organization must be complete (Gamson, 1975). This means that leaders, at all times, need to deal effectively with four different sectors of society. First of all, as we have pointed out above, they must deal with members, those with whom they share common values. Secondly, they must deal with a more and more sophisticated (yet limiting) mass media. For example, a half hour interview may be given to a television station outlining grievances and past activities of a group. However, by the time it is shown on television it will generally take up no more than one minute. The third sector it must deal with is a potential third party which is in favor of the goals of the subordinate group but has yet to become involved (a political reference public). The last sector is, of course, the group that is capable of granting the goals desired by the group (Lipsky, 1973).

Functions of Conflict

We now need to address the issue of the functions of conflict from both a macro perspective as well as from the dominant and subordinate perspective. From the dominant group perspective, conflict is viewed as dysfunctional and disruptive to society.

On the other hand, the existence of a moderate degree of conflict (for periods of time) may have some positive effects. Coser (1956), for example, suggests that conflict in society: (i) sets boundaries between groups by strengthening group consciousness, (ii) permits the maintenance of relationships under conditions of stress, (iii) provides a kind of balancing mechanism in preventing deep cleavages along the social axis, and (iv) allows for a testing of power strength of each group so that accommodation between the groups is possible.

Conflict can be destructive, disruptive and dysfunctional for society. Prolonged conflict (or extremely intensive conflict) can result in the suspension of other social system institutional organizations. Economic institutions may be forced to close, educational systems may be forced to curtail their pure research efforts as the military institutional sphere drains off more and more money, as well as the youth of society. The prolonged existence of conflict in an area may have negative material, social, as well as psychological effects on the people residing in the area.

One of the more neglected areas of investigation has to do with how conflict is viewed and can affect subordinate groups in society. Himes (1966) identifies four dimensions in which conflict can be viewed as functional from the perspective of the subordinate group: (i) structural, (ii) communication, (iii) solidarity and, (iv) identity.

Structural

One of the major functions of conflict from a subordinate group's perspective is that it can reduce the power differential between itself and the dominant group. In reducing the power differential it also restricts the existing status differences. In the process of conflict, the pre-existing vertical status arrangement between dominant and subordinate groups will change to a more horizontal status arrangement. The act of conflict means that the dominant group is no longer in a position to maintain an up-and-down flow of interaction between super- and subordinate. It also suggests that the subordinate group may achieve some of its goals.

Communication

The engaging of conflict, from the perspective of the subordinate group, brings the problem into the focus of collective attention. Newspapers, radio, and television, as well as academics begin to look at, research, and report on the varying subissues that emerge. While it brings the problem out into the open, it also destroys what can be called the "convenience of ignorance." That is, people can no longer say that they didn't realize there was a problem or they didn't know that group "X" was dissatisfied with their lot. The result of this is to elevate the issue into the realm of public opinion both at secondary communication levels (talks, homes) as well as into the political level.

Solidarity

A third function that conflict has is that it can bring the core values of the society into sharp focus and national attention. Many conflicts originate because ultimate values such as "equal opportunity" are not being met. As a result, the call to arms is not based on over-throwing the system, but rather attempting to work within the system and make corrections where necessary. Human Rights codes were introduced to force people into being equal employers and stop discrimination on the basis of sex, race, religion, etc.

Once conflict is indicated, group members begin to sanction others in their group so that the result is increased solidarity. They begin to function as a "we" group. Because external action directed toward specific members will be interpreted as a threat to the entire group, increased consciousness of kind will result.

Identity

Collective identity is produced and maintained through an interactive process of history, ritual and interaction (Klapp, 1972). At the most general level, ethnic identity (race consciousness) is defined as having allegiance to a particular group which is seen as conflicting with another group. The role of conflict and its relation to identity must begin with alienation. To maintain oneself in a group facilitates linkage between the individual and one's reference group. As Pettigrew (1964) points out:

> Recruits willingly and eagerly devote themselves to the group's goals. And they find themselves systematically rewarded (by the group). . . . They are expected to evince strong racial pride, to assert their full rights as citizens, to face jail and police brutality unhesitatingly for the cause. . . . Note, . . . that these expected and rewarded actions all publicly commit the member to the group and its aim. (195-196).

Himes (1966) goes on further:

> In the interactive process of organized group conflict self involvement is the opposite side of the coin of overt action. Actors become absorbed by ego and emotion into the group and the group is projected through their actions. This linkage of individual and group in ego and action is the substance of identity. (10)

As a result of the group action of conflict, the sense of alienation experienced by these groups is dispelled by a new sense of purpose and significance. As Pitts (1974) points out, it is important to remember that identity is a social product. It is a result of purposive actions and an interpretation of actions operating in social relationships (Paige, 1971). As Brown (1935) has suggested:

> A race consciousness group . . . is a social unit struggling for status in society. It is thus a conflict group, and race consciousness itself is a result of conflict. The race of the group, though not intrinsically significant, becomes an identifying symbol, serving to intensify the sense of solidarity. (573)

It should be clear, then, that conflict does not have to be viewed or defined as dysfunctional for society. As defined by a minority group, conflict can be viewed as positive. Conflict, as pointed out earlier, can be viewed as a variable. That is, levels of conflict and their consequences may be positive or negative, minimal or devastating. At one level (the minimal form of conflict) we find actions at the ethnophaulism, stereotyping level. This level of conflict is generally found when ethnic group members have been able (to some extent) to penetrate the institutional structures of the society. More serious levels of conflict would involve informal, illegal forms of discrimination. At an even more serious level of conflict, one would talk of mob violence, riots, or more legalized sanctions such as deportation or expropriation.

The intensity of the conflict is usually higher when initiated by subordinate groups. As Gelfand (1973) points out, the dominant group does not want to engage in overt acts of conflict against the subordinate group. This does not mean that they do not exert force or influence on the subordinate group but rather they are able to do so under the facade of democracy and egalitarianism. The actions taken against Blacks living in Africville (a Black enclave in Halifax) are ample demonstration that the dominant group can destroy a community without engaging in overt conflict with the subordinate group (Clairmont and Magill, 1974).

Conflict, like any other social phenomenon, develops over time. As Allport (1958) stated, violence is an outgrowth of a milder state of mind. In most cases actual outbreaks of violence (defined in the conventional sense of physical injuries to persons and damage to property) take time before they occur. It does not suggest that all members of either group engage in support of the actual violence. In most cases of group violence, less than 10% of the members actually take part in the activity. However, one does find that while the majority do not actually take part in the violence, they do give social support to those members participating. While intense conflictual relations may continue for some extended time, they escalate from minimal forms of conflict, and generally de-escalate after time. (Rapoport, 1974)

Once a social conflict has emerged, the direction of the conflict (greater or less magnitude) will be dependent upon both the social-psychological and organizational changes within the society and the conflicting parties. As commitment to the cause increases, the conflict escalates. This commitment (by both the leaders and the followers) produces heightened in group identity and restricts the realistic evaluation of alternative courses of action (Hermann, 1969; Holsti, 1971).

Leaders also find themselves competing against other more radical or militant rivals, and this places pressure on the existing leadership to escalate the conflict.

Structural changes such as a changing membership (the less militant may leave the organization) and changing beliefs and values of the organization may also produce an escalating conflictual relationship with the adversary.

Kriesberg (1973) also points out that the relation between the conflicting parties is a source for escalating the conflict. Once conflict is evident, points of disagreement or dissatisfaction between the groups expand well beyond the initial focus. Issues which had, up to a certain point, been ignored or given little credence, now begin to assume central import. In fact, these new issues may become more important than the old points of conflict.

The work of Gross (1966) and Gurr (1970) suggests that the introduction of a third party into a two party conflict situation generally has the consequence of escalating the conflict. The introduction of a third party generally results from the fact that as the partisan groups pursue their goals, they infringe upon the interests of a third party. This third party then will enter the conflictual relationship. When this happens, the third group may give support to one side and thereby make it possible for the initial partisan group to continue their conflict. Given that an outsider gives help to one group it is equally likely that a fourth group will enter and provide support for the group without aid.

Conflict does not continue to increase indefinitely and eventually de-escalates in magnitude. From a social-psychological perspective, when expenditures for a goal exceed the rewards of the goal, action will be curtailed. The longer one remains in a conflictual state, the ability to carry out other behavior becomes less and the cost of emitting these alternative behaviors becomes greater.

Organizational changes may also bring about a reduction in the extent of conflict. First of all, internal discord may emerge with regard to the pursuit of a particular goal or the means being used to pursue this goal. Secondly, open negotiations between the two groups may take place so as to decrease the magnitude or even stop the conflict. A third way in which conflict may be reduced is by the inability of one group to continue its conflict behavior. One group may decide that the adversary's coercion has reduced its ability to pursue effectively its goals (Kriesberg, 1973).

Leaders of minority ethnic groups continually monitor the actions of the dominant group. Their actions are not always in accordance with their own needs. They also define the strategies and responses of the opposing group. This assessment is made because the dominant group may give concessions that prove to be illusory and serve simply as devices to maintain domination. For example, the dominant group may react to the subordinate demands in a variety of ways. It may provide symbolic rewards e.g., create a committee to study the issue, of which minority ethnic group members will be a part, or establish "open lines of communication." A second reaction may be to postpone action or to claim external restraint in giving rewards, e.g., the dominant group (or agency) would like to but they cannot because of external constraints. A last type of reaction that can be taken by the dominant group is to discredit the leaders of the subordinate group and thus dismiss their claims.

The actual termination of conflict may be brought about in several different ways. In one way there can be a winner and a loser, and the winner simply imposes its goal onto the loser. A second form of termination is that of withdrawal. Either the two parties break off relations, or one of the two parties withdraws its demands and strategies to pursue the goal. The situation then returns to a slightly changed status quo.

By far the most prevalent termination procedure is that of compromise. Here, mutual concessions are made by the two parties to terminate the conflict for the present time.

Conflict in Canada

There is little doubt that conflict (at various levels) is occurring in Canada. The revival of ethnicity as an important identity (both personal and group) may mean that more conflict will occur. The basis of this conflict may be because of a split labor market, value incongruence, or indirect structural violence.

The race riots in Victoria (1860) involving Blacks, the riots against the Japanese (1900), and the conflict directed towards Hutterites after World War II are all historical examples that show conflict has been a part of the Canadian way of life. More recent acts against visible minorities demonstrate that conflict is not a philosophy that has been discarded by many Canadians. The *Vancouver Sun* (Nov. 1, 1977) has shown that the Canadian Civil Liberties Association study in Toronto (1976) revealed the policy of realtors selling only to

"Whites" when the seller gave these instructions was generally practised. Other forms of lesser conflict are evident in the actions taken by Canadians.

Maclean's (Feb. 7, 1977) has reported that physical attacks against South Asians are reported at a rate of one per week in Toronto. Vancouver has also witnessed a rise in overt conflict against South Asians over the past five years.

Many of the intergroup conflicts that have taken place in the recent past have not involved large scale involvement of members of different ethnic groups. Most incidents have involved single individuals or small groups. For example, in 1973 a Black youth was charged with manslaughter over the death of a White. In 1976 several beatings of Asians were reported taking place in the subway of Toronto. By 1977, reports of "isolated" beatings of Asians and Blacks in the local newspapers were common place.

However, not all conflicts have remained at this level. In Toronto the neo-facist Western Guard Party went public on an anti-Black campaign. They instigated a White Power telephone line (which dispensed racist messages), disrupted Black community meetings and violently interrupted a local television show on which Blacks were appearing. A study of racial attitudes of school children in Ontario revealed that a new pastime for teenagers had emerged—"Paki-busting." In Sydney, Nova Scotia, a notice appeared at one of the local schools announcing an "Annual Nigger Jamboree." The notice stated that "all coons in the school at this time should be beaten to death or at least crippled" (Hill, 1977). Some cars in Alberta bear bumper stickers advising, "Keep Canada Green: Paint a Paki."

More overt collective conflicts have also been evident in the recent past. The overt violence between South Asians and Whites at a Canadian Pacific workshop in 1976 sent several participants to hospital. The same year, in Burnaby, British Columbia, a municipal council meeting was disrupted when a group of local White residents protested the building of a Muslim mosque and social-cultural centre in their neighborhood. The armed confrontation between Natives and Whites near Kenora and the actions of the FLQ from 1963 to 1970 also seem to illustrate that group conflict is not something of the past.

The Canadian public has, by and large, tried to ignore intergroup conflict or treat it as an isolated case, not indicative of a societal trend. A school board in British Columbia banned a film on racism, arguing that it would teach children to become racists. The Alberta provincial government refuses to discuss racial-ethnic conflicts, taking the position that they do not exist. Their continued refusal to support research, conferences, and public discussions of this issue corroborate their policy stance.

After presenting the current picture of conflict in today's society, we find that Canada is a relatively stable society with a minimum of conflict. The major groups that have engaged in conflict during the recent past have been French-Canadians and Native people. The answer to the question of why there has not been more conflict will serve to illustrate our theoretical model previously outlined.

Our first premise was based on the claim that sectors of society have to develop a consciousness of kind. The vast diverse background of immigrants does not facilitate common organization. For example, South Asians do not represent a group with common interests, values, or perspectives of reality. There are real differences between East African Ismailis, Zoroastrian Parsees, and Tamil Speaking Hindus (who may have different nationality backgrounds—Fiji, Mauritius, Uganda, Malaysia, Guyana, Trinidad, Singapore, South Africa, Britain, as well as India, Pakistan, Sri Lanka). We have also pointed out differences within other groups such as Doukhobors (e.g., Independents, Orthodox, Sons of Freedom), and Mennonites (Old Order, Old Colony, Bergthaler, General Conference, Brethren). Unlike the above groups, French-Canadians do have more or less a sense of a common culture that has been able to develop over the years.

We also pointed out that conflicts between groups generally are generated after groups have resided in an area for a relatively long period of time. In many cases, e.g., Asians, groups have not resided in Canada for a long enough time. Tied to this is the fact that visible minority ethnic groups make up a small proportion of the total population. This is not true for the French-Canadian population. While Native people make up a small percentage of the total population, we find that they are concentrated in specific areas of Canada and do make up substantial portions of regional populations. Other groups are spatially concentrated in urban areas but in no way can be considered ghettoized, or reaching what Breton, et al. (1974) call the "saturation point" of racial tolerance.

A third factor identified as important in the escalation or de-escalation of conflict is the leadership. Generally, leadership emerges out of the intellectuals of the subordinate PAG. In the case of French Quebec, the intellectuals have become predominant in the leadership contingent since the late 1950s. They have provided a focus for the masses in terms of identifying the adversary, as well as articulating the concerns of the people. This, of course, has led to a polarization into "we-they."

A Case Illustration—The FLQ (1960-1970)

The FLQ (during the period under consideration) probably consisted of a nucleus of 100 members. A less radical group (involved in support activities of the FLQ core) of about 500 surrounded this activist element.

The central theme developed by the FLQ was that there was oppression, exploitation, and colonization of the Quebecois. Any beginning student would agree that French-Canadians over history have been the victims of injustices and vexations (Pelletier, 1971). According to the FLQ members, the oppressed state of French-Canadians is a result of a "shrewd and deliberate plot between Anglo-Saxon capitalists and internal French-Canadian sell outs."

A content analysis of the material produced over the years by the FLQ demonstrates that they identified the adversary as well as attempted to provide a consciousness of kind. The actual ideology of the FLQ is extremely ambiguous. While it uses many of the words one associates with radical leftists—"lackeys, toadies of the bigshots, society of terrorized slaves, technocratic usurpers, bludgeons of freedom"—the central thrust of the manifestos are devoid of any real substantive actions or philosophy.

However, in the presentation of this ideology, there is the promise of material rewards (higher wages, better jobs) as well as psychic rewards (sense of dignity, control over one's own destiny). The presentation of these messages required the effective use of the mass media. Analysis of the documents seized from the FLQ first of all shows that the members were well aware of this. They provided instructions on how to present slogans, where to present them, and where and how to use the mass media. For example, the style and presentation of the manifesto employs certain expressions and words rather than others. The use of "Franglais" and "joual" is no accident. They believed (perhaps correctly) that this was the most effective style in relating and changing their audience.

The rigidity of beliefs and the separation of the "we-they" for the members began to be evident in the various documents produced by the FLQ in the mid-sixties. For example, one document discusses the possibility of killings in the liberation of Quebec: "The revolutionary must be prepared for everything. We recognize only two classes of people—revolutionary patriots and collaborationists, traitors. There can be no middle ground" (*La Congnée*, publication of the FLQ, December, 1963). Another document states: ". . . you must not believe a single word that comes from a Federalist, for a Federalist is in the first place a liar and in the second place a thief" (*Victoire*, official publication of the FLQ, Vol. 1, #2, December, 1967).

While the FLQ was pursuing its conflictual path, other groups such as the extremist wing RIN (Rassemblement pour L'Indépendance Nationale) began to form the FLP (Front de Libération Populaire) supporting "workers' rights." Some attempts were made by the FLQ to form a coalition with these groups but the organizational structure of the FLQ was not conducive to such structures.[2] The FLQ was successful in getting almost all of the Quebec intellectuals (and many anglophone intellectuals) to object to the government's enactment of the War Measures Act and thus form a kind of temporary coalition.

The result was that structural conditions were conducive to the emergence of a "we-they" perspective. A very effective French-Canadian intellectual leadership (Vallières, 1971) was able to identify the adversary, articulate the goals to be desired, and promise to the people general material and psychic rewards.

The escalation of the conflict started with slogans painted on federal buildings and mail boxes. Fires were then set in various rural CNR stations. Between 1963 and 1967, 35 low power bombs were set by the FLQ. From 1968 to 1970, 60 high power bombs were utilized by the FLQ. In addition to the bombings, electronic and military thefts were engaged in as well as bank robberies to support the movement. By the time British diplomat James Cross was kidnapped and Pierre Laporte killed, 10 other deaths and 50 injuries were attributed (or proclaimed) to the activities of the FLQ. Throughout the seven year period, the conflict escalated and a more black and white (good and evil) image began to emerge.

The existence of a legitimate political party (PQ) provided the FLQ with passive support. For example, PQ member Pierre Bourgault's speech a day after the kidnapping of James Cross stated, "We are five million political prisoners." The PQ did not immediately react in a negative manner to the actions of the FLQ, and when they did, they generally accompanied this stance with attempts to either justify the violence or to at least explain it as not the

---

[2] The FLQ organizational structure was in response to their defined security requirements. The actual number for each cell varied, but each was a quasi-separate entity. The logic behind such a system is that if one cell is discovered and disbanded by police, the members cannot give information about other members.

FLQ's fault, and even as the consequence of the authorities' fault (Pelletier, 1971).

It would not be until the assassination of Pierre Laporte that the PQ and many other groups would speak against the activities of the FLQ. But the act of murdering Pierre Laporte illustrates the conviction of the members of the FLQ—the end justifies any means.

A second factor would also lead to the de-escalation of the FLQ. The organizational structure did not allow itself to achieve the goals set out previously. On the horizontal plane, the organization is divided into semi-autonomous regions, sub-regions and zones. Within each zone a pyramidal structure emerges. The basic unit was the cell (composed of 2-3 persons); three cells formed a group and two to four groups formed a detachment. The result was that communications between members was very difficult. Many of the participants never even knew the names or addresses of those with whom they worked (FLQ document, 1966; Lemoyne, 1964).

The cessation of conflict was brought about through several processes. First of all, internal discord began to emerge in terms of strategies used to obtain the ends. The use of bombings, kidnappings, and assassinations became a matter of concern. Certainly the ethical dualism ideology had been accepted by the core members, but the internalization of this ethic by the masses was not evident.

A third factor that brought about the cessation of conflict was the fact that the federal and provincial governments began to carry on open negotiations with the FLQ. While many of the demands were not eventually satisfied, the fact that negotiations were taking place was important. The eventual revision of the electoral map may have been a result of the conflict. The impact of this act was the change in the perspective of the oppressor.

The last factor to be discussed in the present chapter focuses on the ability of the group to continue its conflictual actions. After the kidnapping and assassination of Laporte, many of the better known leaders were sent to jail, left the country, or legitimized their claims for social change. The invocation of the War Measures Act may have also indicated that continuing the conflict was not in the best interests. As pointed out previously, minority PAG members continually monitor the actions of the dominant group and base part of their actions on their observations.

Conclusion

The evidence clearly indicates that overall conflict is not endemic to Canadian society. However, it does point out that when certain structural conditions are present, conflict can emerge. The recent events of conflict with French and Native people do alert us to one very important structural condition—lack of cross-cutting social affiliation. This idea views a system as a balance of power with overlapping economic, religious, ethnic, and geographical groupings. Because of this overlapping, each group constrains the exercise of power by the other. The result is a mutual group adjustment in the establishment of policy, and implementation of the policy. Out of this process a shared system of beliefs and values will emerge, and compromise will result rather than conflict.

It is not surprising then, that these groups should engage in conflict. In cases involving other minority ethnic groups, we find there is a diversity of membership in specific social-economic-geographic characteristics. In addition, we find that networks between members or organizational structures have not been well developed. This lack of transmission of ideas and information retards the development of a well-developed consciousness of kind. It remains to be seen as to whether or not conflict will be generated as these communication processes are developed. However, as long as the minority ethnic groups continue to develop cross-cutting loyalties and do not develop networks, it is unlikely that serious overt violence will emerge in the near future.

REFERENCES

Allport, G. W. *The Nature of Prejudice.* Cambridge, Mass.: Addison-Wesley, 1958.

Aubert, Vihelm. "Competition and Dissensus: Two types of Conflict and Conflict Resolution," *Journal of Conflict Resolution,* (March, 7, 1963): 26-42.

Blain, Jean. "La voie de la souveraineté," *Liberté,* (March, 1962): 113-121.

Bonacich, Edna. "A Theory of Ethnic Antagonism: The Split Labor Market," *American Sociological Review,* 37 (1972): 547-559.

Breton, R. and A. Breton. "Le séparatisme ou le respect du status quo," *Cité libre,* (April, 1962): 17-28.

Brown, W. C. "Racial Conflict Among South African Natives," *American Journal of Sociology,* 40, (1935): 569-581.

Clairmont, D. and D. Magill. *Africville.* Toronto: McClelland and Stewart, 1974.

Coleman, James. *Community Conflict.* New York: The Free Press, 1957.

Coser, L. *The Functions of Social Conflict.* Glencoe, Ill.: Free Press, 1956.

Dahrendorf, R. *Class and Class Conflict in Industrial Society.* Stanford: Stanford University Press, 1959.

Deutsch, K. "Changing Images of International Conflict," *Journal of Social Issues,* 23(1) (1967): 91-107.

De Vos, George. "Conflict, Dominance and Exploitation in Human Systems of Social Segregation: Some Theoretical Perspectives from the Study of Personality in Culture," in A. de Reuck and J. Knight (eds.), *Conflict in Society.* London: J & A Churchill Ltd, 1966: 60-82.

Gamson, W. *The Strategy of Social Protest.* Homewood, Illinois: Dorsey, 1975.

Gelfand, D. "Ethnic Relations and Social Research: A Re-evaluation," pp. 5-18 in D. Gelfand and R. Lee (eds.), *Ethnic Conflicts and Power: A Cross National Perspective.* New York: J. Wiley and Sons, 1973.

Gladstone, A. "The Conception of the Enemy," *Journal of Conflict Resolution,* 3, (1959): 132-137.

Gross, F. *World Politics and Tension Areas.* New York: University Press, 1966.

Guindon, H. "Social Unrest, Social Class and Quebec's Bureaucratic Revolution," *Queen's Quarterly,* 71(2) (1964): 150-162.

Gurr, T. *Why Men Rebel.* Princeton: Princeton University Press, 1970.

Hermann, C. F. *Crises in Foreign Policy.* Indianapolis: Bobbs-Merrill Co., 1969.

Hill, D. *Human Rights in Canada: A Focus on Racism.* Ottawa: Canadian Labour Congress, 1977.

Himes, J. "The Functions of Racial Conflict," *Social Forces,* 45 (1966): 1-10.

Holsti, O. R. "Crises, Stress and Decision Making," *International Social Science Journal*, 23(1) (1971): 53-67.

Klapp, O. *Currents of Unrest*. New York: Holt, Rinehart and Winston, 1972.

Kriesberg, L. *The Sociology of Social Conflicts*. Englewood Cliffs, NJ: Prentice-Hall, 1973.

Kuper, Leo. "Some Aspects of Violent and Nonviolent Political Change In Plural Societies A. Conflict and the Plural Society: Ideologies of Violence among Subordinate Groups," pp. 153-167 in L. Kuper and M. G. Smith (eds.), *Pluralism in Africa*. Berkeley: University of California Press, 1969.

Lasswell, H. *Conflict and Leadership: The Process of Decision and the Nature of Authority*, 1966.

Lemoyne, P. (pseudonym). The Union of the Revolutionary Forces," *La Cognee*, No. 17, (1964): 15.

Lenski, G. and J. Lenski. *Human Societies: An Introduction to Macrosociology*. New York: McGraw-Hill, 1978.

Leslie, Peter. "The Role of Political Parties in Promoting the Interests of Ethnic Minorities," *Canadian Journal of Political Science*, 2(4) (1969): 419-433.

Lipsky, M. "Protest as a Political Resource," in D. Gelfand and R. Lee (eds.), *Ethnic Conflicts and Power: A Cross National Perspective*. New York: J. Wiley and Sons, 1973.

Lightbody, J. "A Note on the Theory of Nationalism as a Function of Ethnic Demands," *Canadian Journal of Political Science*, 2, (September 1969): 327-337.

Oberschall, A. *Social Conflict and Social Movements*. Englewood Cliffs, NJ: Prentice Hall, 1973.

Paige, J. "Political Orientation and Riot Participation," *American Sociological Review*, 36 (1971): 810-819.

Pelletier, G. *The October Crisis*. McClelland and Stewart: Toronto, 1971.

Pettigrew, T. *A Profile of the Negro American*. Princeton: D. Van Nostrand, 1964.

Pitts, J. "The Study of Race Consciousness: Comments on New Directions," *American Journal of Sociology*, 80 (1974): 665-687.

Porter, J. *The Vertical Mosaic*. Toronto: University of Toronto Press, 1965.

Rapoport, A. *Conflict in Manmade Environment*. Middlesex, England: Penguin, 1974.

Shibutani, T. and K. Kwan. *Ethnic Stratification*. London: Macmillan, 1965.

Sites, Paul. *Control and Constraint*. New York: Macmillan, 1975.

Vallières, Pierre. *White Niggers of America*. Toronto: McClelland and Stewart, 1971.

Weber, M. *The Theory of Social and Economic Organization*. Translated by A. M. Henderson and T. Persons. New York: Oxford University Press, 1947.

Chapter 9

Racism

Levels of Racism

One specific ideology that both includes and extends the process of stereotypes is that of racism. While during the sixties a number of academics focused on this issue, it seems strange that Canadian social scientists in the area of intergroup relations did not find it worthy of investigation. Only recently has there been any interest by Canadians in this issue (Frideres, 1973, 1976; Henry, 1978). While a great deal of controversy has been generated concerning the definition of this concept, some agreement with regard to its meaning has emerged. Generally, it refers to the process of categorizing people on the basis of presumed physiological characteristics. On the basis of these physiological attributes, social and psychological (and sometimes physical) attributes are *causally* correlated with these physiological stimuli. Generally, skin pigmentation is used as the master trait which allows for the causal connection to social-psychological behavior.

When one discusses racism as an ideology (a set of related beliefs held by a person, as well as a statement of what an individual is trying to achieve), one is analysing racism at an individual level. That is, the ideas that an individual has in his cognitive mapping framework. In addition, it should be made clear that two forms of individual racism exist. Kovel (1970) makes a distinction between dominative and aversive individual racism. The former is the individual who acts out bigoted beliefs, while the latter is the type of individual who believes in White race superiority and is more or less aware of it, but does nothing overt about it. This distinction is somewhat similar to Merton's (1949) distinction and relationship between prejudice and discrimination. His four-fold classification (see Figure 1) system shows that one can be prejudiced (attitude) yet can vary in one's behavior (discrimination). Research from various countries (Frideres, 1973) shows that individual racism seems to be on the decline. However, the data also show that in Canada individual racism is alive and well. Particularly, Frideres argues that aversive racism in Canada is virulent and perhaps moving into a dominative form.

FIGURE 1

		Prejudice	
		Yes	No
Discrimination	Yes	1	2
	No	3	4

A second level of racism has been labeled "institutional." Institutionalized racism is defined as those established laws and relationships which systematically reflect and produce differential treatment of various segments in society. While it emerges from the existence of individual racist beliefs, once created it is independent of individual racism (Skolnick, 1966). When a society creates institutions (and institutional relationships) which maintain pre-existing differential treatments toward specific groups, then society no longer needs individuals publicly espousing the virtues of individual racism. It is our view, after careful analysis of Canadian society, that institutional racism is evident, and it promotes and sustains the existing inequality that is present in our social system.

The perspective of institutional racism places heavy emphasis on the importance of history. It is argued that historically, institutions defined and regulated norms, role relationships and sanctions which have now become part of the moral order. Individual racists, because of their belief in the notion of White superiority, fought to attain and sustain social, political, and economic domination over other ethno-social groups. But institutional racism does not exist until "the processes that maintain domination—control of whites over non-whites—are built into the major social institutions" (Fong and Johnson, 1974). The end product, however, shows that institutional racism has produced differential access to power and privilege, subordination, and with institutions and restrictive laws, has shaped and legitimated the stratified system we now have (Jones, 1972; Knowles and Prewitt, 1969).

It is our intention to focus on the emergence of institutionalized racism rather than upon individual racism. Each feeds on the other, and it is our assessment that a cyclical relationship exists in terms of its predominance and obscurity. As the pervasiveness of institutional racism increases in a society, individual racism decreases. However, as the social system tries to correct this built-in structural bias, and institutional racism begins to be challenged, individual racism re-emerges.

When the focus of race relations is taken out of the psycho-dynamic perspective (which has characterized the interpretation of North American race relations for the past 50 years), we must then focus on the institutional structure of that system to explain intergroup relations (Gilbert and Specht, 1972). When this structural focus is taken, it also shows us the import and role of institutions, their structure, their interrelationships, as well as the bureaucratic functions played by them. Bureaucracies have the job of establishing regulations and priorities as well as qualifications for particular positions in our society. Only those individuals able to meet these initial qualifications will be able to participate in the ongoing institutional structure. For example, when Native people suggested that they be hired by the Department of Indian Affairs (with a staff of about 14,000), the response by the Minister of Indian Affairs was that placement was only possible for those belonging to a particular union, and having a particular position and level of seniority in the union. Unless these requirements were met, an Indian could not be hired, and if hired without these qualifications, the union would strike. Yetman and Steele (1971) go even further and point out that even if certain discriminative policies were modified within a specific institution, the inequities in other institutional spheres would continue to perpetuate the inequities. The reasoning behind such an argument is that because of the linkages between these institutions, changes in one segment will result in compensating actions by others. Let us provide an example. Certain post-secondary school systems have attempted to modify their structure in an attempt to increase Indian participation in the education system. These changes involve one or all of the following: entrance requirements, curriculum requirements, residence requirements, special tutoring and special programming. The result of such changes at various schools has been an increase in Native participation, with a commensurate increase in Native graduates. However, the degrees for these persons do not have the same value as regular degrees. Principals of elementary and secondary schools will not give this type of degree an equivalent assessment as the regular degree, and thus employers are hesitant to hire these people. In the end, someone who has an education degree with certain irregularities will not be given the same consideration by potential employers as those who have a regular degree.

In essence, ethnic group subordination is at all levels of institutional spheres, such as the law, education, policy and economy. This last point also illustrates the notion of interaction and accumulation of inequities. In addition to the interaction effects such exclusion produces, Jones (1972) goes on to show how this exclusion accumulates. He points out that missing out at the first level of economic viability perpetuates other economic losses. Once the institutions evolve so as to provide differential opportunities for wealth, power, and authority, then unequal resources will produce unequal qualifications to compete for goods and services and subsequently lead to limited access to goods and services by certain groups. Thus the vicious cycle continues.

A third level of racism is what Jones (1972) calls cultural racism. It is defined as the individual and institutional expression of the superiority of one group's cultural heritage over that of another group. To define this as racism is appropriate to the extent that racial and cultural factors are highly correlated and are the systematic basis for inferior treatment.

Thus far we have attempted to show that racism (at a theoretical level) can be analysed at three levels: individual, institutional, and cultural. At each level the unit of analysis changes and thus the factors to be taken into consideration with regard to an explanation also have to be changed. In addition, it should be emphasized that while aversive individual racism is high in Canadian society, dominative is low. The reason being that institutional racism is pervasive in our society; the institutional structure of our society is such that individuals and groups who are defined as inferior cannot make inroads into the upper echelons of Canadian economic and political structures.

To summarize, the concept of racism embodies the following cognitive mapping (Nash, 1962) structures:

(1) Natural laws exist for man and one of these laws is a "natural" ordering of groups of people.
(2) Races differ in their ability to handle the intricacies (or complexities) of a social system for high levels of development.
(3) A group's "cultural achievement" is an indicator of their innate capabilities.
(4) If an "inferior" race doesn't receive help from a "superior" race, the inferior race will destroy itself and others along with it.
(5) The fight for "equality" among races is a fight against truth.

While certainly the cognitive map of each man on the street may not be a replica of the above, variations will be noticed depending upon region of residence, socialization exposure as well as a number of related experiences the individual undergoes in his lifetime (Banton, 1966, 1979).

It is important to point out that we are not discussing ethnocentrism. Wilson (1973) points out that ethnocentrism is a principle of invidious group distinction whereas racism is a philosophy or ideology of racial exploitation. This distinction is important and is indirectly addressed by Schermerhorn (1970). In his discussion of minimal and maximal racism, Schermerhorn defines minimal racism as when a segment of society claims that darker people are backward or less evolved but only different in degree from the group in control. This definition is more an expression of cultural ethnocentrism rather than racism. However, when maximal racism is defined (darker people are qualitatively different from the control group—not a degree of difference but an absolute difference), Schermerhorn points out the central focus of racism as an ideology.

We have thus far tried to characterize the concept of racism as well as identify the different forms it can take. We have also stated that this ideology is prevalent in our society and continues to remain an issue which is important in explaining some intergroup behaviors. To this end, we will provide the reader with a short historical overview of the emergence of this ideology and conclude with a specific discussion of its emergence in the Canadian context.

Zubaida (1970) identifies three different explanations as to why and how racism as an ideology emerged. They are:

(1) as a result of scientific response to the needs of capitalism;

(2) as a result of racial prejudices of individuals;

(3) as a result of scientific mistakes.

While previous authors have tried to argue for one or the other explanations, it is our claim that they cannot be viewed as independent phenomena. Our approach, as the reader will quickly see, is an eclectic approach and will encompass all three perspectives. The import of any one will vary by time period, but in the final assessment, we feel that all three are necessary to provide a full and complete explanation.

Racism in Comparative and Historical Perspective

If we had to assign a date to the beginning of racism, we would agree with Cox (1948) and suggest that the beginning of the 16th century was the time. Others would certainly disagree with this date and prefer to date it much earlier (Barzun, 1932; 1937) or later (Poliakov, 1968). However, it is our view that these authors confuse the distinction between racism (as an ideology) and the existence of prejudice and the practice of discrimination. We would not disagree with the fact that people have been discriminated against prior to this time. On the contrary, we, as well as many others, could provide a great deal of information confirming the claim.

The Greeks practised discrimination, but their notions of the basic divisions of their society were based upon cultural, not racial, factors. If individuals did not have the Greek culture, particularly the language, they were considered to be barbarians. However, the barbarians were still allowed to enter their culture and attempt to assimilate with the Greeks, with encouragement from the sector in power. Later, during this historical period, there was an active movement by the Greek society to acculturate the barbarians.

The Roman Empire was the next great European power that arose (since it generally consisted of the major population of the world at that time). Again, we do not find evidence of any racial antagonism. Slaves were evident in the system, but slavery was dependent upon where one was born. One became (or did not become) a citizen depending on where one was born. Slaves were of diverse ethnic groups and the distinguishing factor for freedom or slavery was a matter of citizenship. In addition, slaves could attain citizenship, become active and full participants in the system, and increase their social status and power. It seems apparent, then, that racial stigmas were not important at this time.

The impact of the above should be impressed upon the reader. The social relations that occurred were based upon residence, not race. Intermarriage was forbidden only between what Cox (1948) calls "social estate(s)," not biological races. Physiological stigmas were outside the field of perception and social evaluation.

As we view further the European historical process, a succession of invasions of the Roman Empire occurred. The Huns, Turks, and Moors invaded the land (and because of superior weaponry) were able to conquer and subjugate the people. But once again racial (in the biological sense) antagonism did not develop. Religious prejudice (best shown by the Moslem culture) did occur, however. Thus, by the Middle Ages, we still find no biological racial antagonism within the European continent. This seems to be evident by one philosophy adhered to at the time, which was "that the way to handle the Moslem problem is to simply marry them."

At this time Christian Europe viewed the rest of the world in this perspective. They perceived the rest of the world as heathens or infidels. Thus, if we study the causes of the crusades, we will find they were on the basis of economic and religious differences, not racial. However, it should be pointed out that at this time feudalism was dying and economic expansion efforts by the Europeans were beginning.

These Holy Wars (from late 11th to 13th centuries) were based on the notion of conversion. The participants wanted to convert these infidels (by whom they were surrounded) to Christianity. But still (initially) no notion of biological inferiority was attached to these people. What was attached was the notion of cultural inferiority.

The next time period with which we are particularly concerned, is the epoch of discovery in North America. We will examine how racist thought has become central to North American modes of thought and perspectives of social reality. This, of course, brings us around to what we previously stated as the beginning of race relations. Several factors were present in this development.

First, the religion of the two great powers (Spain and Portugal) at that time was based on two related factors: (1) Manifest Destiny and (2) Hamlite Rationalization. These notions carried over to other countries—notably England. The notion of Manifest Destiny was portrayed in several ways but its basic point was that White people were to rule the world or a large portion of it. Several variations of this notion were present and the actual amount of the world to be controlled by Whites varied from one interpretation to another. The Hamlite Rationalization is a belief that certain people are to be subservient to other people.

This idea emerged out of the Biblical story of Ham. Ham, coming home late at night, entered his father's house. His father had been engaged in an orgy and lay drunk and naked on the floor. As Ham and his brother came into the house Ham looked at his father while his brother did not and covered his father. The story concluded with the statement by God that Ham shall have a "mark" placed upon him, his children, and their children's children, etc., and that they shall be servants of the world. Over the years, the "mark" has meant non-White skin and "servants" came to be viewed as a legitimizing factor for the low socio-economic status of non-Whites (Haller, 1971).

Manifest Destiny, the idea of a White man's burden, and the Hamlite Rationalization, in disguised forms, continue to shape White Canadians' values and policies. Manifest Destiny and the Hamlite Rationalization have done much to stimulate the modern-day myth that non-White peoples are generally incapable of self-government. For example, the continuation of the structure of Indian Affairs for well over one hundred years has been partially based on this philosophy and continues to reinforce this belief system.

The usage of the concept Manifest Destiny is helpful in analysing the current White responses to such political movements as "Red Power" and "Black Power." Black and Red Power are based on the belief that Black people (and Red) are capable of governing and controlling their own communities. White rejection of Red and Black Power reflects, in part, the widely accepted White myth that Indians and Blacks are incapable of self-government and must be controlled and governed by Whites.

The belief in a "White man's burden" also has its modern day counterpart, particularly in the attitudes and practices of so-called White liberals busily trying to solve the "Indian problem." The liberal often bears a strong sense of responsibility for helping the Indian find a better life. He generally characterizes these people as disadvantaged, unfortunate, or culturally deprived. Liberal paternalism is reflected not only in individual attitudes but in the procedures and policies of institutions such as the welfare system and most "war on poverty" efforts.

Concurrent with these social and religious ideologies was the rise in biological theories. Perhaps the first element of formal racist theory that was actively invoked was that set forth by Gaines de Sepulveda (a scholar from Mexico). He justified the right of Spain to ruthlessly decimate the native Indian population. Generally, the most salient and specific arguments for allowing this to take place were as follows:

(1) because of the gravity of sins;
(2) because of the crudeness of their natures;
(3) because of the necessity to spread the Christian faith.

Clearly the above arguments fit neatly into the religious ideology of that time. Yet the clearly religious overtones of the above arguments were not entirely racist. Only the beginning of biological criteria was introduced at this time. What was needed now was some clear statement showing how one race was biologically superior to another. Thus, in the years that followed, many "scientific" books were written to show that the native (coloured) population of any geographical area were inferior to the White Anglo Saxon population.

What was needed (and was finally achieved) was for someone to show that the reason for "cultural superiority" hinged upon the "biological" state of the group of people concerned. Thus, the strategy was to show that the reason one's own group was culturally advanced (in specific technological aspects) was due to biological factors inherent for groups of people. The "scientific reasoning" was as follows: one looked at two societies, one being a White controlled system, the other a non-White controlled system, and then made comparisons. Due to selective perception and ethnocentrism, the White society always was defined as superior, since those people who were concerned with such positioning of societies were peoples from White controlled societies. Now, of course, a reason was needed to explain this. This is where the biological aspect of racism comes into existence. These researchers simply claimed that the other society was not as advanced as theirs because of the intrinsic biological make-up of the other society, which made it impossible for them to become superior (Chesler, 1976).

During the early 1500s when pre-Adamite theory (it was argued that Adam was the first Jew but not the first man) was in vogue, the belief was that while *man* was defined universalistically in terms of mental properties, Blacks and Indians were said to lack these properties. For example, Paracelsus in 1520 classified Indians with mermaids and nymphs—all being without souls. Hence, these theories allowed for the idea of different origins. This separate origin of different groups of mankind then allowed for the possibility that some groups were, from their creation, inferior to others (Aldridge, 1973).

By the mid 1600s, two major theories were used to substantiate the origin of color. First of all there was the theory based on purely religious doctrine. The other, however, was based on what was called natural reason. For example, Feijoo (Spanish) argued that the atmosphere was the cause of skin color. However, soon after this (1700s) the "bile" theory (the reasoning was that the bile produced skin pigmentation) was introduced and its most ardent opponent, Le Cat (French) produced a great deal of empirical data rejecting this notion. The end result of these great debates on the role of causal factors related to skin color was that a focusing on biological factors emerged. A new focus on biological factors was thus stimulated to answer the question of why people were different in their cultural structures and mental capacities.

By the mid-18th century, the emergence of anthropology (a combination of the efforts of Buffon—the naturalist—and Blumenbach—an anatomist) began to provide us with our first systematic divisions of mankind. As Poliakov (1968) points out, "this haphazard linking of physical, mental, and moral characteristics is typical of modern anthropology in its early phases" (226).

Others such as Daubenton, Quetelet, and, of course, Linnaeus provided us with well developed techniques for race classification. (For a thorough and concise explication of the scientific theories of races during the second half of the 19th century, the reader should consult the work of Haller, 1971; Gosset, 1965).

Lavater, in the late 18th century, had published a book on physiological measurements of man and their relationship to social behavior, which Morton (from the U.S.A.) took seriously and developed into the concept of *cranial capacity measure*. The basic argument in such a position was that as the cranial capacity increased, man's brain increased, which was an indicator that he was "smarter." As a result, Retzius (Sweden), Gratiolet (France), and Gamper and Gall (Germany) attempted to develop and refine this measurement technique. It was not until the turn of the 20th century that use of the *cephalic index* (the ratio of the greatest breadth of head to its greatest length from front to back, multiplied by 100) was no longer used or considered relevant to the analysis of social behavior. As Gosset (1965) points out, "even Broca (a strong advocate of the cephalic index) came to the conclusion that individual variations are always greater within a given race than between races." Zubaida (1970) suggests that the first book to systematically set out a racist ideology was Knox's *The Races of Men* in 1850, although Gobineau's *Essai* (1853) is perhaps the better known and usually given this dubious distinction.

Out of the cephalic index theory emerged the *cerebral structure and complexity* model. Basically, the idea was that the number and complexity of the brain fissures and convolutions were indicators of superior-inferior races. The research conducted in the 1930s in the United States was able to provide data which upheld this perspective. This research consisted of comparing the structure of Black and White brains. It would not be until a decade had passed that serious methodological errors were discovered in the original research. Two major flaws were pointed out: (i) length of time between death and removal of brain was not controlled for and (ii) the researcher doing the measurements was aware beforehand which brains were Black and which White. When these two factors were controlled for, no differences were ascertained.

Today, a philosophy of *intelligence* (as related to various ethnic groups has emerged. Basically the argument is that some people (usually non-White) have not (cannot) attained a level of intelligence achieved by others (usually Whites). Its most recent and most respected supporter is Jensen (1969). The argument has not been settled although Cavalli-Sforza and Bodmer (1970) and Hunt (1969) make a strong case against the position of Jensen. At this time, it should suffice to say that all of the data are not available to make a decision one way or the other.

Thus far we have identified three factors that have been present in the emergence of racism: religion, biological theory and an anthropological perspective. These factors were present as we moved into the 19th century. In addition to this, of course, was the economic expansion of European countries. European countries had been exploring unknown continents for some time. However, they now began to colonize and exploit the resources of the new worlds. In order to exploit these resources, the colonizing forces had to justify the action they needed to take with the native population, i.e., exploitation, expulsion, or annihilation. Here, then, began a fusion of the prevailing religious ideology, the "scientific" biological differentiation and the political ideology of economic colonialism—capitalism.

The colonization and subsequent settlement of peoples in these new lands emerged out of feudalistic structures. Hence, this new structure would involve not only economic institutions in a society but would interact with each institution in a society. By the 12th century, feudalism was beginning to die as a viable economic mode. Ordinarily, feudalism has been dated from the 9th to the 14th century. This type of system can be characterized as living on *frozen* capital. The status structure in such a society was static, and *tenancy* in some form, constituted the material counterpart of status. Social relations rested upon a principle of tenure which was applied to all people (beginning with the king and continuing down to the serf) (Pinenne, 1933).

The feudal system had an agricultural system (technology) which produced sufficient food surpluses to support large nonagricultural populations. This advanced technology made it possible for a leisure class or elite to exist. This small number of privileged upper class individuals held key positions in the political, religious and educational structures of the society and exhibited strict autocratic rule.

As pointed out above, there was an elite structure (able to maintain an extended family system, acquire formal education and express religious devotion) and land workers (serfs). There was initially no merchant class. Thus, a man's condition was now determined by his relation to the land, which was owned and controlled by a minority of lay and ecclesiastical proprietors.

The organizational structure that best characterizes this time period is that of the estate. These estates usually consisted of about 300 farms (10,000 acres), usually scattered rather than in geographical proximity. The centre of each estate was the customary residence of the landowner. The remainder of the land was parcelled out into a number of divisions (which might contain one or more villages) which were under the jurisdiction of an agent in charge of administration (Sjoberg, 1960).

On the basis of the above structure, it has been argued that: (i) cities were nonexistent (or at least very limited in size), (ii) the idea of profit was unknown, (iii) money had a limited use, (iv) the institutional structure was communalistic, (v) there was no merchant class, and (vi) poverty was considered a result of divine origin and ordained by providence.

As the above structure began to change, capitalism as an organizational structure emerged. It precipitated development of the urban communities of Central Europe. Consequently, it exhibited different attributes than feudalism, such as trade, profit, money, inventiveness, mechanical power, money making as an end in itself, efficiency, capital accumulation, exploitation and individualism.

Along with the emergence of capitalism, Lutheranism (eventuating into Calvinism) also emerged. The relationship to capitalism is certainly close and they complement each other, but again it would be premature to suggest one caused the other. However, the Reformation did undermine old convictions about money and trade as well as strengthen the philosophy of individualism. Basically Calvinism had two major points: (i) it was a gospel of work that exalted sober worldly activity to a "calling," and (ii) a doctrine of asceticism based on the belief that man is a trustee of God.

The relationship between the basic tenets of Calvinism and capitalism is thus: If God created us (trustee) and salvation is the goal of man, how can we determine whether or not we are saved while on earth? The answer provided by Calvinism was that one could take his position (status) on earth as an indirect indicator. In other words, if one reached a high position in society, it was an indicator that you were saved.

The religious ideology (which viewed the non-Whites, i.e., native population, as savages) allowed the White Anglo-Saxon population to view the natives as inferior objects, and later as frustrating as well as dangerous objects. In addition, other parts of the religious ideology, e.g., manifest destiny, allowed Whites to react aggressively toward non-Whites. Since biological racist theories had been well developed by this time (and would later support their position even further by invoking Social Darwinism), treating the native in any debasing manner was justified. As one views the historical process of Anglo-Saxons emigrating into North America, manifest destiny was invoked by the White man in moving into any geographical area. Aboriginal peoples were viewed as impeding progress of the Whites. These people were regarded as an inferior race, and thus discrimination was justified. But perhaps this was all necessary because of the economic development of the European countries.

We should also point out that the French Revolution (Period of Enlightenment) inadvertently produced another rationale that could be utilized by economically expanding countries. This, of course, was the idea that Homo Sapiens could be broken into two groups: human and nonhuman. Thus, if the native non-White population did not have to be viewed as human, then none of the egalitarian modes of thought (embodied in the enlightenment philosophy) had to be afforded to these people. At that time it was utilized as an *ad hoc* explanation for previous behavior, but accordingly would provide a more solid basis for future racist actions (Comas, 1961).

An additional factor which was used (and still is) to foster the development of racism in North America is that of Social Darwinism. This philosophy of evolution and biological development of animals was extended to cover the development of man and eventually to the development of societies and cultures. This began about 1840 and still continues to influence people's thinking. Basically the reasoning of Social Darwinism is as follows: First of all, the nature of man's societies (or cultures) is a product of natural evolutionary forces. Secondly, the notion of survival of the fittest is molded by Social Darwinists to fit social behaviors. Thirdly, the argument is that men begin to struggle with one another (since they are a product of the natural evolutionary forces) and conflict develops. In the end, one group (race) wins over the other. This is taken as clear evidence then that this particular group is superior.

The ideas set forth by Darwin were quickly transformed into what we now call Social Darwinism. This conceptual framework was widely accepted and quickly adopted by major political and economic powers of the day. This position certainly extended beyond the Adamite theory (those who accepted the Biblical theory of creation with regard to Adam and Eve), sometimes referred to as the monogenist theory of creation. Likewise, the groundwork set up by the polygenists (the belief that the descent of a species or race is from more than one ancestral species) prepared a ready acceptance of Darwin's work.

As Comas (1958) points out:

> As Darwin's theory was made public in the years in which the greater powers were building their colonial empires, it helped to justify them in their own eyes and before the rest of mankind; that slavery or death brought to 'inferior' human groups by European rifles and machine guns was no more than the implementations of the theory of the replacement of an inferior by a superior human society. (11)

The result was the haphazard linking of physical, mental, and moral characteristics which now was supported by the educational institutions. While Darwin destroyed the belief that man was an immutable unit, racists adhering to his thesis still could rescue their position by arguing that races were in the process of formation and that separateness was therefore to be encouraged (Banton, 1967: 42).

   Mercantilism (fully developed during the 17th century) also contributed to the emergence of racism. The basic philosophy fitted well into the religious and social fabric of the time. Basically, the three tenets underlying mercantilism were: (i) an overconcern with the accumulation of precious metals by nation states, (ii) the belief that a favorable balance of trade should always be developed, i.e., exports should always exceed imports for a nation-state and, (iii) colonies were to be used for sources of raw materials and outlets for finished products.

   One last factor important in the development of racism needs to be invoked—neutralization (Daniels and Kitano, 1970). This, of course, allows justification or rationalization of certain kinds of behavior which are to a certain extent deviant from the general explicit norms of society. In the context of intergroup relations, this, of course, refers to discriminative behavior toward other groups of people. Since our system calls for equality and freedom for all, this, of course, means that no matter what ethnic group one belongs to (or race) one should be able to fully participate in the system. For example, the Canadian Bill of Rights claims "Human rights and fundamental freedoms shall continue to exist without discrimination by reason of race, national origin, colour, religion, or sex." Thus, when discrimination (or prejudice) is practised by an individual, he must be able to justify his behavior. This, of course, is where neutralization techniques are invoked and used.

   What are some of these neutralization techniques? We have shown how the ideas embodied in religion, capitalism, and pseudo-scientific biological theories along with poor logic, i.e., the emergence of Social Darwinism, have allowed the continuance of racist ideology. They have, in fact fostered the central ideological framework. New techniques have also been added and old ones modified as conditions in the social structure change. A notion like "backlash" is introduced to justify behaviors (of a racist form) by empowered peoples.

   A replacement of the Protestant ethic in the sociological component of culture (from the religious) has also provided needed neutralizations. Since everyone is now supposed to be embodied with this ethic, not holding it is evidence in itself of social abnormality. This, of course, fits neatly into the previously discussed ideology of racism. It then becomes another technique to justify discriminatory behaviors.

   The following figure illustrates the various factors that need to be taken into consideration when discussing the emergence of racism as a competitive

FIGURE 2

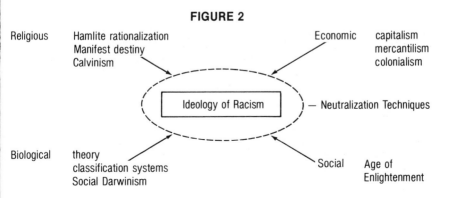

ideology. While each of the factors has contributed to the existence of racism, there is a great deal of controversy as to how much each factor has contributed. Likewise each factor has contributed to the development of racism at various points in time. All of this suggests that racism has been the result of a number of factors interacting with each other over an extended period of time.

Racism in Canada

Thus far we have tried to develop a brief profile with regard to the emergence of racism as an ideology throughout history. Our task now is to trace the emergence of racism in Canada specifically. If we take the date of 1509 as the "beginning of Canada" we will attempt to show that racism did not initially exist in Canada. Several factors were present which precluded its formation in New France. First of all, the French were not colonists in the true sense. Secondly, they were Catholic in their religious ideology. These two factors are extremely important in explaining why the French were able (and still are until this day) to establish better relationships with the Native and non-White peoples of Canada.

Price (1950) argues that the French had little of the racial prejudice so strongly embedded in the Northern European races and their American descendants, so that neither (Canadian) Indians nor the halfbreeds initially experienced serious disabilities. Wade (1970) also points out that the French had none of the English color prejudice. The French government wanted to strengthen their hold on the colony through the process of absorption of the Native peoples, and thus dispatches flowed from Paris instructing the local French-Canadian authorities to encourage Indians to adopt a settled life within the colony, to have their children educated as Frenchmen, and "to promote intermarriage with the object of fusing the two peoples into a single race" (McInnis, 1963: 75).

As the French began to settle into New France, commercial fishing was the initial livelihood. Here, of course, only a minimal amount of contact was made with the Native population and, when contact was made, relationships were on a barter basis.

However, as the fur trade began to expand in form and intensity, the casual contacts of fishermen with Indians along the shore ended, and regular voyages to the rendezvous at Tadoussac at the mouth of the Saguenay began. French traders committed themselves to the exploitation of the Canadian (or Laurentian) Shield. They also committed themselves to a military alliance with the Indians who hunted over the Shield. This alliance was the beginning of the *Laurentian coalition* of Algonquins, Hurons, and French that was to dominate the history of New France until 1701 (Morton, 1963).

During the latter half of the 16th century, the fur trade began to grow. Fashion in Europe dictated that clothes should be trimmed in furs. The fur trade then became one of the occupational mainstays of the new Canadians. France was not interested (initially) in establishing agricultural colonies in this new land. Because France (at this time), ascribed to absolutism and mercantilistic modes of thought, only exploitation of the new land (in terms of raw material) for the mother country was desired. Well-developed, self-sustaining colonies were not desired. As McInnis (1963) points out: "it was the fur trade that was the heart of the economy of New France. . . . But while the fur trade was the chief source of wealth, it was also a burden that hampered the growth of the colony. The real operative factor (establishing harmonious personal relations with the Indians by the French) was the paramount importance of the fur trade. ... The Indian was an essential asset if the fur trade was to prosper or even survive" (57-59).

No large-scale geographical intrusion was made by the French. Even when (1608) the French began to move up river, because of their land ownership design the full extent of their intrusion was not evident to Native people. Land areas were always next to the river bank, extending away from it. But always one edge of the property was adjacent to water. This was generally referred to as the *rang* system of land survey and use.

Price (1950) points out that in the early trading stage the French treated the Indian tribes as independent nations and the Indians on their part usually agreed to these alliances and permitted the French to establish trading posts. Later, when colonization was more strongly marked, the French regarded the eastern Natives as subject peoples and organized their more closely settled territories as *seigneuries*, where the Indians were Christianized, educated, and granted titles to the land which they actually cultivated. This was a policy of peaceful penetration, largely affected by fur trading and mission establishments.

When Champlain established Quebec in 1608 he was careful to ensure that the relationships between French and Indian were cordial. Generally, everything was done to preserve a good understanding with the Indians who visited the trading post, and Champlain wisely perceived that the success of the settlement depended on their friendship. Champlain had learned the fact that Cartier would not have survived the winter in New France if he had not had the help of the Native people.

In addition, as the French moved into the interior (along rivers) of Canada, a reciprocal and somewhat dependent relationship (symbiotic) was established between the two groups of people. The early settlers would not have survived the harsh winters if they had not received help from the Native population. They freely borrowed Indian ideas, cultivated Indian crops and adopted articles of Indian dress and methods of transport. Living close to the land, and with little education, the French pioneers differed only superficially from Indians and mingled with them freely. Indian girls, trained in convents, made excellent wives for isolated farmers and traders as there was a shortage of White women in the colonies (Price, 1950).

The nondeprivation attitude of the powered group (French toward Native peoples) was not developed because they became economically dependent upon certain (Algonquin and Huron) Indian tribes. Only by cultivating their friendship could the furs be transported from central Canada to the Eastern Coast. This is not to suggest that the French always viewed Native people as worthwhile objects. Coalitions of French and Indian were made so as to make war on certain Indian tribes—generally the Iroquois—because they interfered with movement through the trade routes.

Secondly, by 1635, the Jesuits had established many missions within the Indian camps themselves. Their view of the Indians was one of "heathen infidels," but once converted to Christianity the Indians were considered equal to the White man. The religious ideology of Catholicism embraced this notion of brotherhood. It is clear that a dual motive sustained Catholic enterprise in New

France. Missionary zeal was fired by the prospect of converting the Indians to Christianity, and this vision was accomplished by a desire to plant a French Catholic colony as a solid base for the establishment of the faith in the New World (McInnis, 1963: 69).

In addition to establishing the actual base of operation in the Indian village, the priests learned the language, respected most elements of their culture, and generally lived as Indians. Medical techniques were also used by the priests to help the Indians. Again there was no insistence of subordination and relatively little conflict generated in the Jesuits' relationships with certain Indian tribes (Neatby, 1973).

An outstanding feature of the French invasions was Catholic missionary effort. The Recollects began work on the St. Lawrence in 1615, and the Jesuits joined them in 1626. Within twenty years they had won over the Hurons and had established what was virtually a mission state. In addition, the establishment of the missions facilitated the fur trade.

Other factors present also precluded the development of racism. Since fur trading was the main occupation of the early French settlers, "wintering in" was a common practice. This meant that the trappers would live with the Indians over the winter to keep track of the number, size, and quality of furs accumulated. Since most of the early settlers were young French males, social life was limited. Thus, it was not uncommon for these young men to marry Indian women. This was not an act of sexual exploitation but rather one of acceptance of the Indian culture. Families were a result and the father remained responsible for their upbringing.

Industries did not develop in New France because of the protective laws of the homeland (mercantilism). No major industries were allowed to be set up in New France as they were interpreted as a threat to the economy of the homeland. Clearly, then, a high (specialized) division of labor did not develop. As Morton (1963) shows, by 1714 there was textile manufacturing, but most of the industry was in the King's (France) hands. "In consequence, no new staple, either natural or manufactured, was successfully developed for export, and this in turn prevented the commercial expansion of the colonies" (McInnis, 1963: 57). The fur trade was still the central aspect of the economy.

Thus, the needs of New France and the ambitions of the motherland coincided. As McNickle (1957) points out:

> The French in Canada and in the West lost no opportunity to aggravate the fears of the Indians by insisting that the English would not be satisfied until they had completely removed the Indians. The French had not been colonizers, but had been satisfied to trade and build fortified posts to thwart competition. Hence, they could assure the Indians that they were not competing with them for the land. (187)

Colbert wholeheartedly adopted the theory of mercantilism, which was now in full flower. While foreign competition should be excluded, external trade was a source of wealth to be developed by every possible means; and colonies would provide bases for such trade as well as sources of production to supplement the economy of metropolitan France (McInnis, 1963: 48). As Patterson (1972) points out, "the French did not look down on the Indians or other non-Whites as being racially inferior, an attitude which was the reverse of that often characteristic of the British. . . . The religious attachment made it possible for political ends to be served through their personal influence" (60).

When the French were defeated by the British, several conditions were changing. The population of New France had increased to about 60,000. New France was not primarily a mission field, as the French-Canadian historians suggest, but the scene of a commercial enterprise conducted by Frenchmen from France for the material benefit of Old France. On the other hand, the English colonists to the South had turned their backs upon their mother country, and checked by the Appalachian barrier from immediate penetration of the continent, had set about the creation of New England by a colonization effort which dwarfed that of the French.

It was at this time that the Industrial Revolution was beginning. Mercantilism and absolutism and their accompanying modes of thought were in their dying days. Capitalism (through colonial expansion) was now becoming a central form of production. The English were colonists in the true sense. They did not attempt to solely exploit the fur trade which at this time was beginning to dwindle because (a) the market for furs was drying up; (b) beavers were getting scarce and the Indians began to see their way of life changing and reacting in a hostile fashion, and (c) the English were intent upon effectually occupying Canadian soil. This, of course, would allow them to claim it and retain it against other foreign powers. When settlements were made, areas were denoted on maps as strategic and placements of immigrants were made in these areas. This meant that land areas had to be cleared for agricultural enterprises. Rivers had to be stopped or diverted. While the initial English settlements were small, the Indians resisted their encroachments because Natives found themselves continually threatened by the growth of the New England colonies and they formed alliances among themselves (and the French) to resist the English (e.g., the Abenaki Confederacy).

The tie between Indians and French is also evident when one looks at the political ramifications of the process of religious conversion. When the Indians were converted (Christianized) they could then acquire guns and ammunition from the French. Furthermore, the tie of Christianity cut across tribal lines and introduced a new linkage of previously diverse groups. Thus the establishment of many Indian alliances. Indians continually viewed the French as less of a threat to their way of life and ties to the land than the British (Patterson, 1972). It should be pointed out that because the early history of French Canada was written by clerics, the religious basis of the tie with Indians has been over-stressed. However, even when one takes into consideration the political and economic factors, religion still plays an important part (Wade, 1970).

The British settlements did not develop any kind of symbiotic relationship with the Native population. They were supposedly self-contained and self-sustaining and thus they did not need the help of the Native population. Since Native help was not needed, only expansion into new land areas could help them perpetuate their existence. This meant that more land areas (which were agriculturally fit) had to be cleared and this, of course, began to encroach on the Native people's lands. Conflicts between the English and Natives emerged, but not with the intensity of those which took place in the U.S. or even in Western Canada.

The English also had two ideological belief systems which were not present in the French-Catholic culture—Manifest Destiny and the Protestant ethic. The implications of these two belief systems have been discussed previously. It was also the beginning of the Industrial Revolution. As the Industrial Revolution continued, capitalism developed trade agreements between the mother state and the colony. Previously, France had agreements with New France (Canada) that they could not set up industries. All materials had to be processed in the mother country and then shipped back. Even though the French had small shipyards along the river banks, boat building was not a major industry. All of this would now change. English colonies began to set up their own industries. This, of course, made them totally free from any kind of dependence on Native people. This independence would allow non-Natives to view Natives as initially irrelevant, then frustrating, and later as dangerous objects.

Free grants of 50 acres were made to adult male subjects of British origin (increased to 100 in 1853) on colonization roads. This political decision was based neither on sound reasoning nor on sound principles of colonization, but in order to promote settlement where it was deemed advisable that a population should be created.

Farming became an independent and important occupation, both in terms of domestic and international trade, and a surplus of agricultural products was created for the first time. In addition to these trades, there was now the timber trade. At the same time, Canadian society became what it had never really been before the British takeover, predominantly agricultural and rural. As the population increased and need for new land continued, greater pressure was placed on this scarce resource. Natives could choose to fight or migrate. Because of the superiority of weapons held by the British and their ever increasing number, Natives generally chose the latter strategy.

The remainder of the present chapter will attempt to illustrate the pervasive (and sometimes subtle) structure of racism in Canadian society. Because we are dealing with an ideology, we will focus on immigration policy—both proposed and implemented—as an indication of the extent of racism in Canada.

Contrary to most popular opinions, Canada did not have any systematic immigration policies until the late 19th century.[1] As both Hawkins (1972) and Corbett (1957) point out, the British in Canada from 1763 to 1867 never really were concerned with immigration policies *per se*. The first period of policy was basically one of a free entry period (until 1895). The Canadian government felt that the natural forces of supply and demand would sufficiently regulate the size of the migration into Canada. The only input into migration was the promotional activity engaged in by the federal government in Britain as well as providing some payment for the immigrants' transportation. Because almost all of the migrants were from Great Britain and the United States, no restrictive policy was needed.

What immigration policy there was seems to have been contingent upon the

---

[1] It is important to point out that there were some exceptions to this claim. In 1794, Lower Canada passed an act (pushed through by the clergy) stating that "aliens" could not enter Canada. (These aliens were in actuality agents of the French Revolution, Walmsley, 1966: 50) In 1868 another conference was called and the Immigration Act of 1869 was established. A new Act was not passed, then, until 1910 and no changes of that Act occurred until 1952 and this remained until 1969.

steamship companies, HBC and CPR. These companies obviously had much to gain by transporting immigrants to Canada and settling them in various parts of Canada. The government at this time seemed content to leave the colonizing process to these individual enterprises. Not until Sifton (1896) became Minister of the Interior did Canada finally attempt to formulate a coherent, long range immigration policy (Timlin, 1960).

Sifton felt that Canada's future lay in the development of the West, and his immigration policy reflected this. Any groups from Europe which had agricultural occupational skills were asked to settle in Canada. Needless to say, the demographic composition of Canada began to change drastically, yet the color did not. For example, in 1763 Canada was predominantly French (besides Native people). By 1900, the proportion of non-French to French was about three to one. During the years 1867 to 1895 about one and one-half million immigrants entered Canada, most of whom were from the British Isles and the United States.

From the earliest time, Canada's immigration policy has had racist overtones. At various points in time these overtones have become more or less explicit, as we shall soon document. Suffice it to say that any White immigrants willing to participate in the agricultural economy were welcomed to Canada.[2]

Prior to the formalization of immigration policy, evidence is still available to document the racist underpinnings of Canadian society. Slavery, for example, was very prevalent in Canada. The first slave was introduced into New France in 1608, and after 1694 the word "slave" became increasingly common in the civil registers of New France. In 1709 the Intendant (Jacques Raudot) provided an official statement in support of Black slavery (Bartolo, 1976). Most of the slaves lived in or near the city of Montreal. While nearly all of these early slave owners were French, they saw slavery as a temporary condition to be suffered by particular men and women who were victims of misfortune (Tulloch, 1975). Nevertheless, by 1750 there were well over 4,000 Black slaves in New France.

The *Code Noir* (a 446 page volume published in Paris in 1770) was initially drafted to protect the White man from slave violence and to provide an elaborate statement on the treatment of slaves, e.g., sale, religious training, disposition of offspring and rules of intermarriage. The impact of this code on Canadian society was not in the legal sense, since Canadians had come under British rule in 1763, but the impact was important in the informal sense in that it provided a set of rules for Canadians as to how one handled slaves. However, in 1793 Upper Canada confirmed the ownership of slaves. While the statute confirmed ownership of slaves held as of that time, it also stipulated that no new slaves could be brought into the province and that persons subsequently born into slavery would be freed upon reaching the age of 25. It was not until 1834 when all slaves in the British Empire were freed (through the passing of the Emancipation Act) and slavery was abolished in Canada. While formal legislation made slavery illegal, this did not mean that attitudes and behavior toward Blacks took on a more favorable disposition. In the Niagara Falls area (1850)

---

[2] Coupled with this "discrimination" is the fact that Canada (at that time) projected an image of wanting *only* farmers. People from countries with no agricultural skills knew that if you were not a farmer, you might be refused entry or have a hard time establishing yourself in the new country.

Blacks were forced to sit in the back gallery ("nigger heaven") of churches. After 1850, the socio-demographic profile of Blacks entering Canada changed and the extent of White racism increased (Bartolo, 1976). Riots occurred over the segregation of Blacks in a local Victoria theater. Between 1870 and 1930, racism in Canada resembled very closely the form exhibited in the U.S. However, Canadians added one additional biological attribute—Blacks were refused entry into Canada (attempting to settle in Alberta) because authorities argued they were unable to function properly in the cold weather.

Other groups have also been the focus of overt racist action. As we have already noted (Chapter 7), the government passed legal restrictions affecting the Chinese in 1878 and even though action by the federal government disallowing the provincial laws was enforced, the provincial government continued to restrict Chinese immigration. In essence, the laws were changed but the effect was the same—no Chinese could enter Canada (Ward, 1978). The B.C. government continued to restrict Chinese immigrants into their province until 1908. Many of the laws they passed were eventually disallowed by the federal government but by the time they had done so, the B.C. government had passed another slightly different version. The federal government changed their free entry policy in that they imposed a $50 head tax in 1885, doubled it in 1900, and raised it to $500 in 1903. Of the 43,500 Chinese who had come to Canada in 1906, only 12,000 remained by 1922 (Samuel, 1970). As we have seen, when this tax was removed in 1923 the Chinese Immigration Act (1923) cut off Chinese immigration completely. Although eventually male Chinese were allowed to immigrate to Canada, they could not bring their wives and children; this policy remained in effect until 1947.

Japanese have also been the focus of racist actions in their attempts to immigrate to Canada. The special treaties of 1894 (through 1911) with Japan, known as the "Gentlemen's Agreement," systematically excluded Japanese from entering Canada, with the exception of allowing 400 into Canada if they were limited to certain defined classes. The enforcement of the Immigration Act against Japanese during the late 1930s and 1940s also virtually excluded their entry into Canada. In 1950, it was still informally acceptable to exclude Japanese. The following statement, written by an MP at this time, reflects the above charge: "Broadly speaking, we say that anybody who is suitable, desirable and not an Asiatic may be admitted to Canada as an immigrant."

In the early 20th century, British Columbia once again became concerned with increasing migration from India. While specific acts directed solely at South Asians were passed in 1908, the following quote from the Deputy Minister to the Estimates Committee in 1910 summarizes the feeling about non-White immigration:

> The policy of the Department at the present time is to encourage the immigration of farmers, farm labourers, and female domestic servants from the United States, the British Isles, and certain Northern European countries, namely, France, Belgium, Holland, Switzerland, Germany, Denmark, Norway, Sweden and Iceland.
>
> On the other hand, it is the policy of the Department to do all in its power to keep out of the country undesirables which for the purposes of this review I will divide into three classes.

1. Those physically, mentally, or morally unfit whose exclusion was provided for by Act of Parliament last session.
2. Those belonging to nationalities unlikely to assimilate and consequently prevent the building up of a united nation of people of similar customs and ideals.
3. Those who from their mode of life and occupations are likely to crowd into urban centres and bring about a state of congestion which might result in unemployment and a lowering of the standard of our national life.

While neither the law nor the Orders-in-Council passed thereunder absolutely prohibit the landing in Canada of persons belonging to the second and third classes mentioned still their entry has been made extremely difficult by the passing of Orders-in-Council . . . [which] put many obstacles in the way of immigrants from Asia and southern and eastern Europe and, consequently, the numbers coming or likely to come from those countries are correspondingly diminished.

The B.C. government's negative reactions toward Asians paralleled those taking place in the U.S. While it is estimated that less than 400 Asians migrated to Canada in the early 1900s, by 1907/08 the total number was well over 12,000 (of which 63% were Japanese) most of whom were adult males.

Table 1

NUMBER OF EAST INDIAN IMMIGRANTS FROM 1904-11

	Year							
	1904-5	1905-6	1906-7	1907-8	1908-9	1909-10	1910-11	Total
Number	45	387	2,124	2,623	6	10	5	5,200

Source: R. P. Srivastava, "Family Organization and Change among the Overseas Indians," in G. Kurian (Ed.), *The Family in India—A Regional View*, Mouton, the Hague, Paris, 1974, p. 370.

In 1907, anti-Asiatic riots occurred in Vancouver. Late in that year, the Asiatic Exclusion League was formed, and it entered the political arena. By 1908, the B.C. government had forced Prime Minister King to go to the British government and attempt to stop immigration from India. Even though the Indian government discouraged emigration to Canada, it refused to pass legislation to stop people from coming, and that was not sufficient for Canadians.[3]

While the Canadian government had already passed legislation affecting Chinese immigration, it could not do the same with Indians (from India) because they were British subjects (and part of the Commonwealth). Thus, refusing immigrants from India would cause a strain between the Commonwealth nations.[4]

[3] Indians lost the right to vote until 1948. In addition, the Canadian Knights of the Ku Klux Klan were a strong anti-Asiatic force during this time.
[4] Between 1905 and 1914, slightly more than five thousand Indians entered Canada—out of a total of 2.5 million immigrants. Most of the early Indians were Sikhs and at their peak formed less than 0.5% of the provincial population.

However, by 1908 two restrictions were passed concerning East Indian immigration: (i) They had to have $200 upon landing in Canada and (ii) The immigrants had to come to Canada by direct passage (a continuous journey) from their country of birth. Later, an annual quota of 100 was allotted for India. While the first restriction kept most Indians out of Canada, there were some immigrants capable of raising that much money. However, because there were no direct shipping lines between Canada and India, it virtually precluded Indian immigration to Canada.[5] In 1914, nearly 400 Indians attempted to challenge this restriction and chartered a boat to take them directly to Vancouver. All these people had then met the two requirements set up above. After two months of legal battles and actual physical violence, the boat was taken out to sea and returned home without any of the people ever stepping on Canadian soil. There was also at this time a concerted effort made by the government of B.C. to force the existing Indian-Canadian residents back to India. The effect of the formal and informal policy implementation was devastating, and by 1921 only 951 Indians remained in B.C. (Srivastava, 1971)

The policy formulated by Sifton was carried on in the years to follow and as a result there was a more formalized structure created to help develop Canada. This initial restrictive policy has been the foundation for present immigration policy. In 1923 assistance was given to British subjects who wanted to come to Canada. By 1936, a very restrictive immigration policy had developed, and coupled with the depressed economic state of Canada, immigration was almost at a standstill. Only farmers and domestics were allowed into Canada and it was not until leaders of industry became a more viable lobbying force that these restrictions were changed.

However, by the end of the 1930s, the depression had ended and political and social conflict was occurring in Europe. This gave rise to the refugee immigrant. But Canada's immigration policy had not changed. Mainly British subjects (and U.S.A. citizens) with money to support themselves while in Canada were allowed in. Canada was not to change this basic policy until 1952. The following gives an example of the restrictive immigration policy:

> In 1939 . . . the number of industrialists or persons of other occupations admitted by special regulation was 69 (and they had a capital of $4,200,000). (Dept. of Mines and Resources, 1939, 40: 217)

The above seems to suggest that Canada's immigration policy was nonhumanitarian, proagriculture, and was applied unequally for all groups wanting to come to Canada. Specifically speaking, Canada's immigration policy after 1900 was a "closed door" for non-Whites.

The federal government argued that non-Whites, and specifically Asians, were unassimilable and had a lower standard of living than native Whites and thus would be disruptive to Canadian society. Obviously, the mosaic should remain White. As the Green Paper on Immigration points out, "non-Whites were not welcome" (p. 17). Further changes in the policy of the fifties did not change the basic color line. In fact, the immigration regulations that emerged actually rank ordered the acceptable to unacceptable classes of people. The most

---

[5] Indian law prevented the emigration of any contract labour to Canada.

acceptable were from Great Britain; the least acceptable were from India and Pakistan.

In general, until 1952 our conclusion would be that Canada had a non-White exclusion clause built into its immigration policy. "Mackenzie King, Prime Minister for 17 years, said in 1947 that Canada had no intention of changing the 'fundamental composition of the Canadian population' by large scale immigration from the Orient" (Samuel, 1970; 81). Canada seems to have been more concerned with exclusion (and which groups to exclude) than about setting criteria for those people entering our system.

What has happened since 1952? First of all, Canada attempted to develop a long-range immigration policy and secondly, it broadened its admission policies. The notion of "Ethnic Balance" was brought into being. The idea behind this was that no new immigrant groups should disrupt the existing ethno/racial ratio. The implication was that since Canada had not allowed non-Whites into Canada, no more should come in now.

In 1967, the point system was introduced as a just way of evaluating the merits of each potential immigrant to Canada. The point system is based on the philosophy that certain attributes held by individuals will be closely related to successful adaptation to Canadian society, as well as benefiting Canada. Let us illustrate the process for those applicants who are expected to become self-supporting and successfully established in Canada by virtue of their own skills, knowledge, or other qualifications. Nine factors are considered as important in predicting the successful adaptation to Canada as well as ensuring the immigrant will not require assistance from the government. Five of these criteria (education and training, personal qualities, occupational demand in Canada, occupational skill, and education) are considered long-term factors, while the remaining four (arranged employment, knowledge of English/French, presence of a relative in Canada, and general employment opportunities in the area of destination) are considered short-term factors that indicate an applicant's chance of establishing an early foothold in Canada.

The nine factors have a combined potential value of 100 points. When applicants are judged to have at least 50 points, their success in Canada is predicted; less than that will usually result in a negative prediction and thus refusal. For example, up to 20 points can be awarded to the applicant for education and training. Usually one point is given for every year of formal education or vocational/trades training. It should be pointed out that up to 15 points are awarded for the "personal quality" factor. This is essentially the subjective evaluation of the selection officer. And here lies one problem in the point system. Depending upon the selection officer's bias (or views about racial groups), the applicant can receive zero points in this category, thus lessening the applicant's chance of entering Canada. As the saying goes, "If you're White, you're right; if you're Brown, stick around and if you're Black, stand back."

A second issue that has been raised with regard to the point system is that it is based upon criteria established for developed countries. Thus immigrants from underdeveloped countries find it difficult to amass the minimum of 50 points. A third issue centres on the advertisement and availability of offices for immigrants to make applications. Over 30 offices are in Europe with an additional 13 in the U.S.A. while only 5 are in Africa and 8 in all of the Asian countries. All of these factors (representing institutional and individual racism) have reduced, until recently, the flow of non-White immigrants into Canada.

Since 1967, further changes have been made in the immigration policy. All of these changes were to restrict overall immigration as well as to provide more selective criteria for those entering Canada. These changes are reflected in the 1975 immigration statistics which show that 30% of the immigrants in Canada for that year were from Britain and the U.S.A. (19% and 11% respectively). An additional 25% were from Asian countries while only 5% were from African countries. Europe, including Great Britain, contributed nearly 31% of all the immigrants for that year (Green Paper, 1974).

The new Immigration Act became effective April 10, 1978. This new act states, for the first time in Canadian law, the basic principles underlying immigration policy—nondiscrimination, family reunion, humanitarian concern for refugees, and the promotion of national goals. It also provides for an annual forecast of the number of immigrants Canada can comfortably absorb. This annual figure will be arrived at in consultation with the provinces, and will take into account the population requirements, labor market needs, and the availability of social services. The annual figure will be a global limit, not a country by country quota.

On October 24, 1978, the Employment and Immigration Minister tabled the first annual report to Parliament on immigration levels. He established an immigration level of 100,000 for 1979. While any qualified person can apply to immigrate to Canada, special emphasis will be made to encourage entrepreneurs who can create and maintain employment in Canada. For example, in 1977 approximately 1,000 (less than 1% of the total immigration in 1977) entrepreneurs were admitted to Canada. However, they brought nearly 28% ($207 million) of all the funds brought in by immigrants during that year.

The implications of the above changes are that more control will be exercised by both the federal and provincial governments with regard to who is allowed into the country. While an emphasis on entrepreneurs will certainly favor immigrants from "White" (developed) countries, the corresponding changes regarding family reunion and the inclusion of refugees means that non-Whites will also be given an equal chance to immigrate to Canada.

Just how the latter factors will interface with the criterion of labor market needs remains to be seen. As Canada becomes more and more industrialized the need for skilled workers becomes greater. The extent to which refugees and relatives can meet the criteria of skilled labor and entrepreneur has not yet been established.

Conclusion

As a result of the structural factors affecting British settlers into Canada, racism emerged as a normal part of their ideology and philosophy of reality. This ideology has changed in implementation over time but the roots still remain. Racist ideologies have repeatedly been shown to be scientifically incorrect, but they still remain. Its continuance is rooted in the existing institutional structures and interrelationships of Canadian society.

Racism in Canada began with British-Indian relations (which sometimes are referred to as paternalism) which have continued until the present. More recent illustration of this ideology in action centres on the immigration policies and practices of early 20th century and present day immigration policy.

The data presented above consistently show that restrictive and exclusive immigration policies have mostly been directed toward non-White groups, although on occasion they have been directed toward other marginal peoples, e.g., Jews, Hutterites, and Slavs. On the other hand, information is available which shows that the Canadian government acted in near illegal manners in recruiting White immigrants. For example, because at the turn of the century many White European countries had restrictions against their citizens leaving, the Canadian government had to make secret agreements (1899) with an association of German steamship agents (North Atlantic Trading Company) so as to contravene German laws and expedite the migration of German nationals to Canada.

Other acts reflecting a basic racist position are not as clearly stated and must be interpreted in the time context in which they are being issued. For example, the Immigration Act of 1906 (Section 38) authorized the Canadian government to "prohibit the landing in Canada of any specified class of immigrants." Obviously, the language is vague and encompassing. One must look further to see that this section can (and has been) involved almost exclusively against non-Whites. A further amendment in 1910 stated that no person may enter Canada as a landed immigrant if his way had been paid by a charitable society unless that charitable society had been approved by the Canadian government. First of all, this meant that few immigrants from Third and Fourth World countries would be wealthy enough to migrate to Canada, and unless the federal government approved of the charitable organization, they could not even receive help.

We find that racism is a virulent ideology held by Canadians. There is a belief that certain groups (non-Whites) are inferior to Whites and this justifies invidious distinctions and behaviors directed toward them.

REFERENCES

Aldridge, A. "Feijoo and the Problem of Ethiopian Color," in H. E. Pagliaro (ed.), *Racism in 18th Century.* Cleveland: Case Western Reserve University, 1973 pp. 263-277.

Banton, M. "Race as a Social Category," *Race*, Vol. 8, No. 1, (1966): 1-17.

Banton, M. *Race Relations.* London: Tavistock Publications, 1967.

Banton, M. "Analytical and Folk Concepts of Race and Ethnicity," *Ethnic and Racial Studies*, 2, 2 (1979): 127-138.

Bartolo, O. "Blacks in Canada: 1608 to Now," in *A Key to Canada: Part II.* Montreal: The National Black Coalition of Canada, Inc, 1976.

Barzun, J. *Race: A Study in Modern Superstition.* New York: Harcourt, Brace and Co, 1937.

Barzun, J. *The French Race, Theories of its Origin and Their Social and Political Implications.* N.Y.: Columbia University Press, 1932.

Cavalli-Sforza, L. and W. Bodmer. *The Genetics of Human Population.* New York: Freeman, 1971.

Chesler, M. "Contemporary Sociological Theories of Racism," in P. Katz (ed.), *Towards the Elimination of Racism.* New York: Pergamon General Psychological Services, 1976.

Comas, J. *Racial Myths.* Paris, France: U.N.E.S.C.O. 1958.

Comas, J. "Scientific Racism Again?" *Current Anthropology,* 2 (1961): 303-340.

Corbett, D. *Canada's Immigration Policy.* Toronto: University of Toronto Press, 1957.

Cox, O. C. *Caste, Class and Race.* New York: Doubleday, 1948.

Daniels, R. and H. Kitano. *American Racism.* Englewood Cliffs, N.J.: Prentice-Hall Inc., 1970.

Fong, M. and L. Johnson "The Eugenics Movement: Some Insights into the Institutionalisation of Racism." *Issues in Criminology,* 9, 2, Fall (1974): 89-115.

Frideres, J. "Racism in Canada: Alive and Well." *The Western Canadian Journal of Anthropology,* Vol. VI, 4, (1976): 124-145. "Is Racism Dead?" *Anthropological Journal of Canada,* Vol. II, 3, (1973): 2-9.

Gilbert, N. and H. Specht. "Institutional Racism," *Urban and Social Change Review,* 6 (1972): 12.

Gosset, T. *Race: The History of an Idea in America.* Dallas: Southern Methodist University Press, 1965.

Green Paper on Immigration. A Report of the Canadian Immigration and Population Study, Vol. 1-4, Manpower and Immigration, Ottawa, Information Canada, 1974.

Haller, J. *Outcasts from Evolution.* New York: McGraw-Hill, 1971.

Hawkins, F. *Canada and Immigration: Public Policy and Public Concern.* Montreal: McGill-Queen's University Press, 1972.

Henry, F. *The Dynamics of Racism in Toronto.* Research Report, Dept. of Anthropology, York University.

Hunt, J. *Intelligence and Experience.* New York: Ronald Press, 1961.

Jensen, A. "How much can we boost IQ and Scholastic Achievement?" *Harvard Educational Review,* 39 (1969): 1.

Jones, J. *Prejudice and Racism.* Menlo Park, California: Addison-Wesley Publishing Co, 1972.

Knowles, L. and K. Prewitt. *Institutional Racism.* Englewood Cliffs, N.Y.: Prentice-Hall, 1969.

Kovel, J. *White Racism.* New York: Pantheon Books, 1970.

McInnis, E. *Canada: A Political and Social History.* Toronto: Holt, Rinehart and Winston, 1963.

McNickle, D. "Indians and Europeans: Indian White Relations From Discovery to 1887." *A.A.A.P.S.S.* Vol. 31 (1957): 1-11.

Merton, R. K. *Social Theory and Social Structure.* Glencoe Ill. The Free Press, 1949.

Morton, W. *The Kingdom of Canada.* N.Y.: Bobbs Merril Co, 1963.

Nash, M. "The Ideology of Race." *Current Anthropology,* 2 (1962): 285-289.

Neatby, J. "Racism in the Old Province of Quebec," in *Racism in the 18th Century* (Vol. 3), by H. E. Pagliaro (ed.), Cleveland: Case Western Reserve University, 1973. pp. 245-262.

Patterson, E. P. *The Canadian Indian*. Don Mills, Ontario: Collier-Macmillan Canada Ltd., 1972.

Pinenne, H. *Economic and Social History of Medieval Europe*. Harcourt, Brace and Co. N.Y., 1933.

Poliakov, L. "Racism in Europe," in *Caste and Race: Comparative Approaches* by A. de Reuck and J. Knight, (eds.), London, England: J. & A. Churchill Ltd., 1968.

Price, A. G. *White Settlers and Native People*. Melbourne: Georgian House, 1950.

Samuel, T. *The Migration of Canadian Born between Canada and the United States of America: 1955-1968*. Department of Manpower and Immigration, Research Branch, Ottawa, 1970.

Schermerhorn, R. *Comparative Ethnic Relations: A Framework for Theory and Research*. New York: Random House, 1970.

Sjoberg, G. *The Preindustrial City*. New York: Macmillan Co., 1960.

Skolnick, Jerome H. *Justice without Trial*. New York: John Wiley and Sons, 1966.

Srivastava, R. "Family Organization and Change among the East Indians of British Columbia," in G. Kurian (ed.) *Family in India: A Regional View*. The Hague: Mouton and Co., 1971.

Timlin, M. "Canada's Immigration Policy, 1896-1910." *The Canadian Journal of Economics and Political Science*, 26, Nov. 4, 1960, 517-532.

Tulloch, H. *Black Canadians*. Toronto: N.C. Press Ltd, 1975.

Wade, M. *The French-Canadian Outlook*. Toronto: McClelland and Stewart Ltd., 1970.

Ward, P. *White Canada Forever*. Montreal: McGill-Queen's University Press, 1978.

Wilson, W. *Power, Racism and Privilege*, New York: Macmillan, 1973.

Yetman, N. and C. Steele. *Majority and Minority*. Boston: Allyn and Bacon, Inc., 1971.

Zubaida, S. (ed.) *Race and Racism*. London: Tavistock Publishing Company, 1970.

Chapter 10

Dominant Social Control and Minority Subordination

Developing a Model of Ethnic Relations in Canada

The present chapter will develop a model for the study of intergroup relations in Canada as well as focus on specific groups in order to illustrate the processes involved. The model set forth attempts to locate the structure in which intergroup relations take place. Within the structure, we explicate the processes which tie the groups together.

The model to be used in the present analysis of intergroup relations will be based on our conceptualization of how reality is structured. Then on the basis of this structure, we will attempt to analyse the processes that are involved in PAG interaction. Many conceptual and practical problems arise in taking this macro-perspective, in that while the same analytical procedures may be discussed, the actual processes will be different as one moves from region to region and from time to time. Thus, we must involve what Vallee (1971) and Lautt (1973) refer to as regional perspectives. For example, intergroup relations may involve two groups which nominally are labeled the same yet take place in two different regions of our society. French-Canadians, or francophones interacting with British-Canadians will be different as one moves the analysis from Quebec to Manitoba to British Columbia. In this case, perhaps regional identity is the major factor determining the relations, although many other psychological, sociological and demographic factors will bear on the relationship and how it changes (if it does) over time.

Clairmont and Wien (1976) suggest that three different theoretical approaches to intergroup relations have been applied to the Canadian scene. The first approach, *descriptive pluralism*, views intergroup relations as a product of the interaction between intermediate groups. Unfortunately, most of their discussion with regard to this approach is unclear and vague. However, it would seem that this conceptualization views group identity as a result of an individual's affiliation and subsequent socialization within that group. After taking on an identity, group consciousness and loyalty to the group becomes important to the individual, which then determines the relationship.

A second approach has been referred to as the *internal colonialism* or Marxist approach. This framework focuses on the structure and functioning of the economic system. While other structures (and their interrelationships) are studied, the economic institution is viewed as central. The social system is conceptualized as being formed of two social classes—an elite and an oppressed minority. Through control of the political and economic structures of society, the elite is able to exploit the oppressed masses.

The third approach, *evolutionary universalism*, views each society as proceeding in an evolutionary process which, in the end, will be free of any ethno/racial tension or conflict. This position argues that as the structural and cultural basis for prejudice and discrimination disappears, integration will take place. This evolutionary process goes on whenever a system begins to replace ascriptive and particularistic factors by achievement and universalistic attributes.

These theoretical conceptualizations have never been fully explicated nor have they been subjected to a rigorous empirical test. The position to be outlined here will use certain elements from each of the conceptualizations as well as propositions from other theoretical frameworks.

To begin, then, we must outline basic structures that seem to be evident in intergroup relations. However, it is equally clear that groups do not make decisions and carry out actions. It is individuals within an organizational context that carry out the actions. Thus it should be made clear how we wish to handle this problem.

PAGs[1] are composed of individuals who believe (or are told) that they exhibit (or hold) values, life styles and views of reality which are different from other groups of people. For example, minority PAGs working within the Canadian economic structure perceive a disjuncture between the supposed benefits and reality. In addition, they see the continual insistence by the dominant group to assimilate as a potential threat to their group interests and identity. Within this broad organizational context, members set forth goals (explicit and implicit) which are both formal and informal. They then implement these goals as best they can. But how? Obviously each member (individually) would find it difficult to implement decisions that have been made by the group. Thus, each PAG elects (allows) certain members to assume leadership positions. These individuals then carry forth the decisions they (or the group) wish to have implemented. How they attempt to implement these goals is complex. We have chosen a model of "interest groups" as best portraying the processes of how PAGs relate to each other and to other groups based on ethnic, political or religious ideologies.

The actual form and intensity of intergroup relations will be contingent upon the influence of various psychological, social-psychological, sociological and demographic factors (Kinloch, 1979). To facilitate our discussion, we have divided the potential intervening variables into three dimensions. First of all, psychological factors such as "consciousness of kind" (identity) will have an impact upon the organizational structure of a group and its subsequent implementation of decisions made by the masses. If a group is low in "identity" e.g., Scandinavians, certain goals will not be pursued, or pursued in a way which is quite different than those of a group high in identity. Sociological factors, e.g., occupations, will also be important. And a third set of factors—demographic, e.g.,

---

[1] We will use the more general concept "perceived appearance group" (PAG) for the remainder of the chapter. This concept will allow for a more theoretical conceptualization of the processes related to intergroup behavior. This concept facilitates an understanding of intergroup processes beyond just "ethnic groups" and includes ethno-national, linguistic and religious groups.

FIGURE 1

Psychological	Sociological	Demographic
Identity Language View of Reality Religious View Personality Group Loyalty Degree Cohesion	Occupational Structure Immigrant-Native Charter Group Power Roles Reference Groups Contact Competition Racism Economic Structure Independence Group Visibility	Population Size Regional Placement Urbanization Division of Labour Resources

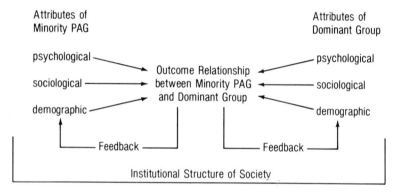

population size, regional placement—will also contribute to structural relationships between PAGs and the dominant group.

Thus, minority PAG leaders must attempt to implement the resources available to them within a specific context to achieve goals (Breton, 1964). Hence the resultant outcome as well as the success of goals (whether local or cosmopolitan) will be retarded or facilitated by the various combinations of the three sets of variables indicated above. The ability to organize these variables in some manner such that a group is able to achieve goals will determine the relationship between the groups. In addition, legitimacy of the organization and its activities will bear upon the success or failure of the group to achieve goals.

All of the above factors will come into play when one analyses about intergroup relations. However, how they are introduced and when as well as how they interrelate with one another has been subject to much debate. It should be pointed out that our state of knowledge does not allow us, at this point in time, to claim that certain factors have greater or lesser weight in determining relations or that the various factors emerge in some causal chain. We only know that the presence or absence of a factor changes (or as one changes) the intensity of each variable it potentially changes the relationship between any two groups. The extent of empirical testing has not advanced to the point of establishing the intricate and complex relationships between various factors. For example, if only three variables (taking on only two values—high/low) were analysed together, theoretically over forty relationships would have to be tested. The addition of a third group or a fourth variable will make the assessment even more complex.

To simplify (not distort) our model, let us first look at a two party situation. One segment of society we will define as dominant i.e., it holds a great deal of power, and the other subordinate (very little power), come into contact. Assuming that the powerful sector does not want to give up power, what will be the subsequent relationship (outcome) between the two, e.g., the structural relationship between two groups at any point in time? A full explication of various outcomes will be discussed in the next chapter.

FIGURE 2

Dominant Group	= D
Subordinate Group	= S
Outcome	= O
Time	= T
Decision	= d

(initial contact) T_1 D relationship S leads to (d) = O_1
$\qquad\qquad\quad$ T_2 D relationship S leads to (d) or (d_1) = O_1 or O_n
$\qquad\qquad\quad$ T_3 D relationship S leads to (d), (d_1), (d_n) = O_1 or O_n

Berry (1958) as well as many others has attempted to delineate a number of outcomes between two groups. For example, the dominant group might decide to segregate the subordinate group from the dominant group. Structured relations might involve the establishment of reserves, the creation of laws to prevent intermarriage, or informal procedures to prevent the subordinate group from taking certain jobs. What we are suggesting, then, is that outcomes are structured relationships between two groups over time which are *conscious decisions* made by each group, which can be a result of "rationale" planning or, in some cases, modified as a result of fortuitous factors. Figure 2 illustrates this process.

Figure 2 illustrates the interaction process of two groups. At time one, the two groups come into contact. The dominant group makes a decision (d) as to what type of relationship (outcome, O_1 should be established. Then at time two, the relationship is assessed and evaluated. If the existing relationship is acceptable, the decision will be to continue with O_1. However if changes in the larger society, subordinate group, or in the dominant group have occurred, then this outcome (O_1) may have to be changed. O_n represents some change.

Deliberate planning can have its problems. In some cases deliberate policy can have results quite the opposite of what was intended. For example, the elaborate Spanish socio-racial (46 categories) classification scheme developed in Mexico, was to make the exact lines of ancestry of descent the major aspect of social status. Two factors mediated against this policy: (i) The elaborate structure made it impossible to enforce and (ii) the gradations between categories were so small it was easy to shift from one category to the next. As a result, the policy was never effective and quickly came into disuse.

In other cases, the policy may become ineffective because of the influence of external factors. For example, slavery in the United States was strengthened initially because of the cotton gin. It created the expansion of cotton production and thus increased the labor demand. However, later (1930 onward) when technological inventions (tractors, cotton pickers) were introduced, it reduced the need for labor and produced massive migration of Blacks to the North. Similarly, in South Africa apartheid is the accepted ideological framework; yet because of the increasing industrialization of South Africa, more skilled labor is needed, which means more non-Whites will have to enter the labor force.

The above examples have been provided to the reader so as to point out clearly that policy planning and program implementation by the dominant group with regard to how they will handle the minority PAG "problem" is not always correct or effective. It also illustrates that the outcomes (and decisions made by a dominant group) cannot be viewed as separate entities in themselves but must be seen in the context of the total society (Hunt and Walker, 1974).

Figure 2 shows a simple dyad relationship between one dominant and one subordinate PAG. Basically, it shows that at some point in time, the dominant group makes a decision as to how it will interact with the specific subordinate group. This, of course, refers to an outcome. Then, as the economy changes, political climate varies, size of population increases (one now has to look at all of the psychological, sociological, and demographic variables introduced previously), the dominant group must re-evaluate its initial decision. If the evaluation is that the status quo will not be upset, it will continue with the initial decision. However, if at this time a decision is made that enough changes have been effected to potentially disrupt the status quo in a manner detrimental to the dominant group's position, then a new outcome will be decided upon. The process is unending. To make the model even more complex, we can introduce three groups. (See Figure 3)

FIGURE 3

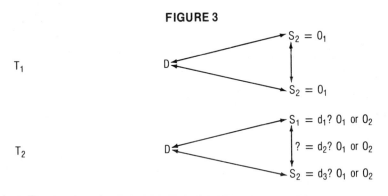

One can clearly see, then, that the model becomes more complex once we begin talking about a situation with more than, say, five groups. The complexity arises by virtue of the fact that while the dominant group makes decisions relative to a specific PAG, the decision may have positive impact for the dominant yet negative for the subordinate. In addition, the decision may indirectly influence a third and fourth group; both negatively, both positively, or some positively and some negatively. Minority PAG members may feel compelled to comply with the dominant group's norm, not because they identify with or have internalized these norms, but because they lack sufficient resources to openly challenge them. If there is minority resistance in such situations, it will likely be very subtle and indirect, frequently an individual rather than a collective endeavor. To add to this complex situation, the subordinate groups carry on interaction between themselves, and they may have positive or negative relations, as well as change over time. (See Figure 4)

FIGURE 4

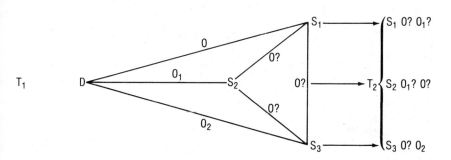

What emerges out of this preliminary discussion of our model is that certain basic assumptions are made which should be made explicit. First of all, dominant groups want to maintain their position in society. For example, groups which hold charter group status have special rights and privileges and they do not give up power (special rights and privileges) willingly (Bachrach and Baratz, 1970). They must retain their position in order to make decisions which will affect them positively. Secondly, both the dominant and minority PAG make decisions. Events that occur which affect both dominant and subordinate groups are not totally a result of fortuitous factors or made by groups with no "consciousness," but rather events which are based on conscious decisions. We do not mean to suggest that these groups will never make errors in deciding specific outcomes, because this does happen. However, once they have made a decision they will carefully monitor each stage (Depres, 1975; Enloe, 1973).

The model to be used portrays a system in which a dominant and subordinate PAG relate to each other over time during which an outcome is established. Over time, these relationships may begin to change because of the impact of psychological, sociological and demographic factors. For example, as immigration patterns change, as birth rates climb, or as urbanization increases, crisis situations emerge during which the dominant group has to redecide what to do. It must decide whether or not immigration laws must be changed so as to preserve (or further change) the composition and ultimately the structure of the society.

An example of this process to redecide would be the creation of a Royal Commission. As Fowke (1948) pointed out in his study of Royal Commissions, this is one major reason for the creation of them. He points out that they secure information to form the basis of legislation, sound out public opinion and, most importantly, allow the airing of grievances, while giving the government a breathing spell before it is required to take action on an issue.

The question now posed is how do the minority PAGs interact with the segments or agencies of the dominant group? In order to answer this question, we must first discuss the structure of minority PAGs. Each minority PAG has its own local, provincial, regional or national organization structure. (See Table 1) Goals are formulated and passed on to the leadership with instruction as to how vigorously to pursue the goals and perhaps specific strategies. If a PAG has only a local organization structure (or perhaps a minimum of structure), its impact in terms of achieving collective goals will be limited in scope as well as content. For example, Chinese members of a community might be able to bring pressure against a specific city council or planning committee in order to achieve a specific goal. The impact, however, will only be indirectly felt beyond the initial

Table 1

CULTURAL ORGANIZATIONS,[1] 1972[2]

	Number of organizations		Number of organizations		Number of organizations
African	8	French	7	Norwegian	8
Arab	13	German	43	Pakistani	3
Armenian	15	Greek	31	Philippine	5
Austrian	4	Haitian	2	Polish	45
Baltic	5	Hungarian	20	Portuguese	12
Belgian	3	Icelandic	6	Romanian	7
Black	11	Inter-Ethnic	19	Russian	10
Bulgarian	2	Italian	66	Scandinavian	3
Byelorussian	4	Japanese	21	Serbian	10
Caribbean	6	Jewish	26	Slovak	11
Chinese	36	Korean	6	Slovenian	8
Croatian	14	Latin American	2	Spanish	13
Czech	12	Latvian	17	Swedish	7
Danish	8	Lebanese-Syrian	4	Swiss	8
Doukhobor	8	Lithuanian	21	Turkish	2
Dutch	20	Macedonian	4	Ukrainian	42
East Indian	15	Malaysian	1	West Indian	3
Estonian	24	Maltese	3	Yugoslav	3
Finnish	18	Moslem	5		

Source: *Perspective Canada*, Information Canada, 1974, p. 282.

[1] In some cases only the head office of an organization is counted even though branches may exist in many centres. Also, if an organization does not advise the Secretary of State's office of its existence it will not be counted.

[2] This is not to be taken as an exhaustive list of organizations. There are only about fifty ethnic groups listed above while we have previously pointed out that there are well over 100 in Canada.

area because of the lack of inter-city, regional, or national organizational structure. Local PAG members who reside in Regina may be unaware of the local Toronto PAG activities and vice versa, even though they may be members of the same ethnic category/collectivity.

However, if the group has provincial, regional and/or national linkages, then a more complex bureaucracy will be established. This, of course, entails the emergence of a structured leadership whose activities fall within the legitimate scope of activities of the larger society. These leaders, then, assume the role status of pressure-interest groups and engage in interaction with the political structure. Until recently, these leaders were considered "universal" intellectuals and were expected to handle a variety of situations and contexts. However, Foucault (1977) has pointed out that more recently, PAGs are utilizing "specific" intellectuals as their leaders. These are individuals who work in specific sectors and at the precise points so as to effect maximum impact on the decision makers. Their jobs are to engage in activities with legitimate political-economic figure-heads and bring pressure against them so as to achieve the goals set forth by the PAG members. Martin (1978) concurs with this model in his analysis of Australia:

> there can emerge ... ethnic communities that function with varying degrees of commitment, varying resources and so on, as multi-interest, identity making and confirming groups. ... They may act as pressure groups in the sense of making claims either directly or indirectly on the government, so as to influence the making or administering of public policy. ... In this form or less overtly, ethnic groups try to take part in the development of community perspectives on their interest and identity. ... (214)

Before we continue, it should be made clear to the reader that we are not suggesting a straightforward, rational model. Organizations made up of people representing a specific PAG do not always rationally evaluate situations, carefully weigh alternatives and then make the most logical or rational recommendations. They, like the rest of us, respond to the social exigencies of every day life. As the stresses of external society impinge upon the group's functioning, reactions are forthcoming.

Initially, the PAG must have some "consciousness of kind". That is, it must be aware of itself as a collective entity (Greeley, 1974). Without this self-consciousness (as a group), discontented people may express their dissatisfaction, but only as individuals, not collectively. In addition, communication between members becomes necessary. The greater the amount of communication (proximity and density of members of the group will certainly affect this), the greater the likelihood that collective identity will emerge. The ethnic press has been one manner in which communication between members may take place in more than one language. Out of this consciousness of kind will emerge a common view of reality and a sense of common fate. However, if this basic structure is not present, then the group will not progress as a group, but, as stated above, progress along individual lines.

The goals that these groups have (assuming now that they have achieved a sense of cohesiveness), are ideas about what might be. Put another way, goals are mental constructs of a future condition which is desired (Kriesberg, 1973).

The articulation of these ideas may be formal (ideology) or informal (inferred from indirect verbal expressions and actions).

The degree of formalization of goals to be set forth by subordinate group · members will, of course, vary according to a number of factors; residential segregation, demographic composition, degree of identification, feeling of consciousness of kind, and communication processes. Certain groups such as the Hutterites have formally codified their goals and have well developed structures by which to carry them out. Ukrainians have also developed techniques for communicating and maintaining a sense of "Ukrainianness" but not to the extent of the Hutterites. On the other hand, Indians (although this is changing rapidly) have not been effective in communicating with other Indians.

PAGs do not exist in a vacuum. They must carry on relations with other PAGs as well as various political and economic agencies (Maklelski, 1973; Nagata, 1964). Thus, the model becomes more than just PAG relations when we begin to introduce the matter of PAGs dealing with municipal, provincial and federal bodies which ostensibly have no ethnic attachment. The importance of such a discussion is seen when groups have loose or no organizational structure in which to relate to these political and economic bodies. For example, Native people are slowly beginning to affect the outcomes when dealing with agencies of the dominant group. This has come about because of the establishment of voluntary associations as well as the emergence of local, provincial, regional and national structures.

PAG Interest Groups

Before continuing our discussion, it would seem prudent to digress for a moment and discuss what is meant by an interest or pressure group. We have used the definition of interest groups set forth by Truman (1951):

> Interest groups refer to any group that, on the basis of one or more shared attitudes (the interests), makes certain claims upon other groups in the society for the establishment, maintenance, or enhancement of forms of behavior that are implied by the shared attitudes. These are shared attitudes toward what is needed or wanted in a given situation, observable, or demands or claims upon other groups in the society. (33-34)

Basically then, interest groups articulate certain demands in the society. They seek to achieve these demands (goals) by bargaining with power groups in the society. They attempt to "transform these demands into authoritative public policy by influencing the choice of political personnel and various processes of public policy-making and enforcement" (Almond, 1961). (See Figure 5)

But with whom do the ethnic interest group leaders interact? We have stated previously that the interaction was with political-economic interest group leaders. "But," the charge will go, "if you look at the political leaders at a municipal, provincial, or even national level, the PAG composition is diverse." Such a statement does not have credence. What has happened in such a statement is that the definition of ethnicity (or whatever label you wish to use) has changed. People talk about Albert Kabroski as an MP or MLA and *assume* he must be Polish. The question is, is he really exhibiting Polish ethnicity via a Polish surname? One needs to look further in the back stages to decide whether

FIGURE 5

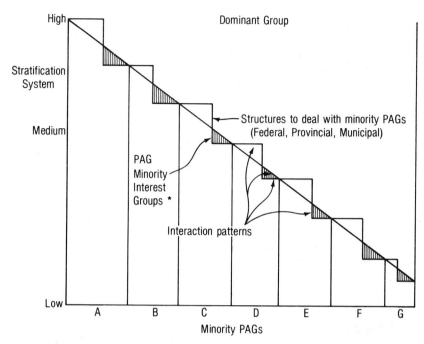

*The effectiveness of the PAG minority interest group will depend on the following major considerations: organizational structure, formalization of goals, and cultural compatibility with dominant group.

or not he is really culturally and ideologically different from the basic Anglo/dominant culture. If he is, then one needs to ask whether or not his constituency is of such a composition that they have voted him in because of their feeling that he would be a good leader and thus promote their interest.

Canadian society is basically one of Anglo structure. Basic institutions have been derived from Great Britain with some modifications to fit the local environment. In addition, these basic political-economic (and other institutional structures) are controlled by English (Anglo) cultural supporters. Only in isolated cases can it be otherwise. We are arguing the fact that even though one becomes a political (economic) leader, just because one has a non-British ethnic name, it does not give evidence that Canada is willing to accept and give equal treatment to non-Anglo groups. People do acculturate and, in some cases, actively reject the traditional culture (see Wuttunee, 1972).

The aim of interest groups is to affect government policy and programs in their favor (Morris and Lanphier, 1977). This suggestion would seem to lead to the argument that interest groups would concentrate their efforts toward an MP or MLA. While this may be true because of the MP's local interest in his/her constituency, in the general case, the MP is the focus only as a last resort by the interest group. In our society interest groups focus on the Ottawa bureaucracy that affects them most directly. This exists at the provincial and municipal level also. However, interest groups also influence government in their annual submissions to the federal cabinet. These annual submissions refer to any policy outputs which the groups consider desirable. Provincial and local interest groups may deal directly with the federal government or channel their appeals through the nation-wide organization of the group. Again the contacts at the provincial and municipal levels are similar to those at the federal level.

It follows, then, that the group must know whether to focus its lobbying efforts at the individual MP, the cabinet, legislative committees, or at the bureaucracy. The context of the issue and where it stands in the public arena will determine which way to go. Erroneous decisions as to what level to focus on will result in unfulfilled goals.

Not all interest groups are effective in their efforts to influence government bureaucracies. The explanation for the failure (or success) of pressure groups lies in basic differences between types of interest groups. Political resources, for example, are spread very unevenly from group to group. In addition, many important interests are in fact unorganized and or inactive and lack determination and persistence in achieving their goal. Likewise one must realize that certain interests tend to be ruled out or are only marginally included in the pluralist balancing process. Many interests are not articulated and many demands are not recognized as important issues by the decision makers. Lastly, there is the bias toward interest groups that is recognized by the government and consulted by it. Institutional interest groups are on one end of the continuum, while issue-oriented interest groups could be placed on the other. The organizational structure of these groups and their goal structure differentiate the two extreme types. Pross (1975) delineates basic differences between the two:

INTEREST GROUPS' ORGANIZATION STRUCTURE

Institutional	Issue
—possess organizational continuity and cohesion	—limited organization and cohesion
—knowledgeable about government sectors which affect them	—poor information about government
—stable membership	—fluid membership
—operational objectives are concrete and immediate	—inability to formulate long-term goals
—credibility of organization important	—goal achievement is important

In making the distinctions in terms of organizational structure, one can already see that issue-oriented groups will be less effective in pursuing and achieving their goals. However, by virtue of having the more effective organizational structure, it allows the institutional group to pursue selective but multiple, broadly defined issues. On the other hand, issue oriented groups can only choose single, narrowly defined goals.

The importance of organizational structure can be seen in analysing the Japanese reactions to Canadian hostility prior to World War II. While these are not the only explanations, they do give some partial illustrations. In 1934 there were well over 230 Japanese religious and secular associations. In addition, any time a crisis for the Japanese emerged, *ad hoc* associations were created. For example, in 1926 the Japanese organized The Amalgamated Association of Japanese Fishermen. This organization was able to oppose, quite effectively, certain federal restrictions on fishing licenses that were being proposed at the time. In addition to internal organizational structures, they were also able to maintain organizational structures (with concomitant communication lines) with the homeland. Because the Japanese Empire had become an ally of Great Britain in 1902, they were, through the Japanese ambassador in Ottawa, able to exert pressure on the federal and provincial governments. These organizations were very influential until the outbreak of World War II. At that time, major legal and social changes were brought into effect partially as a result of external pressures—American policy.

Radecki and Heydenkorn (1976) and Radecki (1977) have also pointed out various functions of Polish organizations. They document that the large, broad-based organizations (e.g., Canadian Polish Congress) have been able to receive recognition from various political institutions and as a result influence the decision or policies affecting this group in Canada. As Radecki and Heydenkorn suggest:

> The leaders of the Congress and of other large independent associations have been recognized as having influence both within their own ethnic community and with the Canadian government, a position which allows them to wage battles and campaigns against restrictive immigration policies, for preservation of the group's status, and upon other such issues. (76).

On the other hand, the Portuguese have not been able to establish strong organizational structures. It is true that wherever a small concentration of Portuguese exist an organization will emerge, but we find that: (i) they are local in orientation and (ii) if more than one exists, a great deal of infighting goes on. There is a lack of unity of purpose in the struggle to protect Portuguese interests. Anderson and Higgs (1976) suggest that Portuguese tend to ". . . look on the clubs (and organizations) not as a vehicle for political or community organization, but to provide them with recreation" (162).

Issue-oriented groups have a small membership with few staff (usually volunteer) to handle the communication that is necessary, while institutional groups have extensive financial and human resources to bring to bear on the variety of issues it wishes to address. It becomes evident, then, that PAGs which are near the institutional end of the continuum will have a greater chance of achieving their goals. They have the ability to use subtle techniques of persuasion (advertising) and to cultivate regular and private meetings with government officials, economic leaders and senior civil servants which increase the likelihood of exerting influence (Porter, 1975; Kelner, 1970; Clement, 1975).

What has been suggested thus far with regard to interest group relations is that the dominant group relates to the subordinate group as a unit. This does not mean that the minority PAG is in fact a homogenous entity. Hence it will be necessary to discuss the emergence of these minority pressure interest groups and the interrelationship of various subgroupings of the minority PAG.

It may be true that specific subordinate groups are homogeneous and have similar values and goals as well as means to achieve them. In such a case, the general model above holds. However, in many cases, PAGs are not homogeneous. Two major dimensions that differentiate will be discussed: (1) economic differences and (2) ideological factions. Again, the boundaries of these two subgroups may be similar but this case is far from common. Figure 6 illustrates the potential subgroupings.

FIGURE 6

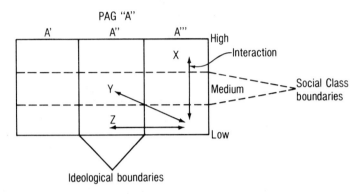

Subordinate groups are no different from the larger system in that their structure also exhibits a mini-stratification system (Wirth, 1945). In the less complex system, the ideological faction system boundaries are the same as the economic. In such a case, each subgroup engages in interaction with the other subgroups. This interaction goes on in an effort for one subgroup to gain power within the group. This, then, will allow that subgroup to represent the entire group as the pressure interest group when it interacts with the dominant group representatives. The necessity for explicating such a model allows the reader to comprehend the fact that intragroup interaction does go on, as well as attempting to illustrate the fact that intragroup relations may involve conflict behavior (Robb, 1978; Rubin, 1976).

In the case where social class boundaries do not coincide, a much more complex set of interactions emerge. The result may be the emergence of a number of subgroups that are continually in conflict in an attempt to represent the entire group. Or, it may, if given the appropriate conditions and time, become a separate PAG or lose its ethno/racial element and simply become a social group or collectivity. In the illustration provided, three factions (X, Y, Z) have been identified. Each faction would be attempting to gain enough power so as to control the other factions and carry on the interaction with the dominant group in a way they defined as appropriate.

The second question posed has to do with the emergence of pressure interest groups. How do these groups emerge and sustain themselves? One of the easiest and perhaps simplest explanations is to claim that some individuals have intrinsic personality attributes that vault them into leadership positions. A second explanation might be that those individuals with charisma become leaders. While both may have a kernel of truth in the explanations, we feel that they fall short of providing us with an adequate explanation of the processes.

We will use a "process" explanation. Generally, the initial stages of leadership formation (and subsequent organization of pressure/interest groups) will begin with individuals in the group defining their position in society as being unsatisfactory (McRoberts and Postgate, 1976). This generally emerges during crisis situations. Once the situation has been defined as intolerable, solutions are needed. Many individuals may offer potential solutions, yet only a few are chosen. It now becomes a matter of who will be identified with what solution because many solutions are tried. Obviously, if a particular solution works (and this does not have to mean an objective change in status of the subordinate group), the individual(s) identified with the solution will be held in high regard by members of the group. However, it may also produce factions as pointed out above.

Normally these solutions to problems begin at the local level and move to higher levels as time goes on. Thus, achieving goals desired by the local groups may allow the individual(s) to move to the next higher level and begin offering further solutions. It is important that the reader understand that this process is not one just involving objective, measurable facts. Thus, the process of establishing pressure groups may take varying lengths of time. This, of course, accounts for the fact that many recent immigrant groups do not yet have established pressure groups. In addition, because of the simultaneous emergence of many potential leaders in a group, it also explains why factions may emerge in specific ethnic groups.

The basic conceptual framework to be used in the present work requires that the reader understand that Canada has two major types of regions: (i) peripheral sectionalism—people uniting behind some common element of a regional culture, i.e., religion, language and (ii) structural sectionalism—people uniting because of class or similarities of occupation (Hechter, 1973).

The importance of making these distinctions is based upon the idea of identity compartmentalization (Lautt, 1973). In terms of our model, this means that an individual has the ability to perform within two cultures at different times with no implication that one is inherently better than the other. Clearly, this becomes important for the individuals residing in a subordinate cultural region. As Lautt (1973) points out:

> Cultural compartmentalization exists in behavioural terms, but individuals are not comfortable with it and do not see it as a legitimate solution to the problem of ethnic conflict and assimilation because the existing values and attitudes towards ethnic groups are not compatible with the behaviour which compartmentalization demands. On the one hand, the dominant cultural group has not conceded that in certain areas of life, different cultural adaptations (i.e., language) are just as legitimate as their own; some of the traits of the ethnic minorities are looked upon as weird, repugnant, or just strange. (139)

On the other hand, for those individuals from a functional region, compartmentalization does not involve cultural identity to the same extent as those from cultural regions. Class, occupation and regional identities all take precedence and to a great extent determine the relationships with other groups as well as the reaction of various minority PAGs to decisions made by the dominant group.

Changes in freight rates are not defined by group members residing in the West as an "attempt to destroy our culture," but rather an attempt by the East to retain their economic superiority. A similar action taken which would affect Quebec would not be defined as such.

The dominant groups will go through the processes of decision-making outlined previously. Once it has made a decision, it then allows for some lag time in order to assess the potential resistance and to allow for further modifications if necessary. The above model suggests that PAGs attain the status of adversary groups which will, of course, involve conflict. As Jackson (1966) points out:

> We see social conflict as a normal and natural outcome of structural processes—of the interplay of power and position, and of boundary-maintenance activity—not as pathological . . . social conflict is an interactional state: that is, the conflicting parties must be in contact and there must be a certain amount of interaction before a state of conflict may be said to exist. (77)

Dominant Social Control Mechanisms

The struggle of a particular PAG to obtain a goal, e.g., language use or a particular language of instruction in certain schools, is not a result of the actions of disgruntled individual malcontents, but rather the result of a struggle for status and identification emerging from their *particular positions and roles in the social system.*

The differentiation between cultural and functional regions is important to understand why certain decisions taken by the dominant group work (or do not work well) with specific PAGs. Hence the application of certain social control mechanisms used against French-Canadians living in Quebec may not be appropriate for those French-Canadians living in the West, Ontario, or in the Maritimes. It also alerts the reader to the understanding that certain specific decisions may be invoked with regard to a range of PAGs.

In discussing techniques of social control, two premises must be kept in mind. First, there is a segment of the population who have power and secondly, they want to maintain it. When we say that a particular group has power, just what are we saying? That is, how do we characterize the concept of power? Before actually stating a definition, we should place some bounds upon the way in which it will be used for this book. First of all, we want to distinguish between actual and potential power. We want to make clear that some groups may have the capacity for activating their resources (assets) but do not do so, either because they fail to realize that they have power, or another group is able to successfully contain the use of power. Secondly, we are limiting the concept of power to activities intended to obtain a desired goal. However, we realize that much power wielding is relatively unintended and its effects are indirect and far reaching (Olsen, 1970: 5).

Two additional points concerning the concept of power must also be stated. Social power can (under many circumstances) be viewed "as a positive factor" in promoting organized social life as well as a negative restriction (Olsen, 1970: 5). The second point to be discussed revolves around the issue of "balance." If both parties exert equal amounts of power, which means that balance is attained, we will still consider this to be power. Whether a group is successful in attaining its goal is not the ultimate criterion for measuring power.

Let us now posit a definition of power: *Power is the ability to use resources to exert social change or overcome resistance to social change in the face of opposition (if it exists).*

In the above definition, we have introduced an additional term which is crucial to the meaning—resources. There are several types of resources that exist. In addition, the kind and amount of resources available to a group will also vary and affect the strength of power a group will exert. Likewise the resources committed and the resistance encountered will temper the degree of power a group has over another group (Olsen, 1970). Resources can consist of tangible goods, such as land areas (reservations) and material possessions (industries), but can also include what Olsen (1970) calls intangible goods: knowledge, skill and legitimacy. For example, Bierstedt (1950) suggests that power stems from: (1) numbers of people (tangible) and (2) the social organization of the people (intangible).

Resources can also be general in nature or highly particular (Wilson, 1973). For example, if the resources can be applied to a number of situations and to a number of people at the same time, then the resource would be defined as general in nature. On the other hand, if resources can only be brought to bear upon one situation, it can be considered specific. One last dimension of resources that should be discussed centres on that of "liquidity" (Gamson, 1968). This simply refers to the ability of the PAG to mobilize the exertion of power. For example, Native people (because of their organizational structure) can deploy many different types of social action within a fairly short period of time. The number of sit-ins, boycotts and action-oriented programs substantiate this claim. On the other hand, groups such as the Jamaicans and other recent immigrant groups do not have this facility.

The reader also needs to bear in mind that the decision to invoke control mechanisms involves a deliberate conscious attempt. That is, the decision chosen by an empowered (or subordinate) group to attain a particular goal is not a fortuitous occurrence. Those groups in power have legitimacy on their side, and one of their central concerns focuses on "norm enforcement" (Firestone, 1971). Thus, definitions of responsible and irresponsible behavior are always made by those in power (Newman, 1973). These definitions, of course, can change (and do change) as the relationship between the powered and non-powered PAGs changes. The long-range goal of the empowered group seems to be a high maintenance of social distance as well as establishing a power differential.

We now want to introduce several concepts necessary to our discussion of social control mechanisms. The major conceptual model to be outlined is heavily indebted to the work of Gamson (1968). Decisions about the degree of discontent that exists within a particular PAG, resources, and the perception of the degree of awareness the PAG has about its resources capability are the three important dimensions.

Degree of discontent

Discontent refers to the degree of acceptance of the moral order that exists in a stable system, i.e., the degree of acceptance (or rejection) of the subordinate PAG to their place in society. If the PAG accepts its position in the society (relative to its place in the institutional orders), it is then considered to be low in discontent.

Resources

The amount of power a particular group has is dependent upon the resources available to or existing with the particular group. Resources include all the things that we discussed previously such as size of the PAG, availability and control of natural and social resources. Other factors may also be considered resources depending upon the organization and development of the larger society.

Perception of subordinate group's awareness level by dominant group

This involves the definition that the dominant group makes about the subordinate PAG's awareness of their resource capability and level of discontent. This of course means that depending on the accuracy of information the dominant group has about the subordinate PAG, decisions will enhance or retard dominant groups' short range or long range goals. Figure 7 explicates the relations among the three factors.

FIGURE 7

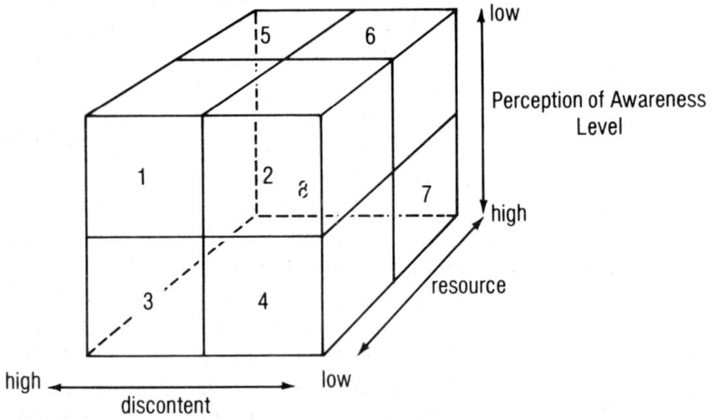

In this model, we are most concerned with the definitions of reality which take place within the existing dominant group. That is, social control mechanisms will be implemented (or not implemented) only if the dominant group defines the situation as warranting such invocation or not. Thus, even though certain minority PAGs may claim that they are highly discontented and have high power potential, if this is not consistent with the definition made by the dominant group, little reaction (in the form of social change) will result.

This, of course, suggests that an "accuracy" dimension must also be introduced into the model. The dominant group, for various reasons, may not define a particular group as high in discontent or high in potential power and thus act toward them in a way which may culminate in a power struggle. Had they defined the situation differently and consequently acted toward them differently, the struggle may have been avoided.

Minority PAGs falling in sector eight (Figure 7) are the most important for the dominant group. They have high resources, are high in discontent, and are perceived by the dominant group as being aware of holding these attributes. An example would be French-Canadians. This means that groups with such attributes must immediately be dealt with if the dominant group is to retain its position. To date, interaction of the dominant group with French-Canadians has not been defined as successful from the standpoint of the French-Canadians. However, with the rise of unemployment, increase in French-Canadian identity, and the use of political social movements such as the Parti Quebecois and FLQ, more and more attention is being paid to this sector of society when decisions are made by the dominant group.

Groups in sector 4 represent the other end of the continuum. These groups are low in discontent, low in resources, and are defined as such by the dominant group. Examples would be Portuguese, Jamaicans and individuals from the Philippines. They have limited resources (small population, low in technical expertise, and low in control of natural and social resources). By not agitating for social change, the dominant group perceives the group as accepting their position in the social system, and as unwilling to change the system.

Other groups/collectivities such as Ukrainians, Jews and Germans can also be placed into the scheme. The important point is that only those groups defined as high in discontent and high in resources will be immediately attended to. Other segments of society such as the Native people, which are perceived as high in discontent but low in resources, will not have any decisions modified for their benefit until their resources are defined as being high.

What are the specific social control mechanisms that are used by dominant groups in a society when action must be taken toward a specific PAG? Two very general distinct techniques are used. The first strategy involves a modification of the decision that was initially made. Thus, once a decision is made, depending on the reaction of the subordinate groups, an interim period is created before the actual decision is put into effect. A present day example is the decision of the dominant group to reaffirm French Canada's right to the legal status of their language. After the decision was made, reactions from other linguistic groups were forthcoming. Rudnetski's minority report within the Bilingual and Bicultural Commission clearly reflects this reaction. The dominant group's response to this discontent was one of modification of the decisions. Presently the system is being changed so that if schools have a specific proportion of any linguistic group and that group requests language of instruction other than English or French, the language of that group must be provided. (see Conclusion).

There are, however, consequences of modification of the original decision to "honor" only French in Canada. One consequence was to increase discontent among other linguistic groups, e.g., Ukrainians. Thus one unanticipated (or in certain circumstances it may be anticipated) consequence is a shifting of discontent from one group to another. However, under certain circumstances this might be a desired outcome. The dominant group may prefer to see some subordinate PAG more contented than other groups because of a similarity of values and interests, or because the group has access to resources (present or potential).

The second general technique attempts to "control the desire of the subordinate PAG to want change." Four subtechniques have been identified: Insulation, Persuasion, Sanction, and Co-optation. As Gamson (1968) points out:

> Such persuasion may involve emphasizing the collective aspects of decisions, making those aspects which involve conflict appear less salient or important. Thus a minority group may be persuaded that the authorities are operating in the interests of the larger collectivity to which both groups belong even if some relative disadvantage is involved for their own subgroup. Thus if they are convinced, they will be more willing to accept temporary setbacks in the belief that 'things will even out in the long run' (125).

Insulation

This technique refers to keeping any minority PAG from effectively participating in the political and economic processes within the social system. In doing this, the dominant group maintains control over the minority PAG's access to resources. This is completed by preventing minority PAGs from acquiring skills and knowledge that could facilitate participation in the larger society. Techniques range from setting up unique governmental programs to limiting educational attainments. Federal agencies such as Regional and Economic Planning have set forth many "programs to help Native people" but they have always been at most, blue collar job preparations. A second example of this process would be the involvement of Native people in the educational institutions of Canada. Presently, the dropout rate is 90% compared to a general dropout rate of about 12-15%.

Few Canadian universities have a Native studies program or other programs that cater to a specific ethno/cultural group. The rationale for noninvolvement issued by universities is that Native people do not have the qualifications to enter university and if special concessions are made, there will be a cheapening of the degree and the cost of providing a special program (with all of the structural supports necessary, i.e., counselors, tutors, additional staff, special residences, etc.) would be prohibitive, and thus other services would have to be curtailed. As a result, about five hundred Native people now attend Canadian universities. If they were equally represented by their percentage in the total population the number would be well over 2,000.

While these institutions may not be blatantly discriminative, the end result is the same. Native people are not allowed into the training institutions of our society and consequently they cannot participate in the decision-making process. In the end, they are effectively controlled in their ability to bring pressure against the dominant group, so that decisions made by the dominant group do not take into consideration the wishes of the minority PAG.

As Porter (1965), Clement (1975) and Kelner (1970) report, few other groups (besides British) are allowed into the elite and semi-elite structure. Kelner finds that in Toronto, the proportion of non-Anglo-Saxon corporate leaders is only about 7%. Non-Anglo-Saxon penetration into other elite areas is somewhat higher but considerably lower than the representation, if total percentage of the population is used as the criteria. Porter, using national data, also shows for earlier time periods the same picture. Only dominant group members (using Canada as the unit of analysis—British-Canadians) tend to be members of the various elite groups in Canada.

Other techniques, such as not allowing Native people to bear arms (historically) or allowing them to exercise the franchise, are examples of insulating an ethnic minority from participation in Canadian society. The creation of reserves and the control of their movements off the reserve are further examples. Blacks, Ukrainians, Japanese, as well as a host of other PAGs have, at one time or another, been exposed to such techniques.

An additional effective and widespread insulation technique is referred to as "selective entry and exit." This, of course, takes place at a macro (societal) level as well as a community level. At a macro level immigration procedures restrict entry of certain groups of people. Those members of a group which (as defined by the dominant group) are seen as potential trouble-makers will not be allowed into the country. Thus, potential deviants and individuals who might at some point in the future organize a social movement against the existing social order will not be allowed into the country.

It should also be pointed out that the image projected by a national state is also a social control mechanism which facilitates the selective entry technique. When Laurier and King were Prime Ministers, Canada was extremely clear in the image it wished to project. Development of the West, agricultural development, and nonurban dwellers were the criteria set forth to decide who would be allowed to enter Canada. Enticing such groups as Ukrainians and Hutterites was clearly a result of such an image projection. The underlying assumption is of course that these groups of people will not pose social problems for the existing social moral order.

> Sifton used the Alien Labour Act to curb the entry of railway construction workers, largely Italians ... who might otherwise enter to work on government subsidized projects.... In 1900, therefore, when the Chinese capitation tax was raised from $50 to $100, he [Sifton] tried to get it increased to $250 or more but failed. He also failed the same year to get the Government to pass an act of the type usually called the Natal Act which would use educational tests in such a way as to bar entry of Oriental labour. (Timlin, 1960: 519)

One of the clearest examples of this process results from the dominant group's reaction to Chinese immigration into B.C. after the 1858 California gold rush. While sporadic antagonistic actions may have been directed toward the Chinese at this time, there is little evidence to suggest that a concerted effort to debar or drive them from the country existed prior to 1870. At this time, relations between Whites and Chinese began to change radically. The emerging hostility was instigated by White working men. At that time, Chinese were being employed at a wage considerably less than that paid to White laborers. As a result of their direct lobbying efforts, the provincial legislature entertained resolutions calling for a $50 annual tax on all Chinese in the province and barring them from working on provincial and federal public works projects.

However, as the employment competition (both real and imaginary) between Chinese and Whites continued, lobbying efforts of the workers increased. In 1876 the B.C. Provincial Legislature did pass a resolution favoring restriction of Chinese immigration and by 1878 included a provision to exclude their participation in public works projects. In addition, they added a quarterly tax of $10 on all Chinese.

By 1884, the B.C. Legislative Assembly passed three Acts: "an Act to prevent Chinese from acquiring Crown lands," "an Act to prevent the immigration of

Chinese," and "an Act to regulate the Chinese population of British Columbia."
As Munro (1971) states:

> The preamble to the last of the Acts sums up the position of the British Col-
> umbia government and the majority of the White settlers:
> Whereas the incoming of Chinese to B.C. largely exceeds that of any
> other class of immigrant and the population so introduced are fast becom-
> ing superior in number to our own race; are not disposed to be governed
> by our laws; are dissimilar in habits and occupation from our own people;
> evade the payment of taxes justly due the government; are governed by
> pestilential habits; are useless in instances of emergency; habitually
> desecrate graveyards by the removal of bodies therefrom; and generally
> the laws governing the Whites are found to be inapplicable to Chinese,
> and such Chinese are inclined to habits subversive to the comfort and well
> being of the community. . . . (47)

While each of these acts was disallowed by the federal government at the
time, the federal government established a royal commission to look into the
question. The final result of the commission (finished in 1885) was that the
Canadian Parliament passed an act to restrict and regulate Chinese immigration into Canada. This restriction act provided a capitation tax of $50 on every
Chinese entering Canada and limited the number any one vessel might carry to
one immigrant for every 50 tons of the carrying vessel.

> The Immigration Act of 1906 contained a section which appeared to prom-
> ise to the Canadian government a considerable expansion of discretion in
> the legal framework governing immigration. Section 30 of that Act
> authorized the passing of orders in Council 'to prohibit the landing in
> Canada of any specified class of immigrants.' (Timlin, 1960: 523)
> . . . the characteristic method used to control entry of Orientals was
> that of passing law after law in the provincial legislature as the Dominion
> Government disallowed one law after another. The process of
> disallowance normally took 8-9 months; by the time the Dominion Govern-
> ment had disallowed one law, the provincial legislature was quite ready
> to pass another, typically unanimously. (Timlin, 1960: 525)

In 1911, American Blacks were turned back at the border and not allowed to
enter Canada. The rationale set forth was that because of the harsh winter
Blacks would not be able to adapt and thus cause a burden for other Canadians.
Interestingly enough, evidence shows that advertisements sent to the U.S.A.
usually focused on the fact that Canada had mild winters (Troper, 1972).

Selective exit can also occur. Deportation at a macro level is a historical fact.
The experiences of Acadians, Germans and Japanese all attest to this fact.
Those individuals of a particular ethnic group which pose threats to the dominant group are placed outside the present nation-state. In January, 1942 the
federal government ordered an evacuation of the Japanese population from the
West Coast. All persons of Japanese descent were forcibly removed from what
was called the defence zone—a zone which extended about 100 miles inward.
No distinction was made between Japanese resident aliens or Canadian citizens
of Japanese descent.

At the end of the war, three orders-in-council (upheld by the Canadian
Supreme Court) were issued under the authority of the War Measures Act,
which stipulated that Japanese nationals as well as Japanese-Canadians (both
native born and those having taken out Canadian citizenship) would be

deported. As a result of this decision, nearly 4,000 were deported. The Canadian government did not rescind the relocation order until 1949.

At a lower unit of analysis, other techniques are readily available for groups in power positions. When selective exit occurs, it implies that troublemakers (or potential troublemakers) have somehow infiltrated (or are attempting to destroy) the existing power structure. But a problem is evident; how can they be handled? Canadian-born citizens cannot usually be deported, but removal of access to resources can be undertaken. The removal can be blatant: simply firing people, removal from one job to another, job relocation, etc. This, of course, poses immediate problems for the existing power structure. The act committed by the dominant group is easily visible for all to see (including the minority PAG which is being represented by the individual), as well as producing immediate negative consequences. Therefore, more subtle techniques are used if possible.

Persuasion

As Gamson points out, persuasion attempts to control the desire rather than the ability to influence. There are several strategies that are available to the dominant group in attempting to control the desire of minority PAGs. One of the most common techniques used involves the *activation of commitment* of the minority group to the social system. For example, during the FLQ crisis, the dominant group pointed out to other subordinate groups' members that they play a vital part in keeping society intact. They were told that they must accept certain temporary setbacks (loss of civil liberties, etc.) so that all of society could benefit. In the invocation of the War Measures Act in 1970, even French-Canadians were told that they must accept their responsibility in keeping the system together. By getting these people to accept this goal, rather drastic measures were able to be imposed upon these people without any negative reactions to the dominant group.

During World War II, Japanese-Canadians were relocated and had their property confiscated (for which they were inadequately or never compensated). They were persuaded (along with other PAGs) that it was in the best national interest for this to occur. And while they (the dominant group) knew that most Japanese-Canadians were good citizens, it was to be viewed as a temporary setback, and that in the long run all of Canada (including the Japanese-Canadians) would benefit. Statements such as "it took them out of the urban ghettos," "it forced them to integrate into Canadian society," and "it introduced them into the economic structure" are all examples of *ad hoc* rationalizations as to why it was an acceptable procedure. After all, Canada was saved. These statements, of course, suggest that persuasion can again be used and with a minimal disruption to the existing power relation.

Selective participation

This is another social control mechanism which is somewhat of a mixture of influence and social control. Free and total participation in decision making, of course, is not possible as this would allow for an equal input of information and equal access to power for all PAGs. However, by allowing PAGs to selectively participate in certain decision-making processes, control is effective. The selective participation of Jews in Canadian society (within one particular institutional order—educational) is perhaps a very good example. The result is that members of a subordinate group can then no longer claim that they "have no voice in affairs which concern them." Secondly, since the participation is selective (both in terms of the people who are allowed to participate and the decisions they are allowed to participate in), any effective resistance to the dominant group's wishes is effectively stopped. As Rosenberg (1971) points out, while Jews have not effectively participated in the upper echelons of the economic or political institutional orders, they cannot argue that Jews are kept from participating in Canadian society. Thirdly,

> under such circumstances, (dominant groups) may encourage increased participation by selected groups despite or even because of the increased influence that it will bring. The new pressures can be then pointed to as justification and defense for failure to take the actions desired by the first group; the second group in turn can be brought to appreciate the constraints which their rival places as the (dominant group). (Gamson, 1968: 140-141).

Sanctions

Negative and positive rewards can be meted out by the dominant group to minority members depending on how they act within the social system. "Responsible" activities carried out by minority members will lead to positive sanctions while "irresponsible" actions lead to negative sanctions. However, as was pointed out previously, definitions of responsible and irresponsible behavior are always contingent upon the dominant group's position. Perhaps one of the most widely used sanctions by the dominant group has been the disenfranchisement of various groups. For example, in 1917 the War Time Elections Act was passed by Parliament. It disenfranchised "every naturalized British subject who was born in an enemy country and naturalized subsequent to the 31st day of March, 1902."

The government's continued battle with the Doukhobors serves as another classic example of the use of sanctions. From 1889 to 1899, approximately 8,000 emigrated to Canada. Three main conditions were set forth by the Doukhobors and accepted by the Canadian government. One, they wanted to live communally; two, be exempt from military service; and three, be consulted regarding matters of their children's education. By 1902, conflict between the Doukhobors and the Canadian government began to emerge. They objected to the oath of allegiance and the registration of land as well as to the registration of births, deaths, and marriages. By 1903, the first nude march occurred and the individuals involved were sentenced to three months in jail.

By 1907, government pressure on the Doukhobors to conform to Canadian laws had increased. Those who refused to individually register their lands and swear the oath of allegiance were evicted. As a result, the incidence of conflict increased. Between 1908 and 1912 about 5,000 Doukhobors moved from Saskatchewan to B.C. where new property was purchased. Because most of the dissidents had moved into B.C. no new problems emerged until the beginning of World War I.

At this time resentment of the Doukhobors on the part of Canadians increased because of their pacifistic ideology. This was, of course, heightened during the war when the Doukhobors refused to take part. Further resentment against the Doukhobors resulted from the fact that they did not wish to send their children to non-Doukhobor schools. In 1920 there was an amendment to the Public Schools Act so that the children could forcibly be sent to school. Fines and seizure of goods resulted when parents failed to send their children to the schools. Between 1932 and 1935 nearly 4,000 Doukhobor children became wards of the B.C. government. Most were placed in foster homes while the remainder was turned over to the Children's Aid Society. They were also fined and they refused to pay the fine. Zubek and Solberg (1952) discuss the results:

> On Premier Oliver's instructions, Mounted Police seized Doukhobor property and sold it at an auction sale for $3,500. The government was not yet satisfied. The fine had been set at $4,600. Eleven hundred dollars worth of cedar poles and railway ties were hauled off to make up the deficit. (109)

During the early 1930s approximately 600 Sons of Freedom were imprisoned on Piers Island for various violations of Canadian laws. By the 1940s and 1950s, the Sons of Freedom were extremely active in various nonlegal activities. During this 20 year period there had been over 3,000 documented violations by Doukhobors. At the request of the provincial government of B.C. an intensive investigation was carried out, with the results of this inquiry published in 1955. Recommendations put forth by the various authors of the report included such strategies as relocating the Sons of Freedom in an area other than the Kootenays or assisting in their emigration to another nation-state. Because of the sharp increase of extra-legal activities engaged in by the Sons of Freedom, the government began to take a "get tough" attitude with increased sanctions to force conformity to the laws which, in some cases, led to mass arrests. By 1962 most of the key members (leaders) of the Sons of Freedom were in prison and, as a result, this movement began to lose its momentum, although renewed activism was apparent in the late seventies.

Another example of sanctions would be the suppression of the German press. In 1903 three German newspapers existed in Western Canada. The largest, *Der Nordwesten* (in Winnipeg), had a circulation of about 20,000 by 1914. The other two, the *Alberta Herold* and *Der Saskatchewan Courier*, were smaller in circulation but nevertheless were important provincial German newspapers.

In 1914 a motion was brought forward by the government that the German language paper should be suppressed and its manager prosecuted for treason or sedition. The motion was rejected not on the basis of its contents but rather because this matter was under the jurisdiction of the Militia Department. However, in 1917 *Der Courier* publishing house at Regina was attacked and windows were smashed. During the next few months several other acts of vandalism were committed against *Der Courier*. By 1918 the Great War Veterans' Association of Canada began to bring pressure against the government urging that all enemy alien newspapers be suppressed. The result of this pressure was that in that year an order-in-council was passed which suppressed all enemy language papers. This order-in-council prohibited the printing of newspapers and other publications in "enemy" languages such as German, Hungarian, Bulgarian, Turkish, Romanian, Russian, Ukrainian, Finnish, Estonian, Syrian, and Croatian.

Sanctions, whether they are positive or negative, applied to minority PAGs are clear attempts by the dominant group to maintain the existing moral order. The effectiveness of the sanction will depend, of course, upon the context and time in which the sanction is employed. Sanctions applied to any one group also serve the purpose of making other groups aware of the consequences of acting in a responsible or irresponsible manner.

Co-optation

One of the most intriguing and complex of social control mechanisms is that of co-optation. This technique does not involve keeping resources from the minority ethnic group but involves yielding access to these resources for the most difficult and threatening minority PAG. This technique, however, generally is not used until other techniques described above have been tried and have failed.

While it involves some risk for the dominant group, in the long run it clearly works to their advantage. The process involves bringing members of a minority PAG into the dominant group power structure. Clearly, in doing so the minority PAG members begin to have access to information previously withheld from them. It then reduces the insulation between the dominant and minority group as well as providing the minority PAG with potential resources. Here lies the risk. It would seem that the minority PAG members could use the newly acquired information for the advancement of their own group goals. However, several factors mediate against this and actually work in favor of the dominant group (and corresponding detriment of the minority PAG). Why should this happen?

First of all, while the social distance between the dominant and minority PAG is reduced and information is gained, once inside the minority PAG members are still subject to negative and positive sanctions of the dominant group. Negative sanctions can be administered to these new members of the dominant group if they do not nominally agree with the group. On the other hand, positive social and economic rewards are forthcoming if the minority PAG member behaves according to the dictates of the dominant group.

Secondly, because of an intense resocialization process, the minority PAG member will take on a new orientation. That is, he will begin to take on the values and norms of the dominant group. Thus, the minority PAG member will begin to identify with the dominant group rather than the original minority group which is attempting to change the system.

One further factor which allows the dominant group to use co-optation is the fact that by yielding access to resources to certain PAG members, estrangement will occur between these individuals and the group they represent. It should be pointed out that those individuals who are leaders of minority PAGs are generally the most vocal, most educated, and most articulate of the group. When these individuals enter the establishment, they are open to the charge of "selling out" by members of the group they represent. This effectively takes away leadership from the minority PAG and seriously jeopardizes their abilities to bring pressure against the dominant group.

Implementation of Social Control Mechanisms

If the above social control mechanisms are available to the dominant group in handling minority groups, under what conditions (and to what groups) would the different techniques be applied?

Gamson (1968) suggests that the level of confidence that the dominant group has in a particular minority PAG (defined by the dominant group) will determine which social control mechanism will be used. If the dominant group defines a particular minority PAG group as having complete confidence in their ability to produce outcomes in their favor (without the minority group doing anything), persuasion will be used. This type of control

> is most consonant with building and maintaining a positive trust orienta- tion. . . . Persuasion only requires convincing the group that they have things well in hand and that it will be well served without pestering the authorities unduly on specific decisions. Other means of control tend to reduce the confidence of solidarity groups. (Gamson, 1968: 181)

When the minority PAG is defined as a neutral group, sanctions (particularly inducements) are used. This group is defined as believing that the dominant group is only "moderately competent and efficient in achieving the goals most desired by the minority group." However, there is also a definition made by the dominant group that the neutral minority PAG has little trust in their making decisions compatible with minority PAG goals.

When the minority PAG is defined by the dominant group as having "no con- fidence" in them, insulation is used. Only when the dominant group defines the minority PAG as seeing them as totally unable to achieve collective goals and unable to be unbiased in decisions will insulation be used.

By using the above social control mechanism with the appropriate PAG, the dominant group is able to maintain its power position in the society. However, it is equally plausible that the above techniques may fail for one reason or another. Since the dominant group is continually forced to define the situation so as to make the appropriate power moves, they also run the risk of misdefining and misapplication. Such an error may not have short run consequences but may have long range implications that change the entire set of relations. By the time the misdefinition is perceived by the dominant group, corrections may not be possible. It is at this point that the minority PAG may begin to reject the ex- isting moral order which has prevented them from attaining equal status in the society. If this does occur, one of the most likely outcomes is conflict.

Summary

We have provided the reader with a macro perspective, to interpret and understand ethnic relations. First of all, a regional perspective must be adopted as defining the context in which the relations are taking place. While few researchers have investigated this variable, a number of people have suggested its import as an analytical and explanatory tool. (Young, 1976; Hechter, 1973; Frideres and Goldenberg, 1977).

The identification of PAGs as pressure (interest) groups is not a novel perspective, but it has not been systematically researched. It is our position that individuals have strong identifications and affiliations with solidarity groups at different levels below the total society, e.g., ethnic groups (Gamson, 1968). In ad- dition, there are few impenetrable barriers in Canadian society that prevent any group from getting some kind of a hearing by the dominant group. In fact, some might argue that dissatisfied groups are encouraged to make demands. For example, Native people have been funded by the federal government to establish organizational structures, e.g., the Native Indian Brotherhood, and COPE.

The effectiveness of these groups is contingent upon a number of factors. Some cannot sustain their organizational structure; some are destroyed by their opponents; some are given recognition but without substance and some become powerful influencing groups. But all must work within the existing legal structure as defined by the dominant group.

Our interpretation of ethnic group relations is one of combining micro and macro factors which influence this relationship. We have also tried to point out that the relations are always in a state of flux. Outcomes at one point in time will not necessarily be in existence at a future point in time. Social systems change over time, and changes in one dimension of the system mean that compensatory changes must be made in other dimensions. We are not suggesting a homeostatic model, but rather that the system must work to continue existence.

A great deal of controversy exists with regard to the social control issue. Many suggest that the relationships between subordinate ethnic groups and the dominant ethnic group are a result of fortuitous factors. Things "just happen" and a relationship emerges. On the other hand, others argue that the dominant group is always calculating how to retain its exploitive situation. Our approach has been to integrate both positions. For example, with regard to the issue of exploitation, the dominant group will exercise self-restraint for several reasons. The dominant group's normative commitment to a set of rules would be violated if an opponent is treated too harshly, or self-interest may require restraint—today's antagonists may be tomorrow's allies. There is, then, a point at which the dominant group must make a decision as to how the group is treated. And this, of course, suggests a "rationale" model.

We once again must point out that we do not see ethnicity as a totally ascribed constant attribute. Rather, we view ethnicity as an emergent phenomenon which is intimately linked with structural conditions and the technological state of the system. It will emerge and become a viable force under specific conditions. As Yancy, et al. (1976) point out:

> This general view also suggests that much of the substance of ethnic culture may be the result of a selective process which consists of a constantly evolving interaction between the nature of the local community, the available economic opportunities and the national or religious heritage of a particular group. (397)

This means that ethnic groups themselves change in organization, consensus of goals, and maintenance of cultural attributes. This also suggests that the dominant group must continually monitor the changes that are taking place so as to best make a decision with regard to that group.

Canada has never been a truly homogeneous society in terms of national and cultural origins of its people. However, the institutional structure of Canada since the mid 19th century has been based upon the assumption that it would become and remain homogeneous. It is clear that differences in the participation of groups in access to knowledge and other sources of power bear out differences in their structural positions; that is, differences among them not only in terms of their dominance or subordination within the same structures, but also in terms of their engagement in different structures (Martin, 1978: 212).

The result is a political system that has developed a set of dominant values, beliefs, and institutional procedures that operate systematically and consistently to the benefit of some groups and to the detriment of others.

REFERENCES

Almond, G. "Interest Groups and the Political Process," in R. Macridis and B. Brown (eds) *Comparative Politics: Notes and Readings*. Homewood, Illinois: The Dorsey Press, 1961.

Anderson, G. and D. Higgs. *A Future to Inherit: The Portuguese Communities of Canada*. McClelland and Stewart and Dept. of Sec. of State, Ottawa, 1976.

Bachrach, P. and M. S. Baratz. *Power and Poverty*. New York: Oxford University Press, 1970.

Berry, B. *Race and Ethnic Relations*, 3rd Edition. Boston: Houghton, Mifflin Co., 1958.

Bierstedt, R. "An Analysis of Social Power." *American Sociological Review*, 15 (December 1950): 730-738.

Breton, R. "Institutional Completeness of Ethnic Communities and the Personal Relations of Immigrants." *The American Journal of Sociology*, LXX, 2 (1964): 193-205.

Clairmont, D. and F. Wien. "Race relations in Canada." *Sociological Focus*, 9(2) (1976): 185-197.

Clement, W. "Inequality of Access: Characteristics of the Canadian Corporate Elite." *Canadian Review of Sociology and Anthropology*, 12 (1975): 33-52.

Depres, Leo. *Ethnicity and Resource Competition in Plural Societies*. The Hague, Paris: Mouton Pub, 1975.

Enloe, C. *Ethnic Conflict and Political Development*. Boston: Little, Brown and Co., 1973.

Firestone, S. *The Dialectic of Sex: The Case for Feminist Revolution*. New York: Bantam Books, 1971.

Foucault, M. "The Political Function of the Intellectual." *Radical Philosophy*, 17 (1977): 12-14.

Fowke, V. "Royal Commission and Canadian Agricultural Policy." *Canadian Journal of Economics and Political Science*, 14 (1948): 160-172.

Frideres, J. and S. Goldenberg. "Hyphenated Canadians: Comparative Analysis of Ethnic, Regional and National Identification of Western Canadian University Students." *The Journal of Ethnic Studies*, 5, 2 (1977): 91-99.

Gamson, W. *Power and Discontent*. Homewood, Illinois: The Dorsey Press, 1968.

Greeley, A. *Ethnicity in the United States*. New York: John Wiley and Sons, 1974.

Hechter, M. "The Persistence of Regionalism in the British Isles, 1885-1966." *American Journal of Sociology*, 79(2) (1973): 319-342.

Hunt, C. and L. Walker. *Ethnic Dynamics*. Homewood, Illinois: The Dorsey Press, 1974.

Jackson, J. "French-English Relations in an Ontario Community." *Canadian Review of Sociology and Anthropology*, 3, (August, 1966.)

Kelner, M. J. "Ethnic Penetration into Toronto's Elite Structure." *Canadian Review of Sociology and Anthropology*, 7, (May, 1970.)

Kinloch, G. *The Sociology of Minority Group Relations*. Englewood Cliffs, N.J.: Prentice-Hall, 1979.

Kriesberg, L. *The Sociology of Social Conflicts*. Englewood Cliffs, N.J.: Prentice-Hall Inc, 1973.

Lautt, M. "Sociology and the Canadian Plains," in *A Region of the Mind*, by

R. Allen (ed.) Canadian Plains Study Centre, University of Saskatchewan, Regina 1973. pp. 125-153.

McRoberts, K. and D. Posgate. *Quebec: Social Change and Political Crisis.* Toronto: McClelland and Stewart, 1976.

Maklelski, S. *Beleaguered Minorities.* San Francisco: W. H. Freeman and Co., 1973.

Martin, J. *The Migrant Presence: Australian Response, 1947-1977.* London: Allen and Unwin, 1978.

Morris R. and C. M. Lanphier. *Three Scales of Inequality.* Don Mills: Logman, Canada, Ltd., 1977.

Munro, J. "British Columbia and the Chinese Evil: Canada's First Anti-Asiatic Immigration Law." *Journal of Canadian Studies,* Vol. 6 (November, 1971): 42-51.

Nagata, J. A. "Adaptation and Integration of Greek Working Class Immigrants in the City of Toronto." *International Migration Review,* 4(1) (1964): 44-69.

Newman, W. *American Pluralism: A Study of Minority Groups and Social Theory.* New York: Harper and Row, 1973.

Olsen, M. (ed.) *Power in Societies.* London: Collier-Macmillan Ltd, 1970.

Porter, J. *The Vertical Mosaic.* Toronto: University of Toronto Press, 1965.

Pross, P. *Pressure Group Behaviour in Canadian Politics.* Toronto: McGraw-Hill Ryerson Ltd, 1975.

Radecki, H. and B. Heydenkorn. *A Member of a Distinguished Family: The Polish Group in Canada.* Toronto: McClelland and Stewart, 1976.

Radecki, H. "Ethnic Voluntary Organizational Dynamics in Canada: A Report." *International Journal of Comparative Studies,* XVII, 3-4 (1977): 275-284.

Robb, J. H. "A Theoretical Note on the Sociology of Intergroup Relations." *Ethnic and Racial Studies,* 1(4) (1978): 465-73.

Rosenberg, *The Jewish Community in Canada.* Toronto: McClelland and Stewart, 1971.

Rubin, F. "Ethnicity and Cultural Pluralism. *Phylos,* No. 2, Vol. 36 (1976): pp. 140-149.

Timlin, M. "Canada's Immigration Policy, 1896-1910." *The Canadian Journal of Economics and Political Science,* 26, 4 (November, 1960): 517-532.

Troper, H. "The Creek Negroes of Oklahoma and Canadian Immigration, 1909-11." *Canadian Historical Review,* (September, 1972): 272-280.

Truman, D. *The Government Process.* New York: Alfred A. Knopf, Inc., 1951.

Vallee, F. G. "Regionalism and Ethnicity: The French-Canadian Case," in B. Y. Card, et al. (eds.) *Perspectives on Regions and Regionalism.* Edmonton: University of Alberta, 1969.

Wilson, W. *Power, Racism and Privilege.* New York: MacMillan Co., 1973.

Wirth, L. "The Problem of Minority Groups," in R. Linton (ed.) *The Science of Man in the World Crises.* New York: Columbia University Press, 1945.

Wuttunee, W. *Ruffled Feathers.* Calgary: Bell Publishing Co., 1972.

Yancy, W., E. Ericksen and R. Juliani. "Emergent Ethnicity: A Review and Reformulation." *American Sociological Review,* 41, No. 3 (June, 1976): 391-403.

Young, Crawford, *The Politics of Cultural Pluralism.* Madison: University of Wisconsin, 1976.

Zubek, J. and A. Solberg. *Doukhobors at War.* Toronto: Ryerson Press, 1952.

Part IV

Minority Responses and Outcomes

Thus far we have only focused on the actions taken by the dominant group in order to maintain (or re-establish) their power position in society. The foregoing discussion would seem to suggest that minority ethnic collectivities are passive acceptors of decisions made by the dominant group. However, we have also suggested that subordinate groups will attempt to influence the decisions already taken (or about to be taken) by the dominant group.

The task before us now is to extend and explicate the theoretical underpinnings of outcomes briefly introduced in the last chapter. That is, what are the different structural outcomes that can exist between a particular subordinate group and the dominant group? We will identify a variety of different responses and outcomes in the next three chapters and provide illustrations for each. This will of necessity involve a historical review as well as some discussion of the contemporary scene.

The reader should keep in mind that when we talk about "responses" or "outcomes," we are being context and time specific. As we will indicate, responses and outcomes can differ for a specific group over time. In addition, different subordinate groups can participate in the same outcome with the dominant group at the same time. We are not advocating a linear or cyclical model nor are we arguing that intergroup relations occur in some ordered sequential pattern that has universal application. For example, we will not suggest, as previous authors have, that relationships between minority ethnic groups move in a stepwise fashion from segregation to pluralism to assimilation to eventual amalgamation.

Our position is in agreement with Schermerhorn (1970) in that we cannot think in terms of universal "serial steps" of outcomes. It is our premise that outcomes between groups are the result of a very deliberate, conscious strategy utilized by the current dominant group. Thus we are arguing that the existing relationships between the dominant and subordinate groups of the system are not a result of random forces acting upon groups of people. People in power positions want to maintain their position, and because they do in fact have power, are able to manipulate and thus control nonpowered people. As Schermerhorn (1970) points out: " . . . 'dominant group' signifies that collectivity within a society which has pre-eminent authority to function both as guardian and sustainers of the controlling value system, and as prime allocators of rewards in the society" (12-13).

Confronted with having decisions imposed upon them, subordinate groups react in a variety of response patterns. Some are actually eager to assimilate, while others seek equality through separation. Still others may accept their assigned status of subordination. The reaction of subordinate groups, like dominant social control mechanisms, may change over time. They may attempt to assimilate at one point, and in time, finding that this is not possible, switch to another response. Their choices (decisions) with regard as to how they will respond generally reflect short-term and long-term goals. These decisions may also be based, to some extent, on a realistic evaluation of their power or potential power. This is not to suggest that this will always be the case. Emotional or habitual responses may also be evident.

The responses and outcomes to be discussed are analysed as separate entities. However, in reality we do not find that they can be conceptually clearly separated; two or more responses may be evident at any one point in time. Our task is to alert the reader to the fact that ethnic minorities do react, and intergroup relations are in fact a two-way process.

One last caution that should be interjected at this point in time is the fact that in discussing outcome, we must make a distinction between what is publicly stated (with regard to outcomes) and what exists. For example, we have noted that Canada has prided itself on its mosaic and looked upon the U.S.A. with an air of superiority because they have pursued a melting pot structure. While hard data comparing the two countries are generally lacking, a number of authors writing on the subject have suggested that in reality, Canada is no more a mosaic (or less a mosaic) than the U.S.A. While the dominant group may publicly espouse the virtues of one model over another, it is quite another matter as to whether or not it does in fact exist.

In general, two basic sociological orientations have been used to explain intergroup behavior and outcomes. The first model focuses on the conflict (oppression) between groups while the opposing model advocates an assimilation (integration) perspective. The first perspective attempts to explain intergroup behavior in terms of a dominant group controlling and (sometimes) oppressing a subordinate group. The assimilationist perspective argues that after encounters of various groups, adjustments will be made by the participants so that harmonious relationships will prevail (Greeley, 1974). The following chapters will review, assess, and interpret both orientations so as to provide a more complete description of responses and outcomes.

The first chapter in this part of the book (Chapter 11) is concerned with ethnic minority group subordination and the lessening or eradication of ethnic minority distinctiveness; the second chapter (Chapter 12) with accommodation between majority and minority, in other words, with maintenance of a status quo; the third chapter (Chapter 13) with ethnic survival or revival; and the book concludes with a chapter on policy implications and a look into the future.

Chapter 11

Subordination and Change

In this chapter we will describe and illustrate several different (but possibly overlapping) responses to, or outcomes of, majority subordination of ethnic minorities, and how this intentional subordination leads to a lessening or complete eradication of minority ethnic identification. First we will review traditional sociological models of ethnic identity change. Then the chapter will proceed to discuss several responses and outcomes representing various degrees of subordination and change along a continuum, from complete removal of the minority (annihilation, expulsion) to extreme subordination and marked loss of minority ethnic identity (assimilation, exemplified in Anglo-conformity), to related but less extreme forms of subordination and change (acculturation, symbiosis, integration, passive submission).

Traditional Sociological Models of Ethnic Identity Change

Sociologists have devoted considerable attention to formulating stages of ethnic identity change. The cycle suggested by Robert Ezra Park in 1926 continues to prove influential in developing ethnic relations theory. According to Park (1926, 1937, 1950), in the relations of races there are cycles of events which tend everywhere to repeat themselves. First, ethnic groups come into contact; there invariably follows competition; eventually some kind of adjustment or accommodation is reached; and finally there is assimilation and amalgamation.

Four years after Park formulated his cycle, E. S. Bogardus (1930: 613) produced one involving the following stages: curiosity towards immigrants, economic welcome (economic integration), industrial and social antagonism (similar to Park's competition), legislative antagonism, fair-play tendencies, quiescence (modification of antagonistic attitudes), and second generation difficulties. This scheme adds little to Park's rather more general model.

Another four years later, W. O. Brown (1934: 34-37) cautiously suggested that race relations have a natural history involving definite stages. After initial contacts of a symbiotic, categoric sort, conflict will emerge, followed by temporary accommodations, a struggle by the minority for status, attitude mobilization and clarification by the subordinates, and eventual solution involving not simply assimilation and fusion but also possibly continued subordination and isolation of the minority. This scheme at least does not suggest inevitable progression toward assimilation.

In 1945 Louis Wirth (347-372) provided a categorization of ethnic minorities based on their ultimate objectives. A minority might be termed pluralistic, if it desired peaceful existence side-by-side with the majority and other minorities. Or it could be assimilationist, if it desired absorption into the dominant group. Or secessionist, if it sought both cultural and political independence. Or militant, if it went beyond the desire for equality to a desire for domination—the total reversion of status.

C. E. Glick (1955: 239) believed that it should be possible to look at race relations as typically involving a sequence of phases, despite his recognition that there are unique features in any given situation of contact between dissimilar groups. He specified that these phases are pre-contact, contact and pre-domination, domination (including accommodation), and post-domination (nationalism and integration). Various social types are associated with each phase. This schema might apply to certain ethnic collectivities in Canada, though—like its predecessors by Park, Bogardus, and Brown—it refers to *race* rather than specifically *ethnic* relations and thus might add some confusion to the discussion. It is debatable whether this terminological distinction was unintentional or deliberate. The earlier writers may have used the popular (and European) designation race as the equivalent of what later sociologists were to call ethnic groups. This was more permissible in the United States, where several major ethnic groups were physically (i.e., racially) distinct, than in Canada, where on the whole cultural distinctions have assumed far more significance than physical attributes.

In providing a model of stages of ethnic minority responses applicable to the Canadian situation, it would seem most appropriate to consolidate these models into a simpler one involving a continuum of minority responses ranging from forced assimilation and passive submission, through acculturation, integration, stratification, accommodation, pluralism and multiculturalism, to social segregation, political separatism, and ethnic revivalism.

Annihilation

Annihilation is one of the most visible and immediate forms of outcome. This outcome has as its central thrust the goal of destroying, in whole or in part, a national, ethnic, or racial group. The destruction may be directed at either the culture of the group (cultural genocide) or at the lives of the individuals (physical genocide). Native people in Canada have been subject to annihilation since the arrival of the French. As Owen, et al. (1967) point out:

> The European fisherman who settled around the shores of the island in the 16th, 17th, and 18th centuries resented their [Indians] petty pilfering, and shot them down at every opportunity, the French even placing a bounty on their heads . . . the Micmac, who united with the French and English settlers, helped to exterminate the unhappy Beothuk Indians of Newfoundland. (188-189)

The above example perhaps best illustrates the more extreme consequences taken toward a particular group. As a result of the above policy, there are no Beothuks living. Another example of physical genocide would be the attempt to do away with Indian people on the Prairies. One strategy used (and still used in South America) was to infect blankets with various diseases that Whites were immune to or had procedures to control, i.e., inoculation. Patterson (1972) points out that this strategy was used on the Prairies with the result that thousands of Indians died. However, physical genocide has never been a popular strategy in Canada and has not been widely used by the dominant group. What has been a more popular and acceptable strategy has been to force the group to take on specific dominant values and culture (cultural genocide).

Again, the relationship of the dominant group with Indians provides us with an illustration. The introduction of reserves for Indians as well as the forced education of Indians illustrate an attempt at cultural genocide. The goal of these policies and programs was to take away old cultural traits or at least make it extremely difficult to maintain these old traits, although it was hoped that the dominant cultural traits would replace these old Indian attributes.

Language, a crucial element in culture, has also been the focus of cultural genocide. The general thought is that if one can destroy the language of the group, then traditions cannot be carried on. Hence it should not surprise us that a number of specific acts with regard to linguistic rights have emerged over time and with reference to specific groups. The most obvious are, of course, those acts against the French, even though their language has attained legal status through the BNA Act. For example, the Manitoba legislature in 1890 and again in 1916 enacted laws against the use of French in schools. In 1912/13, the Ontario Ministry of Education proclaimed that English was to be the only language of instruction in all of the Ontario schools, public or separate. To enforce this, Ottawa discontinued all subsidies for separate schools. Other ethnic groups such as Ukrainians and Germans have also faced these proclamations. In some cases the above has worked well for the dominant group (it has made cultural differentiation difficult to maintain), in others not at all.

Thus far we have focused on the outcome of annihilation as a result of conscious and rational decision making on the part of the dominant group. It is important, then, that we point out that the outcome of annihilation may result even though it was not pre-planned. In the 1800s, whalers from San Francisco came into the Beaufort Sea to hunt whales. However, they discovered that by the time they had stocked their ships with whale oil, winter arrived and their ships were frozen in and unable to return that same year to San Francisco. They wintered in at the mouth of the Mackenzie River. The result was that the Inuit, highly susceptible to measles, contracted the disease immediately. There were a number of epidemics during the 1800s, and in 1903 (one of the last epidemics) nearly one-fifth of the remaining Inuit population died. Other examples of this unintended physical genocide are reflected in the following quote:

> Smallpox ravaged the Indians from the early 1600s until the late 1800s. The Montagnais got it first because they were first in contact with the French at Tadoussac. The earliest outbreak was in 1635 and it swept like a fierce nemesis through the eastern woodlands, spreading over half of the continent by 1700. By 1738 the Sioux, Cree, Piegan and Assiniboine were dying and the stench of rotting corpses hung over the ghost villages of the plains.
> Typhoid fever killed one third of the Micmac in Nova Scotia in 1746. In 1830, influenza swept through the tribes of B.C., inflicting heavy losses. (Symington, 1969: 142)

There is also a relationship between cultural and physical genocide. Again, one must take note of the fact that each form must be interpreted in terms of intended or unintended consequences. As pointed out above, one of the forms of cultural genocide was to establish reserves and stationary housing. This, of course, replaced the teepee and forced the pre-existing nomadic ways of life to change. Because of this change, directly intended to destroy certain cultural traits (cultural genocide), physical genocide resulted. Stefansson (1924) points this out clearly:

> No dwelling could be more sanitary and more likely to forestall tuberculosis than the tepee of the Indians of the Mackenzie Valley. It is not only always filled with fresh air, but it never becomes filthy, because it moves from place to place before it has time to become so; but when a house is built, it cannot be moved. The housekeeping methods which are satisfactory in a lodge that is destined to stand in one place only two or three weeks at a time, are entirely unsuited for the log cabin, which soon becomes filthy and remains so. Eventually the germs of tuberculosis get into the house and obtain lodging in it. The members of the same family catch the disease, one from the other, and when the family has been nearly or quite exterminated by the scourge, another family moves in, for the building of a house is hard work and it is a convenient thing to find one ready for your occupancy; and so it is not only the family that built the house that suffers but there is also through the house a procession of other families moving from the wigwam to the graveyard. (23)

It is still the contention of a number of spokesmen for various subordinate groups that the dominant group is attempting to impose cultural (in some cases physical) genocide onto them. Recent reports with regard to the number of hysterectomies being performed on Native women by White doctors in an attempt to reduce the birth rates suggests that the form of physical genocide may have changed.

With regard to cultural genocide, Natives still argue that they must be able to maintain their way of life, not that imposed onto them by the dominant society. Currently, northern Natives are clearly arguing this in the context of the oil development and pipeline that is proposed to go through the Yukon and N.W.T.

Why would a dominant group choose to implement such a program? In the case of physical genocide, it is normally the result of a belief that no other alternative will work (either in the short or long run). Normally, other alternative outcomes have been tried, but have failed to produce the needed changes as defined by the dominant group. Even if genocide is only partially successful, the result is that the total numbers of the group are reduced substantially and the leadership destroyed, thereby making the group much more manageable and easier to control. It also serves as a warning to other potentially disruptive groups that a similar fate may await them. It should be clear that if this outcome is successful, no further relationships will occur between the now nonexistent (or too small to make it viable) group and the dominant group. However, perhaps partial genocide will suffice for the reasons discussed above, or because some of the remaining members of the group may be used profitably in the economic institutional sphere.

Expulsion

This process involves the relocation of specific individuals in large numbers or sometimes entire subordinate groups. Relocation can take two different forms; internal and external. The former simply refers to geographical mobility taking place within the confines of a particular nation-state, while the latter refers to the relocation (repatriation) of groups outside the political boundaries of the nation-state. Both strategies have been used by the dominant group at various points in time. Perhaps the first use of this process occurred when the Acadians (the original settlers of Nova Scotia) refused to sign an oath of allegiance in 1755. The British forcibly removed them from their farms and loaded them on ships in order to resettle them along the Atlantic coast of the U.S.A. and in Louisiana. Internal expulsion at an early time in Canadian history can be documented when the dominant group reacted to the Native people. If genocide was not practised, internal relocation was almost certain to be implemented. Indians were forced to move from one geographical area to another.

Illustrations of this outcome with other groups would be Canada's treatment of the Germans in World War I and the Japanese during World War II. During World War I, about 6,000 Germans were placed in internment camps across Canada. In addition, about 4,000 were deported. The implementation of such strategies had a profound and lasting impact on Germans as a viable cultural group. The long-term result was that it effectively destroyed the structure of this group, thereby keeping its influence to a minimum. Along with the process of expulsion, other techniques of control were also used (see previous discussion on the suppression of the German press). An unanticipated result of the actions taken against Germans due to the fact that they are phenotypically similar to other WASP groups, was the process of "passing." This concept is normally used to explain the process when ethnic/racial group members of traditionally different phenotypical structures are able to cross racial lines, e.g., Blacks becoming Whites. In Canada, Germans began to pass for other national/ethnic group members, e.g., Dutch, Austrian, and Russian (Ryder, 1955). More recently, Kogler and Heydenkorn (1974) have shown that Canadians of Polish origin have changed to Jewish and Ukrainian as well as to other groups. They have also documented that between the censuses of 1961 and 1971 an increase of 100,000 Ukrainians was noted. Since immigration of people with Ukrainian origin has virtually stopped, this increase suggests that people are changing their identities to Ukrainian. This, of course means that they give up all idiosyncratic cultural traits that would allow others to make an easy identification of them as German. Cultural traits such as language, names, political ideology and in some cases, religion, will be abandoned. In the case of the Germans, they changed their names, stopped talking German (replaced by English) and did not participate in German ethnic festivals and rituals. In some cases, they would publicly deny being German and claim to be some other more acceptable ethnic group. In summary, they denied their traditions and their histories. As a result of these actions (both on the part of the dominant group and the Germans themselves), Germans have become highly acculturated. Only the high rate of immigration of Germans in recent times has allowed them to retain a fairly high rate of mother tongue (German) usage. However, a close inspection of these data will reveal that only the recent immigrants use the mother tongue with any regularity.

The treatment of the Japanese in Canada was similar to that of the Germans, only for a longer period of time and with a greater degree of control. The question as to whether or not the Japanese in Canada during World War II were a threat to Canadian security has been the subject of much debate. Regardless of the answer, the dominant group found that external expulsion was an outcome (used for a period of nearly ten years) that seemed to be effective. While an extended treatment of why the laws were enacted against the Japanese is beyond the scope of this present book, the reader is referred to Ken Adachi's highly readable and penetrating book, *The Enemy That Never Was* (1976). The result of the highly emotional anti-Oriental feelings was the passing of an order-in-council in 1942 that empowered the Minister of National Defence to make any area of Canada a protected area from which enemy aliens could be excluded. This initial law included all Japanese male nationals between the ages of 18 and 45. They were to be removed from this protected area. This area initially was a 100 mile wide strip extending from the Pacific Ocean to the Cascade Mountains (including all off-shore islands) and bound by the Yukon to the North and the Canadian border to the South. Other geographical areas were also defined as protected areas, e.g., the community of Trail, British Columbia because of the mining activities. Another order-in-council empowered the Minister of Justice to control the movements of all persons of Japanese origin in certain protected areas. This included Japanese-Canadian citizens (either native born or those who had taken out Canadian citizenship). It also restricted all Japanese in their type of business or employment, their associations or communications with other persons, and prohibited them from possessing specific articles such as cameras, firearms and radios.

All Japanese were thus to be removed from the protected areas. Initially the plan was to place the males into road camps, and the females and children in internment camps. However, most roads ran close to rail lines, and because Japanese were defined as a threat to national security this lead to an early abandonment of this procedure (although some 2,500 did work in road camps). Hence, most were sent to internment camps in the Slocan Valley of British Columbia, although others were sent to camps in other provinces as far away as Ontario. Others were sent to the Prairie provinces to work with sugar beet farmers. For example, the Security Commission (the structure handling the process of moving Japanese) made an agreement with the Alberta government to accept the Japanese (giving the Alberta government control of the Japanese), and then remove them as "soon as the emergency ceased." As a result, a great number of Japanese were moved to Southern Alberta, Saskatchewan and Manitoba. This is not to suggest that these provinces willingly accepted the Japanese. For example, the city of Toronto refused to accept them initially but later agreed to accept up to 700.

It should be kept in mind that over three-fourths of the Japanese living in Canada during this time were Canadian citizens (either native born or having taken out Canadian citizenship). By 1947, the nearly 22,000 Japanese originally living in British Columbia had dwindled to less than 7,000. On the other hand, Alberta and Manitoba had nearly 6,000, Ontario had nearly 7,000 and Quebec had 1,200.

Because of the strong institutional completeness that existed within the Japanese community before the actions taken by the federal and provincial governments, the results of the relocation were different than for the Germans nearly thirty years previously. In addition, it became clear to the Japanese themselves that because of their different skin pigmentation any attempt to pass would meet with no success. As a result, they once again have built up ethnic enclaves in Canada. However, their networks have remained basically at the local (sometimes regional) level.

Assimilation: Anglo-conformity

What is meant by the term *assimilation*? A precise meaning seems rather elusive, as the term has been repeatedly redefined by sociologists. Park employed the term extensively in his essays (1950, 1952, 1955). He mentioned "the case where societies are formed and maintained by adoption," i.e., immigration, so that "people of a different race and culture take over the traditions and social inheritance of another and an alien people." Assimilation is "a process of interpenetration and fusion in which persons and groups acquire the memories, sentiments, and attitudes of other persons or groups, and, by sharing their experience and history, are incorporated with them in a common cultural life." It is "the name given to the process or processes by which peoples of diverse racial origins and different cultural heritages, occupying a common territory, achieve a cultural solidarity sufficient at least to sustain a national existence." Reuter (1941: 84) defined assimilation as "the process by which persons who are unlike in their social heritages come to share the same body of sentiments, traditions, and loyalties." And according to Fairchild (1944), it is "the process by which different cultures, or individuals or groups representing different cultures, are merged into a homogeneous unit. ... Social assimilation does not require the complete identification of all the units, but such modifications as eliminate the characteristics of foreign origin, and enable them all to fit smoothly into the typical structure and functioning of the new cultural unit. ... Assimilation is the substitution of one nationality pattern for another. ...."

During the 1950s sociologists continued to define and redefine assimilation. Berry (1958: 210) commented that "by assimilation we mean the process whereby groups with different cultures come to have a common culture. ... Assimilation refers thus to the fusion of cultural heritages. ..." A succinct definition was furnished by Cuber (1955: 609): "Assimilation may be defined as the gradual process whereby cultural differences (and rivalries) tend to disappear." Rose (1956: 557-8) regarded assimilation as "the adoption by a person or group of the culture of another social group to such a complete extent that the person or group no longer has any characteristics identifying him with his former culture and no longer has any particular loyalties to his former culture. Or, the process leading to this adoption." Emphasizing a two-way exchange, Fichter (1957: 229) described a "process through which two or more persons or groups accept and perform one another's patterns of behavior. ... It is a relation of interaction in which both parties behave reciprocally even though one may be much more affected than the other." And Simpson and Yinger (1958: 27-28) stressed the distinction between forced assimilation, exemplified in extreme ethnocentrism of the dominant group, and peaceful assimilation.

The refinement of the term assimilation has continued to the present day. Lieberson (1963: 8-11) profitably distinguished between individual and aggregate assimilation: "One can consider an immigrant group as being more or less assimilated by examining the proportion of its members able to speak English or the proportion naturalized. However, there are additional aspects of ethnic behavior that are essentially meaningful only on an aggregate basis. In the existence of ethnic colonies, for example, the behavior of an aggregate is relevant, but not that of a particular individual." Moreover, individual and group assimilation are sometimes in different directions. Lieberson defined an assimilated ethnic population operationally as "a group of persons with similar foreign origins, knowledge of which in no way gives a better prediction or estimate of their relevant social characteristics than does knowledge of the total population of the community or nation involved. Thus we should not call an (urban) ethnic group assimilated if they are highly segregated residentially from the remainder of the total population of a given city." Lieberson has cautioned that in a complex poly-ethnic society such as the United States, selection of a standard population for determining the assimilation of a given ethnic group is somewhat arbitrary; and differences between an immigrant population and the general society are not necessarily due to deviations of the foreign-born from the general social patterns of an area.

M. M. Gordon (1964: 71) outlined seven types of assimilation: first, cultural or behavioral assimilation or acculturation, involving a change of minority cultural patterns to those of the host society; second, structural assimilation, large-scale minority entrance into cliques, clubs and institutions of the host society, on a primary group level; third, marital assimilation, large-scale inter-marriage; fourth, identificational assimilation, the development of a sense of peoplehood based exclusively on the host society; fifth, attitude receptional assimilation, the absence of prejudice; sixth, behavior receptional assimilation, the absence of discrimination; and seventh, civic assimilation, the absence of value and power conflict.

The major distinction produced by Gordon that has had widespread application was that between cultural and structural assimilation. Cultural assimilation is seen as the process whereby members of the subordinate group take on the cultural patterns of the dominant group, e.g., religion. On the other hand, structural assimilation refers to the process where subordinate group members begin to interact with the dominant group at a primary level. The works of Sengstock (1969) and Johnson (1963) are the most widely known applications of such distinctions.

Sengstock (1969), following the same theoretical distinction of Gordon, gives different names to the processes of assimilation. She compares cultural assimilation (the process of losing conspicuous foreign patterns, e.g., language, customs, food habits and value structure changes) and social assimilation (refers to the process of a group retaining its social distinctiveness as a social group after losing the "outside impressions"). Johnson (1963) views assimilation in a similar perspective. She refers to external versus subjective assimilation. External assimilation refers to the outward manners of the immigrant who becomes less distinguishable from the dominant group, while subjective assimilation extends to the psychological structure of the subordinate group member.

It is important to realize that there is a psychological dimension to assimilation. For example, Frazier (1957: 316) has stressed that assimilation involves a subjective element, identification with the general society. Shibutani and Kwan (1965: 21, 121, 352-6, 502-515) have described assimilation as a mental process involving a change of perspective, a re-interpretation of identity, and probably a struggle between traditionalists and advocates of assimilation. Kurokawa (1970: 71) has suggested that for assimilation to occur, the dominant society must accept the idea and the minorities must concur. But, in contrast, Berry (1958: 230-231) has emphasized that assimilation is not necessarily a conscious process; minority group members may become assimilated to an alien culture very gradually and subconsciously.

Considerable confusion in sociological literature seems to have resulted from a failure to distinguish clearly between assimilation as a process and assimilation as a state. In the latter case it could be regarded as the final stage in identity change. In short, the process of assimilation leads to the state of assimilation. In the process an individual is being assimilated, while in the final state he is or has been assimilated. In other words, as Simpson has explained (1968: 438), "complete segregation and total assimilation of a group are opposite ends of a continuum along which may be located varying degrees of limited desegregation; the substantial pluralism found in many communities in Canada; a hypothetical integration which values structural and cultural differences, while insisting upon equal life opportunities for the members of all groups; partial assimilation; individual assimilation; and group assimilation."

The assimilationist ethnic collectivity is one which attempts to integrate itself in the social and institutional structure of the larger society. As Wirth (1945) points out:

> It seeks to lose itself in the larger whole by opening up to its members the greatest possibilities for their individual self development. Rather than toleration and autonomy ... the assimilationist minority works toward complete acceptance by the dominant group and a merger with the larger society. (351)

Full assimilation would refer to the total acceptance of the dominant culture in all of its social dimensions. This would take place if the subordinate groups were allowed membership and participation rights in all clubs and cliques, by social exchanges, and ultimately by intermarriage. It would also mean that the subordinate group would be willing to internalize the values and norms of the dominant group.

According to the most recent statements, assimilation refers to the dominant group's attempt to absorb a minority ethnic group on its own terms without regard to the minority's desires. It is, then, a loss of a minority's identity through merging with the dominant community (Davis, 1978; Kinloch, 1979). Francis (1976: 279), in his discussion of assimilation, refers to the process in which an individual is assigned increasing degrees of membership status in the host society until he becomes indistinguishable from charter members with regard to the distribution of social rewards.

Francis (1976) develops an elaborate schema of assimilation. Again, in viewing assimilation as a process, he identifies the first level as "aspiration." This refers to when members of the subordinate group aspire to achieve membership in the dominant group. A second level is referred to as "transculturation." This involves the subordinate group sharing with the dominant group the essential elements of its culture and their having acquired the skills and qualifications that are expected of dominant group members in analogous situations. The third and final level, "acceptance," occurs when ethnic group members identify themselves and are identified by their associates exclusively with the dominant group. In addition, they share a sense of solidarity with the dominant group members of that society.

The above brief discussion shows that while a number of people have addressed the issue, various perspectives have been used to explain the process. If we can summarize the above, it would seem that two major dimensions have been investigated—the cultural artifact dimension and the psychological dimension. One can give up various modes of dress, foods, lifestyle, and in some cases, language without changing the cognitive framework of the individual. Hence external changes may not be indicative of psychological changes.

The discussion above, then, suggests that assimilation has to be viewed as a continuum. At the least level of assimilation, one would find that there is an acceptance of the political/economic spheres of society as well as other minor attributes of the dominant culture. At the other end of the continuum, we find individuals identifying with (and as) dominant group members and sharing their cultural artifacts. The end result of this level of assimilation would culminate in amalgamation (intermarriage), i.e., there would be no criteria for distinctiveness.

At this point we can summarize some of the numerous suggestions made in the sociological literature of ethnic relations with reference to the conditions affecting the rate of change. First let us examine the conditions serving to hinder or retard assimilation. Differences of the minorities from each other and from the majority in general are significant—in particular, possession of different languages and religious practices. An attitude emphasizing traditionalism is especially important when translated into minority nationalism, ethnocentrism, or any form of organized resistance movement. Social distance of minority from majority, as evidenced perhaps in the low status of the minority, is also significant. This may be combined with spatial isolation and segregation, reducing opportunities for contact between members of the minority group and others. The strength of ethnic subsystems may also retard integration into the general social structure. Finally, we may mention proximity of immigrants to their mother countries and, perhaps related, the constant replenishment of ethnic colonies with new immigrants (Borrie, 1959: 99-100; Price, 1959: 278-280; Shibutani and Kwan, 1965: 475; Warner and Srole, 1945: 72, 95-104; Gordon, 1964: 78).

On the other hand, assimilation may be speeded by such factors as economic integration and economic political opportunities, combined with physical and social mobility. A re-distribution of the once-segregated minorities or the invasion of a former rural settlement or urban neighborhood by members of other ethnic groups lessens segregation; this is particularly true in the case of smaller settlements. Similarity of minority institutions to those of the majority has been emphasized by several sociologists as a significant factor in assimilation. Identity changes through secularization, religious conversion, intermarriage, and racial non-visibility have also been emphasized. And intergenerational changes have been stimulated by public school policies and other government regulations (Dawson, 1936: 378-380; Tumin, 1969: 21-22; Lieberson, 1970; Price, 1959: 279-280; Eisenstadt, 1954: 263-264; Gordon, 1964: 80; Shibutani and Kwan, 1965: 552-553).

More concisely, we would stress that the rate of assimilation by minority group members will be dependent upon the degree of isolation, and the amount of discrimination practised by the dominant group, as well as the ideology held by the dominant group with regard to the capabilities of the various subordinate groups.

However, a few qualifications merit mention; Glazer went so far as to suggest the possibility of a return to the traditional culture after some assimilation (1970: 71-86). M. M. Gordon has recognized the possibility of continuing acculturation without proceeding through the other stages of assimilation which he outlined; but he did comment that once the structural stage has been attained, the other remaining stages will follow (Gordon, 1964: 77, 81). And while some types of ethnic groups will experience assimilation differently from others (such as Zenner's radically changing "corporate" compared to gradually changing "non-corporate" groups) (Zenner, 1970: 72, 105-113), certain sociologists have stressed that assimilation may have relatively little to do with national origins alone (Bernard, 1959: 100; Park, 1926: 5, 353-354).

In discussing the changing direction of assimilation, M. M. Gordon's remarks on Anglo-conformity seem pertinent, even though they were intended to be descriptive of American rather than Canadian society. He has defined "Anglo-conformity" as a broad term "which may be used to cover a variety of viewpoints about assimilation and immigration. All have as a central assumption the desirability of maintaining English institutions . . ., the English language, and English-oriented cultural patterns as dominant and standard in American life." In Gordon's view, Anglo-conformity is one of three central philosophies or goal-systems of assimilation, the others being the melting pot, and cultural pluralism (1964: 85, 88, 98, 104). To a considerable extent all three outlooks continue to coexist in Canada. For example, in the Prairie provinces there has definitely been a gradual shift of emphasis from Anglo-conformity to cultural pluralism, which possibly may now be shifting slowly towards a melting pot attitude. In other words, if we are to differ from Gordon in considering cultural pluralism to be more representative of accommodation than assimilation (a point to which we will return shortly), we would suggest that the general goals stressed by the larger society as a whole and provincial governments in the Prairies have shifted from assimilation (to a particular dominant group, the English-Canadian one) into accommodation (indicated by rather resigned acceptance of the pluralist viewpoint by that group to a considerable extent), and possibly recently into what might best be termed integration (based on a fusion of cultures rather than assimilation to a particular group) (Anderson, 1972: 195-200).

The official Canadian policy towards immigration and assimilation has wavered between Anglo-conformity and cultural pluralism for decades. But Anglo-conformity was the common theme held by the dominant group at least until after World War II. Supporters of this position argued that it was the obligation of the new immigrants to conform to the dominant British institutional structures of Canadian society. If immigrants did not (or would not) do so, they should be excluded from Canadian society (or not allowed entrance into Canada). Individuals supporting this position felt that Western civilization would be destroyed unless the Anglo-Saxon tradition of political and economic structures could be retained (Palmer, 1975). For example, as late as 1949 (if not even more recently) the Canadian federal government's willingness to grant landed immigrant status was still largely dependent on the immigrant's assimilability to Anglo-conformity, though Canada has never had the rigid quota system of the United States (although it has had similar exclusion of Asian immigrants).

The following quotes from *Canada Year Book* illustrate that the central theme of the dominant group has not changed since World War I.

> Canadians usually prefer that settlers should be of a readily assimilable type, already identified by race or language with one or another of the two great races now inhabiting this country. . . . Since the French are not to any great extent an emigrating people, this means in practice that the great bulk of the preferable settlers are those who speak the English language. . . . Next in order of readiness of assimilation are the Scandinavians, Dutch and Germans. . . . Settlers from Southern and Eastern Europe, however desirable from a purely economic point of view, are less readily assimilable. . . . Less assimilable still are those who come from the Orient. (1932: 149)
>
> Since the end of the Second World War, it has been the policy of the Government of Canada to stimulate the growth of the population by selective immigration. Efforts are made to choose immigrants of prospective *adaptability to the Canadian way of life* and to admit them at such times and in such numbers as employment and conditions warrant. (1963-64: 198)

Back in 1931 the Saskatchewan Royal Commission on Immigration and Settlement seemed to cautiously acknowledge the pluralist viewpoint:

> Assimilation . . . is at bottom a problem in adaptation. This, however, is not a one-sided process. It is just as important that we should adapt ourselves to what is best in what the newcomers bring from their home lands, as that they should adapt themselves to what is worthwhile in our economic and cultural life. (199)

There are innumerable examples of English-Canadians dictating their doctrine of Anglo-conformity. The remarks of one exuberant writer (B. M. Frith) from Wakaw, Saskatchewan in 1932 should suffice as an illustration of the direction of assimilation having been toward the British group rather than toward a Canadian identity:

> This district, settled by the pioneers of many tongues and races, has contributed no little part toward the establishment of a social organization built upon British principles in this small corner of a vast new land. Our individual pioneer, be he . . . Hungarian . . . Ukrainian . . . French . . . Pole . . . German . . . has contributed to the growth of this British social organization. . . . Here's to the worth of our pioneers! . . . Here's to the memory of pioneers! You gave of your youth and your worthwhile years to the white-hot iron, which with branding sears the mark of Great Britain's Glory!

Again, according to Hawkes, a Saskatchewan historian writing in 1924, European immigrants:

never really become British, and have no interest in the country outside their material interests; they occupy land, and receive wages, which should by rights belong to our own people; and it is a piece of folly to encourage foreign immigration when there is a surplus population in the British Isles of our own race who could profitably occupy the land, and provide the labour necessary for our development. (678)

During the Laurier regime, Sifton's policy of fairly open immigration from continental Europe to the Prairie provinces was not without its critics. The policy conflicted sharply with the desire of the provinces' population of British origin to preserve Saskatchewan "for English-speaking peoples." Resentment against uncontrolled immigration, especially from eastern Europe, grew steadily through the post World War I years. At the hearings conducted by the Saskatchewan Royal Commission on Immigration and Settlement in 1930, numerous briefs opposing open immigration were submitted. The Saskatchewan section of the United Farmers of Canada suggested that the immigration of farmers be stopped until native-born were better provided for; that there be no solicited or assisted immigration; and that there should be a quota system controlled to some extent by the provincial government. The Saskatchewan Command of the Canadian Legion believed that immigration from continental countries should not exceed immigration from "within the Empire." The Saskatoon Labour Trades Council advocated selective immigration where assimilation was a certainty. The Regina Assembly of the Native Sons of Canada opposed: assisted immigration, whether sponsored by Canada, the immigrants' country of origin, or group interests; special homesteading concessions to immigrants; and granting Canadian citizenship before five years of residence in Canada had elapsed. The Ku Klux Klan in Saskatchewan desired that immigration from "non-preferred" countries in central, eastern, and southern Europe be stopped entirely for at least five years, after which a rigid quota of 2% of the 1901 census should be imposed, except for British, French, and Scandinavian immigrants; that "trained" British and Scandinavian families be allowed to settle on the land; that all handling of immigration be removed from religious organizations; and that any ethnic group settlement be prevented. And the Provincial Grand Lodge of the Orange Order in Saskatchewan added its summary, advocating Anglo-Saxon predominance. It spoke out against the "unwise" policy of bringing in more immigrants than could be easily assimilated "to those British ideals which are fundamental to our national existence." It desired a quota system. It sought to confine immigration to preferred (Anglo-Saxon and Nordic) countries. It opposed group settlement of immigrants (because "it is not conducive to the best interests of our province, nor to the best ultimate interests of the immigrants themselves. . . . It retards the problem of assimilation, and retains distinctions which are detrimental to national unity. . . . We already have evidence of this throughout our province"). It denounced assisted passages for immigrants. It sought a halt to immigrants entering without guaranteed employment. And, finally, it sought provincial government control of immigration and abolition of all colonization organizations (Anderson, 1972: 39-41).

While the Saskatchewan Royal Commission on immigration and Settlement did not appraise the situation in 1930 as negatively as did many of the organiza-

tions submitting briefs, it did recognize that the development of such isolated
bloc settlements was not readily conducive to an integrated Canadian society:

> Throughout the province will be found many group settlements, represen-
> tative of diverse racial stocks. While group settlement has many good
> features, nevertheless there are grave objections to its further develop-
> ment. . . . Doubtless these groups do add diversity and elements of
> richness to the cultural life of the community; and also doubtless by this
> very diversity there is greater opportunity to adapt newcomers to the new
> environment. This, in turn, may result in their more rapid economic pro-
> gress. The warm welcome that may be expected from a racial brother, the
> overcoming of the nostalgia resulting from separation from the homeland,
> as well as other aids, are factors that appear to support group settlement.
> On the other hand, it is the rooted conviction of many of our people that
> group settlement tends to create blocks, thus preventing those intimate
> contacts without which it is impossible to create a sound citizenship.

The commission thus concluded that "homesteading should be discontinued and
remaining Crown lands should be sold preferably to residents of this province,
as a second choice to other Canadians, thirdly to British settlers, and lastly to
other immigrants" (197-98).

In general, Saskatchewan's ethno-religious minorities were on the whole still
quite segregated, at least in rural areas, during the 1920s and 1930s. Hawkes
wrote that the European immigrant "undoubtedly clings to his own nationality,
his own religion, and his own customs. . . . It is too much to expect him to become
a full-fledged Canadian in feeling or in aspiration. . . . It is just as impossible to
turn a mature Pole into a Canadian, as it would be to turn a Canadian into a
Pole. . . ." (1924: 681). And Young wrote "It is unnecessary to labour the point
that blocs of this size permeated with the atmosphere of the Old World and composed of members knit together by the common recollection of neighbourly
association in the past, are inimical to the assimilation of these people. . . . If the
question of assimilation is largely one of contact between immigrants and
native-born, these bloc settlements prevent contact with the native-born"
(1931: 76).

But during the same period at least some assimilation was also already in
evidence. Hawkes admitted that "communalism was breaking-down," that
there was a "great deal of intermarriage between immigrants and the English-
speaking folk," and that "the immigrant in general was anxious to see his
children educated and Canadianized" (1924: 695-6). Similarly, Young wrote
that, though "we are wont to think of the colonies where these people live as
closed districts in which the solidarity of the people is reinforced by their
remoteness from others of different racial stocks and by their lack of contact
with them," nonetheless "they do at times meet others and by virtue of such contact, their customs, attitudes and standard of living are unquestionably
modified, and this to a remarkable extent" (1931: 68). Finally, according to
another study of assimilation by Lysenko, "The transformation which the solid-
bloc community has undergone in the past thirty years is being duplicated in
every Ukrainian community in the country. The old fear, prejudice, ignorance
are being swept away in an irresistible tide of change" (1947: 237).

Gordon (1964: 110-111, 114, 151, 157-58) has suggested that in the United States Anglo-conformity never really reached the point of structural assimilation, due to the resistance of immigrants; moreover, while it is impossible for cultural pluralism to exist without the existence of separate sub-societies, it is possible for such sub-societies to continue their existence even while the cultural differences between them become progressively reduced and even in great part eliminated. What, then, has been the reaction of Canadian ethnic minorities to assimilation?

As a result of the prevalence of the Anglo-conformity philosophy in Canada, a preferential ordering of immigrant groups emerged. Those national groups that were defined as most likely to assimilate and would be able to do so the easiest would be allowed into Canada; those unlikely to assimilate (by the dominant group's definition) were excluded. The end result of such a rank order system placed British and American as the most desirable; Chinese and Blacks the least preferable.

Anglo-conformity as an ideology reached its peak during World War I. However, as Jaenen (1971: 11) points out, Anglo-conformity failed in its most radical manifestations because the non-British groups were too numerous, and they were settled in homogenous communities in many cases. It also failed because the host society was unprepared and unable to absorb so large and so diverse a segment of the population. As Anglo-conformity began to lose its force, a new ideology began to emerge; that of the melting pot philosophy.

This new ideology extolled the virtues of developing a new Canadian culture rather than a continuation of a slightly modified British culture. There was the underlying assumption that if ethnic groups (as social units) disappeared, prejudice and discrimination would become less and eventually disappear. As a direct result, all members of the next generation would have equal opportunities to participate in all dimensions of Canadian life. This position was not only supported by segments of the dominant group but also by immigrant groups such as the Scandinavians and Dutch, for they wanted nothing more than to be accepted as Canadian without adhering to their prior ethno/national affiliation. Other groups also wanting to assimilate made deliberate attempts to hide their ethnic backgrounds.

It would not be until mid-century that the dominant society would begin to seriously doubt the policy of assimilation and begin to move to an outcome of pluralism. And, it would take until the beginning of the 1970s before multiculturalism would become, at least nominally, Canadian federal policy.

With some major exceptions, the dominant sector of Canadian society has felt that assimilation is a preferred and acceptable response by migrants. This implied that these groups would become incorporated into Canadian life as individuals. It was felt that individual immigrants, after a short time in Canada, would change their life styles and accept the existing class/status structure in Canada. The dominant group has always provided opportunities for economic advancement (relative to the economic standing of the immigrants in their homeland), however it has been clear from the time of Confederation that British immigrants would receive preferential treatment, to maintain their dominant position in Canadian society (Martin, 1978).

There have been a number of ethnic minorities that have, at various times in history, tried to assimilate into the larger dominant society. In some cases there has been some success, in others none. In the latter cases, the minority changed to a different response.

Overall, most immigrant attempts at social assimilation have been unsuccessful. Some groups such as the Scots and Scandinavians have been partially successful in assimilating into the larger dominant culture. However, no large scale intrusion into the dominant sector has been evidenced. The dominant group has been able to maintain its superordinate and distinct position in Canadian society. What seems to happen is that individuals from specific subordinate groups are able to assimilate. In this sense there has been a selective, individual assimilation process.

Table 1 suggests the relative rates of assimilation of various ethnic and racial groups. Those groups who have experienced slight subordination developed weak subsystems and have similar cultural and biological traits compared to the dominant group, experience rapid and complete assimilation. At the other end of the continuum, assimilation will take much longer.

Our general conclusion is that while assimilation at the cultural level (for almost all groups) is taking place, assimilation at the structural (social) level is much further behind. The maintenance of group boundaries still seems to exist. The data relevant to endogenous marriages and the existence of ethnic enclaves give support to the claim.

Despite a plethora of studies of assimilation of Canadian minorities, few authors have clearly distinguished between assimilation or loss of ethnic culture and reinterpretation of ethnicity; as Isajiw (1975, 1977) has clearly argued, one can discern ethnic identity *change* without assimilation in the sense of a complete or gradual loss of aspects of ethnic culture. Moreover, there have been relatively few attempts to go beyond mere empirical reporting and to abstract theoretical paradigms for ethnic identity change or persistence (e.g., Anderson, 1975, 1980). The authors taking into consideration exogeneous controls or influences on ethnic infrastructure have been fewer still.

Among others, Li and Bolaria (1979) have argued strongly for an abandonment of simplistic assimilation studies in favor of a more far-reaching causal analysis of structural conditions, particularly as these conditions affect non-White immigrant groups:

> The image of non-Whites in Canada has been frequently distorted by both academics and policy makers. These distortions are based, in part, on assumptions of ethnic lives and cultures that are neither supported by empirical evidence nor theoretical arguments. Until the recent past, however, these assumptions have been unquestionably accepted by sociologists in their construction of assimilation models as basic tools to interpret the meanings of ethnicity. . . .
>
> The first camp within the assimilation school includes those who argue the gradual dilution of cultural traits among ethnic immigrants. Anglo-conformists and melting pot proponents, although differing on their emphasis on Anglo-Saxon culture versus an amalgamated product as the destination, have much in common in this respect—they both argue that immigrant groups are giving up the traits in their assimilation into the new world. Among the second camp are pluralists who stress the persistence of ethnic culture despite assimilation.

Table 1

THE ORDERING OF ETHNIC AND RACIAL GROUPS
(Part A—Left)

Racial Type I—Light Caucasoids			Racial Type II—Dark Caucasoids		
Cultural type	Degree of Subordination	Time for Assimilation	Cultural type	Degree of Subordination	Time for Assimilation
I. English-speaking Protestants (e.g., English, Scots, Canadians)	very slight	one generation or less	I.		
II. Protestants not speaking English (e.g., Danes, Dutch, French)	slight	1-6 generations	II. (e.g., Protestant Armenians and other dark-skinned Protestants)	slight to moderate	6 generations or more
III. English-speaking non-Protestants (e.g., South Irish)	slight	1-6 generations or more	III.		
IV. Non-Protestants not speaking English (e.g., French, Belgians)	slight	1-6 generations or more	IV. (e.g., dark skins of Racial Type I, also Sicilians, Portuguese)	moderate	6 generations or more
V. English-speaking non-Christians (e.g., English Jews)	moderate	1-6 generations or more	V.		
VI. Non-Christians not speaking English (e.g., fair-skinned European Jews and Mohammedans)	moderate	1-6 generations or more	VI. (e.g., dark-skinned Jews and Mohammedans)	moderate to great	very long

Source: L. Broom and P. Selznick, *Introduction to Sociology*. New York: Harper & Row, 1958.

Table 1
THE ORDERING OF ETHNIC AND RACIAL GROUPS
(Part B—Right)

Racial Type III—Caucasoid Mixtures			Racial Type IV—Mongoloids & Racial Type V—Negroids (combined)		
Cultural type	Degree of Subordination	Time for Assimilation	Cultural type	Degree of Subordination	Time for Assimilation
I. _____			I. (e.g., most American-born Chinese, Japanese, Negroes)	great to very great	very long to indefinitely
II. (e.g., small groups of Spanish-Americans in the Southwest)	great	very long	II. _____		
III. _____			III. (e.g., some American Negroes)	very great	indefinitely long
IV. (e.g., most of the mixed bloods of Latin America)	great	very long	IV. (e.g., Filipinos and Negroid Puerto Ricans)	great to very great	indefinitely long
V. _____			V. _____		
VI. _____			VI. (e.g., Orientals and Africans)	great to very great	indefinitely long

Despite the theoretical differences, these divergent views share one important aspect, that it is the *distinctiveness* of cultural origin which is being emphasized, and that such distinctiveness, whether cultural or institutional, is an important determinant in explaining ethnic differences. In stressing the persistence or disappearance of cultural traits and institutions, proponents from both camps in fact recognize the importance of cultural origins in explaining subsequent behaviors of ethnic groups. . . .

The primary objection to the assimilation perspective is not so much whether assimilation as a process, however it is defined, takes place, or whether cultural origin as an attribute, exists or not. Rather, the challenge is based on the frequent allusion that the uniqueness in cultural origin is necessarily the cause of ethnic differences. There are mounting evidence and theoretical dispositions to suggest that the basic assimilationist position is false.

The assimilationist position also suffers from a basic lack of clarity in the way the model is applied. The confusion arises from the causal application of the model as a description *and* explanation of the same ethnic phenomena. . . .

Ironically, assimilation theories frequently represent more idealistic projections of the future than objective realism of the present, or the past. To the extent that they are ethnocentric ideologies centred around the WASP culture, they are . . . mere projections of the dominant ethos of the larger society, an ethos which has too often been taken over uncritically by the sociologist. (411-14)

Undoubtedly some Canadian sociologists would with reason take strong exception to these final suggestions that assimilation theories tend to represent idealistic projections more than objective realism, moreover that they are ethnocentric WASP ideologies. After all, the sociologist studying aspects of the process of ethnic identity change is not necessarily exclusively interpreting his findings as unidirectional assimilation, nor agreeing with Anglo-conformity or some such assimilatory goal set by the so-called dominant society (however that is defined), nor more inclined toward "idealistic projections" than "objective realism." Yet the authors' criticism of ambiguous and tautological assimilation theories, and their advocacy of a structural approach, are well taken.

Related Concepts: Acculturation, Symbiosis, and Integration

While some sociologists, like Gordon, have considered acculturation to be essentially a type of assimilation, or the initial stage of assimilation, other sociologists—and especially anthropologists—have either distinguished between these terms or have preferred to use them interchangeably. For example, according to Redfield, Linton, and Herskovits (1936: 149), acculturation "comprehends those phenomena which result when groups of individuals having different cultures come into continuous first-hand contact, with subsequent changes in the original cultural patterns of either or both groups." Walter (1952) preceded Gordon in viewing acculturation as "a part of the broader process of assimilation"; to him acculturation refers to the "interchange of cultural traits and complexes between or among alien groups" (44, 48). Rose's (1956) definition of acculturation is very similar to his definition of assimilation (see above); he referred to acculturation as "the adoption by a person or group of the culture of another social group, or the process leading to this adoption" (557-558). According to Shibutani and Kwan (1965: 470, 479), "the concept of acculturation refers to the process of acquiring the culture of another ethnic group. This is the initial step in the breakdown of ethnocentrism. . . ." Most significantly, "acculturation may take place without assimilation; minority groups may alter their culture but still retain consciousness of kind. Assimilation refers to both the acquisition of the perspective of the dominant group and the attempt to identify with it."

Banton and Taylor, educated in social and cultural anthropology, have mentioned other terminological refinements. In Banton's (1967) view, "the process of change in the culture of a group of people adjusting to continuing contact with some other group is known as acculturation. Whereas contact normally leads to acculturation, it is conceivable that in certain circumstances the two cultures concerned might be equally balanced and of an inward-looking nature so that a permanent state of peripheral contact could be maintained," in which case we have "symbiosis." (77). And Taylor (1969) has commented, "The situation in which a culture is being modified by the borrowing of customs from one or more other cultures is called acculturation. . . . This term is also applied frequently to the reciprocal diffusion of customs between cultures (155).

As the term symbiosis suggests, and as Shibutani and Kwan (1965) in particular pointed out in describing the relationship between assimilation and acculturation, minority cultures can change without necessarily becoming assimilated. Recognizing this, a number of sociologists—notably Borrie (1959) and his associates and Schermerhorn (1970)—have emphasized the term "cultural integration" rather than "assimilation" to describe cultural change in pluralistic societies. For example, Bernard (1959) has commented that "to say that integration is a happier and more exact term than others to describe the successful inclusion of a new group into an existing society is not idle pedantry. The older term 'assimilation' . . . implies a one-way street in group relations. . . . It will be apparent that this concept of integration rests upon a belief in the importance of cultural differentiation within a framework of social unit. . . ." To which Borrie has added, "There may be economic absorption but cultural pluralism; cultural absorption at some levels . . . yet cultural differentiation and isolation at others (e.g., family customs, diets, etc.) . . . and so on through many permutations which may arise because of variations in the social systems brought into contact through immigration" (1959: 93-94).

Schermerhorn has described integration as "a process whereby units or elements of a society are brought into an active and co-ordinated compliance with the ongoing activities and objectives of the dominant group." Quoting from Coser, he has discussed integration first as a problem of legitimation: "Legitimacy is a crucial intervening variable without which it is impossible to predict whether feelings of hostility arising out of an unequal distribution of privileges and rights actually lead to conflict." Second, integration may be a problem of cultural or value congruence: "When the ethos of the subordinates has values common to those in the ethos of the superordinates, integration (coordination of objectives) will be facilitated; when the values are contrasting or contradictory, integration will be obstructed." Third, integration may be a problem of common or discrepant goal-definitions for subordinate ethnic groups: "Integration involves satisfaction of the ethnic group's modal tendency, whether it be centripetal (referring both to cultural trends such as acceptance of common values, life styles, etc., as well as structural features like increased participation in a common set of groups, associations and institutions) or centrifugal (fostering separation from the dominant group or from societal bonds in one respect or another)'' (1970: 66-73, 77-85).

Passive Submission

The *passive submission* response pattern is evident when a subordinate group comes to acquiesce in their disadvantaged and subordinate status. The group finds it necessary to accept and make the best of the disagreeable elements in their society. The conscious resignation to one's lot or the feeling that "there is nothing one can do" about the situation is perhaps the most common form of passive submission. The ethnic minority simply accepts its fate. As Lee (1976) points out, "The Chinese, in facing second class citizenship appeared content with their low economic position, accepted the discrimination imposed upon them with no public protest" (47). Similarly, with reference to the Japanese in Canada, Adachi (1976) points out:

> Most Japanese did not resist evacuation but cooperated with a docility. Many Japanese did not expect any sort of a "break" in Canada ... [They] ... applied the rationalization of shikata-ga-nai (it can't be helped) in the belief that the fate of a man was tied to forces beyond his control (p. 226).
> In the main, evacuees co-operated with the government officials, suppressed their hostility and frustration, and asked only to be left alone. (230)

While one may accept one's fate, it does not mean that one would like it. For example, the Japanese resented their subordinate status. However, some members may in fact internalize the attitudes associated with their status. These individuals accept the existing moral order without questioning it or doing anything about it.

One form of passive submission that is closely related to internalization of dominant characterization of the subordinate groups is that of self-hatred. This is the process of accepting the dominant group's negative definition of your group, internalizing that attitude and then acting toward the self in that fashion.

REFERENCES

Adachi, Ken. *The Enemy That Never Was.* Toronto: McClelland & Stewart, 1976.

Anderson, A. B. "Assimilation in the Bloc Settlements of North-Central Saskatchewan: A Comparative Study of Identity Change Among Seven Ethno-Religious Groups in a Canadian Prairie Region." Ph.D. thesis in Sociology, University of Saskatchewan, 1972.

Anderson, A. B. "Ethnic Groups: Implications of Criteria for the Examination of Survival," a paradigm presented in a workshop at the annual meetings of the CSAA, University of Alberta, Edmonton, May 30, 1975.

Anderson, A. B. "The Survival of Ethnolinguistic Minorities: Canadian and Comparative Research" in H. Giles and B. St-Jacques (eds.), *Language and Ethnic Relations.* New York: Permagon Press, 1980.

Banton, M. Race Relations. London: Tavistock, 1967.

Bernard, W. S. "The Integration of Immigrants in the U.S.", Conf./26, cited in W. D. Borrie (ed.), The Cultural Integration of Immigrants. Paris: UNESCO, 1959, p. 100.

Berry, B. Race and Ethnic Relations. Boston: Houghton-Mifflin, 1958.

Bogardus, E. S. "A Race Relations Cycle." American Journal of Sociology, 35, 4, (January, 1930).

Borrie, W. D. The Cultural Integration of Immigrants. Paris: UNESCO, 1959.

Brown, W. O. "Culture Contact and Race Conflict," in E. B. Reuter (ed.), Race and Culture Contacts. New York: McGraw-Hill, 1934.

Cuber, J. F. Sociology: A Synopsis of Principles. New York: Appleton-Century Crofts, 1955.

Davis, Understanding Minority-Dominant Relations. Arlington Heights: AHM Publishing, 1978.

Dawson, C. A. Group Settlement: Ethnic Communities in Western Canada. Canadian Frontiers of Settlement series, volume VII. Toronto: Macmillan, 1936.

Eisenstadt, S. N. The Absorption of Immigrants. Glencoe: Free Press, 1954.

Fairchild, H. P. Dictionary of Sociology. Patterson, N.J.: Littlefield, Adams, 1944.

Fichter, J. H. Sociology. Chicago: University of Chicago Press, 1957.

Francis, E. K. Interethnic Relations. New York: Elsevier, 1976.

Frazier, E. F. Race and Culture Contacts in the Modern World. Boston: Beacon Press, 1957.

Frith, B. M. "A Short History of the Wakaw District." Wakaw Recorder, 1932.

Glazer, N. "Ethnic Groups in America: From National Culture to Ideology," in M. Kurokawa (ed.), Minority Responses. New York: Random House, 1970.

Glick, C. E. "Social Roles and Types in Race Relations," in A. W. Lind (ed.), Race Relations in World Perspective. Honolulu: University of Hawaii Press, 1955.

Gordon, M. M. Assimilation in American Life. New York: Oxford University Press, 1964.

Hawkes, J. The Story of Saskatchewan and Its People. Regina: S. T. Clarke, 1924.

Isajiw, W. "Immigration and Multiculturalism—Old and New Approaches," paper presented at The Conference on Multiculturalism and Third World Immigrants in Canada, Univ. of Alberta, Edmonton, Sept. 3-5, 1975.

Isajiw, W. "Olga in Wonderland: Ethnicity in a Technological Society," in Leo Driedger (ed.), The Canadian Ethnic Mosaic. Toronto: McClelland & Stewart, pp. 29-39, 1978.

Jaenen, C. "New Canadians and the Schools," Toronto, Dept. of the Provincial Secretary and Citizenship, October, p. 64, 1971.

Johnson, R. "A New Approach to the Meaning of Assimilation," Human Relations 16, 3 (1963): 295-298.

Kinloch, G. The Sociology of Minority Group Relations. Englewood Cliffs, N.J.: Prentice-Hall, 1979.

Kogler, R. and B. Heydenkorn. "Poles in Canada, in B. Heydenkorn (ed.), Past and Present. Toronto: Polish-Canadian Research Institute, 1974.

Kurokawa, M. Minority Responses. New York: Random House, 1970.

Lee, C. F. "The Road to Enfranchisement: Chinese and Japanese in British Columbia," B.C. Studies, 30 (Summer, 1976) 44-76.

Li, P. and B. S. Bolaria. "Canadian Immigration Policy and Assimilation Theories," in J. A. Fry (ed.), *Economy, Class and Social Reality: Issues in Canadian Society*. Toronto: Butterworths, 1979.

Lieberson, S. *Ethnic Patterns in American Cities*. Glencoe: Macmillan, 1963.

Lieberson, S. "A Societal Theory of Race and Ethnic Relations," in M. Kurokawa (ed.), *Minority Responses*. New York: Random House, 1970.

Lysenko, V. *Men in Sheepskin Coats: A Study in Assimilation*. Toronto: Ryerson Press, 1947.

Martin, J. *The Migrant Presence: Australian Response, 1947-1977*, London: Allen and Unwin, 1978.

Owen, R., J. Deetz, and A. Fisher (eds.). *The North American Indian*. New York: Macmillan, 1967.

Palmer, H. (ed.) *Immigration and The Rise of Multiculturalism*. Toronto: Copp Clark, 1975.

Park, R. E. "Our Racial Frontier in the Pacific", *Survey Graphic*, LVI (May, 1926): 192-196.

Park, R. E. "The Race Relations Cycle in Hawaii," introduction to B. W. Doyle, *The Etiquette of Race Relations in the South*. Chicago: University of Chicago Press, 1937.

Park, R. E. *Race and Culture*. Glencoe: The Free Press, 1950.

Park, R. E. *Human Communities*. Glencoe: The Free Press, 1952.

Park, R. E. *Society*. Glencoe: The Free Press, 1955.

Patterson, E. Palmer. *The Canadian Indian: A History Since 1500*. Don Mills: Collier-Macmillan Canada, 1972.

Price, C. A. "Immigration and Group Settlement," in W. D. Borrie (ed.), *The Cultural Integration of Immigrants*. Paris: UNESCO, 1959.

Redfield, R., R. Linton and M. J. Herskovits. "Memorandum for the Study of Acculturation", *American Anthropologist*, 38(1), (1936).

Reuter, E. B. *Handbook of Sociology*. New York: Dryden Press, 1941.

Rose, A. *Sociology, The Study of Human Relations*, New York: Knopf, 1956.

Rose, A. M. and C. B. Rose (eds.) *Minority Problems*. New York: Harper and Row, 1965.

Rydern, N. B. "The Interpretation of Origin Statistics," *Canadian Journal of Economics and Political Science*, 21: 466-479, 1955.

Saskatchewan Royal Commission on Immigration and Settlement. Regina: King's Printer, 1930.

Sengstock, M. "Differential Rates of Assimilation in an Ethnic Group: In Ritual, Social Interaction, and Normative Culture," *International Migration*, 3(2), (1969): 18-30.

Schermerhorn, R. A. *Comparative Ethnic Relations: A Framework of Theory and Research*. New York: Random House, 1970.

Shibutani, T. and K. M. Kwan. *Ethnic Stratification: A Comparative Approach*. New York: Macmillan, 1965.

Simpson, G. E. Definition of "Assimilation" in International Encyclopedia of the Social Sciences, 1968.

Simpson, G. E. and J. M. Yinger. *Racial and Cultural Minorities: An Analysis of Prejudice and Discrimination*. New York: Harper & Row, 1958.

Stefansson, V. *My Life with the Eskimos*. New York: Collier Books, 1924.

Symington, F. *The Canadian Indian*. Toronto: McClelland and Stewart, 1969.

Taylor, R. B. *Cultural Ways*. Boston: Allyn & Bacon, 1969.

Tumin, M. M. *Comparative Perspectives on Race Relations*. Boston: Little, Brown, 1969.

Walter, P. A. F. *Race and Culture Relations*. New York: McGraw-Hill, 1952.

Warner, W. L. and L. Srole. *The Social Sytems of American Ethnic Groups*. New Haven: Yale University Press, 1945.

Wirth, L. "The Problem of Minority Groups," in R. Linton (ed.), *The Science of Man in the World Crisis*. New York: Columbia University Press, 1945.

Young, C. H. *The Ukrainian Canadians: A Study in Assimilation*. Toronto: Thomas Nelson and Sons, 1931.

Zenner, W. P. "Ethnic Assimilation and Corporate Group," in M. Kurokawa (ed.), *Minority Responses*. New York: Random House, 1970.

Chapter 12

Stratification and Accommodation

This chapter describes situations reflecting some degree of subordination of minority to majority, but where the result is not necessarily a lessening of minority ethnicity. First we will discuss ethnic stratification, clearly involving the maintenance of ethnic minorities in subordinate positions. However, it is important to recognize, in contrast with the responses discussed in the previous chapter (assimilation, passive submission, etc.), that this subordination may serve to strengthen minority ethnic consciousness rather than weaken or destroy it. Secondly the chapter reviews traditional sociological conceptualizations of accommodation, and relates the accommodation of ethnic minorities to pluralism and multiculturalism. This particular response/outcome theoretically should be more indicative of ethnic minority equality with a dominant group (and with each other) than the responses/outcomes discussed previously. However, we would argue that in fact certain Canadian ethnic minorities enjoy more privileges, rights, or equality than others, so that an oversimplified generalization that Canadian society is multicultural is not entirely in keeping with (some would argue far removed from) an accurate sociological appraisal of the situation of ethnic minorities in this country.

Ethnic Stratification

Sociologists have devoted ample attention to the relationship between the subordinate status of ethnic minorities and social stratification. Among the aspects of ethnic stratification discussed by Shibutani and Kwan in their comprehensive book of that title (1965), for example, were symbols of ethnic differentiation (including hereditary traits as status symbols, and auxiliary symbols of ethnic identity); stratification systems; the relationship between ethnic identity and social control; the incorporation of immigrants; and the pattern of conquest and domination. These authors have constructively distinguished between:

(a) *differentiating processes* (e.g., demographic and ecological bases for ethnic stratification; organization of the labor force; differential treatment of minorities as it relates to ethnic identification and the development of group solidarity; the formalization of status gradations, etc.);

(b) *sustaining processes* (e.g., subjective aspects of domination; social distance; the reaffirmation of ethnic categories; the accommodation of stable minorities and their reconciliation to subordinate status; the perpetuation of power differentials; the regulation of social mobility, etc.);

(c) *disjunctive processes* (e.g., upward mobility and marginal status; collective protest; inter-ethnic tension and conflict; minority nationalism and secessionism, etc.);

(d) *integrative processes* (e.g., acculturation, assimilation, pluralism, reduction of social distance, and redefinition of ethnic categorization, etc.).

Clearly, this typology cuts across our own description of a continuum of possible minority responses to dominant social control mechanisms. But it does illustrate, in short order, the complexity of sociological processes covered within the conceptualization of ethnic stratification. Yet even in their extensive discussion Shibutani and Kwan have not mentioned *ethclass*, a term suggested by M. M. Gordon only the year before (1964) as signifying "the subsociety created by the intersections of the vertical stratifications of ethnicity with the horizontal stratifications of social class" (51-54).

Although the interplay between ethnic subordination and social stratification, or the stratification of ethnic minorities, has received extensive coverage in sociological literature, more systematic analyses of ethnic stratification, concomitant with a more sophisticated definition of the concept ethnic stratification, have only emerged in recent years. This newer approach to ethnic stratification tends to focus, perhaps, not simply on the *practice* of ethnic inequality but also on the *ideology* behind these practices. The relationship between stratification and ethnicity is, appropriately, being studied from a *structural* perspective, which attempts, in other words, to account for structural constraints on ethnic minority subordination in society. Increasing attention is being devoted in Canadian sociology (e.g., Bolaria, forthcoming) to, for example, institutional racism manifested in opportunity structures and immigration policies, the split labor market, reserve army of labor, slavery, colonial exploitation and mentality.

Stratification refers to the ranking of categories of people, not the ranking of individuals. Thus, in the case of ethnic categories, the question would be whether or not various ethnic categories can be differentially ranked in terms of position in the Canadian social system (this may involve factors such as income, occupation and education).

Before discussing the evidence with regard to stratification, it might well prove fruitful to discuss briefly some antecedent causal factors. Noel (1968) argues that three major factors are necessary for the emergence of a stratified system: ethnocentrism, competition and differential power.

Ethnocentrism

This concept refers to that view in which one's own group is used as a reference in evaluating all others. Other groups are rated (or scaled) with reference to one's own group. Along with this comparative element, there is the notion of correctness of one's own group. The result is that there is an "over-positive evaluation of one's own group." This view can be expressed in a number of ways, including mythology, personal interaction or the establishment of a double standard.

Competition

This refers to the interaction between two or more social units striving for achievement of the same scarce goal, e.g., land, money. The actual number, significance and commonality of goals being sought will determine the degree (intensity) of competition.

Differential Power

Each group has differential power (resource base). Unless there is a great deal of power differential, one group will not be able to impose its will upon another.

Once these conditions are evident in a social system, ethnic stratification can emerge. As Simpson and Yinger (1967) point out:

> The type of stratification system in a society is of vital importance to its minority-majority relations. Race, ethnicity and religion frequently influence a person's location in the status structure; and the degree to which that structure permits mobility strongly affects the preservation or dissolution of minority groups. (386)

Hence, if ethnic stratification was in evidence in Canadian society, we should see that certain ethnic categories have higher educational attainments, higher occupational prestige or higher incomes. The data presented in the following tables bear on this issue. They show that certain categories consistently have higher education and occupations than other groups.

The data relevant to this issue centre on the distribution of jobs for various ethnic categories. For example, 4.3% of all the jobs in Canada are those of "managers, administrative and related activities." This job classification usually denotes one of high status, commanding high pay as well as other economic benefits. If we now compare the percentage of involvement for various ethnic categories in this job classification, we find that only two ethnic categories have a greater representation than the overall distribution: the British Isles—5.2% and Jewish—10.7%. While other ethnic categories show a lower rate of participation than the total distribution, there is a great deal of variation. For example, the French have 3.7%, Polish 2.8% and Native Indians have 1.5%.

Table 1

NET CONTRIBUTION OR ETHNIC ORIGIN[a] TO LABOR INCOME OF SALARIED MEN, BY ETHNIC ORIGIN—MONTREAL METROPOLITAN CENSUS AREA, 1961

	Deviation from observed average of $4,443	Net contribution of ethnic origin
English—Scottish	+ $1,319	+ $606
Irish	+ 1,012	+ 468
French	−330	−267
Northern European	+ 1,201	+ 303
Italian	−961	−370
Jewish	+ 878	+ 9
Eastern European	−100	−480
German	+ 387	+ 65
Others	−311	−334

a "Net contribution of ethnic origin" means the increase (+) or decrease (−) in dollars to the average wage and salary which is attributable to ethnic origin, all other factors being held constant.

Source: Royal Commission on Bilingualism and Biculturalism, Book III, Part 1, p. 77.

If one ranked the various occupations in Canada by prestige and position, we would find a consistent pattern emerging. Certain groups such as the British Isles are over-represented in high status (prestige) jobs and under-represented in low status jobs. On the other hand, we would find that groups such as Native Indians and Italians are under-represented at the upper social economic levels and over-represented in the lower social-economic occupations.

Perhaps the most dramatic illustration of the impact of ethnicity in our social system is revealed in Table 1. It shows that when all other social factors are held constant and only ethnic background is allowed to vary, there is a difference in income achievement.

The work of Veltman, Boulet and Castonguay (1979) has also shed light on the importance of language, and thus indirectly, cultural differences. Using 1971 census data from Montreal, they analysed the impact of being bilingual, unilingual as well as the use of specific languages in the home.

Table 2

GROSS AND ADJUSTED DEVIATIONS FROM MEAN EMPLOYMENT INCOME BY LANGUAGE GROUP, MALES, MONTREAL CMA, 1971

Language group			Deviations ($)		
Mother tongue	Official language	Home language	Gross[a] (1)	Language Contribution[b] (2)	Background Characteristic[c] (3)
English	Bilingual	English	+2154	+1457	+697
English	English	English	+1813	+1080	+733
Allophone	Bilingual	English	+1569	+581	+988
French	Bilingual	English	+936	+334	+602
Allophone	English	English	+935	-163	+1098
French	Bilingual	French	+235	-67	+301
Allophone	Bilingual	French	-101	-839	+738
English	Bilingual	French	-223	-255	+32
Allophone	English	Allophone	-1147	-1323	+176
Residual	Undefined	Allophone	-1154	-1187	+33
Allophone	Bilingual	Allophone	-1166	-962	-204
French	French	French	-1747	-467	-1280
Allophone	French	French	-1767	-1354	-413
Allophone	French	Allophone	-2011	-1139	-872
Allophone	Allophone	Allophone	-2966	-1845	-1104

[a] Calculated from Table 1 by subtracting the market mean from the mean employment income of each language group.
[b] Regression coefficient for each language group.
[c] Combined effects of age, education, and number of weeks worked.
Note: $R^2 = 0.30$
Source: Special tabulations, 1971 Census of Canada, in Veltman, et al., 1979.
Overall average for entire sample = $7,173.00

The data in Table 2 clearly illustrate that language is a very important contributor to one's income. Column 1 indicates the gross deviation of each language group from the overall average income. Column 2 indicates the contribution of language to the deviation while Column 3 represents the net impact of age, education and number of weeks worked. Column 3 is obtained by subtracting Column 2 from Column 1. The results clearly show that English either as mother tongue, official language or home language is an important determinant of one's income. As Kinloch (1979) points out:

> Minority group relations are a consequence of migration and economic development ... resulting in minority group roles, institutions ... perpetuated through individual socialization and identities ... and rationalized in terms of assumed physiological and psychological inferiority. (196)

Accommodation, Pluralism, and Multiculturalism

Intervening between segregation and the completed state of assimilation is an intermediate response, accommodation, implying the mutual acceptance of at least some integration rather than complete segregation. Accommodation is characteristic of pluralistic societies and multi-national states. Theoretically, a multi-national state should rest upon the principle of sanctioning cultural variability and group differences within the context of national federalism furnishing the means of integrating minorities and encouraging some sort of national unity (Simpson and Yinger, 1967: 28-30). Canada has not been as successful as some other countries in this regard, perhaps largely due to its longstanding and rather confusing status as an officially bicultural and bilingual state, yet a de facto pluralistic society.

There would seem to be some ambiguity in the literature on ethnic relations as to how accommodation relates to segregation and conflict. According to Berry (1958), segregation is essentially a pattern of accommodation. However, Shibutani and Kwan regard accommodation as the outcome of competition and conflict, the establishment of relatively stable patterns of concerted action, involving social isolation despite physical proximity of groups (1965: 119, 263, 280). And Rinder distinguishes between accommodated, segregated, and exotic pluralism (1970: 47). In accommodated pluralism, moderately deprived minorities meet moderate barriers to assimilation with subordinate group identities possessing vital centripetal strengths; they maintain much of their own social orders while articulating with the general economic order either through special skills or the exploitation of neglected work areas. In segregated pluralism, severely disadvantaged minorities, stigmatized as culturally primitive and/or racially different, sustain their identities through maintenance of a traditional social order isolated from that of the larger society (e.g., in a rural setting where their large numbers, comparative isolation, and autonomous institutions support centripetal tendencies). Finally, exotic pluralism is a pluralistic response, lasting perhaps one generation and neither historically nor numerically significant but nonetheless distinguishable, characteristic of identifiable minorities which are neither severely nor moderately deprived. Evidently Shibutani and Kwan's definition and Rinder's accommodated pluralism correspond to our intended definition of accommodation in a pluralistic setting.

Accommodation and pluralism tend to be favored by the second generation, i.e., the sons and daughters of the immigrants. Just as the accommodative stage is an interim between segregation and assimilation, so too does this generation find itself partially acculturated; its culture tends to be more hybrid than completely traditional, and many of its members represent Park's "marginal personality" (Herberg, 1955: 20-21; Shibutani and Kwan, 1965: 200, 284-5; Park, 1950: 318, 375-6; Berry, 1958: 259). The distinctive identities of ethnic minorities tend to persist only as long as they remain positively valued and useful.

Pluralism has been highly valued and defended by many spokesmen of the minorities, particularly Ukrainian-Canadians, as well as some Canadian government representatives and some sociologists. For example, according to Yuzyk, Canadian domestic policy has not subscribed to "a dead uniformity of culture or behavior—nor a fusion of souls in a dead jelly of oneness as dreary as the caked mud of a dried-up slough," the end-product of the proverbial melting pot. Rather, it encouraged citizens and ethnic groups to "be themselves," to "bring their gifts of different cultures to the common Canadian treasury, which constantly enriches our Canadian heritage." While Yuzyk suggests that "the supreme loyalty of each citizen and each ethnic group must of course be to Canada," he also has cautioned that "ancestry should not be denied, discouraged, or suppressed, but rather should be regarded with pride, which is a positive force" (1967: 84-87). The Ukrainians have been stimulated by such public figures as John Buchan (Lord Tweedsmuir), onetime Governor-General of Canada, who advised them (in a speech at Fraserwood, Manitoba in 1939), "You will all be better Canadians for being also good Ukrainians"; and Dr. Watson Kirkconnell, a former president of Acadia University, who commented, "There is nothing so shallow and sterile as the man who denies his own ancestry" (Yuzyk, 1967). Certain sociologists, such as Horace M. Kallen, were advocates of pluralism in the United States during the 1920s. Later sociologists, such as M. M. Gorden and J. M. Yinger, regarded pluralism as democratic yet criticized it as possibly anachronistic and over-enthusiastic (Gorden, 1964: 141-159, 264; Yinger, 1963: 106-7, 110).

The accommodation reponse is evidenced when minority groups desire equality with, but separation from, the dominant group. Minority spokesmen, if not sociologists and political scientists, have tended to equate this reponse pattern with pluralism or multiculturalism. They take the position that different cultures can exist side by side within the same nation-state. Those groups desiring accommodation argue that a pluralistic society has a positive cultural and political value, derived from the existence of the various ethnic minorities and their subsequent interaction with each other as well as with the dominant culture (Smith, 1965; Furnivall, 1948). This positive value emerges, so the theory goes, because each group will contribute the best elements from their cultural heritage to the total culture (n.b. our previous discussion of the notion of a cultural mosaic in Chapter 6). This is perhaps the most pronounced position taken by subordinate groups in Canadian society. With the implementation of the formal multicultural policy in 1971, most ethnic minorities are now claiming that their group should be allowed to retain their cultural traditions.

While some degree of cultural autonomy is pursued, this does not mean that it is pursued independently of other interests. Generally it is expected that if whole cultural traits will be accepted, some degree of economic and political equality will be achieved. Perhaps the best illustration of this reaction is that exemplified by the Hutterites. They have been successful for over half a century in maintaining their cultural distinctiveness while at the same time actively participating in the larger society. Their insistence on remaining culturally separate has not always gone unchallenged by the dominant group, but thus far they have been able to circumvent some decisions made by the dominant group (military service in wartime, taxation, attendance at schools off their colonies, location of colonies, etc.).

The approach to studying pluralism has been carried out from two very different perspectives. On the one hand, there is the equilibrium model which suggests that each society has a number of spheres and systems, e.g., kinship, or the economic system. There is relative autonomy yet balance between these spheres. In addition to the separation of the spheres, there is a strong structure of stable and independent groups intermediate between the individual and the state. This provides for the emergence of a system of checks and balances. The individual participation in these various plural structures fosters a diversity of interests, restrains exclusive loyalties and links the structures together. Thus, the pluralistic system contributes to the integration of the society by promoting the diffusion of common values. This conceptualization of pluralism portrays a social system as a balance of power among overlapping economic, religious and ethnic groupings. Each of these segments of society has some voice in shaping the policy of the social system. Advocates of this type of system argue that society will benefit from this type of structure. Because of the existence of multiple group structures, the most important problems and grievances will be heard, debated and resolved in a democratic fashion.

The second perspective is known as the conflict model. It views society as a mixture of a number of people living side by side, but separately within the same political unit. Each group has its own language, religion; its own view of reality. However, some unifying thread must tie these separate units together. Generally the economic and political structures of the parties will provide that unifying force. However, because each group has different forms of institutions such as education and religion, these different forms become incompatible. As a result of this type of structure (along with the existence of social pluralism), no common values will be evidenced. Hence, plural societies are held together not by integrative forces but by regulative forces. If one views a social system from this perspective, authority, power and regulations are crucial factors in maintaining, controlling and co-ordinating the system. This regulation involves a rigid (and hierarchial) arrangement of the relations between the different units (Furnivall, 1948; Smith, 1965).

Thus pluralism represents a condition in which individuals of common society are distinguished by differences in their institutional structures and social processes. These differences are not distributed in a random fashion but rather clustered. As Smith (1969: 27) points out, "The prevalence of such systematic disassociation between the members of institutionally distinct collectivities within a single society constitutes pluralism."

A society can be said to be plural insofar as it exhibits several characteristics. First of all there is an *absence of value consensus*. This, of course, means that there will be cultural heterogeneity within that system. This suggests that there will be a fair amount of autonomy between the parts of the system. Second, there is usually conflict between the significant corporate groups of the society. Third, social integration is generally achieved through coercion and economic interdependence. Fourth, there will be political domination by one of the corporate groups over the other groups. A last attribute of a plural system will show that there is a primacy of segmental, nonaffective and functionally specific relationships between groups, whereas there will be non-utilitarian, affective ties within the various groups (Van den Berghe, 1969).

The description above would illustrate an ideal type of pluralism. However, it should be noted that pluralism (as an analytical concept) is to be considered a variable, and as such pluralism can vary in form and content, just as other sociological concepts can. Pluralism can also vary in terms of its rate of change. It may be stable (ethnic groups maintaining their identity and resisting assimilation over three to four generations) or transitory (ethnic groups maintaining identity for one or two generations, then assimilating).

Ideal pluralism involves the central idea of maintenance of a distinctive identity while at the same time allowing for full equality to all groups. The equality centres on the moral, legal, political and social dimensions. However, two forms of pluralism have been engaged in by the dominant group. A vacillation between these two forms has been evident for some time. Connolly (1969) explicates the process of what is called syncretic integration. This process occurs when there is an official doctrine espousing the equality of all citizens and allowing individual competition for all economic, educational or political opportunities. The end goal of this strategy is to destroy the pre-national identities and to allow the subsequent emergence of a new all-inclusive national identity.

A second form of pluralism is that of balanced pluralism. In this form of pluralism, each ethnic group is given legitimacy with regard to their identity and structure. Each group is allowed to articulate their cultural and political interests. The competition for scarce resources is achieved through a structured bargaining process.

A pluralistic system involves a number of corporate groups residing within a nation-state with some boundaries. The boundaries may be easily observable, such as political-geographical ones, or obscure—social-psychological boundaries. In either case, each group claims to have some integrity as well as some distinctive traits. Theoretically, this outcome could involve a number of different groups (all equal in power) residing in a nation-state with some degree of autonomy. In practice, of course, this never occurs. Some interdependency does exist between the groups, and this implies some interconnectiveness between the groups. Normally, various groups allow for an all encompassing structure (usually the political/economic) to enable the system to carry on.

One last comment should be made with regard to the notion of boundaries. While clear-cut territorial boundaries do exist (as in the case for Quebec) which allow easy identification of each group, in some cases these clear-cut boundaries do not exist. For example, while there are communities in Canada with small Chinese populations (or in some cases, rural areas), their boundaries are not easily identifiable. However, if one were to establish the network system, we would find that even though they are spatially separated (or isolated), social networks exist which allow for these individuals to maintain their ethno/religious identity.

Pluralism in Canada, now called multiculturalism, began to emerge in the 1960s. One of the first factors to support pluralism was a resurgence in interest of identity for upwardly mobile second and third generation Central and Eastern Europeans. Secondly, the Royal Commission on Bilingualism and Biculturalism sparked a backlash from non-French, non-British Canadians. Then, in 1971, a multicultural policy (within a bilingual framework) was established. Its goal was and still remains to encourage the maintenance of ethnic groups through financial assistance, public recognition of these groups and the establishment of national cultural agencies.

This formal policy of attempting to achieve a pluralistic system assumes that each ethnic group will view this as a procedure by which each group may sustain basic cultural attributes. It is also meant to enable groups to transmit key cultural elements from one generation to the next, and thus allow the survival of the culture.

Canadian society, to a certain extent, exhibits some characteristics of a cultural pluralistic society. This type of system shows mutual toleration or peaceful coexistence of groups with different cultures. Each group in Canada is free (at least theoretically) to develop and maintain its own culture (and in some—but not all—cases the federal government will aid the group) within a framework of the existing Canadian social system. Very little evidence of structural pluralism (participation by different groups in different institutions and informal arrangements rather than in the same ones) seems to be evident. Davis (1978) has pointed out that structural pluralism can vary from what he calls maximal, where participation of the various groups occurs only in one major institution, e.g., economic or political, to minimal, where only one or two institutions are maintained as separate cultural entities.

REFERENCES

Berry, B. *Race and Ethnic Relations.* Boston: Houghton-Mifflin, 1958.

Bolaria, B. S. (ed.) *Oppressed Minorities in Canada.* Toronto: Butterworths, (forthcoming).

Connolly, W. (ed.) *The Bias of Pluralism.* New York: Atherton Press, 1969.

Furnivall, J. S. *Colonial Policy and Practice.* London: Cambridge University Press, 1948.

Gordon, M. M. *Assimilation in American Life.* New York: Oxford University Press, 1964.

Herberg, W. *Protestant, Catholic, Jew.* Garden City, NY: Doubleday, 1955.

Kinloch, G. *The Sociology of Minority Group Relations.* Englewood Cliffs, NJ: Prentice-Hall, 1979.

Noel, D. "A Theory of the Origin of Ethnic Stratification," *Social Problems*, 16, 2 (1968): 18-32.

Park, R. E. *Race and Culture.* Glencoe: Free Press, 1950.

Rinder, I. D. "Minority Orientations: An Approach to Intergroup Relations Theory Through Social Psychology," in M. Kurokawa (ed.), *Minority Responses.* New York: Harper & Row, 1970.

Shibutani, T. and K. M. Kwan. *Ethnic Stratification: A Comparative Approach.* New York: Macmillan, 1965.

Simpson, G. E. and J. M. Yinger. *Racial and Cultural Minorities: An Analysis of Prejudice and Discrimination.* New York: Harper & Row, 1967.

Smith, M. G. *The Plural Society in the British West Indies.* Berkeley: University of California Press, 1965.

Smith M. G. "Institutional and Political Conditions of Pluralism," in L. Kuper and M. G. Smith (eds.) *Pluralism in Africa.* Berkeley: University of California Press, 1969.

Van den Berghe, P. "Pluralism and the Polity: A Theoretical Explanation," in Kuper and Smith (eds.), *Pluralism in Africa.* Berkeley: University of California Press, 1969.

Veltman, C., Jac-Andre Boulet and C. Castonguay. "The Economic Context of Bilingualism and Language Transfer in the Montreal Area," *Canadian Journal of Economics,* 12(3) (1979): 468-479.

Yinger, J. M. *Sociology Looks at Religion.* New York: Macmillan, 1963.

Yuzyk, P. *Ukrainian Canadians: Their Place and Role in Canadian Life.* Toronto: Ukrainian Business and Professional Federation, 1967.

Chapter 13

Survival and Revival

Earlier in this book (Chapter 6), in discussing multiculturalism as an emerging mode in Canadian society, an argument for ethnic change was offset with an argument for ethnic persistence. The present chapter explores ethnic persistence further, focusing on three minority responses/outcomes to dominant control: segregation, secession/separatism, and revivalism. While segregation may be imposed by the dominant society, hence reflecting subordination, it may also be partly voluntary, thus a positive alternative to subordination. More clearly the other responses/outcomes, secession/separatism and revivalism, represent purposive minority efforts to avoid subordination and to re-establish ethnic consciousness.

Segregation

This outcome usually refers to the state of being separate or set apart from other ethnic groups by social norms or by physical/geographical barriers. Normally this outcome is the result of pressures placed upon the subordinate group, and involves only spatial (geographical) isolation. While this is certainly the case in many respects, it must be made clear that not all segregation is involuntary and not all involves spatial separateness. In some cases the segregation may be voluntary, e.g., Hutterites, while in some other cases it may not involve geographical isolation but social isolation. Figure 1 shows the various forms of segregation and examples of each that can be evident in our social system. The forms of segregation, as they apply to one group, may change over time. In addition, different forms may be applied to different groups at one point in time.

FIGURE 1

		Subordinate Group Orientation	
		Voluntary	Involuntary
Forms of Segregation	Physical (spatial)	Hutterites	Indians
	Social	Doukhobors	Jews

First of all, let us look at the voluntary-involuntary dimension. If, from the perspective of the subordinate group, isolation (physical and/or social) is not desired, then one can talk of involuntary segregation. While on the other hand, if the isolation is of the group's own volition, then we refer to voluntary segregation. In addition, because social reality is not easily broken into dichotomies, there will be times when both elements are evident. The Mennonites and Icelanders are good illustrations of voluntary segregation in that they were allowed to settle in blocs. This was not because the dominant group believed in cultural diversity or that they wanted to isolate these groups. It was rather because: (i) it was a way of keeping them in Canada—they could be with their own kind, (ii) it provided for social and economic stability in the developing areas and, (iii) it was an easy way to settle the West. Hence, we once again find ourselves having to assess the processes from a time perspective. At one time a subordinate group may have wished for segregation (for which the dominant group was willing to accommodate) but at a later time not want to maintain this isolation (at which time the dominant group may not acquiesce to the demands).

On the other hand, segregation may be involuntary. Various groups over time have been forced to remain in isolated territories because of dominant group pressure. Indians, for example, have been subjected to segregative processes for many years. Reservations are just one of many clearly demarcated lines that establish physical boundaries between Indians and non-Indians.

With regard to the second dimension of segregation, one must think not only in terms of spatial (territorial-geographical) segregation but also in terms of social segregation. This, of course, refers to social interaction patterns. This means that while spatial segregation may not be present, social segregation may go on. This process, at the individual level, can be referred to as discrimination. An assessment of most urban areas in Canada will reveal that social networks among ethnic groups are usually internal. Anderson and Higgs' (1976) work on the Portuguese demonstrates the extent to which social networks are contained within the group. Other research on the Hungarians (Kosa, 1956), Chinese (Baureiss, 1971), and Blacks (Henry, 1978) all demonstrate that social segregation is a reality in Canadian society.

As illustrated in Figure 1, we see that a variety of combinations can take place. In addition, one group may be both socially and physically separated from other groups in society. Let us begin with an easy, clear-cut example and proceed to a more complex case. In the case of Hutterites, as pointed out above, they would best illustrate a case of both social and physical segregation, with the group itself wanting to maintain their isolation, and where this willingness to be isolated is accepted by the dominant group, although the dominant group would prefer to see the isolation reduced.

Studies of the Blacks in Canada also reveal that segregation has been used against them, but they present a more complex case. From the earliest arrival of Blacks, they were spatially segregated from the surrounding White communities; and the existence of spatially segregated Black communities in Canadian society can be seen from Halifax to the rural areas of Alberta.

As Blacks from the U.S.A. began to emigrate to the West in 1911, first accounts of the influx and impact of Blacks for Canadians came from the mass media. They alerted the general population that a wave (300) of Blacks were entering Canada. This news provoked a debate in the House of Commons which culminated in giving immigration officers the right to bar Blacks from entering Canada on the grounds that they could not adapt to the rigors of the Canadian winters. Such an action was apparently within the power of the Immigration

Act of Canada, and it effectively stopped any further large-scale immigration to Canada by Blacks (Grow, 1974; Thompson, 1979).

Furthermore, other groups not only wanted to stop the entry of Blacks into Canada, but to formally segregate those already in the country. For example, the Calgary and Winnipeg Board of Trade submitted a petition to the federal government which stated that the government should stop further immigration of Blacks into Canada, and that Blacks presently in Canada that were on homestead lands be segregated in a certain defined area or areas from which Whites should be removed. In other areas, such as in Ontario, Blacks were segregated into rural outposts by the action of the White residents. As Winks (1971) points out, the Black resident of Ontario and the West was either dissuaded from certain provinces and regions, or more often, *told* to settle far away from Whites. Even if settlement patterns were not segregated, social interaction patterns were. Very little interaction took place between Black and White "neighbors."

A demographic analysis of an urban centre in Canada will also reveal that a great deal of physical segregation is evident. Each town has its own Chinatown, its own Black ghetto, or its French quarter.[1] However, in these cases interaction patterns are not limited to members of their own kind and interaction patterns cross over ethnic boundaries.

The above examples also illustrate the interrelatedness of the social/physical dimensions. By creating physical segregation, social segregation may follow, while on the other hand, social segregation may not lead to physical segregation. When segregation exists, the ethnic group may remain marginally linked with the larger society, or, alternatively, begin to create its own institutions. This, of course, suggests that if the subordinate group is segregated by the dominant group, one result will be that the group begins to turn inward and develop its own institutional structures (Breton, 1964). Given that a large enough population is able to support these structures (or the fact that they can involve other groups into their institutions at a peripheral level), the ethnic minority will develop solidarity and vitality. Thus, the entire process may lead over an extended period of time to a pluralistic system. This, of course, is dependent upon the group's ability to maintain various religious, educational and welfare institutions. In most cases this is not possible. Some groups, most notably the western French, Jews, Italians and West Coast South Asians (because of unique, distinct cultural factors) have been able to sustain relatively high levels of institutional completeness, while other groups, such as Scandinavians, Poles, and the Lebanese, have not been able to maintain such institutionally complete systems.

Why would the dominant group wish to pursue this outcome? The reasons may vary, as they serve a rationale for the different groups. That is, when this outcome is applied to Native people one rationale may be used, but when applied to another group, a different rationale will be used. The rationale will change as the circumstances and the group changes. In the end, however the overreaching reason will be to retain control over the subordinate groups. Thus

---

[1] The formal term *segregation* is no longer in vogue but rather we talk about *residential concentration*.

it should become obvious that sometimes the stated rationale is of little empirical sociological use to gain an understanding of intergroup behavior. What is apparent, then, is that we must first be able to understand the underlying conditions that precipitate these rationales. It is, like any other social control mechanism, a technique that is dependent upon the conditions of the social structure at a particular juncture in history.

To repeat, it is crucial to observe that segregation, as a minority response to dominant social control, may be voluntary or imposed. We would argue that many cases of relatively segregated ethnic or ethno-religious minorities in Canada are in fact both voluntary and imposed. To illustrate this, let us examine a rural situation, the formation of ethnic bloc settlements in the Prairies, then contrast this with the development of urban ethnic concentrations.

Three main processes by which ethnic, or more precisely ethno-religious group settlements came into being may be distinguished (Price, 1959: 270-272). First, there are organized group settlements, such as those founded by organized bands of political or religious refugees or those founded when organized groups of laborers were brought in to develop a particular area. Second, there are chain settlements, such as those which came into being slowly and sometimes quite fortuitously as the result of chain migration, i.e., the process whereby one or two persons of a particular place in Europe settled in some locality abroad and then established links with their friends or contacts at home. Third, there are gravitation group settlements, formed when migrants who came abroad independently and were drawn together into groups by forces of mutual attraction, such as common dialect or national language, common cultural traditions and customs, common religion, etc. Price had added two qualifications: (i) that the original character of the settlement may change in time, and (ii) that some settlements may be offshoots from an earlier one. There is no doubt that the bloc settlements of the Prairies conform to all of these categories. The Mennonite, Hutterite, and Doukhobor settlements may be described as primarily of the organized type, the Scandinavian ones of the gravitation type, and the French, German Catholic, and Ukrainian-Polish of all three types to an appreciable extent. The establishment of ethno-religious bloc settlements was, in sum, partly due to organized colonization schemes and partly due to rather coincidental gravitation of co-ethnics, while ethnic conflict in both the Old World and the New played a significant part in the creation and perpetuation of ethnic settlements (Anderson, 1977: 188-193).

This settlement process had a profound impact on Canadian society in general and on certain regions of the Prairies in particular. Despite an immigration policy favoring immigrants only from "desirable" countries, by the 1920s Saskatchewan had twice as many immigrants of non-British as of British origin. Vast areas of this province had been incorporated into ethnic bloc settlements; some of the larger bloc settlements included over thirty towns and villages apiece. Ethnic enclaves had become a prominent feature of the Prairies, helping to turn Canadian society into a cultural mosaic largely lacking the strong national identity and melting pot consciousness emerging in the U.S.A. These enclaves were characterized by isolation from other enclaves of different ethnic origins and religious affiliations and from the larger society. Social organization was extremely localized; most bloc settlements had a decidedly local nature, being characterized by the dialects, customs and traditions of particular areas in Europe (Anderson, 1977: 190).

Segregation may be viewed as the first stage in identity change and the immediate result of the formation of bloc settlements. It is theoretically quite possible that some ethno-religious groups in the Prairies still have not progressed beyond this initial stage to any appreciable extent. If the concentration of various ethno-religious groups into compact bloc settlements was largely due to policies of the federal government, railways, and colonization companies (Anderson, 1972, 1977), this concentration must also be viewed as something of a natural process in accordance with the maxim, "birds of a feather flock together." A high proportion of immigrants in rural or urban settings usually live in fairly well-defined ethnic islands. Such cultural islands or segregated ethnic communities are found throughout the world. It may well be that most of them are transitory, disappearing after a few generations, but some manage to retain their cultural uniqueness for centuries. For a long period of time the members of ethnic groups may associate primarily with others of their kind. Even if they are given the opportunity to frequently interact with dissimilar members of other ethnic groups, their contacts with outsiders might be categorical and impersonal. Bloc settlements have tended to promote the development of a strong sense of consciousness of kind (Shibutani and Kwan, 1965: 133, 282-3, 288, 291). An example of this has been the consolidation of national identities; thus in the western Canadian bloc settlements a new Ukrainian-Canadian identity emerged from more localized traditional identification as Galicians, Ruthenians, or Bukovinians, just as a Scandinavian-Canadian identity generally assumed priority over identification as Norwegians, Swedes, or Danes; or a German-Canadian identity was formed with the merging of *Reichsdeutsche* (immigrants direct from Germany) with *Volksdeutsche* (ethnic German immigrants from Russia, Poland, Rumania, Czechoslovakia, Hungary, etc.). But for some, a common Canadian identity has yet to be emphasized or accepted. This is hardly surprising, for at least three reasons. First, in Canada today the demand to identify oneself explicitly as a member of a particular ethnic group is still quite prevalent. Second, biculturalism may have tended to foster multiculturalism (as we noted in Chapter 5). Third, an increasing proportion of recent immigrants to Canada have been non-Whites (as we noted in Chapter 6).

Self-identification is closely related to identification by others, in addition to a consciousness of kind enhanced by living in segregated bloc settlements (Gordon, 1964: 29). Segregation is intimately linked with the degree of differences between the ethnic groups, at least according to traditional sociological theories. Yet it is a most interesting question to what extent these differences are real or imagined, objectively or subjectively defined. In the past sociologists have devised various complicated measurements of group differences to determine national character. For example, the J-Curve of Conformity Behavior, which is a frequency curve drawn to histograms to reveal that the essential attributes of a group, i.e., the characteristics that define the group, tend to follow a J-Curve type of distribution (e.g., loyalty to a particular set of traditions), or Rare-Zero Differentials, indicating that some traits ascribed to a group are rare within the group but never exist in other groups (e.g., a particular peasant costume). Overlapping normal curves, including the Bimodal Curve, show the extent of similarity or difference between groups for a certain common trait (e.g., interest in folk music). Categorical Differentials, measure a single attribute with differential frequency in various groups (e.g., the proportion of youth who are university educated) (Allport, 1954: 93-104). One should note, however, that there would be few cases of group differences marking off every single member of a group from every single non-member. Moreover, indices of similarity or dissimilarity—notably the Bogardus Social Distance Scale—in retrospect seem to have provided relatively little (if any) information on segregation of ethnic minorities from each other in North America (Lieberson, 1963: 39, 135).

What seems crucial in the Canadian case, if not the American, is that the dissimilarity of each group, both to other groups and to the general society, was—and perhaps still is—subjectively felt. Thus, among the principal Prairie ethnic groups, most of the German Catholics, Lutherans, and Baptists, Mennonites, Hutterites, Jews, Poles, and Ukrainians had settled separately in regions of the Ukraine prior to immigrating to Western Canada. German Catholics, Lutherans, Baptists, Mennonites, Hutterites, and Jews all spoke various German dialects; while Ukrainians, Poles, and Russian Doukhobors spoke closely related Slavic languages. The French, German Catholics, and Poles were all Roman Catholics, with Ukrainian Catholics marginally affiliated; German and Scandinavian Lutherans also shared a religion; Mennonites and Hutterites were both Anabaptists. Yet their consciousness of kind, awareness of differences, and segregation were highly institutionalized in the self-centred ethno-religious colonies, at first through churches and related religious-orientated institutions, including schools, if not social organization in general (Dawson, 1936: 378 et seq.).

On the whole, it seems clear that segregation in the bloc settlements of the Prairies has been largely—but certainly not entirely—voluntary. Segregation has been termed involuntary if the minority group is of undesirable status in the eyes of the majority, if it views forced segregation as an insult, if its bloc settlements are havens of refuge from an unfriendly world, if it is subjected to a strict apartheid system, etc. (Shibutani and Kwan, 1965: 283, 415; Berry, 1958: 274, 277; Rose, 1948: 167; Lieberson, 1963: 4-5). But this would appear to have limited applicability to these western Canadian groups. As Shibutani and Kwan have explained, in most cases the formation of ethnic islands is voluntary. People conceive of themselves as living in an alien world, therefore they prefer to form a closed society aimed at maintaining exclusiveness and thereby preserving identity. They prefer to live with what they conceive to be their own kind, to be left alone (Shibutani and Kwan, 1965: 284, 291, 516, 522). Again, according to Lieberson (1963: 4-5), voluntary segregation occurred "if proximity to members of the same group facilitated adjustment to the conditions of settlement in a new country or if the members of an ethnic group simply viewed the residential proximity of members of the same group as desirable. More specifically, in Western Canada the settlement of immigrants in blocs by the government, railways, and colonization companies retarded assimilation and promoted group solidarity, which was then consciously maintained (Kyba, 1968: 105). The threat of assimilation caused minorities to react with an organized effort to preserve those aspects of their various cultures which they valued most highly, giving rise to boundary-maintaining or to what Linton has called perpetuative-rational nativistic movements (1943: 230-240).

Hurd's *Index of Segregation for Racial Origins in Canada* in 1931 did not seem to reflect very well the situation on the Prairies. It reported that the British and French had very low degrees of segregation, the Germans, Dutch, and Scandinavians moderate, and the Slavic groups very high. Indeed, in Western Canada the Slavic groups had effectively duplicated their Old World settings and here, as well as elsewhere in North America, they revealed a marked resistance to change. But in this regard the other groups were not so different. The German language was once spoken over vast areas of the Prairies. Old Colony Mennonites were until very recently—and Hutterites still are—acutely segregated. Rural French-Canadians in the Prairies live largely in compact areas of settlement which are decidedly French in character (Anderson, 1978). If the Norwegians exhibited a marked tendency to concentrate, the Icelanders went so far as to establish their own autonomous republic in Manitoba from 1875 to 1887 (covering 460 square miles around Gimli and complete with its own constitution, law code, and public school system).

While the ethnic enclaves in North America cities may be described as socially isolated, those in rural areas have tended to be isolated physically as well. Segregation may be defined as the act, process, or state of being separate or set apart from others. Physical separation may serve to enhance social isolation. Residence in a common area restricts the possibility of establishing friendly contacts with outsiders, and proponents of separatism may look favorably upon such lack of contact. As Shibutani and Kwan have suggested, "the extent to which a distinctive culture develops among people in a given ethnic category depends upon the degree of their social isolation from others." Moreover, "the extent to which different individuals are able to develop consensus depends upon their participation in common communication channels" (Shibutani and Kwan, 1965: 59, 209, 523, 573-4). In other words, voluntary social isolation, enhanced by physical isolation, makes for the development of a strong consciousness of kind, encouraged by communication within the group but not interrupted by contacts with outsiders (Berry, 1958: 273, 280; Schermerhorn, 1970: 256).

Yet this emphasis of lack of contact between groups can be overstressed. We have already noted how a given group's consciousness of kind is developed largely through the mutual, reciprocal definition of groups as being different and unique. In fact, it is precisely inter-group contact of an unfavorable sort that does a great deal to promote group withdrawal. There is a vast sociological literature on conflict between ethnic groups, out of which we can extract some pertinent suggestions. For example, numerous writers have discussed the self-segregation of minorities as a response to subordination under an unsympathetic majority. Some sociologists have suggested (perhaps simplistically) that the more different the minorities are from each other and from the majority, the greater the conflict. Moreover, they have pointed out that conflict can function to promote consciousness of kind and group solidarity within ethnic settlements. Whether inter-group conflict is inevitable in various circumstances remains a much debated question (Shibutani and Kwan, 1965; Schermerhorn, 1970; Tumin, 1969; Allport, 1954; Price, 1959). In Western Canada the groups considered to be least assimilable to British-Canadian traditions tended to be the ones experiencing the most conflict and also the ones with the most marked sense of unique identity. Old Colony Mennonites regarded the dominant society as sacrilegious, while the latter considered the former an unwanted nuisance. Strictly separatist Hutterites and Doukhobors conflicted with government officials as well as with neighboring farmers over collective farming. (Anderson, 1972: 191-92).

Ethnocentrism, or the exaggerated status-consciousness of a particular ethnic group, and xenophobia, or a group's fear of whatever seems alien to them, were reflected in stereotyping and ethnic joking. Ukrainian and Polish Canadians seem to have borne the brunt of ethnic humor, but for their part they responded with bitter criticism of exploitation by English-Canadians and particularly Jews. Because there are few Jews in contact with people of Ukrainian origin in Saskatchewan, we can assume that this hostility was imported from eastern Europe (Anderson, 1972: 192). Economic competition is central to many discussions of ethnic conflicts. Much conflict ensued from the competition of the various groups for space as their bloc settlements expanded. In particular, in the case of a large bloc settlement encroaching on the territory formerly held by a smaller bloc settlement, the conflict may increase. Considerable evidence of this was found during a study in Saskatchewan (Anderson, 1972); farmers of the smaller settlement were reluctant to sell any land to buyers from the expanding settlement, stereotyping and ethnic joking were common, and a generally mutual mistrust of the intentions of each group was apparent.

It is instructive to contrast the propensity for voluntary and imposed segregation in the rural Prairie settlements with the tendency of ethnic groups to concentrate (voluntarily as well as involuntarily) in certain areas of Canadian cities. We have noted earlier (in Chapter 6) that some ethnic groups in Canada are largely or entirely rural (e.g., Hutterites, Doukhobors, Amish), while many others are mainly urban (Chinese, West Indians, Greeks, etc.). But it is more complicated to ascertain the extent to which ethnic collectivities are concentrated or segregated, much less to figure out whether their segregation is voluntary or imposed. To repeat, Chinatowns are found in all major and some minor Canadian cities. But what proportion of the total Chinese population in each city resides in Chinatown? Concentrations of West Indian immigrants have appeared during the 1970s in Toronto. But what proportion of the total West Indian population of this city live in these particular neighborhoods? Why do some members of ethnic collectivities choose (assuming that they in fact have a choice) to live in ethnic neighborhoods, but others do not? Do immigrants first settle in these neighborhoods (immigrant reception areas), then eventually move out to mixed neighborhoods? To what extent does racial discrimination against non-Whites determine where they can live in the city?

Again, it is our contention that for certain urban ethnic collectivities, just as for ethnic minorities in the rural context, analysing propensity for—and reasons behind—imposed versus voluntary segregation can be very complex; many cases of relative ethnic segregation in Canadian cities involve a complicated interplay between voluntary and involuntary factors. Just to pick one illustration, a high proportion (over 90%) of Jews in Montreal reside in continuous, largely Jewish neighborhoods. Moreover, Montreal Jews (constituting about a third of the total Jewish population in Canada) reveal a high degree of endogamy; relatively few marry non-Jews. The "voluntary" interpretation would suggest, perhaps rather naively yet not completely inaccurately, that Jews tend to be clannish; they like to stick together, and that at any rate most are Orthodox Jews who prefer—or are even virtually required—to live in close proximity to their own synagogues, schools, and other institutions. However, an "involuntary" argument would point out that there has been a long history of anti-Semitism in Quebec, evidenced in the provincial governments, one-time discrimination against Jews at McGill University (particularly in certain faculties), and in real estate policies which effectively prevented Jews from settling (at least in substantial numbers) in traditionally Anglo areas (Anderson, 1967).

On the surface, Canadian ethnic minorities may seem free to settle where they will, in which case any instance of segregation could be seen as entirely voluntary on the part of the minority. But there are many significant constraints serving to limit this freedom: not only racial, ethnic, and religious discrimination, but xenophobia, conservatism, and economic considerations.

Secession

Ethnic groups that adhere to a secessionist philosophy repudiate assimilation and are not content with mere toleration or cultural autonomy. The principal and end goal of such minority groups is to achieve political, as well as cultural independence from the dominant group. It is here that the intellectuals of the minority group may play a crucial role in stimulating an awareness of, and interest in, the group's unique history.

French Quebec best typifies this response. Although one might argue that they have not always held this position, also that many Quebecois are not separatists, it would seem clear that today there is a sizeable proportion of the French population in Quebec which supports this ideological position. McRoberts and Postgate (1976) report that a number of surveys taken in Quebec during the past years have indicated fairly consistently that about one-third of their respondents chose to support the political disengagement of Quebec from the federal system. Just how this sentiment might be translated into action has, until recently, been subject to a great deal of speculation. It would seem, on the basis of responses of French Quebecois to the October Crisis, and to the revolutionary activities of the FLQ, that militant revolutionary tactics would not be acceptable. It would suggest that if the political independence of Quebec was to be achieved, it would have to be through the election of a Quebec government dedicated to a separatist ideology. The election of the PQ and René Levesque as Premier in 1976 (one of the oldtime mainstream separatists) undoubtedly brings closer the possibility of French Quebec achieving its goal of secession, although as we have suggested earlier (Chapter 5) just how fast and in which form (sovereignty-association, complete independence from Canada, or limited autonomy) this goal might be achieved still remains to be determined at the time of writing.

Ethnic Revivalism

A final possible minority response to domination would be revitalization or ethnic revival. This response involves a general rediscovery of a particular group's cultural heritage. Members of the group find that they have, for a variety of reasons over time, lost any major cultural attributes, e.g., language or religion, that distinguish them from the dominant group.

This group begins to rediscover its cultural history and develops bonds with others who also identify with the symbols that represent the group. Members of the group then begin to overemphasize the symbols chosen to represent their group. These symbols take on a heightened positive value and an over-aggrandizement begins to develop. The rediscovered group begins to view its own group as more highly valued than other groups (ethnocentrism).

Native Indians, finding themselves without any distinct, easily observable cultural traits, have chosen to focus on cultural factors normally associated with the Plains Indians (feather bonnets, teepees, powwows, etc.). In addition, they have begun to focus on factors such as aboriginal land rights and pan-Indian identity—which represent some sort of cognitive structure which, while not easily observable, still remains for all Indian people. Various social/political events allow these people to continually reinforce these aspects and enhance their claim that they are a special, unique *perceived appearance group* (PAG).

Similarly, ethnic minority nationalism (involving revivalistic tendencies) has been apparent for at least one Euro-Canadian group: Ukrainian-Canadians. As Anderson (1979) has explained:

> Over 170,000 Ukrainians and Poles settled in compact bloc settlements in the western Canadian prairies. Entire villages moved to Canada, ensuring ethnic self-awareness and a high degree of segregation of the new arrivals from the rest of Canadian society. Ukrainian consciousness in the prairie settlements was doubtless further augmented and inspired by the quest of Ukrainian nationalists in Europe for cultural and political autonomy, official recognition of the Ukrainian language, and permission to have their own schools using that language. Strongly pro-Ukrainian nationalistic sympathies were imported into Canada at the time of the Russian Revolution of 1917 and the ensuing brief period of an independent Ukraine. In Canada, Ukrainian nationalists, anxious to distinguish between Ukrainian and Russian identity, replaced some letters of the Russian alphabet with "Ukrainian" ones. It was also in Canada that the strongly nationalistic Ukrainian Orthodox church regarded the Ukrainian Catholics as "mothered by Rome, fathered by the Polish state." Ukrainian Catholics opposed "Latinization," anxiously preserving their own traditions, liturgy, vestments, and nationalistic accoutrements similar to their Orthodox coethnics. Both Orthodox and eastern-rite Catholic Ukrainians revealed a profound mistrust of western-rite Catholicism, no doubt enhanced by centuries of antipathy toward Polish and Austrian domination. (250)

However, this author has cautioned that:

> Common identity as Ukrainians should not be overemphasized; there were many examples during the early years of settlement in Canada of rivalry, if not at times outright hostility, between these various ethno-religious subgroups within the larger Ukrainian-Polish group. The regions from where most of the immigrants to Canada came—Galicia, Bukovina, Podcarpathian Ruthenia—were within the Austrian Empire; the rest of the

Ukraine lay within the Russian Empire. Thus, the subjugated emigrants thought of themselves first as Galicians, Bukovinians, or Ruthenians; only secondarily as Austrians or Russians. Ukrainian identity was to emerge gradually after they had emigrated; *it was in Canada that they discovered their common identity.* (250-251)

In international perspective, increasing evidence of ethnic revivalism is found among ethnic minorities. In the United States, such militant movements as Red Power, Black Power, and Brown Power (Mexican-Americans or Chicanos) have emerged in recent years. Ethnic revivalism in Europe is not necessarily a recent phenomenon; witness the Gaelic or Celtic revival among the Irish, Scots, and Welsh in the British Isles. But there has been renewed activism among ethnic minorities in many European countries, notably among Basques and Catalans in Spain and France, as well as Bretons, Corsicans, and the Flemish population in France, French-speaking *Valdotains* in the Aosta region and German-speaking *Süd-Tiroler* people in the Alto-Adige region in Italy, and numerous other examples.

REFERENCES

Allport, G. W. *The Nature of Prejudice.* Garden City, NY: Doubleday, 1954.

Anderson, A. B. "Anti-Semitism and Jewish Identity in Montreal," M.A. dissertation in sociology, Graduate Faculty of Political and Social Science, New School for Social Research, New York, 1967.

Anderson, A. B. "Assimilation in the Bloc Settlements of North-Central Saskatchewan: A Comparative Study of Identity Change Among Seven Ethno-Religious Groups in a Canadian Prairies Region." Ph.D. Thesis in sociology, University of Saskatchewan, Saskatoon, 1972.

Anderson, A. B. "Ethnic Identity in Saskatchewan Bloc Settlements: A Sociological Appraisal," in H. Palmer (ed.), *The Settlement of the West.* Calgary: University of Calgary, 1977.

Anderson, A. B. "French Settlements in Saskatchewan: Historical and Sociological Perspectives," paper presented at the Tenth Annual Meeting of the Saskatchewan Geneological Society, Saskatoon, Oct. 21, 1978.

Anderson, A. B. "Ukrainian Ethnicity: Generations and Change in Rural Saskatchewan," in J. L. Elliott (ed.), *Two Nations, Many Cultures: Ethnic Groups in Canada.* Scarborough: Prentice-Hall of Canada, 1979.

Anderson, G. M. and D. Higgs. *A Future to Inherit: The Portuguese Communities of Canada.* Toronto: McClelland and Stewart, 1976.

Berry, B. *Race and Ethnic Relations.* Boston: Houghton-Mifflin, 1958.

Baureiss, G. *The City and the Subcommunity: The Chinese of Calgary.* M.A. Thesis, University of Calgary, 1971.

Breton, R. "Institutional Completeness of Ethnic Communities and the Personal Relations of Immigrants," *American Journal of Sociology,* 70, 2 (Sept. 1964): 193-205.

Dawson, C. A. *Group Settlement: Ethnic Communities in Western Canada* (Canadian Frontiers of Settlements series, vol. vii). Toronto: Macmillan, 1936.

Gordon, M. M. *Assimilation in American Life.* New York: Oxford University Press, 1964.

Grow, S. "The Blacks of Amber Valley: Negro Pioneering in Northern Alberta." *Canadian Ethnic Studies*, Vol. VI, No. 1-2, 1974.

Henry, F. *The Dynamics of Racism in Toronto*. Research Report, Department of Anthropology, York University, 1978.

Kosa, J. *Land of Choice*. Toronto: University of Toronto Press, 1956.

Kyba, P. "Ballots and Burning Crosses," in N. Ward and D. Spafford (eds.), *Politics in Saskatchewan*. Lindsay, Ont: Longmans of Canada, 1968.

Lieberson, S. *Ethnic Patterns in American Cities*. Glencoe, Ill: Macmillan, 1963.

Linton, R. "Nativistic Movements," *American Anthropologist*, 45, (1943): 230-240.

Price, C. A. "Immigration and Group Settlement," in W. D. Borrie (ed.), *The Cultural Integration of Immigrants*. Paris: UNESCO, 1959.

Rose, A. M. and C. B. Rose. *America Divided: Minority Group Relations in the United States*. New York: Alfred A. Knopf, 1948.

Schermerhorn, R. A. *Comparative Ethnic Relations: A Framework of Theory and Research*. New York: Random House, 1970.

Shibutani, R. and K. M. Kwan. *Ethnic Stratification: A Comparative Approach*. New York: Macmillan, 1965.

Thomson, C. A. *Blacks in Deep Snow: Black Pioneers in Canada*. Don Mills, Ont: J. M. Dent and Sons, 1979.

Tumin, M. M. *Comparative Perspectives on Race Relations*. Boston: Little, Brown, 1969.

Winks, R. *The Blacks in Canada, A History*. New Haven: Yale University Press, 1971.

Part V

Conclusion

The concluding chapter, prepared in collaboration with Daiva K. Stasiulis, discusses the current and future policy implications of our analysis of ethnic relations and minority responses or outcomes. How is multiculturalism to actually be implemented by federal, provincial, and municipal governments?

First the emergence of a new multicultural policy (at the federal level) during the seventies is described: why it replaced the former bicultural definition of Canada as an official ideology; what the French reaction has been to this move; and what exactly this multicultural policy intended to accomplish. Then the question of funding this policy is raised, at the federal level as well as for provincial and municipal governments. It is our contention that there has been large-scale wastage, at least on the part of the federal government, of public funds. This is not necessarily intended to suggest a criticism of multiculturalism per se as much as to propose more effective or lasting expenditure in the interest of aiding ethnic minority groups. We regard provincial support of multicultural education to be a step in this direction, although (with Marjaleena Repo) we would question what the content of such an education should be.

Following the lead of Jean Burnet and Wsevolod Isajiw, recent federal multicultural policies are evaluated in terms of their successes and failures. Pertinent literature from a "left" political perspective is then examined, viewing multicultural policies (positively and negatively) as a form of state control. Specifically, the chapter focuses on the selectivity of state (i.e., government) funding of ethnic community organizations, summarizing conclusions drawn from recent and continuing research by Stasiulis and other authors.

A counter-argument for government non-involvement in multicultural spending is presented and criticized.

The chapter concludes with a brief reappraisal of ethnic diversity in Canada.

Chapter 14

Policy Implications*

The Emergence of a New Multicultural Policy

In Chapter 6 we have suggested that Canadian government policies toward ethnic minorities have been continuously in flux between Anglo-conformity, racism, biculturalism, token multiculturalism, pan-Canadian nationalism, separatism, Americanization, etc. As Burnet (1979) has pointed out,

> official recognition of the ethnic diversity of the population as continuing and desirable has been relatively recent. Until the 1960s government policy concerning immigration was based on the principle that those who were admitted into Canadian society should be assimilable into the dominant British and French ethnic groups. Even policy regarding native peoples was dominated by that principle: it was aimed at isolation and gradual assimilation. The immigration policy bore hardest upon those peoples who were considered unassimilable. . . . But beyond rhetoric singularly little support was given by either federal or provincial governments to groups that wanted to maintain their old world heritages. Cultural agencies, with niggardly funding, could afford little attention to any groups other than the British, French and Natives. Private broadcasting in languages other than English and French was strictly regulated, and permitted only when it could be justified in terms of "integration"; the public corporation, the CBC, recognized only English and French; the teaching of other languages, including Indian and Inuit languages, was proscribed, and even the teaching of modern languages was not greatly encouraged. (1-3)

In the post-war period, and especially since the beginning of this decade, the number of state policies and programs in Canada directed explicitly to the incorporation of non-British and non-French groups has grown considerably. The particular ideology of the state, in the sense defined by Poulantzas (1975: 17) as an "ensemble of material practices" with regard to the "other" groups did not emerge as a holistic and fully coherent one, but rather incrementally as a response to a number of economic and political developments.

The state's increased involvement in the field of ethnic relations can be attributed to a process involving three major factors: (1) the growth in federal revenue, (2) the threats to societal integration presented by political develop-

---

* Much of this chapter is excerpted from a paper by A. B. Anderson and D. K. Stasiulis, "Canadian Multiculturalism: A Critique," presented at the Conference on "Ethnicity, Power and Politics in Canada," the Biennial Conference of the Canadian Ethnic Studies Association, Vancouver, October 11-13, 1979.

ments in Quebec, and (3) the growing assertiveness of the more affluent and powerful of the "other" ethnic groups (Palmer, 1976; Loney, 1977).

The Royal Commission on Bilingualism and Biculturalism, set up in response to the growing assertiveness of French-Canadian political nationalism, provided impetus for organized segments of the "other" ethnic groups to articulate the sentiment that the bicultural framework was offensive to non-charter ethnic groups, relegating them to the status of second-class citizens. The ad hoc response of the Commission was to write a fourth book on the "other ethnic groups," leading subsequently in the early 1970s to the adoption by the federal and several provincial governments (Ontario, Manitoba, Saskatchewan, and Alberta) of a formal policy of multiculturalism (Palmer, 1976: 101-2).

Writing on the French reaction to multiculturalism, Isajiw (1975) has commented:

> The other camp is the French, who insist that if there is official recognition of the French language, there should also be official recognition of the French culture. Hence they object to the linking of bilingualism with multiculturalism. Rather, they would prefer linking it with biculturalism. It is not clear how many French-Canadians favour this position, but it appears that by and large in Quebec the ideology of multiculturalism is not popular. On the contrary, it is seen as a policy detracting from the long struggle of French-Canadians to achieve equal partnership with the British-Canadians. Further, as current governmental policy, multiculturalism has been officially linked to the policy of bilingualism. It can be argued that the policy of bilingualism has already given the French some political leverage, and has provided some institutionalized symbolic recognition of equality. (19-20)

On October 8, 1971, the Prime Minister announced the federal government's acceptance of recommendations from the Royal Commission on Bilingualism and Biculturalism directed to federal departments and agencies; and proclaimed a policy of "multiculturalism within a bilingual framework." The government pledged to provide support for such a policy in four ways.

> First, resources permitting, the government will seek to assist all Canadian cultural groups that have demonstrated a desire and effort to continue to develop a capacity to grow and contribute to Canada, and a clear need for assistance, the small and weak groups no less than the strong and highly organized.
>
> Second, the government will assist members of all cultural groups to overcome cultural barriers to full participation in Canadian society.
>
> Third, the government will promote creative encounters and interchange among all Canadian cultural groups in the interests of national unity.
>
> Fourth, the government will continue to assist immigrants to acquire at least one of Canada's official languages in order to become full participants in Canadian society. (House of Commons, Debates, 1971)

In 1972 Stanley Haidasz became the first minister of state responsible for multiculturalism, within the Department of the Secretary of State; however, a completely separate ministry was soon dissolved again only a couple of years later. By 1976 a dramatic overhaul of the federal multicultural office was proposed, which was to allow more concentration on the emerging problem of racial discrimination; yet this move, or at least a move exclusively in this direction, was blocked by the established minorities more interested in preserving their languages and cultures.

A more lasting creation of the federal government has been the Canadian Consultative Council on Multiculturalism, created in 1973. This is a rather complex federal structure with a national executive and five regional branches, and is composed of more than a hundred representatives of various ethnic groups, to advise the minister. By the end of the seventies it had held three national biennial conferences, as well as a number of regional meetings out of which have come many recommendations to government.

The Financial Problem: Funding Multiculturalism

The scope of state funding has in recent years expanded greatly in the domains of ethnic communities, as in the voluntary sector in general (National Advisory Council on Voluntary Action, 1978: 42; Loney, 1977: 456-7). With the inception of the new multicultural policy during the early seventies, the federal government contributed $4,154,000 to its multicultural ministry in 1972/3, and $10,132,000 in 1973/4 (*Canadian Press*, May 18, 1973). While the federal multicultural apparatus has been accused of meaningless squandering of some of its funds (with $3,000 having been granted to a Cape Breton Irish Benevolent Society to teach needlework and $5,000 to the Latvian National Federation to prepare a book on ornaments, etc.), the total budget accorded to multiculturalism has been relatively modest, certainly far below sums expended on various programs to aid industry. The President of the National Congress of Italian Canadians recently expressed dismay at the "miniscule" budget committed to the federal Multicultural Programme for the next five years, commenting that "it must surely indicate the low priority which the government puts on the policy of multiculturalism" (Leone, 1978: 66).

Despite the relatively small size of the budget allocated to multiculturalism, the programs and activities funded through multicultural grants have enjoyed high visibility through advertising in the ethnic press and widespread media coverage given to multicultural events. A cynical interpretation by some critics of the multicultural funding process is that the expenditures made by a particular government on multiculturalism are prompted by the purely political and partisan motive of attempting to garner votes. Although undoubtedly true for the enactment of a large number of government policies, this interpretation of the rationale behind the creation and operation of multicultural policy is overly simplistic, a point that will later be taken up in the critique of multiculturalism from a "left" political perspective.

Provincial Multicultural Policies

Provincial and municipal governments have also contributed to multicultural funding. For example, during the 1973/4 fiscal year alone, Ontario contributed $1.3 million expressly for its multicultural policy directed at immigrants, while that year Toronto gave $150,000 in support of ethnic festivals and other ethnic cultural activities (*Toronto Star*, January 19, 1974).

Burnet (1978: 108) has summarized the provincial multicultural policies in four or five provinces, noting the emphasis placed on education:

> The provinces of Ontario, Manitoba, Saskatchewan and Alberta have in their turn proclaimed policies of multiculturalism, and British Columbia is said to be preparing to follow suit. It is difficult to guess, of course, to what extent the adoption of the federal policy influenced the provinces: the provinces are not given to following Ottawa's lead automatically. However, since the schools are seen as having a key role to play in many of the programmes of multiculturalism and education is under provincial jurisdiction, provincial initiatives are an essential part of any picture. These have involved such measures as appointment of advisory committees or councils on multiculturalism, their members draw from the province's ethnic groups; innumerable conferences, including conferences on curriculum; publications, including multicultural history projects, ethnocultural directories, multicultural resource lists, and periodicals having to do with heritages or multiculturalism; grants for various ethnic or multicultural projects; and in the schools expansion of the teaching of various cultures, and introduction of multiculturalism as a topic into curricula. (1978: 108)

We would argue, however, that with the possible exceptions of Alberta and Ontario, these provinces have not gone far enough in supporting alternative forms of education often demanded, or more politely requested, by ethnic and ethno-religious minorities. Without realistic funding of multicultural education, as represented in second or third language instruction, ethnic-oriented histories and other textbooks, and cultural exchange programmes, it is not likely that decades of discrimination against these minorities, usually assuming the form of enforced Anglo-conformity in the schools, will be offset.

Moreover, while socialization of children to a tolerant and informed view of the cultures of other ethnic and racial groups could make some inroads toward rectifying the racist attitudes of individuals, the racism inherent in the structural and institutional workings of the larger society could quite conceivably remain untouched by such an educational process.

Table 1 reveals the enrollment in second language programmes in elementary and secondary schools. Several comments warrant mention with regard to these data. First of all, we find that for Canada as a whole, less than 40% of all students are enrolled in a second language program. Secondly, with the exception of Ontario, we find a greater number of secondary students enrolled in these programs than elementary students. Thirdly, in the two provinces with the highest number of French mother tongue, we find the highest proportion of students enrolled in a second language (English) program. This confirms the suspicion of many that only French-Canadians are becoming bilingual.

The incorporation of the concept of multiculturalism into the educational process has involved the organization of many sorts of courses in school curricula. A distinction should be drawn here between specifically multicultural classes (teaching about an ethnic culture), ethnic language classes (offered in the language of the ethnic group), and E.S.L. classes (teaching English as a second, third, or fourth language to new immigrants) (Ashworth, 1978).

Table 1

ENROLMENT IN SECOND LANGUAGE PROGRAMMES IN ELEMENTARY AND SECONDARY SCHOOLS, BY PROVINCE

Province and level of education	Students enrolled in second language programmes					
	1970-1971		1973-1974		1974-1975	
	number	%[1]	number	%[1]	number	%[1]
Newfoundland:						
K-6[2]	21,835	21.4	32,520	32.9	33,036	34.2
7-12	37,895	63.9	34,583	56.9	33,031	54.6
Total	59,730	37.01	67,103	42.0	66,067	42.0
Prince Edward Island:						
1-6	3,561	21.2	6,226	41.7	6,148	42.2
7-12	10,794	83.0	8,156	61.2	8,958	69.5
Total	14,355	48.1	14,382	50.9	15,106	55.0
Nova Scotia:						
K-6[2]	12,642	10.4	23,853	21.1	24,424	22.3
7-12	59,955	70.0	59,420	67.0	57,764	61.9
Total	72,597	35.0	83,273	41.2	82,188	40.6
New Brunswick:						
1-6	37,305	61.5	31,997	55.5	36,329	65.1
7-12	42,708	78.2	37,852	70.1	39,318	72.3
Total	80,013	69.4	69,849	62.5	75,647	68.7
Ontario:						
K-8[2]	526,538	38.2	596,820	44.7	609,562	46.0
9-13	252,496	47.5	202,729	36.4	189,426	33.9
Total	779,034	40.8	799,649	42.3	798,988	42.4
Manitoba:						
K-6[2]	42,655	32.9	47,845	38.6	47,224	39.8
7-12	58,389	55.3	45,121	42.3	43,843	41.2
Total	101,044	40.8	92,966	40.3	91,067	40.5
Saskatchewan:						
K-6[2]	6,950	5.2	6,674	5.7	6,208	5.3
7-12	77,928	69.0	56,696	53.3	57,546	54.9
Total	84,878	34.4	63,370	28.5	63,754	28.9
Alberta:						
K-6[2]	58,235	25.7	31,226	9.3	48,418	14.9
7-12	80,607	40.8	63,554	30.7	63,291	30.1
Total	138,842	32.8	125,564	29.9	125,212	29.9
British Columbia:						
K-7[2]	18,558	5.7	31,226	9.3	48,418	14.9
8-12	127,293	66.9	105,664	49.8	96,532	44.5
Total	145,851	28.2	136,890	24.9	144,590	26.8

Table 1 (cont'd.)

ENROLMENT IN SECOND LANGUAGE PROGRAMMES IN ELEMENTARY AND SECONDARY SCHOOLS, BY PROVINCE

Province and level of education	Students enrolled in second language programmes					
	1970-1971		1973-1974		1974-1975	
	number	%[1]	number	%[1]	number	%[1]
Total[3]						
Elementary	728,278	29.1	839,271	34.8	873,270	36.8
Secondary	748,065	55.4	613,775	43.7	589,709	41.6
Total	1,476,344	38.4	1,453,046	38.1	1,462,979	38.6
Quebec[4]:						
Elementary	348,367	41.1	235,500	33.6	249,860	37.0
Secondary	542,026	100.0	599,475	100.0	571,175	100.0
Total	890,393	64.1	834,975	64.2	821,035	65.9

[1] The percentage of the total school population (less the students for whom the minority language is the language of instruction) enrolled in second language programmes.
[2] "K" stands for kindergarten.
[3] The total of all provinces except Quebec.
[4] Includes private schools.
Source: *Perspective Canada II*. Statistics Canada, Printing and Publishing, Supply and Services, Ottawa, 1977, p. 268.

The Province of Alberta seems to have gone the farthest in establishing courses in ethnic languages or about ethnic cultures. In Alberta high schools eight contemporary languages are offered at various levels (Cree, German, Hungarian, Italian, Polish, Russian, Spanish, and Ukrainian); the highest enrollments to date have been in German and Ukrainian classes. By 1980 the province was running ten bilingual public schools (five Ukrainian, three Jewish, and two German) as well as three (Ukrainian) bilingual separate schools. A Language Support Programme, commonly referred to as "Saturday schools," is administered by the Alberta Cultural Heritage Branch. During the 1979/80 school year 4,651 students were enrolled in 71 such schools instructing in at least twenty languages. Nine of these ethno-cultural language schools offered accredited language courses during 1978/79 (five German, two Ukrainian, one French, one Italian) (Pelech, 1980). In addition, the provincial government runs a French-language school system, and francophone Collège St-Jean is affiliated with the University of Alberta. Similar ethno-cultural and French-language schools (écoles designées in Saskatchewan) are found in the other two Prairie provinces.

C. J. Jaenen (1972) has recently appraised the potential for multicultural education in the following appropriately cautious terms:

If we accept the view that Canada is a multi-ethnic and polycultural so-ciety then it would seem to follow that the public school systems of the na-tion ought to reflect this cultural pluralism. Such a conclusion would seem to impose itself if for no other reason than publicly supported school systems should serve all and reflect the educational objectives of the entire community. The tendency in all public or state school systems, however, is towards uniformity and centralization. Uniformity and centralization, whether defended on grounds of administrative efficiency, in the name of equality, or on grounds of scholarly attainment of stated common objectives, discourage educational recognition of cultural pluralism. Thus, one may declare that it is possible for public schooling, equated in the popular mind with education, to retard the development of a unique and significant culture in Canada, to downgrade what is genuinely and authentically Canadian in our life style, and to depreciate the moral, relevant, and innovative aspects of public schooling. (199)

Costa and Di Santo (1972) have added:

Our schools, where much of this harm can be prevented, rather than tapping the rich cultural resources represented by our cultural minorities, are destroying them in the name of uniformity, efficiency and standardization. (249)

However, from a "left" political perspective, Repo (1971) has criticized multicultural schooling as interfering with working class consciousness (a refrain often repeated by theoreticans of the left):

The crucial error is the whole concept of immigrant "culture." The question one has to ask is what is the culture of immigrant labour? And the answer is: the culture of immigrant labour consists of hard work, long hours, poor pay, a lot of children, a lot of illness, and premature old age, *all of which constitute a typical working class fate.* The language of that experience is incidental. *This* culture is indeed the one to be taught in schools and everywhere else, but not a second should be wasted on transmitting some superficial features from the past society of the immigrant into his present existence. The immigrant worker should integrate with his new society, learn its language and history, learn about the ideology of immigration (i.e. why he was brought here), and learn about the history and conditions of his own class in Canada. It goes without saying that he should participate in the over-all struggles of his class in this country.

Any demand for ethnic schools and programmes will only lead into a hopeless ghetto mentality on the part of the immigrant, and into a permanent isolation and alienation from the Canadian context. It would make it totally impossible for the working class to communicate with each other on the work-place and in the neighbourhood. This is ideal from the establishment's perspective, because the more divided and fragmented the working class is, the stronger the present power structure becomes. (17)

Federal Multicultural Policies: Successes and Failures

Jean Burnet, an individual much involved in the formulation and assessment of Canada's recent cultural policies, has noted the achievements of federal multicultural policies. The commitment of the government in this field is demonstrated by the relative durability of multicultural structures and agents such as the minister of state responsible for multiculturalism (since 1972), and the Canadian Consultative Council of Multiculturalism (since 1973), and by the fact that "the budget allocated to multiculturalism has been increased in times of fiscal constraint" (1978: 107). Moreover, the multicultural bodies have been actively engaged in a number of ventures:

> The Multiculturalism Directorate has carried on liaison activities with ethnic communities and with the ethnic press; initiated and developed studies and research, including a series of histories on ethnic groups; assisted the Canadian Ethnic Studies Association to develop as a full-fledged society with two regular publications; sponsored activities in the performing and visual arts; assisted in programmes aimed at retention of non-official languages and given grants for a vast array of other projects. (Burnet, 1978: 107)

Yet Burnet has also raised a number of pertinent criticisms of federal multicultural policies during the past seven years (1978: 107-12). She notes the "uncertainty, suspicion and dissatisfaction regarding the policy" among diverse sectors of the population—including groups in Quebec, Anglo-celts and many others. She points out the disjuncture between attitudes—an explicit approval of the multicultural policy, and behavior—the rejection of the policy as indicated in the continuation of discrimination. In addition, the policy which was framed under pressures from ethnic groups of European origin and designed to meet their concerns, such as language maintenance, has not kept pace with the changing patterns of immigration and the concerns of the new visible minorities which have to do with human rights, especially in the job market, rather than cultural or linguistic rights.

A more general problem with multicultural policy is the lack of consistency, clarity and continuity in both its interpretation and administration. Since October 1971 there have been no fewer than four ministers responsible for multiculturalism. Even more problematic is the lack of clarity and consensus concerning the aims of the policy and the means by which they are attained among the politicians, public servants and the leaders of ethnic organizations who are all involved to greater or lesser degrees in the formulation and implementation of multicultural programmes (Burnet, 1978).

Isajiw (1975) had earlier expressed the dangerous potential multicultural policies hold for becoming a strategy of "containment of the other ethnic groups, similar to that of colonial pluralism":

> It appears to me that the relevant leaders of the British groups still see the policy in this manner. As long as ethnic differences can still be retained in museums, exhibited as entertainment or hidden in "do-it-yourself" projects, no institutionalized recognition of equality is necessary. If however, ethnic pluralism in Canada is a phenomenon which reflects the structure and processes in society as a whole, then this old-fashioned interpretation of the policy is inadequate. In the long run it will fail to articulate the tensions which the continuing process of ethnic differentiation evoke. (20-21)

However, Isajiw goes on to question only the "interpretation and application of the policy" rather than its basic presuppositions (21).

About fifteen years ago, a prominent Canadian sociologist, John Porter (1965) argued that: "Ethnic and cultural differences are a fraud perpetrated by the

British upon all other Canadians in order to keep them in their place." This view, in our opinion, is overstated and denigrating to the very real differences in values, customs and language held by diverse groups of Canadians. However, Porter's statement implies a process of manipulation of ethnic and cultural distinctions which we would agree does occur and can be observed in analysing the exogenous structural constraints imposed on ethnic communities. A clearer understanding of multicultural policy is facilitated by relating it to the general process of state intervention in advanced capitalist societies.

Multiculturalism as State Control

A critique of multicultural policies can be constructively related to our earlier discussion of dominant social control mechanisms (Chapter 10). The comprehension of the rationale for—and the effects of—multicultural policy requires locating the state's practices with regard to explicitly ethnic concerns in the framework of a larger understanding of the development of the state in capitalist societies. This framework was first suggested by O'Conner (1973) and further developed by other theorists working in the Marxist tradition (e.g., Wolfe, 1977; Panitch, 1977; Mahon, 1977; Loney, 1977). According to O'Conner (1973):

> the capitalistic state must try to fulfill two basic and often mutually contradictory functions—*accumulation* and *legitimization*. ... This means that the state must try to maintain or create the conditions in which profitable capital accumulation is possible. However, the state also must try to maintain or create the conditions for social harmony.

The process involved in multiculturalism of state agencies attempting to link themselves with ethnic organizations is related to the legitimization function of the state, i.e., to its attempt to maintain social harmony. However, the regulation of inter-ethnic relations also implies a third state function, that of *social coercion*—that is, "the use by the state of its monopoly over the legitimate use of force to maintain or impose social order (Panitch, 1973: 8). An active process of legitimation on the part of the state occurs when the state recognizes the demands emanating from segments of the nondominant classes which control some strategic resource—such as the ability to command votes or to cause social disruption (Wolfe, 1977: 145, 150). The ability of the state to openly coerce intransigent forces is largely enhanced if the populations which are objects of state coercion are relatively powerless in economic and political terms.

Within any historical conjuncture, the state may engage in a diversity of actions and policies vis-a-vis ethnic groups which are manifestly contradictory to each other in intent—exercising its coercive function in immigration matters and widespread police harassment of certain ethnic and racial groups while at the same time providing resources for various self-help and cultural projects to ethnic organizations, thus gaining legitimacy from these ethnic populations. In general terms, it might be said with regard to the Canadian state's stance to the social, economic and political incorporation of its nondominant ethnic groups, that prior to the Second World War, there was a tendency to enforce, through legislation, the "vertical mosaic" or to allow the dominant forces in the society at large to do so unhindered. The more usual response in the contemporary period has been, (i) to alleviate, through legislation and the development of special agencies, the strains of racism and ethnic inequalities which threaten the social stability of Canadian society or the legitimacy of its government, and (ii) to actively foster and control the formation of previously neglected ethnic interests and guide their incorporation into the state and civil society.

Multiculturalism, concerned as it purports to be with the achievement of equality (to the point where Burnet (1978: 108) views this as the ultimate aim of the policy), has addressed itself to the problems of racism, particularly within the provincial jurisdiction of education. Powerless, however, to legislate against discrimination, multicultural bodies have confined themselves for the most part to an advisory role and to "developing understanding among peoples" (*Islander*, October 1, 1974: 1, 3).

In terms of their output, multicultural state agencies have been much more active in representing the interests of organized ethnic bodies while concomitantly regulating their activities. Mahon (1977), examining the federal civil service, has delineated how this simultaneous process of representation and regulation of nondominant interests functions. Within the state, there exists an unequal structure of representation. Dominant interests are represented in departments with greater power and authority such as the Department of Finance, which establishes relations with all important sectors in the Canadian political economy. Fractions of subordinate classes are represented in lower-ranking departments such as Labour, Health and Welfare, and Indian Affairs and Northern Development. The departments representing subordinate interests tend to have more delimited mandates, less relative autonomy, and fewer resources. Moreover, within them, the regulation of specific interests in reaching a compromise suited to the national interest, which corresponds to the class interests of the hegemonic faction of the dominant class, predominates over the mere representation of sectional, i.e., ethnic, interests. Within the state, "all social forces achieve a form of representation. (However) the relations among the representatives express the inequalities established in civil society" (Mahon, 1977: 193).

Using Mahon's suggestive framework, one can better understand the role of government agencies connected with the multicultural policy in representing the interests of non-dominant ethnic groups. A number of indices point to the *relative* insignificance of the state's attendance to the real and articulated interests of Canada's non-charter ethnic groups. These include the modest budget accorded to multiculturalism (especially given the size of its constituency), the lack of relative autonomy of multicultural agencies (e.g., an absence of separate ministries at the federal or provincial levels) and its delimited, though vague mandate.

The vagueness of the mandate of multicultural bodies makes it amenable to as narrow an interpretation as a particular minister of state for multiculturalism cares to make. For instance, the last Liberal minister Norman Cafik's statement that "multiculturalism was not established to create a new kind of society, but to reflect the society which we already have" (Donaldson, 1979: 38), implies little scope indeed for significant social change.

If one examines the four fundamental principles enumerated by the federal government concerning multiculturalism, the one referring explicitly to government intervention in alleviating socioeconomic inequities reads:

The Government will assist members of all cultural groups to overcome *cultural* barriers to full participation in Canadian society (Canadian Consultative Council on Multiculturalism, 1975: V).

In the instance of multicultural policies, the state is claiming to meet not only the expressive, more explicitly "ethnic" needs of ethnic collectivities, but also the potentially oppositional demands for social, economic, and political equality of new immigrant or marginal groups. However, given that the claim to represent these politically volatile needs is articulated in the context of agencies and policies which emphasize *cultural* contributions or transformations, this strategy of state intervention can be seen as one of depoliticizing issues concerning the needs and objectives of nondominant ethnic groups.

The process of regulation of the activities of ethnic communities occurs through a multifaceted process involving state funding, but also government appointments of ethnic community leaders, consultations between community leaders and government representatives over certain issues and the formulation of legislation, attendance by government officials at important ethnic social and policy-making events (e.g., conferences, banquets, cultural and religious celebrations) and socialization of community leaders to the ethnic policies of the state (through their attendance at state multicultural conferences, and through government advertisement in ethnic newspapers). It is in the relationship of dependency established when an ethnic organization accepts funds from a government agency that one can observe the most serious effects of state intervention in ethnic community affairs.

The Importance of State Funding of Ethnic Community Organizations

State funding becomes an especially attractive source of financial support for ethnic associations having no independent economic base either in the form of ownership of capital or the receipt of large and regular membership dues. Funds from the government are sought, however, not only for their efficacy role, i.e., for the means which they provide for carrying out organizational activities. They are also valued for the legitimacy that is given to associations by government recognition (Loney, 1977: 468). This legitimizing role of government funding may be viewed as particularly important for subordinate or marginal ethnic groups who are still suffering from lack of prestige accorded them in an earlier era of Anglo-conformity (Palmer, 1976).

Recent studies examining the role of government in the granting process have made the self-evident but often neglected point that government grants are given to groups whose programmes meet the objectives of the grantor (Rosenblugh in Loney, 1977: 463; NACVA, 1978: 169). Thus, for instance, organizations truly interested in maintaining the culture of a group may be given less priority by multicultural agencies than those sponsoring *multicultural* programmes of cultural sharing.

Not only the type but also the scope of organizational activities may be severely curtailed by the nature of government funding. For instance, the trend in federal funding has recently been toward non-recurring project grants rather than sustaining grants which would sustain a voluntary association over the long run. This granting predilection works to the disadvantage of nascent and deprived groups. The groups that will likely obtain support are the larger and well-established ones which already possess organizational continuity and cohesion and therefore are able to sustain the expenses involved in the process of applying for grants and developing project proposals. The short-term nature of these project grants permits little achievement towards any specific social goals. Often enough funds are provided only for the initial phases of a project—such as a feasibility study (*Islander*, January 15, 1974: 4). Projects are often funded for the immediate results they yield or the high public visibility that can be given them (e.g., conferences). The highly bureaucratized process of applying for government funds and accounting for their expenditure drains the leadership of organizations of valuable time and energy, which could otherwise be more directly utilized in the pursuit of the organization's objectives.

Not only the mere fact of state funding to associations, but also *where* in the associational structures of ethnic communities funds are funnelled, has an impact on the community's organizational behavior. The state, hoping to achieve the greatest impact for its dollar, will attempt to channel funds into the most representative organization, often the organization that is or claims to be the national umbrella organization. The government stipulates that in order for ethnic organizations to qualify for sustaining grants (group development-operational supports) from the minister of state for multiculturalism, they must be national. By bestowing funds to ethnic associations which have some semblance of national organization, the intent of the federal government may be to foster structures which will further nationalist sentiments and feelings of gratification for the federal government. This propensity to fund the national umbrella organization within the community is aided by its often moderate stance on most controversial issues and its professional, responsible leadership. The state's choice to financially support the national organization often occurs *despite* its lack of legitimacy amongst the leadership and rank and file of other community organizations, which attempt to compete for the same government funds. The recognition of this trend in funding is important in light of the criticism voiced by opponents of multiculturalism who point out the dangers of fostering fragmentation or disunity in the support of ethnic group activities by the state. The diversity of groups funded by the state does *not* reflect the legitimate differences in terms of culture, language, religion, social class, or political orientation existing within the organized segment, let alone the total population of ethnic community, as recent research on South Asians and Blacks in Toronto has clearly indicated (Stasiulis, 1979).

The fact that government agencies are becoming incorporated into the interorganizational networks of ethnic community organizations and are doing so in such a way as to be pre-eminent in their relationship with the funded organization, is crucial to an understanding of that organization's structure and activities. State funding can affect: (i) social cohesion within the organization, (ii) character of leadership, (iii) mass-elite relationships, (iv) leadership tasks, and most importantly, (v) the objectives and activities of the organizations (Stasiulis, 1979: 16-19).

From the perspective of the ethnic collectivity as a whole, within which one can imagine a number of possible organizations, potentially linked in various ways to each other and carrying on a variety of activities, only some organizations and actions will be undertaken, largely determined by the state support given to them. Although government funding may prove attractive for certain segments of an ethnic population, the fear of losing their autonomy may prevent other segments from approaching government agencies in the first place. The efforts of the more determinedly autonomous segments to link various organizations and associations into a unified community may be barred from doing so by the co-optation of some organizations by government agencies. Thus, the repercussions of state intervention in the funding of ethnic community associations extends well beyond the individual organizations funded to impact upon the inter-organizational network(s) of the ethnic community as a whole.

Our contention that the process of social control by the state of ethnic community activities works, and works relatively well, is not meant to imply a conspiratorial or reifed view of the state or the ruling class whose interests it best represents. First of all, there are undoubtedly well-intentioned and dedicated individuals employed by state multicultural bodies who wish to promote tolerance, justice and equality within this society and are not cognizant of the extent to which their agency's activities inhibit more far-reaching efforts towards these goals. Secondly, many of the consequences of state intervention on the ethnic communities may in fact be unintended. Thirdly, the co-opted individuals from the ethnic communities may be either naive about the consequences of state funding (rationalizing the acceptance of certain funds which meet their objectives), or ripe for co-optation. One Black organizational leader pointed out the complementarity of the generally conservative interests of Black, middle class professionals in Black organizations and government bodies:

> Black professional leaders exploit the situation by joining community organizations to get a sense of what is happening at the grass roots level. They are able to get credibility and use it to buttress their own situation, in terms of getting more status and prestige. They've now become entrenched and become part of the institution (i.e. the Board of Education). Most of them are very conservative because they're very unsure of their position and they will defend the institution and call others upstarts and provocateurs (Interview conducted by D. K. Stasiulis with a leader of a Black organization in Toronto, July 1979).

During the present time, as the state responds to the deepening recession by cutting back on funds for a wide range of social programmes, the purse for multiculturalism and the sponsoring of ethnic activities is likely to diminish. Interviews with leaders of South Asians and Black leaders of prominent community organizations in Toronto carried out by Stasiulis revealed that for these leaders, the dwindling government funds appeared much more salient and visible a problem than the changes incurred by the acceptance of state funds. We would hypothesize, however, that with widespread cutbacks some of the effects of state funding are not likely to change drastically, as long as some funds remain accessible to organizations, and as long as the state continues to propagate the multicultural ideology (which is the most favorable ideology towards "other" ethnic groups to date). It seems that the anticipation of some aid from the government and the formation of numerous other types of relationships with the state play an almost equal role in modifying the activities of community

organizations as does the actual receiving of government funds by an organization. It is not merely the funding of ethnic organizations, but the tendency to feed
into the potential or actual inter-organizational structures of ethnic collectivities, in which one can locate the most weighty consequences of the present
mode of state intervention for ethnic communities.

The Argument for Government Non-Involvement

We would be remiss to entirely ignore the fact that, while spokesmen for certain
ethnic minorities have been insisting on increased government spending at all
levels on multiculturalism (or in the case of the French on biculturalism), other
Canadians have been adamant about government non-involvement. In a recent
editorial in Maclean's (April 14, 1980) Larry Zolf stated this latter position in
rather blunt terms.

Supporting Diefenbaker's "One Canada" crusade for unhyphenated, unghet-
toized Canadianism, Zolf has argued that multiculturalism for all means Canadian culture for none; "the state has no place in the balalaikas of the nation, nor
in its scullcaps, turbans or sheepskin coats." He believed that multiculturalism
tends to make us lesser Canadians, or as he put it "second-class citizens riding
steerage in the Canadian ship of state."

Attacking what he regarded as wasteful government spending, Zolf has commented that Trudeau made a federal minister out of a "professional Polish
politician" (Haidasz), and put millions of taxpayer dollars into Liberal government advertisements in ethnic newspapers or into "the silly subsidizing of
Ukrainian choirs, Swedish meatball movies and Lapland yak calls." Ostensibly,
Zolf has argued, the purpose of multiculturalism through the spending of the tax
dollars was to save the ethnics and their cultures from extinguishing themselves
in a future American-type melting pot. However, he has continued, multiculturalism does not preserve ethnic culture. After all, ethnic Canadians have
been doing that for themselves, at no expense to the Canadian taxpayer, for
years. In Zolf's view, Canadian taxpayers should have to subsidize the cultural
heritages of only one-third of the nation (we can assume that Zolf does not consider people of privileged British or somewhat less privileged French origin to
qualify for multiculturalism). According to Zolf, an ethnic Canadian culture that
cannot survive without taxpayers' subsidization will not be around for very
long. "Multiculturalism," he has written, "is just plain wrong. It is terribly
wrong to keep Canadians along racial lines; to do so officially with taxpayers'
money is monstrous." He has suggested that Canadian ethnics should preserve
their cultures on their own, without tax dollars, and that their native cultures
would flourish in the pride of self-help and self-identity. Arguing for a single
Canadianism, Zolf (following Diefenbaker) has based this on cementing two
cultures (i.e., biculturalism) rather than "400 cultures in search of a people."

Zolf has portrayed multiculturalism, not entirely incorrectly, as a political
ploy to secure votes for the Liberal Party. However, he has gone on to point out
that multiculturalism encourages double loyalties, thus "gives the fledgling
Canadian Identity, already frail and wan, near fatal kicks in its most sensitive
organs." In fact, multiculturalism encourages the reverse of what it claims to
accomplish. Instead of making subordinate ethnic minorities equal to the
charter (founding) peoples, it ensures their subordination because it "centres

them out, ghettoizes them and then inevitably makes them feel inferior." Multiculturalism encourages ethnic segregation and prevents assimilation to "the rich English and French cultures that are and must remain the dominant cultures of this country if Canadians and Quebecers are to jointly survive as a nation." In short, what Zolf has suggested is cutting off any sort of government support of the ethnic diversity in this country so that preferably all these ethnic cultures could blend into a goal of Anglo-conformity (or possibly even franciza-tion).

We would counter with the argument that this position is hardly an enlight-ened appreciation of Canadian ethnic diversity. It would serve to perpetuate dominant social control of ethnic minorities rather than to acquiesce to the minorities' rightful claims as full Canadian citizens to government support of their own schools, language programmes, teaching of ethnic history, and the like. We have argued that there is a good deal more to multiculturalism than simply folk dancing or eating ethnic foods. Any realistic multicultural policy for Canada must seriously combat racism and discrimination, domination and sub-mission. The central fallacy in the bicultural tradition, which a multicultural policy was to replace, is that it stressed that some ethnic minorities—the British and to a lesser extent the French—were to enjoy more privileges or rights than others. Reference was made to these founding races while Native and other ethnic groups were excluded.

Ethnic Diversity in Canada: A Re-appraisal

Not without an ample degree of caution, we would conclude that the position of ethnic minorities in Canada has been changing, generally for the better.

Canadians of British background have for the most part retreated to their proper place as a minority—collectively the largest minority in the country, but still a minority. Hopefully their traditional position as the dominant society will continue to be de-emphasized in favor of recognition that they too are a mi-nority. Hopefully, too, Canada will continue to down-play its traditional tie to British imperialism, which surely must be recognized once and for all as a thing of the past.

The French at long last have succeeded, it would seem, in pushing for more recognition of their unique place in Canadian confederation, or if this effort fails, as an independent state. Quebec is not, never has been or never will be simply another province. It is very clearly a nation-state within a rather ill-defined confederation. For much of Canadian history, French minorities outside Quebec have been denied the full realization of their linguistic rights in the schools, media, courts, etc. They have had to fight bitter, prolonged, and repeated battles for whatever concessions were granted them by the Anglo ma-jority or minority. This should and must come to an end. At the same time, as with Anglo-Canadians, the French in some regions must realize that any notion of charter status will likely be questioned by ethnic groups which outnumber them, such as German-Canadians in all four western provinces and Ukrainian-Canadians in the Prairies.

Native people, currently undergoing rapid urbanization with a concomitant change in life style and values, have made many advances in recent years, not the least their growing politicization. But on the whole they still have innumerable serious problems to overcome: too many Native people are still affected by dire poverty, alcoholism, unemployment, and a host of other problems. Native organizations are constructively pushing not only for improved living conditions but also for constitutional reform, land claims, and the recognition of the Native status of intermarried Treaty Indian women.

Other ethnic minorities have recently been successful—but as yet only in small measure—in establishing their own schools and language programmes, such as in Alberta and in the largest cities (Toronto and Vancouver as well as Greeks in Montreal). It is our conviction that for multiculturalism to gain any success in the Canadian context it must be incorporated in meaningful ways into public school curricula. Finally, if established ethnic minorities (other than British or French Canadians) have been fairly successful in overcoming discrimination against them, Canada has a long way to go to eradicate racism and prejudice against newer arrivals, non-Whites and Native people. If this country has at times had reasonably generous immigration and refugee policies (most recently the admission of tens of thousands of Vietnamese), we would do well to remember that Canada has also had a long history of official racism directed against Asians (e.g., discriminatory immigration policies, exclusion, imprisonment and deportation) as well as ample evidence of popular opposition to non-White immigrants. It is hoped that Canadians will be able in the future to rise above such narrowmindedness. It is already very much to the credit of Canada that it has succeeded in incorporating such a human diversity into one country. The challenge now must be to have the adaptability to translate this diversity into socio-political forms which represent fair recognition of the aspirations of Canadian ethnic minorities.

REFERENCES

Ashworth, Mary. *Immigrant Children and Canadian Schools.* Toronto: McClelland & Stewart, 1978.

Burnet, Jean. "The Policy of Multiculturalism Within a Bilingual Framework: A Stocktaking," *Canadian Ethnic Studies,* Vol. X, No. 2, 1978, pp. 107-113.

Burnet, Jean. "Myths and Multiculturalism," paper presented at the annual meetings of the Canadian Society for the Study of Education, Univ. of Saskatchewan, Saskatoon, June 6, 1979.

Costa, E. and J. DiSanto. "The Italian-Canadian Child, His Family, and the Canadian School System," in N. Byrne and J. Quarter (eds.), *Must Schools Fail?* Toronto: McClelland & Stewart, 1972.

Donaldson, Gordon. "Our Costliest Cult," *Quest,* May, 1979.

Isajiw, Wsevolod W. "Immigration and Multiculturalism—Old and New Approaches," paper presented at the Conference on Multiculturalism and Third World Immigrants in Canada," Univ. of Alberta, Edmonton, Sept. 3-5, 1975.

Islander, October 1, 1974 "Multicultural Council criticized at meeting," pp. 1, 3.

Islander, January 15, 1974 "Responsible leadership needed now," p. 4.

Jaenen, C. J. "Cultural Diversity and Education," in N. Byrne and J. Quarter (eds.), *Must Schools Fail?* Toronto: McClelland & Stewart, 1972.

Leone, Laureano. Brief presented by the National Congress of Italian Canadians to the third Canadian Conference on Multiculturalism, Ottawa, 1978.

Loney, Martin. "A Political Economy of Citizen Participation," in L. Panitch (ed.), *The Canadian State*. Toronto: University of Toronto Press, 1977.

Mahon, Rianne. "Canadian Public Policy: The Unequal Structure of Representation," in L. Panitch (ed.), *The Canadian State*. Toronto: Univ. of Toronto Press, 1977.

National Advisory Council on Voluntary Action to the Government of Canada (NACVA) *People In Action*, Ottawa: Minister of Supply and Services Canada, 1978.

O'Conner, James R. *The Fiscal Crisis of the State*. New York: St. Martin's Press, 1973.

Palmer, Howard. "Reluctant Hosts: Anglo-Canadian Views of Multiculturalism in the Twentieth Century," in *Multiculturalism as State Policy* (report of the Second Canadian Conference on Multiculturalism, Ottawa), 1976.

Panitch, Leo. "The Role and Nature of the Canadian State," in L. Panitch (ed.), *The Canadian State*. Toronto: Univ. of Toronto Press, 1977.

Pelech, Fiona. "Heritage Language Programs in Alberta," paper presented at the Conference on "The Central and East European Community in Canada: Roots, Aspirations, Progress, and Realities," University of Alberta, Edmonton, March 13-15, 1980.

Porter, John. *The Vertical Mosaic*. Toronto: Univ. of Toronto Press, 1965.

Poulantzas, Nicos. *Classes in Contemporary Capitalism*. London: New Left Books, 1975.

Repo, Marjaleena. "The Fallacy of 'Community Control' ", *Transformation: Theory and Practice of Social Change* I, 1: Jan.-Feb. 1971.

Stasiulis, Daiva K. "The Respresentation and Regulation of Ethnic Group Interests Within the Canadian State," paper presented at the annual meeting of the Canadian Sociology and Anthropology Association, Univ. of Saskatchewan, Saskatoon, June 1-4, 1979.

Wolfe, Alan. *The Limits to Legitimacy*. New York: Free Press, 1977.

Zolf, Larry. Podium: "Mulling over Multiculturalism," *Maclean's*, April 14, 1980, p. 6.

Index